Human–Computer Interaction Series

Editors-in-chief

Desney Tan, Microsoft Research, USA

Jean Vanderdonckt, Université catholique de Louvain, Belgium

HCI is a multidisciplinary field focused on human aspects of the development of computer technology. As computer-based technology becomes increasingly pervasive – not just in developed countries, but worldwide – the need to take a human-centred approach in the design and development of this technology becomes ever more important. For roughly 30 years now, researchers and practitioners in computational and behavioral sciences have worked to identify theory and practice that influences the direction of these technologies, and this diverse work makes up the field of human-computer interaction. Broadly speaking it includes the study of what technology might be able to do for people and how people might interact with the technology. The HCI series publishes books that advance the science and technology of developing systems which are both effective and satisfying for people in a wide variety of contexts. Titles focus on theoretical perspectives (such as formal approaches drawn from a variety of behavioral sciences), practical approaches (such as the techniques for effectively integrating user needs in system development), and social issues (such as the determinants of utility, usability and acceptability).

Titles published within the Human– Computer Interaction Series are included in Thomson Reuters' Book Citation Index, The DBLP Computer Science Bibliography and The HCI Bibliography.

More information about this series at http://www.springer.com/series/6033

Panagiotis Germanakos • Marios Belk

Human-Centred Web Adaptation and Personalization

From Theory to Practice

 Springer

Panagiotis Germanakos
Suite Engineering UX,
    Products & Innovation
SAP SE, Walldorf, Germany

Department of Computer Science
University of Cyprus
Nicosia, Cyprus

Marios Belk
Department of Computer Science
University of Cyprus
Nicosia, Cyprus

ISSN 1571-5035
Human–Computer Interaction Series
ISBN 978-3-319-28048-6   ISBN 978-3-319-28050-9   (eBook)
DOI 10.1007/978-3-319-28050-9

Library of Congress Control Number: 2016931418

Printed on acid-free paper

This Springer imprint is published by SpringerNature
The registered company is Springer International Publishing AG Switzerland.

Foreword

Many of the roots of today's personal and collective computing can be traced to some of the seminal work of the Stanford Research Institute and Xerox's Palo Alto Research Lab from the 1960s and 1970s. Since this time, amazing progress, as predicted by Moore's law, has relentlessly driven inventions into the hands of billions of people worldwide. Businesses have been able to leverage technology solutions to drive dramatic efficiencies and new capabilities at scale. Beyond technical capabilities, early visionaries like Doug Engelbart and Alan Kay envisioned an even higher purpose – one in which computing could be a personal and shared medium to augment human capability and to amplify human creativity. From the beginning, the early vision of personal computing was human-centred.

In 1972, Hasso Plattner and the cofounders of SAP brought together a deep expertise in technology and quickly uncovered some unmet needs of businesses. With this expertise and understanding, SAP created a real-time data processing application for financial accounting known as RF and later known as R/1. Many years later, I would learn from Hasso that one of the keys to SAP's early success was a third dimension that the cofounders added to their technology and business understanding. This was an approach that the cofounders took to better understand and define the problem at hand before jumping into the solution. They worked on-site with potential customers trying to deeply understand work of the end users for whom they were building their solutions. They observed, asked many questions, and even helped perform the tasks of their end users. They coded on-site and often sought feedback about the applications that they were building directly from the end users who would be using their software. From SAP's beginning, the early key to success was human-centred.

Back then; there was no terminology for this methodology. Now, terms such as human factors, human computer interaction, user experience design, and design thinking describe the theory, vocabulary, application, and values in the software industry. In fact, when Hasso Plattner first read about design thinking in 2004, he quickly saw the potential to bring an SAP which had grown significantly from its humble beginnings back to its human-centred roots. Today, a growing number of organizations are trying to learn and scale creativity through the application of design thinking and human-centred methodologies. This is especially true in the information technology industry. I have called it the "humanization of IT." Whether in academia or in business or from theory to practice, if we commit to continue the quest of the visionaries that came before us, to augmenting human capabilities through technology innovations, the keys to success will be human-centred.

Chief Design Officer, SAP SE   Sam Yen, Ph.D.
Consulting Associate Professor,
Hasso Plattner Institute for Design at Stanford
(a.k.a. the "d.school")
Palo Alto, 2015

Preface

The rapid evolution of heterogeneous and ubiquitous technologies in recent years, along with the growing demand for automation of services and content delivery, generated a number of new communication opportunities, interaction concepts, and information structures. Nowadays, the role of the computer and the Internet has been upgraded to an indispensable auxiliary tool for the harmonious and orderly everyday human action. However, in this era of wireless communication, pervasive computing, and Internet of Things, there is an increased likelihood that technology will drive developments into directions with no clear reasoning and strong grounds at its basis. There is the risk that the pure technological-driven developments will not contribute to the solution of real problems and concerns that could be proven beneficial for the end users. Today, this is already, at some extent, visible through the "war of apps," in which various organizations release updates of applications with the latest technological, visual, or interaction design enhancements driven by their strategic objectives, such as their strong presence in the market, rather than systematically investigating and analyzing methods for comprehensively capturing the real needs and requirements of users that could bring real innovation and quality to them.

In this respect, the need for research and development of adapted and personalized multi-contextual interfaces and systems becomes today even more evident. Researchers and practitioners alike can take advantage of the philosophy, benefits, flexible models, and techniques of these research areas and create hybrid solutions that could adequately support the generated specialized use cases to the benefit of the unique user. Each user has unique traits, abilities, perceptual preferences, experiences, etc., that directly affect every interaction process. It is therefore of paramount importance to increase the quality of the information delivery and navigation support in order to increase users' comprehension, usability, and decision-making during task execution. This could be achieved by defining more accurate user-centred models and by developing intelligent personalization and adaptation algorithms and interfaces that can ensure effective information management, communication, and presentation.

At a broader extent, the vast amount of dynamic data produced by systems and services should not be driven only by pure data and task models, but rather should be processed in a user-centred manner. In turn, user-centred approaches must not consider only traditional profile elements of the user (i.e., age, experience, profession, tasks, interests, time, location) or technology characteristics (i.e., displays, connectivity, processing power, interface, and data entry) but also other intrinsic human factors such as visual, cognitive, and/or emotional values that can constitute inclusive user models based on which these data can be interpreted to the benefit of the unique user. Furthermore, adaptation and personalization should not focus only at a design level for enhancing users' interaction and usability, but at the same time at a level where intelligent techniques will be able to decide for the volume and kind of information that need to be delivered given the particular multi-contextual objectives and needs of various users (i.e., deciding on the why, what, when, and how).

It is true that one-to-one Web-based content provision probably is a functionality of the distant future. However, the existing underlined challenges of comprehension and orientation difficulties suggest the direct adoption of guidelines and practices that will enhance the design and development of interactive hypermedia applications and systems. This could provide more usable and qualitative content and services adjusted not only to the respective execution environments but also to the heterogeneous needs, requirements, skills, and perceptions of users.

Henceforth, the main objective of this book is to study all the important theoretical dimensions and technologies that govern the relationship between human and computer communication, from the adaptation and personalization viewpoint, suggesting methods and techniques that can promote the robust interaction among the two entities in various application domains.

More specifically, it focuses on state of the art that covers a large number of topics in the area of adaptation and personalization of the content and navigation, processing and communication, and human factors, providing pragmatic references, analyses, new methodologies, architectures, and evaluation methods that tend to approach the subject more thoroughly. It further provides latest suggestions and solutions placing emphasis on step-by-step practical guidelines of developing adaptation and personalization algorithms and interfaces of hypermedia applications and services taking advantage of users' intrinsic individual characteristics, preferences, behaviors, and needs.

Our Standpoint: From Theory to Practice

Many books in the areas of adaptation and personalization, user modeling, HCI, or user-centred design primarily focus upon the presentation of a good amount of current research works in their respective sub-domains of investigation; they deal with latest technologies and systems for content adaptation, and they report sound techniques, algorithms, practical examples, and evaluation methodologies. They also propose a diversity of aspects helping someone to generate new ideas in their fields as well as interaction designs which are, however, mostly driven by a technological viewpoint, subjective beliefs, or qualitative assessments. All these angles are of great value and importance that definitely set the grounds for more optimized practices toward adaptation and personalization.

Nevertheless, traditionally, the main efforts in academia and business were focused on how to tackle the well-known gap between research results and practical designs. Consequently, most of the works, white reports, and/or materials are presenting either solid theoretical backgrounds and models or technological frameworks and routines, making it difficult for someone, most of the time, to find any tangible connection between the two "ends" in a single unit of reference.

In this respect, our main concern in *Human-Centred Web Adaptation and Personalization: From Theory to Practice* is to present a consistent end-to-end standpoint toward the interdisciplinary fields of adaptation and personalization, discussing the convergence of the pertinent human-centred theoretical dimensions, challenges, and constraints, with the models, methods, and technologies that researchers and practitioners can use as a practical guide for the development of their systems and applications. We discuss how they can handle the arising complexity, and we suggest guidelines not only at an architectural level but also at a user interface design level. As a success factor we consider the broader perspective we have tried to adopt toward the subject matter, avoiding where possible, to emphasize on stand-alone nonreusable approaches (e.g., present communication interactions and multi-applicable components that align their functionality depending on the application area and the distinct contextual elements that might be composed of, like, e-learning, e-commerce, usable security, intelligent interfaces, etc., but having always the user in the centre). We elaborate on the adaptation and personalization process in dynamic environments from the user perspective, employing psychometric tools and algorithms, and we describe an open framework that has the ability to adapt the content presentation, navigation, and resources to various contexts based on human-centred design guidelines and adaptation effects.

This holistic and interdisciplinary approach is expressed through the overarching flow of the book that is intentionally structured from *theory* and *principles* to *practice*. These three phases approach the subject rigorously giving the reader an understanding of how the fuzzy humanistic nature (user) can coexist with the deterministic technological presence (system) revealing the links and subsequent interaction processes to the benefit of the former.

For Academia and Business

This book could also be used as a textbook since it cites numerous scientific works and sources for an additional variety of insights and guidance in each discussion topic or as a reference (handbook) redirecting to a selection of our most influential publications till today for more comprehensive and focused descriptions. We believe that its scope is suitable for both the academic and business sectors and aims to attract the attention of an interdisciplinary audience between researchers and professionals working in the broader fields of information communication technologies (ICT), Web adaptation and personalization, user modeling, human factors, user experience, services, e-commerce, education and technology, and usable security. It provides extensive theoretical and practical information and support for scientists, teachers, students, human factor professionals, ICT professionals, service providers and developers, product designers, and general users. The audience can further gain knowledge from the tangible experiences, new ideas, practical guidelines, and research results with regard to all aspects (theory, applications, and tools) of bringing quality into content and interactions into various contexts of use for adaptation and personalization. More specifically, as core milestones of the book, among others, we pinpoint the following:

1. An enhanced reference on user modeling, introducing a comprehensive user model that extends the notion of existing ones, in a way that incorporates intrinsic human factors, which serve as the primal personalization filtering element of any type of content. The main aim is to help researchers understand how visual, cognitive, and emotional factors can function together under a common model for increasing personalization quality.
2. A detailed description of an open and interoperable Web-based framework that can serve as a guide for researchers and practitioners on how to bridge the theoretical human perspectives with the rigid reality of technology and the generation of intelligent adaptation rules for personalization.
3. A set of step-by-step practical guidelines and examples of designing adaptive and personalized components and user interfaces based on distinct human factors. It is of particular value for researchers, providers, and Web designers and developers to gain a competitive advantage in their market.
4. A broad evaluation in three heterogeneous application areas (i.e., learning, commerce, usable security) and presentation of a number of study designs and results that will increase the understanding of (young) researchers and students on how to handle samples and apply qualitative and quantitative analysis in this area.

Henceforth, we could say that the main benefits concentrate on the top-down approach realized in this book (from theory to practice), through the identification of the human-centred theoretical implications on the information space, their interpretation into tangible design guidelines, and the guidance for a more apt development of personalization techniques, intelligent algorithms, recommendation models, and real-time paradigms. We are confident that this way we can improve the user experience of various task executions and interactions, minimize complexity and frustration, and provide valuable solutions that will remain.

Heidelberg   Panagiotis Germanakos
2015   Marios Belk

Acknowledgments

This book presents the capstone outcome of our interdisciplinary research journey (started 12 years ago, or so), unfolding the experiences and lessons learned in the intersection of the research disciplines of adaptive hypermedia, Web personalization, user modeling, and cognitive psychology. The idea for this book emerged as the number of failures, success stories, and the acquired knowledge matured up to a level worth to be told, as the consistent efforts at a basic and more applied level with continuous investigation, analysis, experimentation, and results implied that they can offer a meaningful holistic alternative perspective in this era (for many) of technological determinism. Throughout this period, our research (entailing as cornerstones our Ph.D. years) focused primarily on two aspects: to investigate the impact of human factors in interactive systems with the aim to more inclusively meet the unique users' requirements for increasing the quality of user experience through adaptation and on the specification, analysis, design, and evaluation of human-centred solutions in an attempt to develop usable and intelligently designed user interfaces and mechanisms that enable personalized user interactions.

In the context of this research, we worked closely with several people to whom we are sincerely grateful. Without their constant support and encouragement, such an endeavor would be simply not feasible. The fruitful and productive collaborations and the endless discussions and ideas can be realized in the numerous contributions and scientific findings and publications reported in this book.

First, our sincere gratitude goes to our two respectful Ph.D. supervisors, Dr. Konstantinos Mourlas, Associate Professor at the Department of Communication and Media Studies, National and Kapodistrian University of Athens, and Dr. George Samaras, Professor at the Department of Computer Science, University of Cyprus. Apart from motivating us throughout our research endeavor, so to find ourselves in a challenging and highly interesting academic environment, we are thankful for their valuable research, intellectual, and scientific guidance in the development of our research work as well as in the development of ourselves as research scientists.

Parts of the research reported in this book have been driven by the Ph.D. works of Dr. Nikos Tsianos and Zacharias Lekkas at the Department of Communication and Media Studies, National and Kapodistrian University of Athens. We have collaborated consistently with Dr. Tsianos and Mr. Lekkas in many aspects of this work as well as in the context of their own Ph.D. research works. Among other contributions, Dr. Tsianos has significantly contributed in understanding and investigating the impact of human factors in the e-learning domain, whereas Mr. Lekkas has contributed in the design of the emotional dimensions of the suggested human factor-based user model reported in this book. More specifically, through his model on emotional regulation, we were able to grasp the importance of coupling the constructs of emotional arousal with the "rational" system of individuals and the benefits that their result can have in computer-mediated interactions. We thank both for their excellent cooperation, quality and fruitful discussions, and work conducted during this research endeavor.

We would like to express our appreciations to our lab fellow, Dr. Panayiotis Andreou, Lecturer in Computing at the University of Central Lancashire, Cyprus, for his unrelenting help and support throughout the duration of our research work. Panayiotis has been a true source of inspiration, always more than willing to take time out in order to help us and make effective discussions during crucial times in our research work. We are also thankful to Dr. Andreou for helping us design the reported framework and the respective formalizations of the user model and the adaptation procedures. His expertise in database systems and algorithms was indeed valuable for realizing many technical aspects of this work.

Many thanks go to Dr. Efi Papatheocharous, Senior Researcher at the Swedish Institute of Computer Science, for the great collaboration, her professionalism, and the endless discussions we had throughout the years. Her expertise in software engineering and artificial intelligence significantly contributed in designing the user modeling mechanisms reported in this book and realizing the challenging task of implicitly modeling human factors based on navigation behavior of users.

Our sincere appreciations go to Dr. Christos Fidas, Lecturer at the Department of Cultural Heritage Management and New Technologies, University of Patras, for introducing us to the area of usable security and the need to understand users in this realm for designing and developing more usable and user-centred security mechanisms. Through the fruitful discussions we had and his insightful ideas and high expertise in human-computer interaction, Dr. Fidas has significantly contributed in understanding how human cognitive factors can be better realized in user authentication and CAPTCHA mechanisms, helping us in turn to create the suggested human-centred design guidelines and adaptation effects in the context of usable security reported in this book.

We would like to express our special thanks to Professor Andreas Demetriou and Assistant Professor George Spanoudis of the Department of Psychology, University of Cyprus, for their efforts and productive discussions we had, especially at the early stages of this research work that helped us in conceiving and developing the human factor-based user model.

We also thank our lab fellows at the Department of Computer Science, University of Cyprus, namely Dr. Dimosthenis Georgiadis, Dr. Christophoros Panayiotou, and Dr. Christophoros Christophorou for their endless support and great ideas throughout the years of our collaboration.

A big thank you goes to various students at the Department of Computer Science, University of Cyprus, for the productive collaboration that helped in implementing many technical aspects reported in this book, namely, Anna Sialarou, Kyriakos Georgiou, Georgia Kleanthous, Marios Constantinides, Argyris Constantinides, Andreas Hadjidemetris, and Elena Efstathiou. Many thanks go to various students of the University of Cyprus and the National and Kapodistrian University of Athens for voluntarily participating in several user studies and for their valuable feedback. Also, we would like to acknowledge the academic and technical support of the Department of Computer Science, University of Cyprus, and the Department of Communication and Media Studies, National and Kapodistrian University of Athens, that provided the support and equipment needed for conducting our research throughout the years.

Furthermore, we would like to thank SAP SE, and in particular the Department of Suite Engineering UX, Products and Innovation, in Walldorf, Germany, for providing the grounds of further clarifying the existing gaps between the academic research outputs and their realization in complex business settings and processes as well as the benefits their amalgamation can offer. It is clearly recognized that once a sound synergy exists between the two worlds, the solutions and the human-computer interactions enabled by them will be able to provide an indisputable added value to the end user no matter the context of application.

We would also like to thank the national research funding programs, the Hellenic PYTHAGORAS, E.P.E.A.E.K. II, the Cyprus Research Promotion Foundation, and the University of Cyprus research committee for internal research funds, as well as the structural funds of the European Union, that financially supported this research endeavor through a number of research projects during the years.

Last but not least, we would like to thank our families for their unconditional love and support all these years as well as our friends for their patience and understanding for the hours we were not able to be with them.

Book Overview

Human-Centred Web Adaptation and Personalization: From Theory to Practice is organized in three main phases as shown in the Table of Contents. The first phase, namely, *THEORY: The Human in the Centre of Web Personalization*, draws an overview of the current digital era stressing the demand for user-friendly and personalized systems and services to the benefit of the unique users. It elaborates on the current communication reality which is driven by new challenges, opportunities, interactions, and structures of information representations. It brings human factors in the centre of attention, highlighting their importance toward the more prominent application of adaptation and personalization in various context areas. It reviews and presents a number of theories and models with respect to human cognition, attention, emotions, and learning and how these can be extracted, modeled, and interpreted in a way that could add value to systems and services by enhancing their content presentation and navigation. Phase 1 includes two chapters. Chapter 1 introduces the technological shift toward single-point data access and continuous communication and new principles of interaction led by current technologies (e.g., Web 2.0, Web 3.0, cloud-based, and the Internet of Things). It reapproaches the area of human-computer interaction underlying the new user requirements that reinforce the design and development of user-centred and personalized interactive hypermedia systems and applications. Consequently, it underpins the importance of adaptation and personalization and the needs, challenges, and problems entailed in the delivery of personalized information and multipurpose user interactions. Chapter 2 makes a reference to the importance of human factors in Web adaptation and personalization, pinpointing their dynamicity and how they can influence the design of multipurpose interactions and interfaces. It places emphasis on specific cognitive and emotional (e.g., anxiety) factors that influence information processing, learning, and decision-making. The main concern is to identify their impact/consequences on the information space in various contexts and how these can be utilized in adaptation and personalization systems and services in order to increase their effectiveness and efficiency.

The second phase, namely, *PRINCIPLES: Web Adaptation and Personalization Processes and Techniques*, attempts to inclusively elaborate on the process of adaptation and personalization of hypermedia environments. It presents an extensive investigation of the adaptation and personalization fields (based on existing state-of-the-art research and reviews), on the analysis of parameters and contexts identifying relationships between these two areas of research, on the importance of user modeling and methods of extraction, and on systems, technologies, and methodologies assigned to a number of application areas trying to approach the topic from a more global perspective. It lastly overviews an adaptation and personalization framework that realizes the mapping of specific theoretical human factors and dimensions with the more deterministic nature of technologies, algorithms, and functions. Phase 2 is composed of three chapters. Chapter 3 analyzes the concept of user models, as a key component of adaptation and personalization systems. It presents its requirements, characteristics, implicit and explicit user data collection methods, and user model generation techniques and makes a reference to a comprehensive user model that incorporates on top of the "traditional" user characteristics and specific cognitive and emotional factors. Chapter 4 refers to adaptation and personalization as a process liable to alleviate the arising difficulties and complications when users interact with various hypermedia environments. It further analyzes existing issues and challenges that influence this research field and presents an extensive review of the two subsequent research domains of Web personalization and adaptive hypermedia, with the related methodologies, techniques, and technologies. A reference is also made to selected state-of-the-art adaptation and personalization systems that were proposed throughout the last 20 years. Chapter 5 overviews an open and interoperable adaptation and personalization framework, namely, mapU, by emphasizing on its modules, components, and technologies used. The main objective of this chapter is to serve as a guide of how a number of interdisciplinary elements, attributes, and functionalities can coexist and enhance usability, satisfaction, and user experience delivered via its intelligent user interface to a number of heterogeneous contexts of interaction.

The third phase, namely, *PRACTICE: A Practical Guide and Empirical Evaluation in Three Distinct Application Areas*, consists of three chapters. Chapters 6, 7, and 8 bring together the aforementioned interdisciplinary research, concepts, models, and technologies and investigates how these can be applied in three heterogeneous contexts of use, i.e., e-learning, e-commerce, and usable security. These areas have different characteristics (e.g., purpose, motivation, communication models, data structures, audience, etc.), peculiarities, and constraints that need a different methodological approach. These characteristics are briefly described at the beginning of the respective chapters to the extent that justify the analysis and development of the corresponding adaptation and personalization algorithms and interfaces. Furthermore, it suggests a number of human-centred practical design guidelines, of how researchers and practitioners can take advantage of each one of the human factors and develop user-centred algorithms, components, and interfaces that could increase usability, learnability, satisfaction, and user experience in these contexts. Finally, it presents a set of empirical evaluations showing in detail study designs and data analyses as well as the corresponding impact and related discussions.

In each chapter we include an abstract, an introduction, and a summary to directly guide the reader and increase his familiarization with the contents. We also try to consistently correlate (by adding dedicated sections in the main chapters) the various theoretical concepts and models of human factors discussed, to the adaptation and personalization process, emphasizing on implications, interpretations, and methods of use. We believe this way the reader can have a more clear understanding of how different areas are blended and he will be able to recognize the benefits, impacts, and limitations to more inclusively frame the respective concepts and techniques in their context of use.

Contents

Abbreviations

3G	Third generation
4G	Fourth generation
ADL	Absolute Distance of Links
AJAX	Asynchronous JavaScript and XML
ANN	Artificial neural networks
AOI	Area of interest
ASP	Active Server Pages
AWD	Adaptive Web Design
B2B	Business to business
B2C	Business to consumer
BAI	Beck Anxiety Inventory
BPN	Back-propagation network
C2B	Consumer to business
C2C	Consumer to consumer
CAPTCHA	Completely Automated Public Turing test to tell Computers and Humans Apart
CLR	Common Language Runtime
CNF	Conjunctive normal form
CPE	Cognitive processing efficiency
CSA	Cognitive style analysis
CSS	Cascade Style Sheets
CTA	Cognitive test anxiety
DAML	DARPA Agent Markup Language
DASS	Depression Anxiety and Stress Scale
DIH	Decision Integration Hypothesis Theory
E-CSA-WA	Extended Cognitive Styles Analysis-Wholistic Analytic
EEG	Electroencephalography
ELSIN	European Learning Styles Information Network
FIS	Fuzzy inference system
FIT	Feature Integration Theory
GAI	Geriatric Anxiety Inventory

GEFT	Group Embedded Figures Test
GOMS	Goals, operators, methods, and selection rules
GPS	Global Positioning System
GST	Guided Search Theory
HCI	Human-computer interaction
HHI	Human-human interaction
HIP	Human interaction proof
HTML	Hypertext Markup Language
HTTP	Hypertext Transfer Protocol
ICT	Information and communication technologies
ID	Identification
IDE	Integrated development environment
IIS	Internet Information Services
ILS	Index of Learning Styles
IoT	Internet of Things
IP	Internet Protocol
IT	Information technology
ITS	Intelligent tutoring systems
JIT	Just-in-time complier
JSON	JavaScript Object Notation
KLM	Keystroke-Level Model
LISP	LISt Processing
LSI	Learning Styles Inventory
LSQ	Learning Styles Questionnaire
MLP	Multilayer perceptron
MSIL	Microsoft Intermediate Language
NFC	Near Field Communication
OCR	Optical character recognition
OIL	Ontology Inference Layer or Ontology Interchange Language
OSIVQ	Object-Spatial Imagery and Verbal Questionnaire
OWL	Web Ontology Language
PC	Personal computer
PDA	Personal digital assistant
PHP	PHP: Hypertext Preprocessor
PIN	Personal identification number
QoS	Quality of service
QR	Quick response
RBAC	Role-based access control
RDF	Resource Description Framework
RFID	Radio-frequency identification
RWD	Responsive Web Design
SHOE	Simple HTML Ontology Extensions
SMS	Short Message Service
SQL	Structured Query Language
STAI	Stait-Trait Anxiety Inventory

SVG	Scalable Vector Graphics
TMAC	Team-based access control
TV	Television
UPPC	User perceptual preferences characteristics
URL	Uniform Resource Locator
UX	User experience
VICS	Verbal-imagery cognitive style
W3C	World Wide Web Consortium
W4	Wireless World Wide Web
WMC	Working memory capacity
WMTB-C	Working Memory Test Battery for Children
WoT	Web of Things
WWW	World Wide Web
XHTML	Extensible Hypertext Markup Language
XML	Extensible Markup Language

Part I
Theory: The Human in the Centre of Web Personalization

Chapter 1
Personalization in the Digital Era

Abstract According to a recent claim by IBM, every day we create 2.5 quintillion bytes of data – so much that 90 % of the data in the world today has been created in the last two years alone. These data come from a variety of sources and in diverse formats creating an ecosystem that apart from the many benefits and opportunities it offers, generates a number of problems and complications that might hinder and disorient people in their daily interaction with online information. In this respect, non-personalized systems and applications fail to meet the needs and goals of different users. The necessity for adaptation and personalization of today's fast growing and dynamic computing systems, content and services is now even more recognizable since they can offer alternative solutions that could adequately support the increasing multi-purpose requests and desires of users. This chapter overviews the major influential dimensions and aspects around this uncontrolled and vague ever-expanding digital reality, and tries to sketch the shift of viewpoints towards new research challenges in creating adaptive and personalized interactive systems that consider the human in the 'centre'. Main aim is to provide a first understanding of the context and dynamics around adaptation and personalization, and motivate the reader to appreciate the role of the user and individual differences in the design and development process of such systems.

Keywords Human-computer interaction • User-centred design • Adaptation • Personalization • Challenges

1.1 Introduction

Today, the computer and the Internet constitute the cornerstone of any modern society supporting the daily human activities and enabling new intelligent methods of fast and easy communication. The growing role of the Internet as a communication medium is highlighted, beyond the obvious living experience, by the high volume of research on practical directions like the development of tools and algorithms that can handle processes and messages generated from a wide number of heterogeneous platforms and technologies, as well as on the more theoretical ones which are ranging from concepts and designs that aim to increase the familiarity and usability

© Springer International Publishing Switzerland 2016
P. Germanakos, M. Belk, *Human-Centred Web Adaptation and Personalization*,
Human–Computer Interaction Series, DOI 10.1007/978-3-319-28050-9_1

of the multi-modal interfaces, to the investigation of the effects of the digital divide in specific societal contexts.

Similarly, the World Wide Web (WWW or Web) has become a platform for deployment of complex applications of increased interactivity, as it takes the form of a medium used for multifaceted and important tasks like commercial and governmental transactions, social intercommunication, collaborative work, learning and information retrieval. Within this realm, adaptation and personalization of interactive systems is considered a promising research direction as it is sufficient that the consequences of a system that will not offer the expected user experience, hinder the interactions of users, or create false expectations and not effective use, will generate frustration and decrease its acceptability. In this context, one of the most important and challenging issues is to support users, engaged on tasks related to their everyday processes, through adaptive and personalized human-computer interface designs and applications.

Adaptation and personalization, which could be considered as a central practice of Human-computer Interaction (HCI), is therefore pronounced as the main ingredient of future online services and applications which are expected to offer a rich set of computing and communication services to users in a broader context, representing unprecedented opportunities to access, manipulate, and share information as well as to accomplish tasks through heterogeneous devices and contexts of use. In this regards, adapting the functionality and the content, of an interactive system, into an assemblage that specific users are able to understand and use intuitively in order to perform specific tasks is a challenging endeavor. It entails understanding and modeling of human behavior for diverse user groups and stakeholders, with regard to structural and functional user requirements. These, in turn, need to be translated into usable human-computer interaction designs and workflows that aim to minimize user cognitive loads, perceptual and learning efforts and erroneous interactions.

Taken into consideration that users of the World Wide Web do not necessarily share common conventions, cultural, and cognitive backgrounds and contexts in which specific decisions are required to be taken we propose in this book that adaptive and personalized systems and user interfaces could provide a viable alternative in order to ensure simplicity and ease of use offering equal chances for participation by all. Adaptive user interfaces provide an alternative to the "one-size-fits-all" approach of static user interfaces by adapting the interactive system's structure, navigation, terminology, functionalities and presentation of content to users' perceptions and level of knowledge with regard to any type of information or service, aiming to increase the usability of the interface and provide a positive user experience.

This book studies the important theoretical dimensions and technologies that govern the relationship between human-computer communication, from the adaptation and personalization angle, suggesting methods and techniques that can promote the robust interaction among the two entities in various application domains. Throughout the book, we have the standpoint that the application of adaptation and personalization should always have the human (user) in the centre. This expands the focus of current approaches that might consider traditional user characteristics (as for example needs and/or requirements), and gives emphasis on how intrinsic human individual characteristics could be explicitly considered with respect to users' interactions with any kind of interface. Henceforth, we have coined the term 'Human-centred Adaptation and Personalization' since we tackle the subject from a more holistic and interdisciplinary perspective bringing human factors in the centrum and discussing methods for creating inclusive user models, intelligent algorithms and techniques for specialized use cases that increase user experience and usability.

In addition, our main concern, amongst others, is to present in the best possible way the co-existence of the two worlds, of theory and practice, in the adaptation and personalization area, and how researchers and practitioners can benefit depending on their area of application. Therefore, we move beyond standalone and isolated attempts, investigating methods and techniques of how a high level understanding (or the extraction) of specific human factors can be put into practice and provide the desired adaptive and personalized outcome. This could be achieved by (a) defining accurate human-centred models based on users' perceptions, behaviors, abilities, experiences, etc.; and (b) creating adaptation and personalization algorithms, interaction principles and smart interfaces that can handle the increasing complexity of data structures and the high volume of information.

1.2 Rethinking Human-Computer Interaction

The link between humans and the latest technologies and computational systems is now tighter than ever. This reality has led to the birth of a new interdependent dimension that signifies how people communicate. Primarily, it influences how people function with respect to their individual processes, collaboration patterns, working activities, and/or what habits they create for their life style. The present exchange of messages between people over the existing communication frameworks of interaction does not anymore only occur in the physical environment but mostly in the electronic one. This yields a number of new features and limitations which are continuing to proliferate, with respect to the design and capabilities of the social (hyper) media and software systems, the simplicity of use, the friendliness and usability of the user interfaces and so on. The coexistence of the human with the computer, with the necessary theories and viewpoints has started long time ago, but apparently there was not the corresponding technological setting in place that would support them to evolve. More specifically, the term "Human-Computer Symbiosis" has been introduced and widely studied by JCR Licklider back in the 60s (Licklider 1960), which although was a pioneer direction considering the technological advancements of this epoch, only in recent years under this frame of digital holism could be entirely feasible. The objectives of this symbiotic state of human-computer expressed by Licklider, were:

- To enable computers, that until then supported only the solutions of standard problems, to facilitate the standardized form of thought and intellect;
- To enable people and computers to make decisions and to control complex situations, while creating a more flexible relationship with the specific software programs.

To get a clearer picture of these concepts we will introduce the basic theoretical aspects of human and computer systems/communication. However, main purpose of this book is not to thoroughly analyze all the attributes that characterize these two ends. Such an endeavor has been quite inclusively undertaken by many researchers until today (Dix et al. 2003; Preece et al. 2011; Ritter et al. 2014). It is considered though of importance to study these factors that govern their relationship and promote thereby the human-computer communication in a robust interaction. This way, it will be easier to understand the paradigm shift that influences this relationship and the necessity of developing adaptive and personalized interactive hypermedia processes and environments in today's digital era.

The analysis of this dimension falls under the research area of HCI, which together with the Human-Human Interaction (HHI) – it refers to the interpersonal communication between people who participate in complex HCI environments – attempt to define the borders of this relationship. As the term implies, the HCI consists of three parts: The human-user dimension, the computer itself and the ways these two entities work together (communicate). By working together, we mean how humans interact with computers and how computers are designed and developed in order to manage a successful interaction with human beings. To start with, when we refer to HCI today, we do not have necessarily in mind a single user with a personal computer. The term "user" might refer to a specific user, a group of users working together, exchanging messages in a social context, or a number of users in an organization where everyone is engaged in some part of a task or process. The user is anyone who is trying to complete a task using the technology. By the term "computer", is meant any technology that varies from a conventional personal computer to a large scale computing system, a process control system or an embedded system. The system may contain computational components as well as other people. With the term "interaction" we mean any communication between a user and a computer, regardless of whether it is direct or indirect. The *direct* interaction is associated with dialogue, feedback and control throughout the lifetime of a task. The *indirect* interaction can refer to background or batch and off-line processing. The important and common aspect to all these scenarios is that the user needs to interact with the computer in order to achieve an action or process.

To better understand the objective of HCI, we should try more generically to approach this relationship and the underlined differences between the human and the computer. We must focus on the way in which people understand the space, and therefore receive a stimulus that they process and respond, as opposed to a conventional computer. According to Licklider, people are flexible, able to plan themselves under unexpected circumstances and based on the new information they receive. In contrast, computers follow a more linear functionality, based primarily on how they have been programmed that they should "react" per occasion. The behavior of the computer is determined by the cause, with a predetermined operation based on the data entered. This we cannot say that it is the case in human behavior. Hence, even though the various relations of input/output information can be modeled quite well in a computer, in contrast, there is currently no concrete modeling of human behavior which is governed by various sensory and perceptual dynamics. The operation of a computer could well be seen as predictable while the prognosis of human reactions as particularly dynamic and difficult. These findings, although their lapidary presentation, can portray the diversity of these two entities and hence the possibility of researching towards a harmonized relationship between the human and the computer. In any case, it is exactly this diversity that characterizes human-computer systems (Gallatay 1986), that prompted the development of the field of HCI (Balint 1996), with models and techniques that allow each entity to complement the other in what is difficult or impossible for one or the other to accomplish respectively.

Nowadays, the research area of HCI is a key point of reference in the design and implementation of any application, from a simple icon to integrated information systems, weapon systems, navigation systems, and others. Especially, in computer science and system design its value must be recognized as a fundamental and universally applicable theory. The area of HCI is the thematic area of informatics that studies the design, development and evaluation of interactive computer systems, that is systems that interact with their users (ACM SIGCHI, "Curriculum for Human-Computer Interaction", Special Interest Group on Computer-Human Interaction Curriculum Development Group, New York, 1992), for which a system designer must consider their responsibilities, objectives and activities throughout the process. For all the other sciences, HCI can be seen as a specialization even though it can provide important and insightful information.

1.2.1   Repositioning the "I" in HCI

The rapid technological development along with the advancement of the information technology – that is, according to Oxford dictionaries, the use of systems (especially computers and telecommunications) for storing, retrieving and sending information – stress nowadays the need to redefine the factor of "interaction" in the relationship of HCI and to investigate new dimensions that could be proven more efficient and applicable in the present technological ecosystem. As it is commonly perceived, today's reality enables the formulation of more flexible and hybrid communication models between humans (users) and technologies since the former interact with and through many different devices which in turn present a particular level of intelligence themselves. We have therefore escaped from the strict one-to-one relationship to more open and scalable collaboration models which create many opportunities but at the same time increases the complexity of this coexistence.

The evolution, utilization and growing ubiquity of heterogeneous technologies (such as, bar codes, Quick Response (QR) codes, Near Field Communication (NFC) tags, etc.) along with the growing demand for automation of services and content delivery during the last years, generated the potential for new interaction concepts and information structures to arise. Interactive computing technologies such as sensors, actuators, and interactive graphical displays have become increasingly common in the everyday life's settings that humans interact such as cars, houses, or consumer products (e.g., residential smart meters, smart appliances, smart energy-aware systems, smart cars and gas-stations, smart fridges, etc.). The convergence of mobile, cloud, big data, and social media, bring the Internet in the centre, as a central hub that enables context-aware ubiquitous platforms, middleware and applications to proliferate. This realization has been gradually supported by new technologies that have been only recently introduced and became quickly largely common, like short-range wireless communications, RFIDs and real-time localization, allowing the Internet to penetrate into the real world of physical objects. Today we are living in the era of Internet of Things (IoT) that allows physical devices to seamlessly communicate through the Internet. More specifically, IoT refers to uniquely identifiable objects and their virtual representations in an Internet-like structure (Ashton 2009). Or, in a more free interpretation it refers to the connection of all devices and/or people, identifiable through unique IDs (i.e., IPs), over an advanced multi-purpose real-time network. Similarly, we are witnessing a fast-growing progress in the Web technologies. The trend, almost 25 years ago, towards desktop computing has been transformed into a digital revolution with the appearance of Web browsers and the resulting explosion of the World Wide Web. The Web started only as an idea in the late 80s with the introduction of the HTTP protocol and the Web 1.0 by Tim Berners-Lee in 1989, found at the time at a definition stage where open markup languages and hypertext (as the first version of the HyperText Markup Language (HTML) in 1990) made the content available (or better accessible) to users. Since then, it has been progressed very fast to its second generation, called Web 2.0, in 2004, supporting internet-based services, collaboration, social networking/communication and sharability among users, and then to Web 3.0 in 2006, enabling machine-facilitated understanding through computational intelligence techniques and data semantics. Consequently, the World Wide Web has reached today, to refer to its latest "edition" as Web of Things (WoT) which describes the software architectural styles and programming patterns that allow real-world objects to be part of the Web. The WoT is inspired from the embedded Internet connectivity and it is about reusing well-accepted and understood Web principles to interconnect the quickly expanding ecosystem of embedded devices, built into everyday smart things (Pitsillides 2014). Inevitably, as the field continues to evolve at an astonishing pace, with new technologies to be introduced continually, and with existing ones to become obsolete almost as soon as they appear, this reality brings networking and usable communication devices in the centre of attention while it could be characterized as a mass-market phenomenon of our economy.

On these grounds, the coexistence of the multi-purpose technologies and devices, which are based on heterogeneous semantic grounds, create a reality which is composed of vast amounts of data and specialized use cases that users need to understand in order to co-operate and act. A reasonable sequence of questions would be: How do we define these kinds of interactions which are created among the specialized devices and the users? For example, how do we handle the interaction data generated from a smart fridge or a smart car and the intuitive embedded actions undertaken on our behalf? What happens in case of failures and how can we ensure the continuous controllability to the user? The massive production of data makes people neither to feel happy nor safe. In contrast, it creates an overwhelmed situation with more facts and complex decisions that they need to take with regard to a particular functionality. In order for a user to feel inclusive and productive to this new digital reality, he must maintain the controllability over the processes and/or the collaborative environments he participates. This implies that new interaction methods and workflow models need to be defined with respect to the user per se, the content (smart objects) and the various processes, since users could be characterized more emotional and are interested for the interaction design, rather than the features and representations of data, which give meaning just to applications. Moreover, the latest interface technologies offer new possibilities of interactions in the style and kind of information presentation (e.g., reasonable, rational, arbitrary, sequential, haptic, visual, auditory, communicative, etc.), in which previous research findings may not fit with respect to user preferences and needs, underlying the importance of revisiting the current knowledge repositories and the design and development principles.

Designers, professionals and practitioners need to understand the possibilities and limitations of computing technologies and multi-modal interfaces at a sufficient level to be able to engage in a constructive analysis and to create feasible interaction concept proposals for products and services. Many users today would agree that the manufacturers of computer applications and interactive software systems have only recently started to pay consistent attention to ensure that their products and services are developed in a user friendly manner. On the other hand, there are several designers of computer systems and applications still arguing that computers are extremely complex to design so to manufacture products that will deliver services as required while at the same time to offer an ease-of-use and simple accessibility.

1.2.2 HCI Meets Adaptation and Personalization: Influential Research Disciplines

HCI's main objective is to optimize human's and computer's performance not as two separate entities but rather together as a common system. The research towards that direction requires the synergy of many disciplines that try to understand the issue of HCI and to contribute with relevant approaches and insights accordingly, given their different scientific focus. We could say that these disciplines belong to three main overarching areas that is, anthropology, sociology and information science, including disciplines as cognitive and social psychology, social sciences, communication theory, linguistics, computers science, mathematics, engineering to mention but a few. In this book, we will mainly focus on the convergence of the areas of cognitive psychology and computer science, emphasizing on how particular factors and techniques can work together to provide adaptive and personalized interactive hypermedia environments, design guidelines and experiences that engage users of the current technological generation into a usable and pleasant interaction.

The area of cognitive psychology is the one that has contributed significantly towards that direction, proposing cognitive models that are associated with a better understanding of information processing and more generally of processes that govern the interaction. Apart from its primary subject matter, to study the thought (when it was founded as a science by Wundt in Leipzig in 1879), cognitive psychology's intention is to investigate the cognitive processes that support cognitive abilities. Users develop different principles, ideas and perceptual/mental models concerning each interaction. They use different methods of information acquisition and learning as well as they employ different strategies for knowledge retainment with respect to their experiences and abilities (different "cognitive models" such as for example, "left brain" and "right brain" oriented people). Cognitive psychologists attempt to give generic answers to questions related to mechanisms that support cognitive and emotional processes, to mechanisms that are responsible for collection and processing of information, and to investigate cognitive functions such as perception, recognition, storage and recall of information, understanding, and problem solving. Hence, any of the findings, theories or suggested models deeply affect the scope of HCI, since they interpret at some extent the possibilities and limitations of the human nature in relation to this interaction (human-computer). As Davou (2000) points out, beyond the main differences of the various proposed approaches, which stem from the broader scientific viewpoint of each one (or from small or large variations in the main object of study, i.e., whether it is the subject, message, frame, space, time etc. in the centre), common point of all is the realization that communication requires at least two sides, which depending on the model, are called the *source* and the *receiver*, or the *transmitter* and the *receiver*, with their respective connotations to designate each method. Thus, various models of HCI, which are primarily affected by the above scientific dimensions and cognitive psychology approaches, have been proposed in the light of the communication between these two sides (human-computer) and the necessary interaction devices (e.g., input/ output, user interfaces, etc.), permitting the transfer or movement of information from both sides.

At a higher-level, these models describe the interaction with a computer including various stages of human behavior, such as expressing an intention and executing an action; and the different levels of an activity, such as the goal to improve a text and the intention behind every low-level action like the natural execution of a command (Norman 1986). The most important models that proposed and supported the creation of the usability evaluation methods of interfaces are the Model Human Processor (Card et al. 1983), the Goals, Operators, Methods, and Selection rules

(GOMS), the Keystroke Level Model (KLM) and the model of the seven stages of Norman (1986).

The design and further development of user interfaces is critical as they are the midpoint in communication with an application, and may affect the overall usability and reliability of a system. The aftermath of a poor interface design is, among others, the increased number of errors in data entry and system operation, the inaccessible functionality, the users' frustration and low productivity, the system failure (due to its rejection by the user), and the disorientation and inability of users to achieve core objectives and tasks.

At this point we should not omit to make a reference to cultural and ethnic differences of various individuals that affect significantly this process. Such a direction, even though it is not in line with the main scope of this book, might be of particular interest for the reader for further investigation since it gives a more global perspective of the multi-level influence that human cognitive development might have and adds on to the challenge to more inclusively study humans' dynamic nature. According to Röse, intercultural HCI design describes the user and culture oriented design of interactive systems and products taking into account the cultural context of the user depending on the tasks and the usage of a product (Heimgärtner 2012). In more generic terms, as culture we define a "*complex whole which includes knowledge, belief, art, morals, law, custom, and any other capabilities and habits acquired by man as a member of society*" (Tylor 1974). Given the diversity of existing cultures around the world and the globalization of information technology applications and services, the investigation of cultural aspects and their effects on human-computer interactions are shifting in the centre of attention lately (Ferreira et al. 2013; Nöll et al. 2015). With respect to cognition, research has shown that cultural characteristics affect extensively human behavior, cognitive development and personality traits that define humans as individuals (Thrower 1999; Tomasello 2000). Specifically, a high number of philosophical and historical essays, as well as a large number of intra- and cross-cultural user studies have shown that culture affects the development of human cognition and cognitive processing styles and abilities (Cui et al. 2013; Varnum et al. 2010; Engelbrecht et al. 1997).

On the side of computer science, the area of artificial intelligence is the one that traditionally deals with the study and understanding of human intelligent behavior on the assumption that intelligence can be better analyzed if we try to reproduce it. The pioneers of artificial intelligence were inspired by the idea that computers and computer programs could serve as an appropriate metaphor for understanding and reasoning. In the context of adaptation and personalization, many research attempts are using computational techniques that share roots with the suggested cognitive models to dynamically adapt the content presentation and functionality of an interactive system based on implicitly retrieved user models that contain multipurpose information about the user.

Nonetheless, simply developing rich and elaborated personalization and user modeling techniques is not adequate in today's highly complex and dynamic computing environments. Although personalization has shown to be the key for improving usability and user experience, it is of critical importance to measure how and why users would benefit. Apparently, individuals are different from each other, but an undeniable issue that is required to be resolved for successful personalization, is to understand the underlying theories that could guide research endeavors in producing practical and measurable outcomes. This approach has been inspired by the individual differences research; in the words of Kyllonen and Stevens (1990), a person may differ from another in "...*fundamental cognitive abilities that affect the overall integrity of the individual's cognitive information processing system*". It should be noted, though, that such differences are expected to manifest when a certain amount of information processing load is imposed on the user, which consequently involves interactive hypermedia environments and Web systems that present a certain degree of complexity. A first approach would be to identify the levels in which individuals demonstrate considerable differences, such as demographics, social, mental abilities, personality, goals, needs, and experience, and to build a cohesive user model by including characteristics that would be proven to be important in affecting behavior and performance.

User models figure as the kernel of adaptation and personalization systems and at a more theoretical level they could be considered as the component that at some extent joins the objectives of the two areas of computer science and cognitive psychology in the field; since they refer to the collection and maintenance of all the user characteristics, that include also behavioral patterns, cognitive, emotional and perceptual preferences, etc. User modeling embraces various challenges: (i) What characteristics of the user are considered important to be included in the user model; (ii) how to represent them; and (iii) how to extract and maintain them in time. Given that these user characteristics might change over time, as well as, that in many cases, users are unwilling to provide such information, explicit user model generation approaches usually result in user models that become inaccurate over time. The topic of user modeling will be extensively discussed in Chap. 3 of this book, but it is necessary to adequately underpin at this stage the important contribution of artificial intelligence, by utilizing more sophisticated approaches, in the implicit and dynamic generation of user models as an answer to the abovementioned problem,. Such cases are the interaction activities of users which may be utilized by data mining and machine learning techniques (like cluster analysis, classification, decision trees, and artificial neural networks) to recognize regularities in user paths, to predict user preference or estimate the probability that users will like particular items and consequently integrate them in a user model.

A thorough literature review on how data mining techniques can be applied to user modeling in the context of (mostly the Web) adaptation and personalization systems may be found in Eirinaki and Vazirgiannis (2003); Pierrakos et al. (2003); Mobasher (2007) and Papatheocharous et al. (2014). To give a brief idea for their potential, the reported data mining techniques enable pattern discovery through clustering, classification, association rules, and Markov chains for the Web personalization purposes. Clustering or fuzzy clustering techniques group users together that share common characteristics or similar navigation behavior (Nasraoui et al. 2008; Castellano and Torsello 2008; Castellano et al. 2007). Classification techniques map user information (e.g., interaction data) into one of several predetermined classes which usually represent different user models (Wu et al. 2007). Association rule techniques aim at generating associations and correlations among sets of items (Linden et al. 2003; Su and Khoshgoftaar 2009). Markov chains are used to represent the transitions of users within the Web environment (Parka et al. 2008; Cadez et al. 2000; Yang et al. 2003) and they are utilized for indicating the next page users might navigate based on their current location and previous navigation paths.

Although the discipline of artificial intelligence has found its way in the area of HCI and more specifically in the context of adaptation and personalization of users' everyday interactions over the various devices and multi-modal interfaces, there are still open research issues and weaknesses with regard to fundamental influential factors, such as the behavioral drivers and navigation interaction of users in executing task-oriented reasoning processes. Furthermore, the critics on artificial intelligence approaches are not few, with a representative viewpoint the one of Hubert Dreyfus (1972) who, by generalizing, has argued that there are many things that computers cannot do yet, because they operate in a binary logic which differs substantially from human reasoning. Dreyfus argues that the binary conversions of symbols in the machine logic are still too far from mimicking the human thought. Therefore, even though it is commonly accepted that we can manage or better model the interaction between machines easier, due to the fact that their informational requirements are usually more deterministic and can be easier modeled by people (Balint 1996), it seems that such an argument is not true for people themselves, and inevitably capturing the dynamic human behavior and the influencing cognitive and/or emotional processes at an adequate extent is still a challenge of the far future.

Nevertheless, on the grounds of this realization, and with the transition to the digital age, it is of high risk future solutions to follow computer-centred rather than human-centred extensions. Therefore, it is considered imperative the embracement of the needs, preferences and capabilities of the people and not solely of the parameters that frame the technology evolution per se (Norman 1996). In this respect, we should explicitly note that in this book we consider the human as the central "character" in any reference on interactive systems since he is the one for which computer systems are designed and his evolved requirements, contexts and special interaction dynamics should guide the human-computer communication.

1.3 The Need for User-Centred Design in Interactive Computing Systems and Interfaces

The human-computer co-operation according to Suchman (1987) may be considered from two angles: The *emulation approach*, which is based on the logic that computers should be enriched with human-centric skills if we want to enhance human-computer cooperation, and the *complementing approach* based on which we must accept that the computer is not a human and that the human-centred design should 'exploit' this diversity by developing new methods for interaction and cooperation. In particular, human- or user-centred design has received great attention lately by the research community as well as by many business organizations. Nowadays, there are various tools and methods in the market that are used to increase the understanding of the users' requirements and the process of their tasks execution in order to better support the design, development and evaluation of the systems, components, and/or interfaces they interact. Using these tools practitioners are trying to collect information like: *What users do?*, *What users say?*, *What disrupts a workflow?*, *What supports users' work?*, etc.

User-centred design approaches focus on interacting iteratively with the end-users, especially for identifying and validating user requirements, designing system prototypes as well as for evaluating them. The aim is to investigate thoroughly what users require from a novel system design and how the system can support them in accomplishing specific tasks effectively, efficiently, and with a certain degree of user satisfaction. An important aspect of this process is to model a user interaction with a user interface. A good design practice aims to establish common grounds among designers and users related to aspects of user-system interaction by formalizing the information architecture of the interactive system and by specifying the interaction flow for accomplishing specific tasks. A well-used and simple approach to modeling interactive systems is to analyze the users' actions in several levels of abstractions and identify on each level the most appropriate terminology, content presentation and interaction flow.

There are many text books and white reports written with respect to user-centred design, with their content and process steps to vary depending on the strategies and the priorities of the respective researchers and organizations. A further analysis and elaboration on the subsequent items that constitute this perspective would be out of the scope of this book. However, for the sake of completion, we should mention that the user-centred rationale drives the viewpoint of this book. Such a process methodology is also vital and should be applied for the design and development of adaptation and personalization systems, following four overarching principles (Preece et al. 2011): (a) Identifying needs and establishing requirements, placing emphasis on who our target users are and what kind of support an interactive product or service could usefully provide; (b) developing alternative designs that meet those requirements, describing conceptual models that show what a product or a service should do, how it will behave and how it will look like; (c) building interactive versions so that they can be communicated and assessed, using any kinds of prototypes that users can interact identifying problems in the early stages of design; and (d) evaluating them, i.e. measuring their acceptability, based on given criteria such as the number of errors the users do, how fast they complete a task, how appealing the product or a service is, how well it matches their requirements and so on.

To sum up, early focus on users and tasks, emphasis on their participation in the design process for ideation and evaluation, setting specific usability criteria and iteration are the keys to success for (adaptive) interactive systems. The users develop different structural and functional mental models and thus they need individual scaffolding. Forming a mental model related to system interaction embraces a seven step iteration cycle (Norman 2013): Forming the goal, forming the intention, specifying an action, executing the action, perceiving the state of the world, interpreting the state of the world, and evaluating the outcome. The users form a conceptual intention related to their goal and try to adapt the intention to the features provided by the system and from these user-perceived features, the users try to perform their actions. Subsequently, the users attempt to understand the outcome of their actions by evaluating the system response. The last three stages help the users to develop and refine their mental models of the system. The whole process is repeated in iterations of user actions and evaluations which results in developing and refining their mental models by interpreting the system's response. The development and maintenance of user mental models is a dynamic and continuous process, especially related to novice and average users who are still in the process of developing these models based on empirical system interaction. Once these models are created, then the users interact with the system in more automated ways, faster, and more efficiently. Ineffective practice of this syllogism usually leads to "one-size-fits-all" approaches, and poor designs of adaptive interactive systems and interfaces that present a questionable usability, functionality, efficiency, reliability, maintainability, or simply... do not work!

1.4   The Concept of Web Adaptation and Personalization

The growth in the size and use of internet as communication medium has changed the way content and services are designed and implemented during the last decade. In this new digital era, the hypermedia content is frequently divided into nodes of information and semantically enhanced links implementing a hypermedia structure where users have the freedom to navigate and discover themselves the required information. Services are embedded in similar structures and new hypermedia technologies determine the platform that will be used for the implementation of a wide range of applications, like commerce, entertainment and communication, learning and education. Multimedia applications have abandoned the low level of interactivity and they have moved to higher levels of (user) interaction, incorporating hyper linking techniques that result in many cases to more complex hypermedia environments.

The traditional sequential access of information has been replaced by new navigational features of hypermedia where nodes can be visited in a variety of ways generated by multi-purpose channels and devices (forming routes in hierarchical, star or mesh structures). These practices often lead to navigation difficulties, as users get overwhelmed by unnecessary information which might eventually lead towards searching for stimulating rather than informative material. In an ocean of a few billion Internet nodes, Web searching and retrieval of relevant information for each user has become extremely difficult and an increasingly time consuming process for him. The user is left helpless to find the information he seeks through the Internet portals, which are providing in a hierarchical order a list of possible connections per module (categorization), hoping that he will find quickly the right path and will successfully reach the desired leaf of this complex tree. Of course, there is the option of using one of the various search engines available today, and with the use of keywords to receive instantly some results which are however usually hundreds or even thousands of possible destinations for the user who is striving to find the right one to follow. Furthermore, locating and visiting the desired destination – or the content provider that covers the user's interests – it is still not the ultimate solution to the problem, since there is the increasing realism of content overlapping with additional topics and links that are irrelevant to the user and which may ultimately lead him to cognitive overload. In such a case, the user feels confused and disoriented since he diversifies from his initial navigation towards extracting the desired knowledge from an Internet node. The average user should be able to easily and quickly discover the information or services he is looking for from the vast information pool that characterizes todays Internet.

Additionally, the diffusion of the Internet as a medium that enables users not only to navigate but also to create and promote new content has led to an information explosion where the problem no longer merely lies in whether there is the specific information or not and how it is retrieved from the Internet nodes that is stored, but also in the way it will be presented in the heterogeneous interests and "unique" needs of the end-users. Potential visitors can differ in interests, language or age with different skills in the use of new technologies while they might use different devices to access the Internet. Therefore, the content must be more communicative and user friendly with the ultimate aim of creating a 'smart' Internet with applications and services that will serve users based on their needs, capabilities and preferences. The ongoing utilization of wireless accessibility to the Internet through mobile devices of any nature (i.e., mobile devices, tablets, TVs, car LEDs, etc.), makes the above need of fast search and easy retrieval of information even more intense and important as a success factor of the wireless technology. The content should not only be properly adjusted/displayed according to the interests of the end-user but should also be adapted to the constraints imposed by the device itself (i.e., screen size, wireless connectivity, processing speed, bandwidth interface – Panayiotou and Samaras 2006).

To alleviate such navigational difficulties, researchers have put huge amounts of effort to identify the peculiarities of each user group and design interfaces, interaction methods and systems that could deliver adaptive and personalized interactive experiences. Research on adaptive interactive systems (Schneider-Hufschmidt et al. 1993) can be traced back to the early 1990s where researchers from the hypertext and hypermedia community recognized the drawbacks of static hypermedia in a variety of application areas (Brusilovsky 2001) and explored various ways to adapt the content presentation and functionality of such systems to the needs of individual users. With the exponential increase of users and information on the World Wide Web in the mid-1990s (ISC 2014), the need to provide adaptive and personalized content to the heterogeneous needs and preferences of users became evident. Within this realm, researchers from the Adaptive Hypermedia community used the Web as an attractive and challenging platform for applying their research, and since then, the majority of research on adaptation and personalization systems has been applied on it (Brusilovsky 2001; Brusilovsky and Maybury 2002). The field of adaptation and personalization systems has received even greater attention from the research community in the last years with the appearance of new applications and services in the new digital reality of big data and IoT, bringing up the necessity for a dynamic execution of processes in continuous changing environments.

An *adaptive* (or adapted) interactive system is any interactive system which is capable to automatically or semi-automatically adapt its information architecture, functionality and user interface as a response on implicit or explicit gathered data which are related with the users themselves (e.g., behavioral patterns), their interaction with the system or the context of use in which interaction takes place. It is a process that is triggered by the system (computer driven) and not directly by the user (user driven) as it happens in the case of *adaptable* systems, where the users explicitly intervene and customize the content and structure of, e.g., a Web-site, by changing the fonts, colors or size of an object, or re-organizing data items. Adaptivity and adaptability very often co-exist in a system, with the utter goal to increase its functionality and improve the users' experience by providing personalized and bootstrapped interactions.

In general, adaptive systems and networks cover a wide spectrum of applications with similar behavior and properties where the term adaptivity can be met in three different variations:

1. *Adaptivity of content and services.* In this category content and services have to be adapted according to user preferences and system constraints. Adaptive hypermedia, Web personalization and intelligent user interfaces are some of the main representatives of this category where content, navigation and appearance/ aesthetics have to be adapted according to: (a) The user model; and (b) the device characteristics of the user (e.g., monitor resolution, bandwidth allocation, etc.) also referred as Quality of Service (QoS) constraints. Adaptive and personalized services share in this case the same basic goal, to provide users with the content they want or need without requiring them to ask for it explicitly. Thus, adaptivity of content and services is the provision to the individual of tailored products, Web-based content, multimedia-based services, information or information relating to products or services. The issue of adaptivity of content and services is a complex one with many aspects that need to be analyzed. Such issues include, but are not limited to: (a) What content to present to the user; (b) how to show the content to the user; (c) how to ensure the user's privacy; (d) how to create a global personalization scheme. At the higher level, adaptivity of content and services is realized in one of two ways: (a) Services or Web-sites that require users to register and provide information about their interests and needs; and (b) Services or Web-sites that only require the registration of users so that they can be identified. At the lower level, adaptivity of systems and processing is required for the implementation of such applications and services.
2. *Adaptivity of systems and processing.* The current interest on systems and processing is focused on the ability of these systems to adapt their execution at run

time according to changing system requirements and requests that arrive from the dynamic and complex runtime environment where other objects or processes are running concurrently sharing the same computational power as well as other resources. The emphasis here is not given to the adaptive content but to the adaptive execution of the processes. The traditional systems although they perform well in static information spaces they are inadequate for new and evolving environments like multimedia servers, streaming media presentations, ubiquitous computing, soft real-time systems, agent computing and grid computing. Recent research has given interesting results in the above areas where new operating systems and programming environments have been implemented supporting high levels of adaptivity without sacrificing the predictability and the correctness of the system during execution.

3. *Adaptivity of networks and communication.* Current interest in network technology is focused on the development of new distributed applications like distributed multi-media information systems, media streaming, desktop conferencing and video-on-demand services. Each such application needs adaptive behavior and QoS guarantees, otherwise users may not accept them as these applications are expected to be judged against the quality of traditional services (e.g., radio, television, telephone services). Some of these issues become even more complicated once viewed from a mobile user's perspective, when wireless communication media and mobile device constraints are involved and the demand for adaptive communication "anytime, anywhere and anyhow" is presupposed. The emphasis here is given at the communication and transportation of information and the ability of the network resources and protocols to adapt their transmission according to the communication needs and the characteristics of the connection of the individual user and the others. The mobility of the user, the variation of bandwidth during communication, loose connections and the network congestion are some of the main factors that adaptation should take into account.

The main focus of this book is placed mainly upon the first category, highlighting the high-level research goals of adaptation and personalization systems which are concentrated around two main issues; the appropriate user modeling, dealing with what information is important to be incorporated in the user model and how it can be represented and extracted, and the appropriate adaptation procedures, dealing with which adaptation types and mechanisms are most effective to be performed and how they can be translated into adaptive user interface designs in order to improve the system's usability and to provide a positive user experience (Germanakos et al. 2007).

As we have seen earlier, the key in the context of adaptive interactive systems is the "unique" user and accordingly the apt formulation of effective and highly maintainable user models. It is assumed that each individual carries his own specific demographic and psychographic characteristics, interests and preferences, all of which cannot but affect his relationship with communication at all levels (from interpersonal to mass). The architecture of an adaptive interactive system (or an adaptive Internet in more generic terms), and what it represents, makes it possible to personalize the "message" under each unique user – a very important step forward in relation to a general classification of many common/social groups as might arise from the theories of "audience reception" of the communications research field. The inherent difference also lies in the fact that it is no longer considered how each audience understands the message, but how each person will receive the message that he is interested, and if possible on a form that complies with the inherent characteristics of the user. Therefore, through this adaptation it is possible someone to refer to the receipt of personalized messages.

Indeed, as it will be demonstrated through this book, the process occurs at the receiver and not at the provider side of the respective message. But, in order for adaptation and personalization to have an effect in such a way that will meet the needs and requirements of each user, he must first provide some characteristics (either implicitly or explicitly), that define his user model and will consequently support the whole process. Depending on the application and the domains in which it figures (information, entertainment, education, commerce, etc.), it is possible that the features, on which the whole process of adaptation is based upon to vary. In more generic terms, *adaptation* is a particular functionality that distinguishes between interactions of different users within the information space (Eklund and Sinclair 2000); while a system can be classified as *personalized* if it is based on hypermedia, has an explicit user model representing certain characteristics of the user, has a domain model which is a set of relationships between knowledge elements in the information space, and is capable of modifying some visible or functional parts of the system, based on the information maintained in the user model (Brusilovsky 2001, 1996).

However, how willing is a user to enter this information? How difficult and time consuming is this process for him? How familiar is he with the diversified environments of data entry and at what degree he can reconcile with the concept of security? In simpler terms, some of the studies conducted make reference to the use of multiple models for a specific user depending on the status he is currently found (Panayiotou and Samaras 2006). In this context, key determinant factors of each model creation might refer whether the content visited during the navigation over the Web by the user relates to work or fun, or what is the connection speed (high or low) during this process. Accordingly, the user will accept, for example newsletters that will satisfy his interests based on his current status/role of functioning, saving him from information that could distract him and thus estrange him from the use of Internet.

Certainly, the urgency for adaptation and personalization of today's fast growing and dynamic computing systems is even more visible since it can offer crossbreed solutions that could adequately support the increasing multi-purpose needs and requirements of users. The construction of the user model, the various personalization methods and adaptation techniques as well as algorithms, paradigms and methods of study working together under a common umbrella in order to provide a unique user experience is a major research direction and challenge. The characteristics and limitations incorporated in them seem to be influential in every information communication through Internet interaction yielding multifaceted and interdisciplinary questions, equally fundamental for the present book.

1.5   Current Problems and Challenges: An 'Out-of-the-Box' Thinking

Undoubtedly, it is now assumed that any reference in mass or mediated communication channels also involves the use of the Internet, which is estimated that grows by at least one billion pages per day. Of course, someone can never be certain about the exact pace of growth since by the time he reads these lines any statistical analyses are considered already obsolete. The opportunities and the potentials underlined by its flexible structures, the alternative ways of interaction and the concentration of huge volumes of data it provides certainly offers now a big advantage compared to earlier times. Every user can grasp the information he needs and can access any service and application often in real time from any device, at any time and upon request. Nonetheless, at the same time, the observed rising amount of information and the high complexity of interactions introduced, amongst others, by the continuous advancement of new and multipurpose technologies may intensify the problems of users' orientation and affect their perceptions and understanding leading often to overwhelming situations.

We are living in an era of wireless communication, pervasive computing and IoT, and we believe it would be of interest to the reader to dedicate the remaining of this section to the latter concept, as the latest revolutionary overarching fact, trying to envisage the arising challenges for adaptive interactive systems and applications in such a reality. The IoT is a network of real-time interconnected agents that is everywhere reproducing its own intelligence. Its main philosophy is based on the Internet but it employs more advanced connection concepts, interaction methods, functionalities, algorithms and technologies under a common framework to justify its existence. This differentiation creates huge challenges that sometimes are difficult to grasp. From a more futuristic perspective, many believe that it has the potential to become a global brain, since billions of users every day feed it with intelligence. A global brain where, in simple terms, each cell is a human/user, each neuron the message he sends and the synapses the interaction. The yielded accumulated information from this process maintains its presence and contributes to the formulation of its collective intelligence that will keep growing. It could be characterized as a living organism that will continue to evolve until it achieves a human-like consciousness (or awareness, i.e., to understand events and correlate them with goals) and be able to monitor itself. If we paraphrase the words of Neil Armstrong, after all, maybe *the Internet was the small step for the human and the IoT the giant leap for the mankind* (Germanakos 2014).

In more practical terms, the IoT could have a bipolar meaning: On one hand it might refer to a connected world based on the proliferation of a number of intelligent devices and services that bring smartness in an ecosystem, enhancing communication, increasing speed, social inclusion, etc. On the other hand there is always the challenge of how can people handle this new situation which inevitably creates a new reality around and for them. Such a reality, at a far extreme, is liable to affect their (subjective) perception and create questions with regard to what is right and wrong, since the convergence of the physical and the virtual life becomes even more intense. The triggers and stimuli that users receive from their environment, based on which they comprehend, decide and act, consist of different attributes and schemata of information that inevitably lead to different analysis, since they assign different values and meanings to concepts and facts. The features and functionality of this 'network of things' will create a different understanding for the flow of information from one agent to another (as agents we mean entities that might represent, i.e., humans, machines, robots, intelligent proxies and algorithms) that its acceptability and impact will need to be evaluated with different rules and regulations. This technological shift constitutes a phenomenon that, the concern to take over and drive solutions and concepts towards a direction with not significant impact to the end-users, is now more obvious than ever. Metaphorically speaking, we might witness obsessive attempts, driven by a ruthless corporate competition, to build the perfect car but in the end to not have the control over the steering wheel to drive it where we want. Because, simply there is no time to include the end-user in the whole process of design and development. Hence, most of the expectations and needs will be stirred with even more assumptions and subjective perspectives and not with the ingredients of real problems and pain-points that could yield actual requirements and solid user models. In the "game" of innovation, in evolution, there is no room for compromization when tackling a particular use case or issue and should not, by any means, be driven by the viewpoint of the technological advancements that might constrain a solution, distort a demand or worst, build something with no significant purpose.

In this respect, the need for research and development of adaptive and personalized multi-contextual interfaces and systems comes even more onto the surface. A key challenge for the new generation of tools and services is to provide an enhanced positive user experience, satisfying the unique user, since software will undertake a big part of the market. In fact, the conceptual and architectural designs of the developed technological solutions will change radically, bringing software and sensors closer together. Ultimately, a complete solution will be composed by a sensor, processor, radio, and operating system in one place (however, it is still not clear how the operating system will be positioned in this setting, as it is not clear how the whole economic system will function and where it will balance). Servers have already been transformed into virtual servers, since they are not anymore figuring as a central point of a system with physical presence. They are gradually designed for specific jobs/functionalities and are virtually found, i.e., on the cloud. These solutions will be mostly intelligent tools and services (or even services that provide intelligence) that they should have capabilities, such as: Real-time response on numerous device endpoints, end-to-end security and compatibility, integration and interoperability with other IT systems, end-to-end management, etc.

On the other hand though, simplicity is the key word for the end-user. The users should be able to use the next generation applications without being necessary to undergo through training, change their way of thinking or their everyday life activities. Now, the need for user modeling, adaptation and personalization is even more recognizable since this research area through its philosophy, methods and techniques can create hybrid solutions that could adequately support the generated specialized use cases to the benefit of the end-user. Each user has unique knowledge and experiences, traits, abilities, etc., that directly affect another through the interaction process. It is therefore critical to increase the quality of the information delivery and navigation support in order to escalate users' comprehension, usability and decision making during tasks' execution. It is necessary to establish user models, which consolidate all the pertinent characteristics under an inclusive schema by which a "smart" system will personalize the content. At first, a key criterion for adaptation till to date in most hypermedia applications is the user experience, taking into account the degree of familiarity with the cyberspace and the pursued objectives. For example, as long as a "smart" system "knows" that a user is novice in computer use, activates the navigation support, simplifies or disables hyperlinks that can become disorienting, leads directly the user to a potential objective, reduces the amount of information potentially excessive, and so on. Similarly, having the user stated his various interests, it is possible to reach this material that relates mostly to his preferences and purpose, and even presented in an adaptive manner (i.e., regulate the quantity of information).

Nevertheless, with the continuous progress of new technologies, even if a user model is known and defined, there is a basic discord on how to use and operate successfully an end-to-end process; since there is a plethora of special features and limitations on how to process and present the data. Due to this, the difficulty of offering homogeneous information increases rapidly. On one hand we have the coupling of all those elements that make up a user model and on the other the diversity of technological structures and devices that are required to carry the desired effect at specific time frames and in predetermined format. The rising questions therefore are focused upon whether there should be a categorization of user models, to the benefit of a more deterministic technological implementation, and if so, to what extent? In such a case, are we referring to a user-centred design of systems considering users' intrinsic characteristics or are we limited to a fuzzy approach towards systems analysis and development? Also, what are the points that need to be improved or developed to provide integration and interoperability among these technologies to better transfer the required information to the user? These challenges give a more clear meaning to the synergy of the two areas of HCI and knowledge data discovery and management (HCI-KDD 2015). At a lower level there is the necessity for optimized artificial intelligence techniques that will efficiently extract and enhance the clarity of large data sets (big data) and on the other hand there is the need for inclusive user models based on which these data can be interpreted to the benefit of the user.

Finally, with the existence of the IoT we are inevitably referring to a new challenge regarding data prevention and security, since IoT refers to a digital ecosystem totally different than the ones we are familiar with. It embodies millions of real-time edge nodes, which constitute a system similar to a biological one and probably we should start considering other prevention or recovering strategies and methods. It is obvious that antivirus solutions as we know them today will not be effective enough, since the requirements and philosophy based on which they have been built will not be applicable anymore. We must shift our way of thinking and create intelligent security algorithms that will consider the characteristics of the new reality and will adapt their functionality accordingly. In a similar way with what the body does for defending ad-hoc localized attacks we should develop more adaptive antiviruses to tackle diverse multi-objective attacks. For instance, a today's antivirus tries to restructure (or reorder) some lines of code of an infected module of a program in order to restore it and enable a system to be up and running smoothly again. An attack to the network of IoT could affect (or infect) only a designated area of it which is composed of multiple layers of information, different scope programs and hardware components and a spontaneous diagnosis for the symptoms should be initially taken place, before the adaptive algorithm decides which methods to evoke for the assembly of the viable dynamic cure that will be applied.

1.6 Summary

This chapter has introduced the theoretical and technological context of the current digital era and discussed the research field of HCI, with the disciplines that influence the human-computer communication, emphasizing on the paradigm shift of 'interaction' by referring to the new characteristics and viewpoints that shade this term. We have highlighted the existing overarching challenges of comprehension and orientation difficulties when users interact with multipurpose data and services, and although one-to-one content provision may be a functionality of the distant future, we have proposed that the design and development of adaptation and personalization systems and applications based on user-centred models could be considered as a necessary step towards that direction. We believe that including users, as the primary 'actors', during the design and development process can result to usable and qualitative solutions and interfaces, adjusted to their heterogeneous requirements, skills and perceptions, that consequently will increase their acceptability and will ensure a long term sustainable presence. We introduced therefore the concept of 'human-centred adaptation and personalization', and thinking out-of-the-box we presented some of the respective problems and challenges that researchers and practitioners might have to consider in the current ecosystem of IoT. Our main purpose is to provide readers with a holistic approach that could motivate, stimulate ideas, generate knowledge and fruitful discussions towards innovative researches and practices.

The remaining of the book is structured around the following broader concentration points:

1. Next chapter makes a reference to the importance of human factors in adaptation
   and personalization processes by presenting a number of theories related to
   human cognition and information processing as well as to emotionality with
   respect to anxiety and learning process (Chap. 2). Researchers and students will
   be able to gain a first insight on the pertinent models, constructs, extraction
   methods and implications, as well as to expand further their knowledge through
   the supportive references and bibliography.
2. It thoroughly discusses user modeling principles and methods of extraction
   (Chap. 3), introducing a comprehensive user model that extends the notion of
   existing ones; in a way that incorporates intrinsic human factors, which serve as
   the primal personalization filtering element of any type of content. We believe
   that this chapter will communicate to researchers and practitioners the importance of defining accurate and inclusive user models building on the understanding of how visual, cognitive and emotional factors can coexist under a common
   representation schema for increasing personalization quality.
3. It reviews the most prominent adaptation technologies and personalization categories, their impact on content and user interfaces, and presents a selection of
   current state-of-the-art systems (Chap. 4). This chapter can help researchers and
   practitioners to draw a strong background at a more practical level in the field.
4. Chapter 5 details an open and interoperable human-centred personalization
   framework, namely mapU that can serve as a guide for the reader on how to
   bridge the theoretical human perspectives with the deterministic reality of technology and the generation of intelligent adaptation rules for personalization.
5. Finally, we suggest a set of step-by-step practical guidelines and examples of
   designing adaptive and personalized tools and interfaces based on distinct human
   factors (Chaps. 6, 7 and 8). These chapters could be of particular benefit for
   researchers, service and content providers, Web designers and developers to gain
   a competitive advantage in their market. In parallel, we present a broad evaluation in three heterogeneous application areas (i.e., learning, commerce, usable
   security), elaborating on a number of study designs and results, that will increase
   the understanding of (young) researchers and students on how to handle samples
   and apply qualitative and quantitative analysis in this area.

References

Ashton K (2009) That 'internet of things' thing. RFID J 22:97–114
Balint L (1996) Computer-mediated interpersonal communication. In: Day D, Kovaks D (eds)
    Computers, communication and mental models. Taylor & Francis, London
Brusilovsky P (1996) Adaptive hypermedia: an attempt to analyse and generalize. In:
    Brusilovsky P, Kommers P, Streitz N (eds) Multimedia, hypermedia, and virtual reality.
    Springer, Berlin
Brusilovsky P (2001) Adaptive hypermedia. User Model User-Adap Inter 11(1–2):87–110
Brusilovsky P, Maybury M (2002) From adaptive hypermedia to the adaptive web. Commun ACM
    45(5):30–33

Cadez I, Heckerman D, Meek C, Smyth P, White S (2000) Visualization of navigation patterns on a web site using model-based clustering. In: Proceedings of the ACM SIGKDD international conference on knowledge discovery and data mining, ACM Press, pp 280–284

Card S, Moran T, Newell A (1983) The psychology of human computer interaction. Lawrence Erlbaum Associates, Hillsdale

Castellano G, Torsello M (2008) Categorization of web users by fuzzy clustering. In: Proceedings of international conference on knowledge-based intelligent information and engineering systems. Springer, Heidelberg, pp 222–229

Castellano G, Fanelli A, Mencar C, Torsello M (2007) Similarity-based fuzzy clustering for user profiling. In: Proceedings of international conference on web intelligence and intelligent agent technology workshop, IEEE/WIC/ACM, pp 75–78

Cui G, Liu H, Yang X, Wang H (2013) Culture, cognitive style and consumer response to informational vs. transformational advertising among East Asians: evidence from the PRC. Asia Pacific Bus Rev 19(1):16–31

Davou B (2000) Thought processes in the age of information: issues on cognitive psychology and communication. Papazissis Publishers, Athens. ISBN 960-02-1389-5

Dix A, Finlay J, Abowd G, Beale A (2003) Human-computer interaction, 3rd edn. Prentice Hall, Upper Saddle River. ISBN 978-0130461094

Dreyfus HL (1972) What computers can't do: a critique of artificial reason. Harper & Row, New York

Eirinaki M, Vazirgiannis M (2003) Web mining for web personalization. J ACM Trans Internet Technol 3(1):1–27

Eklund J, Sinclair K (2000) An empirical appraisal of the effectiveness of adaptive interfaces of instructional systems. Educ Technol Soc 3(4), pp 165–177. ISSN:1436-4522

Engelbrecht P, Engelbrecht P, Natzel S, Natzel S (1997) Cultural variations in cognitive style: field dependence vs field independence. Sch Psychol Int 18(2):155–164

Ferreira C, Salgado L, de Souza C (2013) A vocabulary to access users' cultural perspectives in human-computer interaction. In: Proceedings of the IFIP TC13 conference on human-computer interaction (INTERACT 2013), Springer, pp 314–322

Gallatay AM (1986) Natural and artificial intelligence. Elsevier, Amsterdam

Germanakos P (2014) User modelling, adaptation, and personalization (UMAP) in the era of pervasive computing and big data: challenges of the future. Panel position statement, UMAP 2014. Aalborg, 7–11 Jul 2015

Germanakos P, Tsianos N, Lekkas Z, Mourlas C, Samaras G (2007) Capturing essential intrinsic user behaviour values for the design of comprehensive web-based personalized environments. Comput Hum Behav J. Special issue on Integration of Human Factors in Networked Computing. doi:10.1016/j.chb.2007.07.010

HCI-KDD (2015) HCI and knowledge discovery & data mining. Available online at http://www. hci4all.at/expert-network-hci-kdd/. Accessed July 2015

Heimgärtner R (2012) Cultural differences in human-computer interaction: towards culturally adaptive human-machine interaction. Oldenbourg Wissenschaftsverlag, Berlin/Boston

ISC: Internet Systems Consortium (2014) Available online at http://www.isc.org. Accessed July 2015

Kyllonen PC, Stevens DL (1990) Cognitive abilities as determinants of success in acquiring logic skill. Learn Individ Differ 2(2):129–160

Licklider JCR (1960) Man-computer symbiosis. IRE Trans Hum Factors Electron, HFE-1(1):4–11. Reprinted in In Memoriam: Licklider JCR (1915–1990) Taylor RW (ed) Digital systems research center reports 61, Palo Alto, 1990

Linden G, Smith B, York J (2003) Amazon.com recommendations: item-to-item collaborative filtering. J IEEE Internet Comput 7(1):76–80

Mobasher B (2007) Data mining for web personalization. In: Brusilovsky P, Kobsa A, Nejdl W (eds) The adaptive web. Springer, Heidelberg, pp 90–135

Nasraoui O, Soliman M, Saka E, Badia A, Germain R (2008) A web usage mining framework for mining evolving user profiles in dynamic web sites. J IEEE Trans Knowl Data Eng 20(2):202–215

Nöll T, Köhler J, Reis G, Stricker G (2015) Fully automatic, omnidirectional acquisition of geometry and appearance in the context of cultural heritage preservation. ACM J Comput Cult Herit 8(1), 28 pages

Norman DA (1986) Cognitive engineering. In: Norman DA, Draper SW (eds) User centered systems design. Lawrence Erlbaum, Hillsdale, pp 31–61

Norman DA (1996) Design as practiced. In: Winograd T (ed) Bringing design to software. Addison-Wesley, Reading, pp 233–247

Norman D (2013) The design of everyday things. Basic Books, New York

Panayiotou C, Samaras G (2006) Mobile user personalization with dynamic profiles: time and activity. On the move to meaningful internet systems 2006: OTM 2006 workshops (PerSys 2006), Montpellier, 29 Oct–3 Nov 2006. Proceedings, Part II, pp 1295–1304

Papatheocharous E, Belk M, Germanakos P, Samaras G (2014) Towards implicit user modeling based on artificial intelligence, cognitive styles and web interaction data. Int J Artif Intell Tools (IJAIT), World Scientific, 23(2):21 pages. doi:10.1142/S0218213014400090

Parka S, Sureshb N, Jeonga B (2008) Sequence-based clustering for web usage mining: a new experimental framework and ANN-enhanced K-means algorithm. Data Knowl Eng 65(3):512–543

Pierrakos D, Paliouras G, Papatheodorou C, Spyropoulos C (2003) Web usage mining as a tool for personalization: a survey. J User Model User-Adap Inter 13(4):311–372

Pitsillides A (2014) The web of things: towards smart pervasive environments. Keynote talk in the 2nd international workshop on smart city and ubiquitous computing applications (SCUCA 2014), in conjunction with the IEEE WiMob 2014, Larnaca, 8 Oct 2014

Preece J, Rogers Y, Sharp H (2011) Interaction design: beyond human-computer interaction, 3rd edn. Wiley, New York. ISBN 978-0470665763

Ritter FE, Baxter GD, Churchill EF (2014) Foundations for designing user-centered systems: what system designers need to know about people. Springer, London. ISBN 978-1447151333

Schneider-Hufschmidt M, Kühme T, Malinowski U (1993) Adaptive user interfaces: principles and practice, Human factors in information technology. North-Holland, Amsterdam

Su X, Khoshgoftaar T (2009) A survey of collaborative filtering techniques. Adv Artif Intell Article 4, 19 p

Suchman L (1987) Plans and situated actions: the problem of human-machine communication. Cambridge University Press, Cambridge

Thrower T (1999) The relationship between culture and cognitive style: a review of the evidence and some reflections for the classroom. Mid-West Educ Res 12(2):36–44

Tomasello M (2000) Culture and cognitive development. Curr Dir Psychol Sci 9(2):37–40

Tylor EB (1974) Primitive culture: researches into the development of mythology, philosophy, religion, art, and custom. Gordon Press, New York

Varnum M, Grossmann I, Kitayama S, Nisbett R (2010) The origin of cultural differences in cognition: the social orientation hypothesis. Curr Dir Psychol Sci 19(1):9–13

Wu X, Kumar V, Quinlan JR, Ghosh J, Yang Q, Motoda H, McLachlan G, Ng A, Liu B, Yu P, Zhou Z, Steinbach M, Hand D, Steinberg D (2007) Top 10 algorithms in data mining. J Knowl Inf Syst 14(1):1–37

Yang Q, Huang JZ, Ng M (2003) A data cube model for prediction-based web prefetching. J Intell Inf Syst 20(1):11–30

Chapter 2
Human Factors in Web Adaptation and Personalization

Abstract Research on modelling intrinsic human characteristics with the outer scope to enrich the adaptation and personalization process has matured noticeably over the past several years. Designers of adaptive interactive systems are now personalizing the hypermedia content to users' needs and preferences by considering the inclusion of components that take into account cognitive and emotional factors, in an attempt to eradicate known difficulties that occur in traditional approaches. Cognition and emotions play a central role in guiding and regulating interactions, navigation, and learning behavior as well as in increasing performance, accuracy and satisfaction. This happens by modulating numerous cognitive and physiological activities to the benefit of the unique user. In this regards, in this chapter we discuss the theoretical assumptions and influence of dominant cognitive typologies, as well as the way that individuals process their emotions, during key HCI activities that support information processing, decision making, problem solving and learning. We further present methods of extraction and a number of implications that could provide a practical insight on the development of adaptation and personalization rules and designs. At this point we should bring into the reader's attention that given the high complexity and vagueness of subsequent human constructs, the selection of the appropriate cognitive and/or affective theories and models should be primarily in accordance to the context, situation or the goals of each research.

Keywords Human factors • Individual differences • Human cognition • Information processing • Human emotions

2.1 Introduction

The effort to introduce human individual differences in the design of adaptation and personalization systems by creating user models and adaptation mechanisms that will be able to regulate information processing factors to the benefit of the unique user, is a challenging direction towards human-centred interfaces. Such an endeavor is mainly hampered by the fact that there is very limited experience regarding which characteristics are the most important in Web interactions (Tsianos et al. 2012). The

© Springer International Publishing Switzerland 2016
P. Germanakos, M. Belk, *Human-Centred Web Adaptation and Personalization*,
Human–Computer Interaction Series, DOI 10.1007/978-3-319-28050-9_2

term individual differences is indeed very broad, since it could include from genet-
ics to personality; thus, it should be mentioned that the way that it is used in the
context of this book derives from the field of differential psychology. The term
(initially in German, Psychologie der individuellen Differenzen) was proposed by
Stern (1900), in order to summarize the research on mental differences, in coordination to a notion of "general psychology". The emergence and proliferation of the
individual differences research is not however directly linked to cognitive research;
in fact, researchers from the fields of differential and cognitive psychology have
often opposed each other, especially on whether psychometrical approaches are
truly related to human cognitive structures (Glaser and Pellegrino 1978). Also, it is
rather indisputable that, for the most part, individual differences research was based
on (or provided a basis for) the study of intelligence (Dillon and Watson 1996). A
common focal point of the theories of intelligence originate from the work of
Thurstone (1948), who claims that there are certain distinct basic mental abilities
(factors), in which people differ at some extent. All this work was at a large extent
summarized by Caroll's (1993) very influential meta-analysis, which led to the
development of his three stratum theory. A review by Deary (2001), on a relatively
recent state of research on intelligence, revealed that individuals predominantly differ in the following abilities (the definitions are cited from McGrew 2009, p. 5–6):

- Visual (and spatial) ability: "The ability to generate, store, retrieve, and transform visual images and sensations".
- Verbal ability: "The breadth and depth of a person's acquired store of declarative
  and procedural reading and writing skills and knowledge".
- Memory (short-term): "The ability to apprehend and maintain awareness of a
  limited number of elements of information in the immediate situation (events
  that occurred in the last minute or so)".
- Processing speed: "The ability to automatically and fluently perform relatively
  easy or over-learned elementary cognitive tasks, especially when high mental
  efficiency (i.e., attention and focused concentration) is required".

Even though these intelligence factors are highly stable throughout a person's
lifetime, fluid reasoning, memory, and speed tend to deteriorate with high age. Such
psychometric theories of individual differences are indeed much elaborated and
complicated. However, we consider that a broad and thorough understanding of
how people differ when required to perform mental tasks is necessary in order to
subsequently narrow down the number of possible user attributes that could be used
in an adaptation and personalization scheme.

Furthermore, during the years researchers were interested in the way individuals
process their emotions and how they interact with other elements of their information processing system. Theorists from a variety of orientations tend to agree on two
emotional processing systems with considerable conceptual overlap: A schematic,
associative and implicit system that has connections with bodily response systems
and involves fast and automatic processes, and an abstract propositional 'rational'
system that is analytical, reflective, logical, and relies on high-level executive functions. The former system is susceptible to biological mechanisms and is often

manifested in the form of anxiety and stress. The latter system relies on logic and rationality. Research on emotions is by far more complex and unpredictable in comparison to research in cognition mainly due to the dynamicity and the difficulty of identification, extraction and interpretation of the subsequent factors and events. In addition, the lack of consensus in the definition of emotions and the diversity of individuals' reactions to particular situations makes it almost impossible to generalize or to articulate more deterministic approaches of investigation. The behavior and responses of a person to a particular stimulus might be driven by psychophysiological changes, personality traits, subjective experiences, etc., that lead to diverse expressions and a wide range of related activity patterns hard to formulate. However, in many cases researchers were able to develop systems and processes that could simulate at some extent the human affective states and adapt their behavior accordingly. In this book, we will discuss specific emotional factors that have a direct influence in the learning process, proposing a multi-layer model that combines constructs with respect to emotional regulation and arousal. The human brain tries to maintain a state of homeostasis between these two levels, the cognitive and the physiological. Affect and emotional experience is acting as a catalyst that facilitates this balance but if it cannot be properly controlled, it hinders the cooperation between these two systems and leads to emotional outcomes that cannot be managed or regulated by the brain. The affective element of the model includes the concept of anxiety which is an emotion characterized by subjectively unpleasant feelings of tension, worried thoughts and physical changes like increased blood pressure over anticipated events or stimuli, and emotion regulation which is the way individuals perceive and control their emotions. Individuals attempt to influence which emotions they have, when they have them and how they experience and express them. By combining the affective state of the individuals with their regulatory mechanism we can reach into a conclusion of how emotions influence their performance and the outcome of their behaviors.

In our view, the aforementioned areas of cognition and emotion are a good starting point for the study of their respective effects in adaptive interactive systems. They are composed of constructs that refer to habitual or preferred modes of thinking, perceiving, and remembering (Tennant 1988), or to consistent individual differences in preferred modes of organizing and processing information and experience (Messick 1984). Interactive systems require both visual and verbal (reading) processing of information, affecting the high-level cognitive factors of the human brain, such as cognitive styles, in the way individuals process and remember information and primarily affect preference and performance in hypermedia systems, while at the same time maintain awareness of different elements (i.e., hyperlinks). On the other hand, persons with limited abilities in elementary cognitive processes, such as working memory capacity, may face increased difficulties in such systems, generating for example excessive cognitive loads during interactions or increased levels of emotional arousal resulting to imbalance situations, of what is expected from them and their perceived ability to meet those expectations (or demands). These assumptions do not necessarily imply that more intelligent persons excel during interactions with a system; each individual may have different strengths and/or weaknesses, and perhaps the employment of personalization techniques could result in providing tailor-suited environments.

A thorough presentation and analysis of all the cognitive and emotional theories and models that connect to the various levels of information processing is not in the scope of this book. Rather, our main effort in this chapter is to discuss a number of factors that we believe primarily influence information processing with respect to the decision making, problem solving and learning. Our main concern is to create a basic theoretical understanding pertinent to the utilization of those factors and their effects in the design and development of specific use cases of human-centred adaptation and personalization models and rules. Similarly, the reader could exploit and integrate alternative theories and/or routes of application depending always on his research directions and the distinctiveness of his studies.

2.2   Human Cognition and Information Processing

Historically, the research attempts of cognitive psychology concentrated upon the study, with the use of scientific research methods, of the human perception and cognitive processes that take place in the human mind during information processing (Davou 2000). At the beginning of the twentieth century, the investigation of the mechanisms that affect the learning process was one of the main research directions for cognitive psychologists, who tried to design research procedures that would emulate the methods of pure and applied sciences, in an effort to establish psychology as "real" science. This view point led to the primacy of the phenomena that could be observed and more specifically to the correlation of the stimulus with the measurable results of a behavior. However, the intermediate processes of the mind and the mechanisms during the learning process could not be directly observed deflecting from the aims and objectives of this research. The limited association of stimulus with the response, as well as the difficulty of making predictions and evaluations based on rigorous experimental methods, formed the core of behaviorism which became the dominant theoretical approach to the processes of learning (Hock 1999). It is worth to mention, that a cornerstone theory regarding the processes of learning and cognition, opposing the dominant theories of behaviorism at the time, is the one proposed by Tolman (1948) who introduced the concept of cognitive maps. A cognitive map is a mental representation which serves individuals to acquire, code, store, recall, and decode information about the relative locations and attributes of phenomena in their everyday or metaphorical spatial environment.

Nevertheless, the so called "cognitive revolution" was realized with the development of the computer in the 1950s which had a significant influence in psychology. The computer provided the grounds for researchers to use it as a metaphor through of which they could compare the human mental processing, by representing non-observable processes in an observable manner (computer-mind analogy). This comparison was used as a means for better understanding the way information is processed and stored in the human mind. The information processing perspective, which was an alternative theoretical approach taking over the so far theories of behaviorism, was based on the idea that individuals apply a more thorough processing of the information they receive, rather than simply responding to a stimuli they are presented with. Since then, the information processing theory (referring, for many, to the "software level" when associated with the human brain) has become one of the most prominent psychological theories that describes the process of learning, which can be defined as a change in a person's mental structures that creates the capacity to demonstrate different behaviors (Eggen and Kauchak 2007). More specifically, it emphasizes on how a stimuli from the environment goes through the processes of attention, perception, and storage throughout a series of distinct memory stores (Lutz and Huitt 2003). The organization of information in computing systems is proportionate with the inclusion of knowledge in the human brain, which supports the argument for efficient learning with the use of electronic environments.

Inevitably, cognitive psychology, as one of the main disciplines of cognitive science, is associated with the research fields of computer science, and more specifically with artificial intelligence, following a parallel path in developments; exchanging research data and theoretical approaches. In particular, artificial intelligence used theoretical models of cognitive psychology to understand and simulate human perception and processing while contributing decisively to demonstrate to what extent these models are effective. Furthermore, throughout the history of cognitive psychology, the field of artificial intelligence attracted psychologists and contributed to the development of theories driven occasionally from a different reasoning (Flanagan 1991), such as:

- The growth of computational power enables practitioners and researchers to simulate human behavior and address complex and hard to solve problems.
- This field is dominated by the concept of information processing and application rules.
- Computers use and interact with symbols on various levels.
- In the case of artificial intelligence, psychological events can be realized in various ways without being characterized by the physical manifestation of cognitive processes, but by their role in the operating procedure.

In addition, many argue that the metaphorical relationship between computing and cognitive psychology has contributed for the educational effectiveness of hypermedia due to the structural similarities in the organization of information (Swindler 2001).

Nonetheless, despite the promising convergence and results of artificial intelligence and the information processing model, over the past decades, researchers recognized that computers can only serve as a loose and pretty general model of human memory, which is related to the specifics of how the brain actually codes or manipulates information as it is stored in memory (human memory is one of the primary areas of cognition and is discussed in the next section).

At a secondary level (also called as the "hardware level" of the human mind), that dictates the relationship of cognitive psychology with neuroscience; research works concluded that learning and information processing depend upon inherent structural parameters (Graber 2000). This predicts individual differences in learning and processing abilities among individuals, constituting a subject of interest for adaptation and personalization systems too. Specifically, the network of the human brain is estimated to consist of 10–100 billion neurons, out of which each one of them has the specialized ability to process specific information, and is triggered when a stimuli is associated with the encoding ("programming") of each neuron. Incoming information is fragmented into very small pieces and processed by specialized neurons, and then, if necessary, regenerated. The possibility to develop logical associations depends in turn on the electrical connections between neurons, synapses. Accordingly, the cognitive response to a stimulus depends on the presence or not, and the number of available synapses between the existing information associated with the stimulus and the ability to formulate new synapses (Graber 2000). Furthermore, the failure of processing new information may be related mostly with the physiological parameters of an individual rather than the behavioral ones. That is because even though the structure of the brain between people is broadly similar, the number of connections vary, and although they link to external stimuli, there is a tendency of repetition, and the trigger of existing synapses, rather than the creation of new ones. In addition, during childhood, the human brain is highly receptive to new input of information due to the large number of nerve recipients, transmitters and connections. In adulthood, the synapses that are not used become inactive. Thus, practicing and training of mental abilities broadens the possibility of processing information.

To the extent that neuroscience can portray the way information is recorded at the level of "hardware", cognitive functions are not independent of the physiology of the human brain, but rather they affect how each person perceives and processes information. These differences can also relate to the learning process, even though it is not clearly discernible because of the high complexity of the human brain and the relationship between the "hardware" and the "software" of the human mind.

2.2.1   The Role of Human Memory

Over the last fifty years, a high number of works have focused on understanding human cognitive processes, proposing various models, definitions and interpretations on the structure of an internal information processing system. Researchers have attempted to describe the basic architecture of this system, defining as 'information', any stimulus that is newly processed or is already exploited by the human mind to comprehend objects, events and situations (Anderson 1990). The study of memory and its relationship or integration to human cognition was at the time in the centre of most research directions in cognitive psychology. The various suggestions and perspectives tried to formulate a consensus on several aspects of information processing, mainly emphasizing on how the brain encodes, stores and retrieves information from the memory. These approaches, triggered many times by

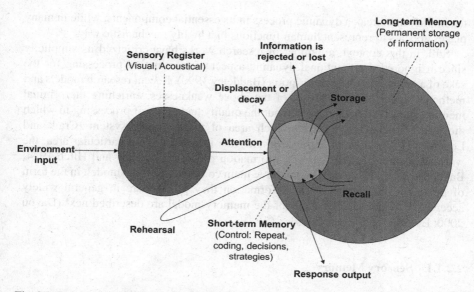

Fig. 2.1 Representation of the multi store model of memory (Atkinson and Shiffrin 1968)

conflicting realizations, refer to memory as a multi-faceted, limited capacity, mechanism that maintains a number of connections, representations, or structures which are related to the accumulated life-time perceptions and/or mental experiences of a person. The stored information is liable to change or manipulated when new stimuli or knowledge is acquired, while the interaction of the new information with the stored information could be demonstrated as a top-down, bottom-up or a combination of the two, system (Miller et al. 1960; Gibson 1979; Driscoll 2001; Eliasmith 2001; Winn and Snyder 2001; Huitt 2000).

Despite the disagreement and the different angles of view on many levels of understanding, it seems that there is an agreement among most cognitive psychologists on some basic principles, which are derived from an inherent consistency of cognitive processes during execution (when individuals process information – Huitt 2000). This agreement or homogeneity was proposed through the Multi Store Model of Memory of Atkinson and Shiffrin (1968), which has been widely used for explaining how information is processed by humans. The Multi Store Model of Memory suggests that memory is made up of a series of stores and it consists of three separate components (see Fig. 2.1): *The sensory register*, in which sensory information enters memory (e.g., acoustical, visual information); *the short-term memory* (also called working memory), which receives and holds input from both the sensory register and the long-term memory; and *the long-term memory*, where information which has been rehearsed in the short-term memory is stored indefinitely. In case rehearsal does not occur, information is forgotten, lost from short-term memory through the processes of displacement or decay. This model is forced to simplify and break a dynamic process in its essential components, while in many places appears to represent human functions in a highly mechanistic way.

Still, in this context, a number of research works have criticized its simplicity since it ignored the functional dynamic aspect of information processing for the sake of a structural, linear description (Baddeley 1990). Recent research models and methods suggested replacement of the above weaknesses, enriching the original memory model with statements about the quality and depth of processing in which the information is submitted in each area of the cognitive system (Craik and Lockhart 1972), or highlighting explicitly the importance of a particular area, the working memory for the current information process (Baddeley and Hitch 1974; Baddeley 1986). Nevertheless, the three main components of the model, in the form of treatment and nature of the information they process are in general widely accepted. The main components of the memory model are described next (Davou 2000; Eysenck and Keane 2005).

2.2.1.1 Sensory Memory

Any stimulus that is coming from the individual's surrounding environment and detected by the human senses is briefly available in sensory memory. This temporary retention of information as they enter the brain is also called sensory buffer, because it concerns information detected by the senses and not yet processed further in the human brain for processing and interpretation. An unlimited amount of information can be put into sensory memory but being only active for a limited amount of time, since as the person is continuously in communication with the environment, new information is constantly shifting and entering while removing the old. The detection of the information in sensory memory is also related to the concept of attention, and the information is further processed to a subsequent stage in short-term memory. This refining capacity of sensory memory has the advantage to "withstand" the unrestricted flow of information but also a key disadvantage is that, when the rate and intensity of inflow of such information increases, and exceeds the decay rate or shifting "useless" information, its effectiveness and efficiency is dropped, causing confusion.

2.2.1.2 Short-Term Memory and Working Memory

Due to the high number of sensory input from the environment, much of the information in sensory memory decays and is forgotten. Once information is attended, it is transferred to the short-term memory. In contrast to sensory memory where a high number of information can be active, in short-term memory the time and capacity is limited. According to Miller (1956), short-term memory might contain from 5 to 9 objects active at the same time (7 ± 2). More recent studies have refined and extended these findings and further confirmed the limited capacity of short-term memory. At

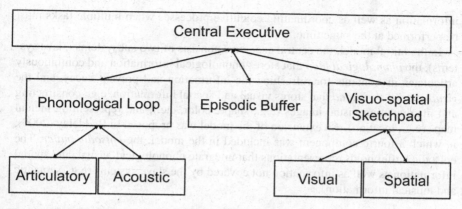

Fig. 2.2 Baddeley and Hitch's working memory model (1974)

this stage, the information stays for a longer time active than in the sensory memory. The information may be contained in the short-term memory for up to 30 s. Apart from the limited capacity and the limited life time of information, a third character- istic of short-term memory is its high fragility (Eysenck 1988). In particular, the information in short-term memory is not yet permanently "registered" in the cogni- tive system. Information is maintained in this part of the system and undergoes the required processing, which will either lead to permanent storage (in long-term memory) or will be rejected from the human mind. This temporary hold of informa- tion is fragile and easily disrupted by other incoming information (or existing, retractable information), so that a possible distraction can lead to confusion or total loss of information. Short-term memory is the area where new and current informa- tion is entered and processed in the human mind, but also associated with existing information an individual has in long-term memory that is drawn to use as a refer- ence framework for the classification and interpretation of new information. Given its limited capacity, short-term memory is unable to retain a lot of information con- currently active for processing, which eventually might cause the problem of "over- load" of the cognitive system in case a high number of information is being presented and processed.

The conception of working memory grew out of the literature on short-term memory (Baddeley 1992, 2012) as an empirical model of cognitive functions used for temporarily storing and manipulating information. Although short-term mem- ory and working memory are used interchangeably in many occasions, short-term memory could be referred as the simple temporary storage of information, whilst working memory as the combination of storage and information manipulation (Baddeley 2012). Baddeley and Hitch (1974) proposed the multi-component model of working memory (see Fig. 2.2) which consists of a *central executive* that is the central system for pointing attention to relevant information, removing irrelevant information as well as coordinating cognitive processes when multiple tasks must be performed at the same time.

In the initial model, the central executive consists of two subsystems (slave systems), the *phonological loop* that stores phonological information and continuously articulates its contents for refreshing the information and prevent decay, and the *visuo-spatial sketchpad* that stores visual and spatial information, e.g., constructing and manipulating visual images (e.g., shape, color, etc.), and representing mental maps (e.g., location). An extension of the model was proposed in Baddeley (2000), in which a fourth component was included in the model, the *episodic buffer*. The episodic buffer holds representations that integrate phonological, visual, and spatial information as well as information not covered by the slave systems (e.g., semantic and musical information).

2.2.1.3　Long-Term Memory

Long-term memory is the final stage of Atkinson and Shiffrin's human memory model (Atkinson and Shiffrin 1968). In this stage, information remains for a long period of time or indefinitely. In short-term memory, newly entered information is associated with older, related information retrieved from the long-term memory which is further organized and interpreted for giving meaning to the information. In the long-term memory, this new and processed information is stored in a wider network of knowledge for each person. Opinions of researchers differ on the duration of stay of information in long-term memory. Some consider that once the information is entered into this form, this information is never removed or lost by an individual's cognitive system. Others argue that there is a possibility that information might be "lost" from long-term memory, in case the information is not placed in the correct position within the network of information already available to the person, or in case this information has not created strong bonds with other existing information (Baddeley 1990; Eysenck 1988). Nevertheless, it is agreed that the information entered in long-term memory is maintained throughout the life-time of the individual and serves as a knowledge base on which the new information is decoded, i.e., compared, interpreted and organized (Loftus and Loftus 1980).

Long-term memory is comprised of *explicit memory* and *implicit memory* (Atkinson and Shiffrin 1968). Explicit memory (declarative memory) refers to information that is consciously available. Explicit memory has three subdivisions: *Episodic memory* that refers to memory for specific events in time (e.g., remembering a person's name and incidence of interaction with that person); *semantic memory* that refers to factual information (e.g., the meaning of words); and *autobiographical memory* that refers to information regarding events and experiences of an individual. Implicit memory refers to procedural information about the body of the person, e.g., how to brush the teeth, how to swim, etc.

2.2.2 *Visual Perception*

Visual perception is of vital importance in our everyday lives, since it enables individuals to move around freely, to recognize other people or objects, to read books, to identify depth and proximity or to watch videos and movies. Similarly, visual perception, as well as the concepts of visual search and visual attention (as described in the following sections), are some of the most important factors that influence the area of HCI. As it is known, the most common human-computer communication medium is the screen of a device, where through the optical channel a user perceives the information that is presented. The use of graphics on the computer screen enables the representation of images which resemble real objects causing the same cognitive recognition procedures as those followed in the real world. *Visual perception* as defined by Sekuler and Blake (2002, p. 621) is *"the acquisition and processing of sensory information in order to see, hear, taste, or feel objects in the world; also guides an organism's actions with respect to those objects"*. Even though it might be considered as an inherent "automatic" ability that many times is ignored, visual perception is a complex process that is supported on the one hand by the functioning of the optical sensor (eye, neural pathways, and the brain), and on the other hand by the cognitive functioning of understanding the receptive stimuli. The eye receives the stimuli in the form of light, which stimulates the light-sensitive retina at the back of the eye, in which thousands endings of the optic nerve are concentrated, that in turn help to transfer the visual stimulus to the corresponding brain centre. Understanding the visual stimuli is the process that allows us to recognize three-dimensional objects, their relative distances, the color, the brightness, etc. A big number of theoretical approaches that investigate this process support that individuals perceive the surrounding world by combining the receptive stimuli based on their prior knowledge and experiences generating meaning and images (Marr 1982). Our expectations and context may affect our visual perception, while the post-processing of the visual stimulus and our past experience allows us to see the images stable while we move in space, the color and brightness of objects unchanged as light is constantly changing. It also allows us to understand that the size of objects does not change, although those get eventually visually smaller when we are moving away from them. Nevertheless, there is still a major controversial theoretical issue based on which psychologists usually are divided. This is expressed through the understanding whether the perception starts by the stimulus itself (and the information related to it), known also as 'bottom-up' or 'direct theory' of perception (Gibson 1966), or it is more 'indirect' a.k.a. 'constructivist' or 'top-down' theory (Gregory 1970), that refers to the use of contextual information (increasing meaning) in the pattern recognition or in our perception of reality.

The Gestalt psychology has also influenced significantly the study of how individuals perceive visual components and how they are organizing them. Gestalt theory, which contributes mostly to the concept of the perceptual grouping, tries to understand the ability of individuals to acquire and maintain meaningful perceptions in a rather chaotic world by forming a global whole with self-organizing abilities. Its principles (or laws of organization) support that the human mind maintains a perception of the visual stimuli that gives value to the whole (standing as a reality on its own) irrespective of the parts that it consists of (Wertheimer 1923; Koffka 1935; Kohler 1947). The Gestalt principles are briefly summarized as follows: (a) Principle of *proximity*, objects that are close to each other are formulating groups; (b) principle of *similarity*, objects which are similar with respect to their shape or color belong to the same group; (c) principle of *closure*, objects (or regular figures) that are not complete tend to be perceived as a whole by individuals (our mind fills in the visual gap); (d) principle of *continuity*, the elements of objects that are aligned within an object tend to be grouped together perceived as an integrated whole; (e) principle of *common fate*, the elements that move towards one (the same) direction or in the same speed are perceived as elements of a common group that moves towards that directional line or path; and (f) principle of *symmetry*, the elements (or areas) of objects contained between symmetrical limits appear (or perceived) to create solid coherent shapes.

The Gestalt principles have a direct application in HCI and the design of interactive hypermedia systems since their usability and acceptability by the users depend at a large extent upon whether: They facilitate grouping of similar objects or shapes, they connect the details of figures or content on reasonable ways when information is missing (e.g., surfaces presented as homogeneous regions rather than as scattered spot phenomena), they provide meaningful descriptions on activities, they use metaphors and identical terminology on prompts, menus, help, etc., they maintain consistent sequence of actions in similar situations, and so on.

2.2.3 Visual Search

According to Peterson et al. (2001), *"From the time we wake in the morning until we go to bed at night, we spend a good deal of each day searching the environment. For example, as we drive from home to work, we scan the roadway for other automobiles, pedestrians, and bicyclists. In the office, we may look for a coffee cup, the manuscript we were working on several days ago, or a phone number of a colleague that we wrote down on a scrap of paper. In short, much of our life is spent searching for information relevant to the task at hand"*. The processes included in these activities have been studied under the light of *visual search*, in which a target lying in our visual field can be detected rapidly. In the process of visual search, subjects usually have an optical material that contains a number of objects (groups of objects or a different field size). The cognitive target is presented to them during the search effort, and their objective is to decide whether the target is located within the available visual field (display). Visual search is comprised of three widely known theories, the *Feature Integration Theory*, the *Guided Search Theory*, and the *Decision Integration Hypothesis*, which are described next.

2.2.3.1 Feature Integration Theory

The Feature Integration Theory (FIT), proposed by Treisman (1988, 1992), distinguishes the features of the objects (e.g., color, size, specific direction lines) from the objects themselves, providing the following cases:

- There is an initial instant parallel process in which the visual features of the objects existing in the environment are processed simultaneously, and there is no dependence from the concept of attention.
- Then a serial process is taken place in which the features are combined to formulate objects.
- The sequential process is slower than the original parallel process, especially when the object group is particularly large.
- The visual features may be combined focusing on the location of an object. This focus of attention (focused attention) referred to as "union" ("glue"), creates unitary objects from the available features.
- The combination of features can be affected by the stored knowledge (such as, bananas are usually yellow).
- In the absence of focused attention or relevant prior knowledge, the features of different objects are combined randomly, producing "illusory conjunctions".

The theories of Treisman and Gelade (1980) have been tested and proven to be valid since the experiments suggested that the combination of the features of an object require the process of attention, otherwise the lack of focused attention produces illusory conjunctions (random combination of features – Treisman and Schmidt 1982). Their research indicated that there were a significant number of illusory conjunctions when attention was sparsely distributed, but not when the stimulus was presented in focus (focal attention). On the contrary, Duncan and Humphreys (1989, 1992) argued that the theory of Treisman was quite limited. In particular, they supported that the repetition of visual search is based on two factors that they were not included in the initial version of the FIT: (i) The similarity of targets and non-targets; and (ii) the similarity between non-target, and the attribution which is much higher when the similarity is high. Additionally, Humphreys et al. (1985) demonstrated that visual search may be instant when the non-targets are all the same. According to the FIT, the fact that the target was determined by a combination or association of the visual features (for example, a vertical and a horizontal line), could be interpreted that the visual search was affected to a great extent by the non-targets. Therefore, Treisman and Sato (1990), based on the above reviews, developed further the FIT, arguing that the degree of similarity between the targets and the conditional distractors affect the visual search time. In 1993, Treisman (1993) proposed a more complex version of the FIT, in which there are four types of attentional selection. First, there is a selection depending on the location that includes a relatively wide or limited "window" of attention (broad or narrow attention window). Secondly, there is a selection of visual features, which are divided into surface-defining features and shape-defining features. Third, there is a selection which is related to the basis of object-defined locations. Fourth, there is a selection during the final stages of the process which determines the object file and which controls the response of an individual. In this way, the attentional selectivity can function at different levels given the demands of a task.

2.2.3.2   Guided Search Theory

Driven by the FIT, Wolfe (1998) developed the Guided Search Theory (GST). He replaced the assumption of Treisman and Gelade (1980), that the initial processing is necessarily parallel and the subsequent processing to the individual serial, introducing the logic that processes are conventionally more or less efficient. Wolfe (1998) supported that there should be no influence of the group or of the visual field with respect to the target tracking time in case that the parallel processing is used, in contrast to the use of serial processing where the influence of the group size plays a major role.

According to the GST, the initial processing of basic features produces an activation map which is a representation of visual space in which the level of activation of each item at a location reflects the possibility that the location contains a target. Therefore, if we assume that someone is looking red, horizontal targets, the feature processing would activate all red and horizontal objects. Attention will then turn to objects based on the level of activation, starting with those that are more activated. The above assumption allows us to understand why the search time period is longer in case some non-targets share one or more features of the target stimulus (Duncan and Humphreys 1989). The notion of activation map provides a realistic manner in which the visual search can be performed more effectively ignoring the stimuli that do not share some of the features with the target stimulus.

2.2.3.3   Decision Integration Hypothesis

Palmer and colleagues (Eckstein et al. 2000; Palmer et al. 2000), proposed the Decision Integration Hypothesis theory (DIH), considering that the processes involved in feature and conjunction searches are more or less similar. In particular, Palmer et al. (2000) considered that the parallel processing is contained in both search types. These assumptions were presenting an opposite standing point compared to those of the original formulation of FIT. Palmer et al. (2000) argued that observers create internal representations of the target and the distractor stimuli. These representations are "noisy" (internal response to any given item differs from trial to trial). The performance on a visual search task involves decision making based on the discriminability between the target and the distractor stimuli. The main question that arises is: Why the visual search is less effective when associated with searching conjunctions rather than with feature searches? According to Eckstein et al. (2000), conjunction searches are more difficult because there is less of a distinction between the target and the distractor stimuli. Visual search is basically slower when it comes to large groups of objects because the complexity of the decision making process is greater when there is a wide range of items in the visual field.

2.2.4 Visual Attention, Speed and Control of Processing

Visual attention is defined as a process of concentrating on a discrete aspect of information (visual or auditory). During this process attention is deviating from any other (not pertinent) objects in order to achieve effective engagement with the particular object (James 1890). A high number of researches have focused on visual attention since it is considered as one of the most important human sense and because visual objects can be precisely controlled and manipulated (e.g., display time, shape of the object, etc.) for investigating and understanding the concept of visual attention (Eysenck and Keane 2005). Several research works (Vecera et al. 2014; Corbetta and Shulman 2002; Posner 1980; Posner and Petersen 1990; Yantis and Jonides 1990) suggest that attention is split in two main types: the *goal-driven*, which is voluntary, endogenous and directed from the target, and the *stimulus-based*, which is involuntary, exogenous and directed by the stimulus. Depending on whether the objects of attention are one or more, attention can be focused or divided. In the latter case, peripheral vision is used in which visual information is viewed from outside the centre of the gaze, e.g., when viewing the movements in a room while talking to a person.

The process of visual attention may be divided into two successive stages: the pre-attentive stage and the limited-capacity stage. In the *pre-attentive stage*, the information goes through a parallel processing from the entire field of view, and determines areas of interest through it (determines important visual elements). The pre-attentive stage of vision subconsciously defines objects from visual primitives, such as lines, curvature, orientation, color and motion and allows definition of objects in the visual field. The *limited-capacity stage*, which is based on the aforementioned pre-attentive mapping, performs a high-level processing which is driven by some more generic criteria. When items pass from the pre-attentive stage to the limited-capacity stage, these items are considered as selected. Interpretation of eye movement data is supported by the empirically validated assumption that when a person is performing a cognitive task, while watching a display, the location of his gaze corresponds to the symbol currently being processed in working memory and, moreover, that the eye naturally focuses on areas that are most likely to be informative (Gulliver and Ghinea 2004).

From the perspective of individual differences in human cognition, various theories exist that aim to describe and explain how and why individuals differ in attention (Demetriou et al. 2013). Researchers attempted to understand attention and the functioning of the human mind in terms of more basic processes, such as control of processing and speed of processing (Demetriou et al. 2013). *Control of processing* refers to cognitive processes that can identify and concentrate on goal-relevant

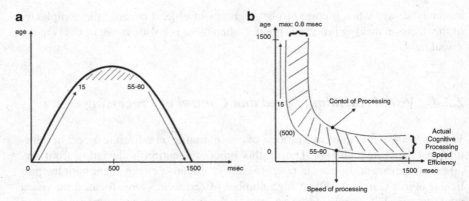

Fig. 2.3 (**a**) Speed of processing (Germanakos et al. 2008). (**b**) Actual cognitive processing speed efficiency (Germanakos et al. 2008)

information and inhibit attention to irrelevant stimuli. Control of processing is also closely related to the individual's *speed of cognitive processing* which refers to the maximum speed at which a given mental act may be efficiently executed. Speed of cognitive processing and control of processing are directly related to a person's age, as well as to the continuous exercise and experience, with the former to be the primary indicator. Therefore, as it is depicted in Fig. 2.3a (Germanakos et al. 2008), the processing development speed increases non-linearly in the age of 0–15 (1500 ms), it is further stabilized in the age of 15–55–60 (500 ms) and decreases from that age on (1500 ms). However, it should be stated that the actual cognitive processing speed efficiency is yielded from the difference (maximum value 0.8 ms) between the peak value of the speed of processing and the peak value of control of processing, as it is depicted in Fig. 2.3b (Germanakos et al. 2008).

Various research works argue that the aforementioned cognitive processes have an effect on comprehension, learning and problem solving (Conway et al. 2002; Shipstead and Broadway 2013; Demetriou et al. 2002; Unsworth and Spillers 2010; Klingberg 2009). They are mainly used in mental tasks, such as arithmetic tasks, e.g. remembering a number in a multiplication problem and adding that number later on, or creating a new password and using that password later for authentication, or recognizing the distorted text of a CAPTCHA mechanism.

Studies revealed the relationship between cognitive processing abilities and working memory capacity (Conway et al. 2002; Polderman et al. 2006). Enhanced speed of information processing facilitates access to information that is sustained in the working memory system (Baddeley 1992). In addition, enhanced speed of processing enables individuals to handle more efficiently information flow during problem solving, because information can be represented, interpreted, and integrated before it is lost through decay or interference (Hale and Fry 2000). On the other hand, enhanced working memory capacity enables individuals to represent and process more information units at the same time enabling them to construct more complex concepts or relations.

Table 2.1 CAPTCHA and text-recognition complexity correlations based on task performance

Working memory	Speed and control of processing	CAPTCHA complexity
Limited	Limited	Baseline
Limited	Enhanced	Higher
Enhanced	Limited	Higher
Enhanced	Enhanced	Higher

The relationship between control of processing and working memory capacity is also well documented (Shipstead and Broadway 2013; Engle 2002; Kane et al. 2007). Working memory capacity predicts the ability to rapidly focus attention (Heitz and Engle 2007). For example, individuals with enhanced working memory capacity are less susceptible to Stroop interference (Hutchison 2007; Unsworth and Spillers 2010). Working memory capacity also predicts the ability to avoid being distracted by powerful stimuli. For example, a study conducted by Conway et al. (2001) investigating working memory capacity effects within the cocktail party phenomenon, revealed that individuals who detect their name in an irrelevant message have relatively limited working memory capacities, suggesting that they have difficulty blocking out, or inhibiting, distracting information. Furthermore, in the context of personalizing the complexity level of text-recognition CAPTCHA challenges, in terms of number of characters, text distortion and noise used in the challenge, working memory capacity and speed and control of processing influence differently the performance in tasks completion. In particular, a study conducted in Belk et al. (2013a) showed that cognitive processing abilities of users (i.e., speed of processing, controlled attention and working memory capacity) strongly affect task performance in different complexity levels of solving text-recognition CAPTCHA challenges. For example, speed and control of processing, or working memory capacity could be used to decide the level of CAPTCHA complexity that should be provided to users to balance security with usability. Table 2.1 shows that users with limited working memory capacity, or limited speed and control of processing should be provided with a baseline complex CAPTCHA since these types of users need significantly more time to complete a highly complex CAPTCHA challenge. On the other hand, users with enhanced cognitive abilities could be provided with a highly complex CAPTCHA, and thus increasing the security of the mechanism at a minimum cost to usability, since they solve both baseline and highly complex CAPTCHA similarly in terms of task completion time. Nonetheless, analysis of results indicate that speed and control of processing are a more determinant factor affecting user performance in CAPTCHA since enhanced working memory capacity users performed with no significant differences in the baseline complex CAPTCHA, compared to limited working memory capacity users. A within-group analysis of enhanced working memory capacity users revealed that speed and control of processing abilities might affect performance in regard with working memory capacity since the majority of them had limited and medium levels of processing speed and control.

2.2.5 *Learning Styles*

Learning styles represent a particular set of strengths, techniques and preferences that individuals employ during the learning process (on how they learn). For many years, research on learning styles has generated great interest but also divergent viewpoints (Coffield et al. 2004), since they are widely varied, and some of them fail to exhibit satisfactory reliability and validity (Markham 2004). In this respect, many researchers have criticized the scientific basis and theories of learning styles and their influence on educational learning (Coffield et al. 2004; Henry 2007; Curry 1990). However, as empirical research often demonstrates, learning style and the definition of specific learning strategies is an important factor in the computer mediated learning process, facilitating individuals to achieve more effective learning (Tsianos et al. 2006; Boyle et al. 2003), though not always in an expected way (John and Boucouvalas 2002). It has been argued that the distribution of learning material in ways that match learners' ways of processing information is of high importance, since it *"can lead to new insights into the learning process"* (Banner and Rayner 2000). Regarding these individual differences, there have been many attempts to clarify cognitive and learning parameters that correlate to the effectiveness of learning procedures, often leading to comprehensive theories of learning or cognitive styles (Cassidy 2004). Within the context of educational psychology, theories of learning styles have been developed, addressing the issue of individual differences in learning, or more specifically the perception, processing and retaining of information, while they also serve as a link between cognition and personality (Sternberg and Grigorenko 1997). Learning styles, as a term, are frequently used interchangeably with cognitive styles (described in more detail in the next section), which are *"consistent individual differences in preferred ways of organizing and processing information and experience"* (Messick 1984). Nevertheless, learning styles and cognitive styles are broader concepts that incorporate a greater number of not mutually exclusive characteristics, in which learning styles rather focus on learning than on cognitive tasks (Cassady 2004).

Curry's 3-layer onion model (Curry 1983) classifies learning styles in a way that they are not mutually exclusive, but co-exist in different levels of learning processes. Specifically, moving from the inside to outside, the innermost layer is called *cognitive personality style*, and is the most stable trait. The middle layer is the *information processing style*, whilst the outermost consists of *instructional preferences*. Theories that fall in the inner layer are mostly related to cognition or traditional personality research, while more learner-centred approaches fit in the middle layer. The outer layer is more unstable, and it should be mentioned that according to Sadler and Riding (Sadler-Smith and Riding 1999) it is affected by the inner layer. However, the Dunn and Dunn model (1985) that belongs to the layer of instructional preferences exhibits high reliability and validity, but its implications are not easily related to Web-based environments. On the basis of this onion model a number of learning styles' models has been proposed in the literature (the reader can find a more thorough classification in Atkins et al. 2001).

Kolb's Learning Styles Inventory (LSI – Kolb and Kolb 2005) has been widely used for personalizing E-Learning hypermedia systems (Milosevic et. al. 2007; Botsios et al. 2008). The Kolb's LSI proposed four distinct learning styles associated with four stages that students go through during a learning cycle: (i) Students initially gather solid experience on an issue; (ii) based on this experience students make (internal) reflections on the issue; (iii) they create abstract concepts and make generalizations; and finally (iv) they test in practice (experimentally) new knowledge and provide explanations for new situations. In his model, Kolb proposed that each individual shows preference for one of the four stages of the cycle, which uses at a greater extent and gives the appropriate learning style. Accordingly, the Kolb LSI distinguishes an individual's learning style as: (i) *Convergers*, individuals that prefer to discover possibilities and relationships, concentrate better when studying alone and better understand through abstract thinking; (ii) *divergers*, individuals that prefer real life experience and discussion, are imaginative, like brainstorming and group work, prefer observing; (iii) *assimilators*, individuals that solve problems with deductive reasoning and have the ability to create theoretical models; and (iv) *accommodators*, individuals that solve problems by carrying out plans and experiments, challenges theories, are adaptable and work based on gut feeling rather than logic.

Another learning style theory is the Felder/Silverman Index of Learning Styles (ILS – Felder and Silverman 1988) which has also been widely used for personalizing E-Learning hypermedia systems (Graf and Kinshuk 2009; Papanikolaou et al. 2003). The Felder/Silverman ILS distinguishes students into one of the following learning style dimensions: (i) *Sensing learners* that are concrete, practical, oriented towards facts and procedures, or *intuitive learners* that are conceptual, innovative, oriented towards theories and meanings; (ii) *visual learners* that prefer visual representations of presented material (e.g., pictures, diagrams, flow charts), or *verbal learners* that prefer written and verbal explanations; (iii) *active learners* that learn by experimenting and working with others, or *reflective learners* that learn by thinking things through and working alone; and (iv) *sequential learners* that work linearly, orderly and learn in small incremental steps, or *global learners* that have a holistic approach in learning and learn in large leaps.

Other popular learning style models include among others Neil Fleming's VARK model (Leite et al. 2009) which distinguishes learners as visual learners, auditory learners, reading-writing preference learners and kinesthetic learners or tactile learners, and Honey and Mumford's Learning Styles Questionnaire (LSQ – Honey and Mumford 2006) that made two adaptations to Kolbs' experiential model to reflect managerial experiences of decision making/problem solving, and proposed four dimensions (Activist, Reflector, Theorist and Pragmatist). An extended review of other learning style models (including cognitive style models) can be found in the report of Coffield et al. (2004) that reviewed the literature on learning styles and examined the 13 most influential models.

2.2.6   Cognitive Styles

Research on cognitive styles is an area of human sciences to explain empirically observed differences in information mental representation and processing. Different theories have been proposed over time suggesting that individuals have differences in the way they process and remember information. Due to the multi-dimensional nature of cognitive styles, a global definition has not been given to date. Nevertheless, in a recent global E-Survey of 94 individual style researchers and experts (Peterson et al. 2009) of the ELSIN network (European Learning Styles Information Network) who were asked to comment on the state of the field and their own understanding of the phenomenon being studied, the majority agrees that *"cognitive styles are individual differences in processing that are integrally linked to a person's cognitive system. More specifically, they are a person's preferred way of processing (perceiving, organizing and analyzing) information using cognitive brain-based mechanisms and structures. They are partly fixed, relatively stable and possibly innate preferences"*.

The work of Riding and Cheema (1991) is considered an important turning point for cognitive style research (Peterson et al. 2005), that made a survey of approximately thirty different cognitive styles and concluded that most of the proposed theories measured two broad style dimensions: (i) A *Verbal/Imager* dimension that refers to how individuals process information and indicates their preference for representing information verbally (Verbals) or in mental pictures (Imagers); and (ii) a *Wholist/Analyst* dimension that refers to how individuals organize information and indicates a preference of structuring information as a whole to get the big picture (Wholists) or structuring the information in detail (Analysts). We next describe these two dimensions.

2.2.6.1   Verbal/Imager Dimension

One of the most widely accepted theories of human cognition is the Dual Coding Theory (Paivio 2006; Paivio and Csapo 1973). It suggests that visual and verbal information (respectively, image-based and text-based) is processed and represented differently and along two distinct cognitive subsystems in the human mind; the visual and verbal cognitive subsystems. Each subsystem creates separate representations for information processed which are used to organize incoming information that can be acted upon, stored, and retrieved for subsequent use.

Many psychology studies have reported that pictures are better recognized and recalled by the human brain than textual information, referred as the picture superiority effect (Anderson 2009; Ally and Budson 2007; Brady et al. 2008; Paivio and Csapo 1973). Paivio's Dual Coding Theory explains the picture superiority effect that pictures are more perceptually rich than words which lends them an advantage in information processing. Pictures are processed and represented as they are perceived (e.g., color, shape, etc.) but are also represented automatically as words (e.g., *"picture of a car"*), and thus have two representations for the same picture being observed. In contrast, textual information is not automatically represented as a picture without explicit instruction or additional mental effort. The redundant representation for pictures (two representations instead of one) increases their processing efficiency and memory strength. In addition, the picture superiority effect might be explained by the fact that pictures are mentally represented along with the features being observed, whereas text is visually sparse and represented symbolically, where symbols might have a different meaning depending on the form of the text, which requires an additional processing for the verbal subsystem. For example, 'X' may represent the Roman numeral 10 or the multiplication symbol (Biddle et al. 2012).

Nevertheless, other research findings claim that the picture superiority effect does not always hold and is affected by various factors (Oates and Reder 2010; Reder et al. 2009; Brady et al. 2008; Robertson and Köhler 2007; Whitehouse et al. 2006). For example, Oates and Reder (2010) claim that the picture superiority effect only occurs when a picture affords a meaningful textual label that discriminates it from other pictures. This way the picture can be represented efficiently and effectively in its dual form (visual and verbal). Results of their study reveal that abstract pictures are not memorable as single words since the visual stimuli is difficult to identify, and hence, a generation of a consistent textual label is not easy or possible. Robertson and Köhler (2007) have further provided evidence that the ability to label a picture affects its processing and memory. In their study, they assessed 4–6 year old children and reached the conclusion that whenever children could successfully name aloud the picture during encoding were more likely to remember it later.

In this context, as an effort to explain the aforementioned empirically observed differences in users' mental representation and processing of information, many researchers have developed theories of individual differences in cognitive style from the perspective of dual coding theory (Riding and Cheema 1991), and consequently, argue that individuals have differences in the way they process and remember information. In particular, individuals may process verbal information more efficiently than visual information (Verbals), whilst others the opposite (Imagers). Although it is likely that individuals switch strategies depending on the nature of the task, studies have revealed that individuals consistently prefer one or the other strategy (Riding and Cheema 1991). Furthermore, ability might affect preference towards a particular strategy in that if a particular mode of processing is more efficient for a person then it is more likely to be preferred.

2.2.6.2 Wholist/Analyst Dimension

The Wholist/Analyst dimension is strongly related to the theory of field dependency/independency proposed by Witkin (Witkin 1962; Witkin et al. 1977) which is considered one of the most important and highly researched cognitive styles (Rezaei and Katz 2004; Riding and Cheema 1991). In particular, Witkin distinguished individuals being field dependent and field independent in which he describes field independence as *"an analytical, in contrast to global, way of perceiving which entails a tendency to experience items as discrete from their backgrounds and reflects ability to overcome the influence of an embedding context"*. For example, when confronted with problems, some individuals are good at extracting things from the context and prefer to handle them in a more analytical way. In contrast, individuals termed as field-dependent cannot abstract an element from its context and are intended to handle problems in a holistic way.

Accordingly, Riding and Cheema (1991) proposed the Wholist/Analyst dimension and classified users to the cognitive typologies of Wholist or Analyst which are respectively mapped to the field dependent and field independent typologies of Witkin. Their different characteristics and implications on hypermedia systems are the following: (i) Users that belong to the *Wholist* class view a situation and organize information as a whole, proceed from the whole to the parts and organize information in loosely clustered wholes. Wholists have high assertiveness, and especially in extreme types, they are decisive; while (ii) users that belong to the *Analyst* class view a situation as a collection of parts, stress one or two aspects at a time, proceed form the parts to the whole and organize information in clear-cut groupings (chunking down). Analysts have low assertiveness and especially in extreme types, they are indecisive.

2.2.7 Elicitation Methods of High-Level and Elementary Cognitive Processes

Elicitation methods for high-level information processes include mainly questionnaires where participants express their experiences and preferences, and psychometric tests that measure response times of participants on specific aptitude tasks. In the case of learning styles, popular elicitation tools include Kolb's Learning Style Inventory (Kolb and Kolb 2005), the Felder/Silverman Index of Learning Styles (Felder and Silverman 1988) and Honey and Mumford's Learning Styles Questionnaire (Honey and Mumford 2006). In the case of cognitive styles, self-reported questionnaires usually ask the participants to rate their preference towards a verbal versus visual mode of processing. Example ratings would be *"I have a photographic memory"* or *"My verbal skills are excellent"* (OSIVQ – Blazhenkova and Kozhevnikov 2009). However, for the reason that questionnaires showed relatively low internal reliability and poor predictive validity (Blazhenkova and Kozhevnikov 2009; McAvinue and Robertson 2007), objective measures through the development of psychometric tools have emerged, such as response time in solving cognitive tasks that require verbal or visual processing. In particular, psychometric tools have been proposed that typically require from the participant to provide an answer to text-based or image-based statements. Depending on the response time of each answer, the ratio of means or medians between the verbal and visual statements is computed and further used to classify the participant to a

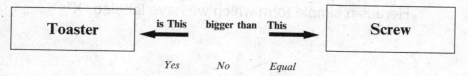

Fig. 2.4 Example of an imagery item in the word form (Peterson et al. 2005)

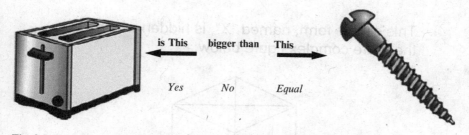

Fig. 2.5 Example of an imagery item in the picture form (Peterson et al. 2005)

particular group; Verbal or Imager group. Popular psychometric tests that highlight differences in the Verbal/Imager dimension include the VICS test (Peterson et al. 2005) and the CSA test (Riding 1991). Figures 2.4 and 2.5 illustrate an example of the VICS test in which individuals are presented with a set of cognitive verbal and imagery tasks. Figure 2.4 illustrates an example of an imagery item, in the form of a word, while Fig. 2.5 illustrates the same core imagery item as in Fig. 2.4, but this time in the form of a picture. Main aim is to illustrate the pictures and words in a different format and not in content, aiming to investigate if users respond differently to the picture and word based stimuli.

Measurement of Wholist/Analyst tendencies primarily involves the dis-embedding of a shape from its surrounding field (Riding and Cheema 1991). Some of the earliest methods include the Rod-and-Frame Test in which participants are required to determine the upright position of a rod; the Body Adjustment Test, in which subjects judge their body position in different fields (e.g., defining their body position in rooms with tilted walls and chairs); the Rotating Room Test, in which subjects adjust a room to the true vertical position; and the Group Embedded Figures Test (GEFT – Witkin et al. 1971), in which participants are required to find common geometric shapes in a larger design (Fig. 2.6). Also, computerized tests include the CSA test (Riding 1991) and the E-CSA-WA test (Peterson et al. 2005) in which participants are required to judge whether two geometrical figures are identical or not, and decide whether a geometrical figure is embedded in a larger complex figure. The reader may also refer to Kozhevnikov (2007) and Riding and Cheema (1991) for a review on older questionnaires and psychometric tests.

Here is a simple form which we have labeled "X":

This simple form, named "X", is hidden within the more complex figure below:

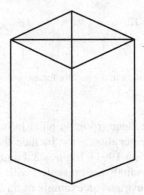

Fig. 2.6 Sample item from the GEFT booklet (Witkin et al. 1971)

In recent years, there have been also many research attempts that employed computational intelligence techniques to dynamically extract and/or correlate cognitive styles with users' navigation behavior. Frias-Martinez et al. (2007) utilized a number of clustering techniques to understand human behavior and perception in relation with cognitive style, expertise and gender differences of digital library users; Antoniou and Lepouras (2010) studied the connection between the way people moved in a museum and the way they preferred to approach and process information cognitively; Hsu and Chen (2011) investigated how learners' cognitive style affect their navigation behavior through data mining techniques as well as analyzed how navigation behavior may influence performance in education environments; and Kinley et al. (2010) explored the relationships between Web users' searching behavior and their cognitive style. Finally, a more recent study of Belk et al. (2013b) revealed a relationship between the Wholist/Analyst dimension and the users' navigation behavior in terms of linearity/non-linearity. In particular, results revealed that Wholists tended to follow linear hyperlink sequences within online encyclopedia articles, in contrast to Analysts who did not reveal any significant differences in navigation behavior.

For the more elementary processes, a typical measure of cognitive processing control is the Stroop task which requires individuals to name the color in which a word has been printed, while ignoring the word itself (Stroop 1935). Conflict arises when the color of the word and the word itself are incongruent, e.g., the word "blue" is printed in red color. Individuals must override the dominant aspect of the stimuli (the tendency to read a word) with the processing of their weaker, but goal-relevant aspect (the recognition of ink color). In this respect, the difference between the two kinds of measures is taken as an index of inhibition, which is the basic component of control of processing (MacLeod 1991; Stroop 1935). Individuals being faster indicating the printed color of the word tend to have more efficient controlled of processing.

As we have seen earlier, working memory is a system that consists of the central executive that controls the two slave systems (visuo-spatial sketchpad and phonological loop), plus the episodic buffer that provides a temporary interface between the slave systems and the long term memory. In order to identify the capacity/storage of each subsequent sub-system, participants could go through a series of working memory span tests. At first, the test of Demetriou et al. (2013) could be used for measuring both the central executive function and the verbal storage ability (phonological loop span), providing an indication of individuals' working memory ability. Undertaking this assessment test, individuals are required to store the last word of a series of consecutively presented (written) sentences, while deciding at the same time whether the meaning of each sentence makes sense or not. The test gradually becomes more difficult, since the number of sentences increases from two (first level) to nine (last level). There are six series of sentences in each level, and the participants have to remember correctly the last words of four at least series in order to proceed to the next level. Secondly, a working memory test to measure the visuo-spatial sketchpad could be used (Demetriou et al. 2013). A total of 21 figures are presented to the individuals, with increasing complexity as the test progresses. Each figure is presented for about 2 s before it disappears, and thereupon the participant has to identify the figure among five highly resembling ones. Each correct answer allows the user to continue to the next figure, until he fails to retain the visual information due to the increased complexity. In total, individuals are classified as "low", "medium", or "high" accordingly, with respect to their ability, based on a calculated aggregated score of all tests.

2.2.8 Implication of Cognitive Aspects on Adaptation and Personalization

The discussion of the aforementioned individual differences leads to our proposal concerning the implementation of adaptation and personalization systems and interfaces that can appraise human cognitive factors. A short practical overview of selected theoretical dimensions/models is discussed next. The implications of those in the hypermedia environments can be utilized as a set of personalization parameters and adaptive mechanisms that can reconstruct and adjust any content and/or service based on the capabilities and the condition of the user.

From the perspective of learning styles and more specifically of the LSI paradigm, Kolb's 4 types are drawn from two independent scales: Concrete experience vs. abstract conceptualization, and reflective observation vs. active experimentation. People-oriented types are those that tend to concrete experience rather than abstract conceptualization, which in terms of personality theories are rather 'feeling' than 'thinking'. Therefore, as it is clearly defined by the theory, divergers' and accommodators' individual characteristics demonstrate a strong preference in group working, since collaboration may be a necessary prerequisite for maximizing learning performance. It also could be argued that the present modus operandi of E-Learning systems in general favors types of learners that prefer working alone (convergers and assimilators), than those who are people-oriented. Implications for designers could be summarized in the equal distribution of the different types of learners, and in further motivating convergers and assimilators to participate. For example, if for any reason a group of learners consists only of these latter two types, then a Web-based educational environment's functionality may be impaired.

As described previously, Riding and Cheema (1991) identified two independent dimensions of cognitive styles, by integrating a large volume of pre-existing style research into their theory: Verbal/Imager, and Wholist/Analyst. The first dichotomy represents individuals' preference for receiving and processing information in either visual or verbal mode, while the second refers to a corresponding preference for information in whole or in parts; individuals without preferences are classified in each scale as intermediates. The implications of the Verbal/Imager dimension are rather clear; the Wholist/Analyst dimension, however, is derived from Witkin's construct of "psychological differentiation" (Witkin et al. 1971, 1977), and its implications are somehow more complex. In a nutshell, Analysts are better at active analysis and perception differentiation, tend to act independently, are self-oriented and self-reinforced, and develop their own strategies. Wholists prefer social interaction and collaboration, while they require external direction, reinforcement, feedback, defined goals and specific structures.

More specifically, various studies revealed that the Verbal/Imager dimension is particularly related to the content representation within hypermedia systems (Ghinea and Chen 2008). Their different characteristics and implications on hypermedia systems are the following: (i) *Verbals,* represent information verbally, focus their attention externally and are stimulating. Individuals being Verbals prefer and perform better when hypermedia content is presented in the form of text. Verbals also have great reading accuracy and are better at recalling acoustically complex and unfamiliar text (Laing 2001); and (ii) *Imagers* represent information in mental pictures, focus their attention internally and tend to be passive. Imagers prefer and perform better when the hypermedia content is provided in the combination of graphical and textual representation, but do not perform efficiently when an exclusively verbal representation is provided (Ghinea and Chen 2008). On the other hand, the Wholist/Analyst dimension is particularly related to the way hypermedia content is structured, and has an effect on users' learning patterns and navigation behavior within hypermedia systems. A recent work of Chen and Liu (2008), which investigated the effect of field dependency dimension on users' learning patterns within Web-instruction programs, revealed implications of cognitive style on users' preferred ways of using different navigation tools and display options. In particular, field independent users tended to actively group relevant concepts utilizing an alphabetical index tool of the hypermedia system, while field dependent users tended to be passive and relied on hierarchical maps to build relationships among different concepts (Chen and Liu 2008). Regarding the available display options, field independent users were capable to extract relevant information from the detailed description because they have a tendency to use their own internal references, while field dependent users preferred to get concrete guidance from examples, since they heavily rely on external cues. Finally, field independent users browsed fewer pages to directly get to relevant topics for completing their tasks, while field dependent users tended to build an overall picture by browsing more pages because they use a global approach to process information.

Regarding more elementary cognitive processes (i.e., working memory, controlled attention, speed of processing), existing research works have shown that individual differences in such human cognitive processing abilities have an effect on problem solving and comprehension (Conway et al. 2002; Shipstead and Broadway 2013; Demetriou et al. 2002; Unsworth and Spillers 2010; Klingberg 2009). Thus, bearing in mind that human-computer interactions are processed on a cognitive level, such individual differences could be important for personalizing content and functionality to the needs and abilities of users. Accordingly, we consider that adaptive interactive systems can be manipulated in a way that could compensate for certain individuals' limited levels of speed of processing, control of processing and working memory, mainly by restructuring the content; presenting more explanations; additional navigation support; reducing the number of simultaneously presented stimuli and the volume of content (preventing cognitive overload); and by providing information at a slower pace, to mention but a few techniques. These methods are essentially personalization techniques that could be employed in almost every (complex enough) interactive system, though their efficiency can only be validated through empirical research. Chapters 6, 7 and 8 present guidelines and empirical findings of applying such individual differences (i.e., cognitive styles and elementary cognitive processes) in personalizing content and functionality of various interactive systems in different application domains.

2.3 Emotions and Learning Process

Over the course of time, a combination of developments in statistical know-how and the evolution of thought within psychology enabled the refinement of measures, and subsequently the assessment of more specific factors in the field of individual differences like different kinds of ability, cognition (discussed previously) and emotion.

Especially, the concept of emotion (and affect) is perhaps the most extensive, complex, and yet dynamic research field of psychology, with many extensions, conflicting views and unanswered questions over time. Main attempt is to identify the unique character of individuals describing properties of behavior which concern the individual's typical ways of coping with life events (Lewis and Haviland-Jones 2004). Throughout the years, there are a number of definitions assigned to emotions with respect to their nature, management and control. Indicatively, Darwin (1872) defined emotions as subjective feelings, separating them into those caused by external conditions and those caused by physical conditions such as hunger and pain. Oatley argued that an emotion occurs when an event is evaluated against a target giving priority to some goals in relation to others. Often emotions are accompanied by different types of thought, expression, and physiological response, and can be put on hold or compete with alternative courses of action (Oatley 2001).

Many researchers used to believe that emotional processes were beyond the scope of a scientific study, until recent advances in cognitive science and psychology suggested that there is nothing mystical about emotions. In general, emotions can influence our logic in situations of fear, panic or love as well as our decisions in normal situations, since mere laws and regulations do not have any practical application without the interference of emotions in the two high cognitive processes of humans, that is decision making and perception. They are affected by someone's knowledge and goals, and according to surveys, have a very central role in rational thought. Together with emotional experience, emotions are useful in learning and decision making, since the preconceptions that are related to previous emotional experiences of comparable situations facilitate the efficient processing of knowledge and reasoning necessary for current conscious decisions. Scientists believe that the emotions involved in ideas, designs and every experience is stored in our memories. The positive emotions encode the knowledge related to efficiency, opportunities and anything associated with positive results, while they might increase internal motivation. The negative emotions encode the knowledge of failure, the risk and anything related with negative results.

In principle, the nature of emotions is considered much more basic than the one of logic and intelligence (Vesterinen 2001; D'Mello et al. 2005; Ahn and Picard 2005), and their role much more influencing with respect to human behavior. The American physician and neuroscientist Paul MacLean proposed and studied extensively back to 1990 (MacLean 1990) a three-layered model of the human brain which essentially describes three separated brains that exist in our skull. These brains, even though are developed in separate times in our growth cycle toward higher thinking, it seems that they are interconnected and are not entirely discrete. These are: the *neocortex* brain (the outer layer – that has been studied most compared to the other two), a place in the brain where the majority of the processing of perception is taking place and contains the visual cortex and the auditory cortex; the *limbic* brain (the middle layer), found in the centre of the brain and is the place of emotion, attention and memory (records positively and negatively charged memories); and the *reptilian* brain (the innermost core), responsible for the control of breathing, heartbeat, basic sensory motor functions, instinctive behavior and motivation.

As mentioned in the introduction, we are interested in the way individuals process their emotions and how those are related with other elements of their information processing system, during decision making, problem solving and learning. With the direct or indirect inclusion of technologies in peoples' daily lives it is expected that a sophisticated system will be able to provide consistent communication opportunities that will support a seamless interaction between the users and the various applications and services. Systems should be able to perceive information related to user needs, preferences, characteristics, and even emotional states and conditions. Norman (2004) argued that in order for media to communicate better with people they need to be able to understand our emotions and in order to do that they need to have emotions as well. According to Picard "*if we want our computers to be really smart, to adapt to us as users, and to interact of course with us, then they must develop the ability to recognize and express emotions, to have empathy, and have what is called 'emotional intelligence'*" (Picard 2000). The applications proposed by Picard are based on classification and perceptual mechanisms of bodily responses from people using the machine (e.g., facial expressions, gestures, eyegaze, body temperature, blood pressure, etc.). Of course, given the complexity of emotional and cognitive structures and their further modeling and evaluation, these approaches are still found in early stages or refer to individual efforts (that mostly belong to the area of Affective Computing and Artificial Intelligence).

From the scope of adaptation and personalization, incorporating emotional constructs in the development of user models is deemed necessary, since they could contribute to more comprehensive solutions especially in relation to the fields of education and training. Adaptive interactive systems belonging to these areas of concern are of particular interest, since educational hypermedia (along with on-line information systems) are the most popular (accounting for about two thirds of the research efforts), out of the six in total applications areas that have been identified since 1996 with respect to adaptive hypermedia systems (Brusilovsky 2001). Apart from their research popularity and significance, these systems vary in terms of adaptation effects, personalization techniques and user modelling characteristics even if they might share the same educational or learning objectives and principles in their backbone. Designing educational settings that utilize individual differences and emotional characteristics in their personalization approaches during learning process may increase the effectiveness of users' academic performance, comprehension capabilities and satisfaction (Germanakos et al. 2008; Tsianos et al. 2009). Learning is acquiring new or modifying existing knowledge, behaviors, skills, values, or preferences and may involve synthesizing different types of information, even emotional ones. Emotions and affect are a vital part of a continuous mental process and as such the whole learning procedure is influenced by them. A user's behavior during learning process is altered by affective elements in problem solving routines, judgement and decision making (Bechara et al. 2000; Levenson 1999), as is performance in cognitive processing tasks. Decision-making and problem solving are cognitive processes where the outcome is a choice between alternatives, and could be regarded as an indirect way to make inferences to a person's learning pattern since learning includes continuous decision making and problem resolution.

The literature reveals three models that study the link between emotions and learning (D'Mello et al. 2005): The Stein and Levine model, the Kort, Reily and Picard model, and the Cognitive Disequilibrium model.

In this section we emphasize on the emotional factors that have a direct influence in learning and the processes that take place during the acquisition of knowledge. We discuss the theoretical grounds of emotional concepts that are easily generalized, inclusive and provide some indirect measurement of general emotional mechanisms. These sub-processes manage a number of emotional factors like anxiety, boredom effects, anger, feelings of self-efficacy, user satisfaction, etc. In this regards, we developed a theory primarily discussed in (Lekkas et al. 2011a) that focuses on *emotion regulation*, the way in which an individual perceives and controls his emotions, and *emotional arousal*, which is the capacity of a human being to sense and experience specific emotional situations (Lekkas et al. 2011b). We put emphasis on anxiety, which is probably the most indicative factor and can be proven significant in determining design attributes in Web-based educational systems with respect to HCI practices such as usability and aesthetical aspects. We also consider psychometric challenges as well as the complicated matter of quantifying and subsequently mapping emotions in the adaptation and personalization process of interactive systems as shown in Chap. 5.

We hypothesized that by combining the level of arousal of an individual with the moderating role of emotion regulation, it is possible to clarify, at some extent, how a user's affectional responses hamper or promote learning procedures. Thus, by personalizing on affect, the educational concept, we can avoid stressful instances (by reducing the negative effect of high levels of anxiety) and take full advantage of the users' cognitive capacity at any time. An effort to present an extensive discussion and/or to construct a model that predicts the role of emotion, in general, is beyond the scope of this book, due to the complexity and the numerous confounding variables that would make such an attempt rather impossible. However, there is a considerable amount of researches concerning the role of emotion and its implications on academic performance (or achievement), in terms of efficient learning (Kort and Reilly 2002), and we believe that even a reference around the proposed lines would give an adequate insight to the reader with respect to this application area of adaptive interactive systems.

2.3.1   Emotion Regulation

For the proposed theory we are trying to combine various levels of analyses and form a typology that will help us circle effectively the cognitive and affective mechanisms of the brain. In order to apply a purely psychological construct to a digital platform we adjust the various theories concerning cognition and emotion having in mind to make our psychological model flexible and applicable to users' models, needs and preferences. In order to manipulate the emotional parameters according to user characteristics, our research goes through the stage of extracting quantified elements that represent deeper psychological and affective abilities. The latter cannot be directly used in a Web-based environment, but a numerical equivalent can define a user characteristic (e.g., basic emotions like sadness, anger, etc., cannot be directly measured and adequately described unless they do not go through the necessary standardization and quantification, e.g., to be presented on a standardized scale).

Theorists from a variety of orientations tend to agree in two emotional processing systems. There is a considerable conceptual overlap in their formulations:

- A schematic, associative and implicit system that has connections with bodily response systems. This mode involves fast and automatic processes such as priming and spreading activation. It often involves large numbers of memories in parallel. It is not wholly dependent on verbal information – visual, kinesthetic or other cues could provide the basis for priming or activating an emotional memory.
- An abstract propositional 'rational' system that is analytical, reflective, logical and relies on high level executive functions. It is primarily based on verbally accessible semantic information.

Individuals can utilize these two systems to process information. The first system relies on experience and intuition. In particular, individuals consider issues intuitively and effortlessly. Rather than reflect upon the various considerations in sequence, individuals form a global impression of issues. In addition, rather than apply logical rules or symbolic codes, such as words or numbers, individuals consider vivid representations of objects or events. These representations are filled with the emotions, details, features, and sensations that correspond to the objects or events. Finally, learning is equated to ascertain associations from direct experiences.

The second system, in contrast, relies on logic and rationality. In particular, individuals analyze issues with effort, logic, and deliberation rather than rely on intuition. To decide upon issues, they rely on logical rules and symbolic codes. The context (de-tails, features, and emotions) that correspond to objects or events are disregarded. To facilitate learning in this system, individuals learn the rules of reasoning that are promulgated in society.

Recent neuroscientific findings are consistent with these multi-level conceptualizations. LeDoux (1998) has reviewed evidence suggesting that emotion networks have direct anatomical connections to both the neocortex and the amygdala. Events that are highly emotional are likely to be registered at both subcortical and cortical levels. The subcortical route is shorter and rapid whereas the cortical route is longer and slower. In the subcortical route sensory information goes from the thalamus directly to the amygdala. In the cortical route information is sent from the thalamus to both the cortex and hippocampus and is then projected to the amygdala. As noted by Samoilov and Goldfried (2000) these recent findings support a qualitative distinction between cortically based and subcortical levels of information processing. They imply that not all emotional responses are mediated cortically; rather, some may by initiated without any cognitive participation: *"Emotional responses can*

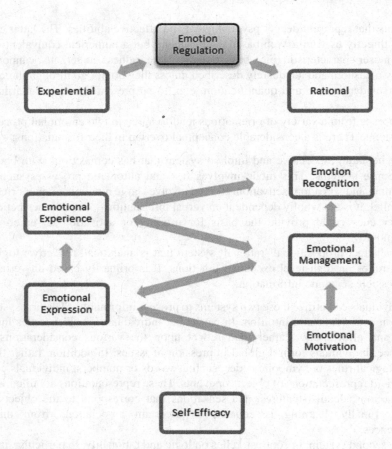

Fig. 2.7 The emotion regulation model (Lekkas et al. 2011a)

occur without the involvement of the higher processing systems of the brain, systems believed to be involved in thinking, reasoning, and consciousness" (LeDoux 1998).

Therefore, at first, we focus on the cognominal construct of emotion regulation and we are investigating its connection with cognitive processing tasks, decision making and problem solving styles. We focus on emotion regulation as an emotional mechanism and not on a number of basic emotions because experiential emotion regulation can provide some indirect measurement of general emotional mechanisms since it manages a number of emotional factors like anxiety, boredom effects and frustration. Our model of emotion regulation includes as well two levels of processing in relation to the aforementioned concept of processing but we consider that these two levels are connected closely with each other and that information is processed not only in a serial way but also concurrently. It is composed of two base elements (see Fig. 2.7 – Lekkas et al. 2011a) as discussed below.

2.3.1.1 The Experiential Level

The *experiential level* is the actual emotional experience and emotional expression of the individual (the capacity of a human being to sense, experience and express specific emotional situations). More specifically, emotional experience is the covert emotional condition that a human is experiencing as a result of a stimulus or information of such kind, while emotional expression is the overt reaction of such a stimulus, the behavior that follows the experience.

The study of emotional experience and emotional expression has a long history, which dates back to the 1870s with scientific investigations undergone by Charles Darwin (Darwin 1872). Darwin's work emphasized the biological utility of emotional expression. Thus, it contributed to the development of an evolutionary-expressive approach to emotion, which suggests that emotion exists because it contributes to survival (Oatley 1992). Emotional experience, emotional expression and emotional arousal have been conceptualized as three primary components of emotion (Kennedy-Moore and Watson 1999), with emotional reflection as a secondary component, involving thoughts about the three primary components.

Expressive confidence involves the skillful production of situation-appropriate emotional expressions. Individuals high in expressive confidence have been found to be in good control of their emotions, as well as experiencing and expressing positive emotions with family and peers (Gross and John 1998). These assets probably result in them being better liked by others, with whom they interact. In contrast, individuals high in negative expression are more likely to experience and express negative emotions, possibly with the consequence that they are less well liked.

Our model of emotion regulation distinguishes mechanisms surrounding the experience of emotions, from those surrounding the expression of emotions. Whilst in practical terms this is probably a seamless process, we believe it is conceptually useful to distinguish experience from expression. We hypothesize that it is more fundamental and harmful to control emotional experience, than to control emotional expression. The expression of emotions is behavioral. Thus, the mechanisms surrounding it, involve the real and imagined consequences of expression, cultural and family rules for acceptable expression. These mechanisms may be different from those involved in emotional experience, which is of course experiential, rather than overtly behavioral. Such emotional experience may involve feeling too much intensive emotion, feeling inappropriate emotion, or feeling numb. Also important, is how the initial negative stimulus is registered, whether emotions are experienced as a gestalt, rather than separate somatic constituents and understanding the causes and meaning of the emotional experience. In short, it could be said that emotional experience points more towards a stimulus event, and expression more towards the behavioral response.

In summary, emotion regulation is not so much concerned about whether emotional expression is right or wrong but more with what mechanisms underlies successful and unsuccessful processing. Failure to express emotions may be integrally related to failure to properly process an emotional event. However, this is only one important part within a more complex process, as emotion regulation is regarded as the overall concept within which, emotional expression simply constitutes the final stage.

2.3.1.2 The Rational Level

The model would be problematic without a regulatory mechanism of emotion. For this reason we included also the *rational level* of emotion regulation which is the multiple ways with which the individual recognizes and manages emotions. It is comprised of the notions of emotion recognition, emotional management and emotional motivation. These are the three (out of five) scales that comprise the emotional intelligence construct which has been introduced based on the research conducted by Goleman (1995), who defined emotional intelligence as the ability to recognize our own emotions and those of others, to motivate ourselves and to properly manage our emotions in our relations; and Salovey and Mayer (1990), that around the same lines referred to emotional intelligence as the ability to assess, manage and express our emotions (and those of others) and the ability to make use of them. Emotional Intelligence seems to be a possible predictor of the aforementioned concepts, and is a grounded enough construct, already supported by academic literature. Many researchers believe that emotional intelligence is a personality trait that is related to performance (Lyons and Schneider 2005; Newsome et al. 2000; Day and Carroll 2004). Specifically, people with high emotional intelligence, perform better both at work (e.g., interviews, management, academic issues, to groups and cognitive tasks) and in the various activities of daily living. In this regards, we selected these scales since the factors that deal with human to human interaction (like empathy) are not present in Web-based applications – at least for the time being. So, respectively, emotion recognition is the ability to realize the true nature of an emotion as it is and to feel it in the appropriate degree. Emotional management is the ability to manipulate and to control an emotion while emotional motivation is the ability to transform an emotional experience into a motivational urge.

We believe that the two systems, the experiential and rational, composing our model can interact. If someone during the stage of emotion recognition realizes intuitively that the emotion that is about to be triggered will have a negative and unpleasant emotional experience as an outcome, then it will be implicitly transformed to a different emotion so that it will be easily manageable in the next stage. The human brain prioritizes based on the principles of self-regulation and not on the search of objectivity and truthfulness.

For the sake of completeness, we need also to refer to an additional concept which is called *self-efficacy*. Self-efficacy plays a critical role in how we think, feel and behave, and for that reason it seems that is directly connected with the two systems of our model. It is defined as people's beliefs about their capabilities to produce and perform (Bandura 1997). These beliefs determine how people feel, think, motivate themselves and behave.

2.3.2 Emotional Arousal

As we mentioned earlier *emotional arousal* is the capacity of a human being to sense and experience specific emotional situations. Our main conceptualization for incorporating this dimension in our theory derives from Russell's Circumplex Model of Affect (Russell 1980), who proposed that all affective states arise from two fundamental neurophysiological systems, one related to valence (a pleasure–displeasure continuum) and the other to arousal, or alertness.

The emotional state of a user at any given moment is susceptible to constant variations due to factors that are either triggered within a specific environment or may as well be extraneous and unrelated to human-computer interactions. As a result, users may experience a wide range of emotions while interacting with hypermedia content, both positive and negative. In parallel, research on emotions has shown that the association of certain emotions to specific events may have a significant impact on information processing and/or on the consolidation of newly acquired information (Ochsner 2000; Kensinger 2004; LaBar and Phelps 1998). Hence, the monitoring and identification of users' emotional state while interacting with hypermedia content could be useful, since it would allow the employment of corresponding personalization techniques in order to reduce the influence of negative emotions. However, identifying human emotions with high accuracy is a complex procedure, whereas altering the emotional state of a user is even more challenging.

Our model approaches emotional arousal of users by giving emphasis on anxiety as the core element of this construct. In combination with the moderating role of emotion regulation, we are interested initially in clarifying their relationship and investigate the possibility of a unified typology. Thus, we are mainly interested in the different forms of anxiety (state and trait anxiety (Spielberger et al. 1983), cognitive test anxiety (Cassady and Jonhson 2002), and computer anxiety (Desai 2001)), and its manifestations as an increase of stress and negative emotional arousal with consequent negative effects on learning performance (Hamilton 1985). It has to be clarified that we use anxiety as a reaction to stress which could be considered as an adverse reaction that people have to excessive pressures from different sources or other types of demand placed on them (Health and Safety Executive 2007). Although the terms stress and anxiety are typically used interchangeably in everyday conversation, there is a difference. Stress, unlike anxiety, is a response to daily pressures. While stress is a response to a specific stressor, anxiety has no identifiable root. For the purpose of the current research we refer to anxiety as a more suitable notion, since it is related with the mental outcome of an intervention and not on the pure physiological reaction. Nevertheless, there is still a question about the role of primary/secondary emotions, and their cognitive and/or neurophysiologic intrinsic origins (Damasio 1994). Emotions influence the cognitive processes of the individual, and therefore have certain effect in any educational setting. Again, bibliographic research has shown that anxiety is often correlated with academic performance (Cassady 2004), as well with performance in computer mediated learning procedures (Smith and Caputi 2005). Subsequently, different levels of anxiety should have also a significant effect in cognitive functions.

Anxiety is an unpleasant combination of emotions that includes fear, worry and uneasiness and is often accompanied by physical reactions such as high blood pressure, increased heart rate and other body signals like shortness of breath, nausea and increased sweating (Kim and Gorman 2005). Anxiety can be regarded either as generated set of emotions (short term "state anxiety") or as a predisposition (long term "trait anxiety"). The anxious person is not able to regulate his emotional state since he feels and expects danger all the time. Barlow (2002) describes anxiety as a cognitive-affective process in which the individual has a sense of unpredictability, a feeling of uncertainty and a sense of lack of control over emotions, thoughts and events. This cognitive and affective situation is associated as well with physiological arousal and research has shown that an individual's perception is influenced in specific domains such as attentional span, memory, and performance in specific tasks. In relation to performance, the findings are controversial but there is a strong body of research which supports that anxiety is strongly correlated to performance and academic achievement (Spielberger and Vagg 1995; Spielberger 1972), as is test anxiety (Sapp 1993).

Test anxiety is a situation-specific form of personality anxiety, which refers to the set of phenomenological, physiological, and behavioral responses that accompany concern about possible negative consequences or failure in an evaluative situation (Spielberger and Vagg 1995). Test anxiety has two major components: worry and emotionality, and the cognitive component of test anxiety is regarded as the defining component of test anxiety (Cassady and Jonhson 2002). Worry is the cognitive concern about performance and emotionality is somatic reactions to task demands and stress (Schwarzer 1984). At different temporal phases (pre-evaluation, active evaluation, and post-evaluation) of an evaluation, individuals with different experiences of test anxiety are disadvantageously influenced by worry associated with the consequences of failure. According to the cognitive interference theory, which has been used to interpret the effects of test anxiety on subdued cognitive performance, cognitive interference refers to worry that interferes with performance by distracting an individual from the goal and high levels of worry are often associated with low levels of performance (Sarason et al. 1990).

The third form of anxiety that we include in our theory is *computer anxiety*, which is directly related with the emotional state of a user during any interaction since it is perceived as a "state anxiety" and not as an inherent feature of his personality. It seems that computer anxiety (Wilfong 2006) affects a very large number of people in today's technological reality and should be considered during the identification and formulation of users' emotional models. It is defined as a negative emotional state and/or a negative (cognitive) experience of a person while uses a computer or he thinks a future use of the computer. People with computer anxiety show symptoms of phobia and psychological instability that leads to the gradually lesser use of computers by them. The current "demand" for the everyday interaction with various digital devices and hypermedia content intensify even more these symptoms that without any preventing techniques in place might result in worsening the existing condition they found in leading to dissatisfaction, anger (also known as computer anger), frustration, or physical actions, such as violence. Possible factors related to computer anxiety and anger according to researchers are the experience in computers, computer use, self-efficacy and the expected results (Wilfong 2006). To sum up, individuals attempt to influence which emotions they have, when they have them and how they experience and express them (Bechara et al. 2000). By combining the affective state of the individual with his regulatory mechanism we can reach into a conclusion of how emotions influence someone's performance and the outcome of his behavior. Our main hypothesis is that the moderating role of emotion regulation reduces the negative effect of high levels of anxiety, and should be taken into account in an adaptive interactive system during the learning process.

2.3.3 Methods of Extracting Emotions and Anxiety

Within the context of research studies on emotion and HCI, corresponding systems have been developed using physiological measurements for identifying users' emotional state (including anxiety) either by employing biometric sensors and/or psychometric questionnaires.

The most commonly used biometric sensors are those measuring galvanic skin response (also referred as skin conductance or electrodermal activity), heart rate, and blood volume pulse. Ward and Marsden (2003) have examined users' physiological responses to different Web-pages. The sensors that were used provided measurements of skin conductance, heart rate, and blood volume pulse. According to their findings, during periods of inactivity, heart rate and skin conductance are reduced, while blood volume pulse tends to increase. During performing simple tasks, there is only a small variability in all three measurements, indicating low levels of emotional arousal. Unexpected events, however, triggered intense variations (increase of heart rate and skin conductance, decrease of blood volume pulse), as a result of higher emotional arousal. In another study (Villon and Lisetti 2007), the physiological measurements were mapped on the circumplex model of affect (Russell 1980). The physiological variables were skin conductance, skin conductance level, skin conductance responses, heart rate, and heart rate variability. This study supports that heart rate is indicative of valence, while skin conductance is related to arousal. Electrodermal activity, facial electromyography and heart rate were the physiological variables in a study that involved the presentation of two versions of a computer-based simulated mobile environment to users (Mahlke et al. 2006). These two versions were designed in a way that each would evoke different emotional responses; correlations between arousal, valence, and the physiological measurements were found. A rather different approach involved the integration of electromechanical film sensors in a chair, in order to measure variations in heart rate (Anttonen and Surakka 2005). According to the findings of this study, the physiological responses were correlated with the emotional valence (positive, neutral, and negative) of the stimuli that were presented to users. Biometric sensors were also used in an online communication system (Wang et al. 2004), using galvanic skin response and blood volume pulse sensors. In this study, it was also supported that galvanic skin responses are indicative of arousal, while blood volume pulse is related to valence; the latter however was considered as very difficult to measure in an accurate way.

On the other hand, one possible implementation of a Web-based system interfaces that can appraise such human characteristics, is through the use of a series of online tests and questionnaires that can assess the psychological abilities and properties of the user (Picard 2000). The number and the type of tests used vary depending on the scope of each research work. For example, the Beck Anxiety Inventory (BAI) is an accredited anxiety inventory with a focus on somatic symptoms of anxiety, aiming to elicit symptoms such as nervousness, dizziness, inability to relax, etc. It includes a total of 21 items that are administered via self-report in which respondents indicate how much they have been bothered by each symptom over the past week (Beck and Steer 1993). The Depression Anxiety and Stress Scale (DASS) is a 42-item self-report questionnaire which measures the negative emotional states of depression, anxiety and stress. Each scale contains 14 items, divided into subscales of 2–5 items with similar content. The Depression scale assesses dysphoria, hopelessness, devaluation of life, self-deprecation, lack of interest/involvement, anhedonia, and inertia. The Anxiety scale assesses autonomic arousal, skeletal muscle effects, situational anxiety, and subjective experience of anxious affect. The Stress scale assesses difficulty relaxing, nervous arousal, and being easily upset/agitated, irritable/over-reactive and impatient. Respondents are asked to use 4-point severity/frequency scales to rate the extent to which they have experienced each state over the past week (Lovibond and Lovibond 1995). Lastly, the Geriatric Anxiety Inventory (GAI) is a validated instrument for anxiety that is specifically targeted on older adults. It consists of 20 "Agree/Disagree" items designed to assess typical common anxiety symptoms. The measurements of somatic symptoms with the instrument are limited in order to minimize confusion between symptoms common to anxiety and general medical conditions. The GAI is not designed strictly as a diagnostic tool, but rather to assess anxiety symptoms in general (Pachana et al. 2007). Most of these tests are available in a variety of languages, including multiple dialects.

In order to validate our theory and accurately grasp the complexity of anxiety, apart from the use of biometric sensors (Tsianos et al. 2010; Psaltis et al. 2014), we utilized a number of standardized psychometric tests adapted to the needs of each anxiety type discussed above. For the general (core) anxiety measure we used the Stait-Trait Anxiety Inventory (STAI – Spielberger et al. 1983) which is an accredited and widely used anxiety inventory. It is obtained through a self-report questionnaire aiming to measure the presence and severity of current symptoms of anxiety and a generalized propensity of a person to be anxious. The questionnaire includes 40 items that measure two sub-scales which are allocated to the State Anxiety Scale (S-Anxiety) and the Trait Anxiety Scale (T-Anxiety). The S-Anxiety measures the current state of anxiety, asking how respondents feel "right now" using items that measure subjective feelings of apprehension, tension, nervousness and worry.

The T-Anxiety evaluates relatively stable aspects of "anxiety proneness" including general states of calmness, confidence, and security (for the purpose of our study only the trait scale was used).

Apart from the trait scale of STAI test we employed also a situation-specific measure of anxiety (i.e., educational), using Cassady's Cognitive Test Anxiety scale – 27 items (Cassady and Jonhson 2002). The Cognitive Test Anxiety scale measure focused on only the cognitive domain of test anxiety, formerly referred to as worry. The cognitive domain includes the tendency to engage in task-irrelevant thinking during test taking and preparation periods, the tendency to draw comparisons to others during test taking and preparation periods, and the likelihood to have either intruding thoughts during exams and study sessions, or have relevant cues escape the learner's attention during testing (Cassady 2001). This way, we can see the differences between the individual's evaluation of anxiety and what actually happens during the task. Individuals with high trait anxiety, report heightened perceptions of negative outcomes across a range of possible contexts and scenarios (Lerner and Keltner 2000), so they tend to be subjective and negative to their judgement.

In addition, we used self-reported measures of state anxiety (current anxiety) taken during the assessment phase of the experiments (so to collect measurements of the subjects in different circumstances during tasks' execution), in time slots of every 10 min (six time slots). Users had to self-report their levels of anxiety using an indicative bar that is embedded in the user interface of the adaptation and personalization interactive system we developed (see Chap. 5).

Lastly, we measured emotion regulation with a questionnaire developed by us (Cronbach's α that indicates scale reliability reaches 0.718 – Lekkas et al. 2013). The test consists of 25 items that measure emotion recognition, emotional management, emotional motivation, emotional experience and emotional expressions as discussed earlier.

In general, the use of psychometric questionnaires in user modelling procedures is a valid form of measurement regarding learners' predispositions towards developing high levels of anxiety in a Web-based learning environment, at least as shown by previous research findings. Through such an approach, however, the variability of learners' emotional state remains evasive, whereas the notion of a system that dynamically adapts on individuals' fluctuating emotional state cannot be realized.

2.3.4 Implications of Anxiety in Adaptive Interactive Environments

Computer systems and applications become better and more sophisticated every day and they can already perceive information related to user needs and cognitive (at most) related preferences. However, adaptation and personalization systems (especially in constraint and directive educational settings) should be able to assess human needs and affective elements, and investigate the inner and deeper relations that exist between them, through the use of methods that influence the environment according to the emotional condition of a user (Barlow 2002). In such a way, an emotionally tense or unstable individual will be able to receive the hypermedia content based to what he considers appropriate (easier to control and manipulate) for his working, decision and/or learning model.

Emotional and decision factors during the learning process can be proven significant in defining user behavior in Web-based educational applications and interfaces, taking into consideration psychometric challenges, as well as the complicated matter of quantifying and subsequently mapping emotions on a digital environment. Most theories of choice assume that decisions derive from an assessment of the future outcomes of various options and alternatives through some type of cost-benefit analyses. The influence of emotions on decision making is largely ignored. We often have different preferences as to our approach, varying between thinking and feeling. When we use reason to make decisions, we seek to exclude emotions, using only rational methods and perhaps even mathematical tools although emotions exist in the first stage of our decision making procedure and are followed by reasoning. The foundation of such decisions is the principle of utility, whereby the value of each option is assessed by assigning criteria (often weighted). Web-based educational systems until recently tried to integrate tools that aid users in a purely rational process (E-Learning and Decision-support systems). There is a whole range of decision making that uses emotion, depending on the degree of reason that is included in the process. A totally emotional decision is typically very fast. This is because it takes time (at least 0.1 s) for the rational cortex to get going. This is the reactive (and largely subconscious) decision making that you encounter in heated arguments or when faced with immediate danger. User behavior is in its final analysis a decision making process and the nature of its activity is strongly correlated with emotions, that is why the role of emotions is extremely important.

The mediating role of technology can help the designers to understand the emotional mechanisms of users more inclusively and adjust the hypermedia environments more efficiently to their needs. One possible implementation of an adaptive educational system's interface that can appraise human emotions is through the use of a set of parameters that can adapt according to the emotional condition of the user and his preferred style of action. A certain emotional condition demands a personalization of equivalent proportions. The user will have the capability to respond emotionally either after being asked in a specific moment or after a decision from the system, with respect to content presentation and navigation, based on his user model and his preferences is being made. Such a system should be designed in a way that can create a detailed model for every user and can provide two basic services. One application-based that is related to the user interface, the navigation, usability and aesthetical appearance, and one content-based that has to do with the learning objects, the allocation of content, the depth and the dissemination of information. Using these, the user interface will take the form that the user wishes so, helping him to work effectively, to learn more efficiently and less anxiously.

At a practical level, we hypothesize that emotion regulation and arousal are negatively correlated and therefore we propose that an individual with high emotion regulation would usually have low arousal levels because of his ability to control and organize his emotions. Henceforth, a possible development of personalization rules should adhere to the assumption that users with high anxiety levels lacking the moderating role of emotion regulation, are in a greater need of enhancing the aesthetic aspects of an adaptive educational system, while users with low anxiety levels focus more on usability issues.

Researching on emotions and the impact on decision making and problem solving during the learning process is only the first step towards a more broad understanding and modelling of user patterns of behavior. Such research results can enrich current viewpoints during user requirements collection and analysis and could be further used as more specific design guidelines. A related discussion is also taken place in Chap. 6 of this book.

2.4 Summary

The basic objective of this chapter was to introduce a number of dimensions of individual difference, coming from different research areas but all of which have a distinctive impact when users interact with the hypermedia information space. We have attempted to approach the theoretical considerations and create a basic understanding at first with regard to cognition and those mechanisms that influence information processing, decision making, problem solving and learning. We have analyzed core high-level cognitive factors, such as learning and cognitive styles; and more elementary cognitive processes, like human memory (working memory and long-term memory), visual search and attention, and speed and control of processing. According to related findings, it may be supported that interactive systems that apply adaptation and personalization techniques that consider any of these cognitive characteristics in their user model have a significant positive effect on users' interactions, assisting them, amongst others, in locating and processing information more efficiently (see Chaps. 6–8). Our rationale behind using the respective cognitive constructs derives from the fact that their impact is compatible to the structure and form of the hypermedia content. Therefore, human-centred solutions should be able to match their environments to individuals' information processing preferences, increasing users' levels of comprehension, accuracy, performance, satisfaction while at the same time minimizing cognitive overload and disorientation.

It is generally accepted that the cognitive elements are more straightforward (compared to emotional), since they are easier to measure and easier to quantify; and we have already reached a level in which we can make inferences about how users with different cognitive abilities and preferences can be aided or guided through an adapted and personalized system and/or user interface.

With respect to the role of emotions in hypermedia environments, it may come as no surprise that emotional factors are important in the decision and problem solving during the learning process. The emotion regulation constructs comprise characteristics that people often exhibit in their decision making. Therefore, we have seen that by combining the emotional arousal (affective state – with focus on anxiety – and trait) of an individual with his regulatory mechanism (experiential and rational emotion regulation) we can reach into a conclusion of how affect influences his performance and the outcome of his behavior. It has been argued that positive affect increases motivation, attention, pleasantness, participation and engagement, while negative affect is highly involved with boredom, fear, anger, displeasure and distraction. These findings could be considered insightful enough even if, for the time being, applied at more directive and highly controllable environments as the ones related with Web-based learning.

Finally, we presented methods of extraction of specific cognitive and emotional processing factors and referred to the implications that the theoretical and empirical representations can have for the design of similar applications, interactions and user interfaces. We believe that this direction could be useful to the reader at a more theoretical level that investigates, at some extent, the connection between cognition and emotions with respect to information processing and at a more practical one of how their impact can be translated into designs, adaptation rules algorithms that can generate more effective and usable interactions and systems.

References

Ahn H, Picard WR (2005) Affective-cognitive learning and decision making: a motivational reward framework for affective agents. In the 1st international conference on affective computing and intelligent interaction (ACII 2005), Beijing, China, 22–24 Oct 2005

Ally BA, Budson AE (2007) The worth of pictures: using high density event related potentials to understand the memorial power of pictures and the dynamics of recognition memory. NeuroImage 35:378–395

Anderson JR (1990) Cognitive psychology and its implications, 3rd edn. Freeman, London

Anderson JR (2009) Cognitive psychology and its implications, 7th edn. Worth Publishers, New York

Antoniou A, Lepouras G (2010) Modeling visitors' profiles: a study to investigate adaptation aspects for museum learning technologies. Comput Cult Herit 3(2):1–19

Anttonen J, Surakka V (2005) Emotions and heart rate while sitting on a chair. In: Proceedings of the SIGCHI conference on human factors in computing systems, Portland, Oregon, USA, pp. 491–499

Atkins H, Moore D, Sharpe S, Hobbs D (2001) Learning style theory and computer mediated communication. ED-MEDIA 2001 world conference on educational multimedia, hypermedia and telecommunications. In: Proceedings of 13th international symposium, Tampere, Finland, 25–30 June 2001, pp 71–75

Atkinson RC, Shiffrin RM (1968) Human memory: a proposed system and its control processes. In K W (ed) The psychology of learning and motivation: advances in research and theory, vol. 2, Academic Press, New York

Baddeley A (1986) Working Memory. Clarendon Press, Oxford

Baddeley A (1990) Human memory: theory and practice. Lawrence-Erlbaum Association, London

Baddeley A (1992) Working memory. J Sci 255(5044):556–559

Baddeley AD (2000) The episodic buffer: a new component of working memory? Trends Cogn Sci 4:417–423

Baddeley A (2012) Working memory: theories, models, and controversies. J Annu Rev Psychol 63:1–29

Baddeley AD, Hitch G (1974) Working memory. In: Bower GH (ed) The psychology of learning and motivation, vol 8. Academic Press, London

Bandura A (1997) Self-efficacy: the exercise of control. Freeman, New York

Banner G, Rayner S (2000) Learning language and learning style: principles, process and practice. Lang Learn J 21(Summer 2000):37–44

Barlow DH (2002) Anxiety and its disorders: the nature and treatment of anxiety and panic, 2nd edn. The Guilford Press, New York

Bechara A, Damasio H, Damasio AR (2000) Emotion, decision-making, and the orbito-frontal cortex. Cereb Cortex 10:295–307

Beck AT, Steer RA (1993) Beck anxiety inventory manual. Harcourt Brace and Company, San Antonio

Belk M, Germanakos P, Fidas C, Holzinger A, Samaras G (2013a) Towards the personalization of CAPTCHA mechanisms based on individual differences in cognitive processing. In: Proceedings of the international conference on human factors in computing and informatics, SouthCHI, 2013

Belk M, Papatheocharous E, Germanakos P, Samaras G (2013b) Modeling users on the world wide web based on cognitive factors, navigation behaviour and clustering techniques. J Syst Softw 86(12):2995–3012. Special Issue on Web 2.0 Engineering

Biddle R, Chiasson S, van Oorschot P (2012) Graphical passwords: learning from the first twelve years. ACM Comput Surv 44(4), 41 pages

Blazhenkova O, Kozhevnikov M (2009) The new object-spatial-verbal cognitive style model: theory and measurement. Appl Cogn Psychol 23(5):638–663

Botsios S, Georgiou D, Safouris N (2008) Contributions to adaptive educational hypermedia systems via on-line learning style estimation. Educ Technol Soc 11(2):322–339

Boyle EA, Duffy T, Dunleavy K (2003) Learning styles and academic outcome: the validity and utility of Vermunt's inventory of learning styles in a British higher education setting. Br J Educ Psychol 73:267–290

Brady TF, Konkle T, Alvarez GA, Oliva A (2008) Visual long-term memory has a massive storage capacity for object details. Nat Acad Sci 105(38):14325–14329

Brusilovsky P (2001) Adaptive hypermedia. User Model User-Adap Inter 11:87–110

Caroll JB (1993) Human cognitive abilities: a survey of factor analytical studies. Cambridge University Press, Cambridge

Cassady JC (2001) The stability of undergraduate students' cognitive test anxiety levels. Pract Assess Res Eval 7(20)

Cassady JC (2004) The influence of cognitive test anxiety across the learning–testing cycle. Learn Instr 14:569–592

Cassady JC, Jonhson RE (2002) Cognitive test anxiety and academic performance. Contemp Educ Psychol 27(2):270–295

Cassidy S (2004) Learning styles: an overview of theories, models, and measures. Educ Psychol 24(4):419–444

Chen S, Liu X (2008) An integrated approach for modeling learning patterns of students in web-based instruction: a cognitive style perspective. ACM Trans Comput Hum Interac 15(1), Article 1, 28 pages

Coffield F, Moseley D, Hall E, Ecclestone K (2004) Learning styles and pedagogy in post-16 learning. A systematic and critical review. Learning and Skills Research Centre, London

Conway ARA, Cowan N, Bunting MF (2001) The cocktail party phenomenon revisited: the importance of working memory capacity. J Psychon Bull Rev 8:331–335

Conway ARA, Cowan N, Bunting MF, Therriault DJ, Minkoff SR (2002) A latent variable analysis of working memory capacity, short-term memory capacity, processing speed, and general fluid intelligence. J Intell 30:163–183

Corbetta M, Shulman GL (2002) Control of goal-directed and stimulus-driven attention in the brain. Nat Rev Neurosci 3:201–215

Craik FIM, Lockhart RS (1972) Levels of processing: a framework for memory research. J Verbal Learn Verbal Behav 11:671–684

Curry L (1983) An organization of learning styles theory and constructs. In: Curry L (ed) Learning style in continuing education. Dalhousie University, Halifax, pp 115–131

Curry L (1990) One critique of the research on learning styles. Educ Leadersh 48:50–56

Damasio AR (1994) Descartes' error: emotion, reason, and the human brain. Putnam Publishing Group, New York

Darwin C (1872) The expression of the emotions in man and animals. D. Appleton and Company, New York

Davou B (2000) Thought processes in the age of information: issues on cognitive psychology and communication. Papazissis Publishers, Athens. ISBN 960-02-1389-5

Day LA, Carroll AS (2004) Using an ability-based measure of emotional intelligence to predict individual performance, group performance, and group citizenship behaviours. Personal Individ Differ 36:1443–1458

Deary IJ (2001) Human intelligence differences: a recent history. Trends Cogn Sci 5(3):127–130

Demetriou A, Christou C, Spanoudis G, Platsidou M (2002) The development of mental processing: efficiency, working memory and thinking. Monogr Soc Res Child Dev 67(1):1–155

Demetriou A, Spanoudis G, Shayer M (2013) Developmental intelligence: from empirical to hidden constructs. Intelligence 41:744–749

Desai MS (2001) Computer anxiety and performance: an application of a change model in a pedagogical setting. J Instr Psychol 28(3):141–149

Dillon A, Watson C (1996) User analysis in HCI-the historical lessons from individual differences research. Int J Hum Comput Stud 45(6):619–637

D'Mello KS, Craig DS, Gholson B, Franklin S, Picard R, Graesser CA (2005) Integrating affect sensors in a intelligent tutoring system. In affective interactions: the computer in the affective loop workshop at 2005 international conference on intelligent user interfaces, AMC Press, New York, pp 7–13

Driscoll M (2001) Psychology of learning for assessment, 2nd edn. Allyn & Bacon, Boston

Duncan J, Humphreys GW (1989) A resemblance theory of visual search. Psychol Rev 96:433–458

Duncan J, Humphreys GW (1992) Beyond the search surface: visual search and attentional engagement. J Exp Psychol Hum Percept Perform 18:578–588

Dunn R, Dunn K, Price GE (1985) Learning Styles Inventory (LSI): an inventory for the identification of how individuals in grades 3 through 12 prefer to learn. Price Systems, Lawrence

Eckstein MP, Thomas JP, Palmer J, Shimozaski SS (2000) A signal detection model predicts the effects of set size on visual search accuracy for feature, conjunction, triple conjunction, and disjunctions displays. Percept Psychophys 62:425–451

Eggen P, Kauchak D (2007) Educational psychology, windows on classrooms, 7th edn. Pearson Merrill Prentice Hall Publishing, Upper Saddle River, pp 202–227

Eliasmith C (ed) (2001) Memory. Dictionary of philosophy of mind. Washington State University, Pullman

Engle RW (2002) Working memory capacity as executive attention. J Curr Dir Psychol Sci 11:19–23

Eysenck M (1988) A handbook of cognitive psychology. Lawrence Erlbaum Assoc, London

Eysenck WM, Keane RM (2005) Cognitive psychology – a student's handbook, 5th edn. Psychology Press/Taylor & Francis Group, New York

Felder RM, Silverman LK (1988) Learning and teaching styles in engineering education. Eng Educ 78:674–681

Flanagan O (1991) The science of the mind, 2nd edn. MIT Press, Cambridge

Frias-Martinez E, Chen SY, Macredie RD, Liu X (2007) The role of human factors in stereotyping behavior and perception of digital library users: a robust clustering approach. User Model User-Adap Inter 17(3):305–337

Germanakos P, Tsianos N, Lekkas Z, Mourlas C, Samaras G (2008) Realizing comprehensive user profile as the core element of adaptive and personalized communication environments and systems. Comput J, Special Issue on Profiling Expertise and Behaviour, Oxford University Press. doi:10.1093/comjnl/bxn014

Ghinea G, Chen SY (2008) Measuring quality of perception in distributed multimedia: verbalizers vs. imagers. Comput Hum Behav 24(4):1317–1329

Gibson JJ (1966) The senses considered as perceptual systems. Houghton Mifflin, Boston

Gibson J (1979) The ecological approach to visual perception. Houghton Mifflin, Boston

Glaser R, Pellegrino JW (1978) Uniting cognitive process theory and differential psychology: back home from the wars. Intelligence 2(3):305–319

Goleman D (1995) Emotional intelligence: why it can matter more than IQ. Bantam Books, New York

Graber DA (2000) Processing politics. The University of Chicago Press, Chicago

Graf S, Kinshuk (2009) Advanced adaptivity in learning management systems by considering learning styles. In: Proceedings of international workshop on social and personal computing for web-supported learning communities, (SPeL 2009), September 2009, Milan, Italy, pp 235–238

Gregory R (1970) The intelligent eye. Weidenfeld & Nicolson, London

Gross JJ, John OE (1998) Mapping the domain of expressivity: multimethod evidence for a hierarchical model. J Pers Soc Psychol 74(1):170–191

Gulliver SR, Ghinea G (2004) Stars in their eyes: what eye-tracking reveals about multimedia perceptual quality. IEEE Trans Syst Man Cybern A 34(4):472–482

Hale S, Fry AF (2000) Relationships among processing speed, working memory, and fluid intelligence in children. J Biol Psychol 54:1–34

Hamilton V (1985) A cognitive model of anxiety: implications for theories of personality and motivation. Issues Ment Health Nurs 7(1–4):229–250

Health and Safety Executive (2007) Managing the causes of work-related stress: a step-by-step approach using the management standards. Health and Safety Guidance, HSE Books, Norwich

Heitz RP, Engle RW (2007) Focusing the spotlight: individual differences in visual attention control. J Exp Psychol 136:217–240

Henry J (2007) Professor pans 'learning style' teaching method. The Telegraph. Online Article

Hock RR (1999) Forty studies that changed psychology, explorations into the history of psychological research, 3rd edn. Prentice-Hall, Upper Saddle River, pp 108–109

Honey P, Mumford A (2006) The learning styles questionnaire, 80-item version. Peter Honey Publications, Maidenhead

Hsu Y, Chen S (2011) Associating learners' cognitive style with their navigation behaviors: a data-mining approach. In: Proceedings of the international conference on human-computer interaction: users and applications (HCII 2011). Springer, pp 27–34

Huitt W (2000) The information processing approach. Educational psychology interactive. Valdosta State University, Valdosta

Humphreys GW, Riddoch MJ, Quinlan PT (1985) Interactive processes in perceptual organization: evidence from visual agnosia. In: Posner MI, Morin OSM (eds) Attention and performance, vol XI. Lawrence Erlbaum Associates Inc, Hillsdale

Hutchison KA (2007) Attentional control and the relatedness proportion effect in semantic priming. J Exp Psychol Learn Mem Cogn 33:645–662

James W (1890) Principles of psychology. Holt, New York

John D, Boucouvalas AC (2002) Multimedia tasks and user cognitive styles. In: International symposium on communication systems networks and digital signal processing (CSNDSP 2002)

Kane MJ, Conway ARA, Hambrick DZ, Engle RW (2007) Variation in working memory capacity as variation in executive attention and control. In: Conway ARA, Jarrold C, Kane MJ, Miyake A, Towse JN (eds) Variation in working memory. Oxford University Press, Oxford/New York, pp 21–48

Kennedy-Moore E, Watson JC (1999) Expressing emotion. Myths, realities, and therapeutic strategies. The Guildford Press, New York

Kensinger EA (2004) Remembering emotional experiences: the contribution of valence and arousal. Rev Neurosci 15(4):241–251

Kim J, Gorman J (2005) The psychobiology of anxiety. Clin Neurosci Res 4:335–347

Kinley K, Tjondronegoro D, Partridge H (2010) Web searching interaction model based on user cognitive styles. In: Proceedings of the international conference of the computer-human interaction special interest group of Australia on computer-human interaction (OZCHI 2010), ACM Press, pp 340–343

Klingberg T (2009) The overflowing brain: information overload and the limits of working memory. Oxford University Press, New York

Koffka K (1935) Principles of Gestalt psychology. Harcourt, Brace & Co., New York

Kohler W (1947) Gestalt psychology. Liversight, New York

Kolb AY, Kolb DA (2005) The Kolb learning style inventory – version 3.1 2005. Technical specifications. Experience Based Learning Systems, Inc., Hay Transforming Learning, Boston, Hay Group

Kort B, Reilly R (2002) Analytical models of emotions, learning and relationships: towards an affect-sensitive cognitive machine. Conference on virtual worlds and simulation (VWSim 2002)

Kozhevnikov M (2007) Cognitive styles in the context of modern psychology: toward an integrated framework of cognitive style. Psychol Bull 133(3):464–481

LaBar, Phelps EA (1998) Arousal-mediated memory consolidation: role of the medial temporal lobe in humans. Psychol Sci 9(6):490–493

Laing M (2001) Teaching learning and learning teaching: an introduction to learning styles. New Front Educ 31(4):463–475

LeDoux J (1998) The emotional brain. Touchstone, New York

Leite WL, Svinicki M, Shi Y (2009) Attempted validation of the scores of the VARK: learning styles inventory with multitrait–multimethod confirmatory factor analysis models, Educational and Psychological Measurement, 70(2):323–339

Lekkas Z, Tsianos N, Germanakos P, Mourlas C, Samaras G (2011a) Emotional web-based design: the concepts of emotional experience and emotional expression. In: Proceedings of the IADIS international conference on interfaces and human computer interaction (IHCI 2011), Rome, Italy, 24–26 Jul 2011, pp 283–290

Lekkas Z, Tsianos N, Germanakos P, Mourlas C, Samaras G (2011b) The effects of personality type in user-centered appraisal systems. In: Proceedings of the 14th international conference on human-computer interaction – HCI international 2011 (HCI 2011), Orlando, Florida, USA, 9–14 Jul 2011, LNCS 6761. Springer, Berlin/Heidelberg, pp 388–396

Lekkas Z, Germanakos P, Tsianos N, Mourlas C, Samaras G (2013) Personality and emotion as determinants of the learning experience: how affective behavior interacts with various components of the learning process. In: Proceedings of the 15th international conference on human-computer interaction – HCI international 2013 (HCI 2013), Las Vegas, Nevada, USA, 21–26 Jul 2013, LNCS 8005. Springer Berlin/Heidelberg, pp 418–427

Lerner JS, Keltner D (2000) Beyond valence: toward a model of emotion specific influences on judgment and choice. Cogn Emot 14:473–493

Levenson RW (1999) The intrapersonal functions of emotion. Cogn Emot 13:481–504

Lewis M, Haviland-Jones JM (2004) Handbook of emotions, 2nd edn. The Guildford Press, New York

Loftus E, Loftus G (1980) On the permanence of stored information in the human brain. Am Psychol 35(5):409–420

Lovibond SH, Lovibond PF (1995) Manual for the depression anxiety stress scales, 2nd edn. Psychology Foundation, Sydney

Lutz S, Huitt W (2003) Information processing and memory: theory and applications. Educational Psychology Interactive, Valdosta, GA

Lyons BJ, Schneider RT (2005) The influence of emotional intelligence on performance. Personal Individ Differ 39:693–703

MacLean PD (1990) The triune brain in evolution: role in paleocerebral functions. Springer, US. doi:978-0306431685

MacLeod CM (1991) Half a century of research on the Stroop effect: an integrative review. J Psychol Bull 109:163–203

Mahlke S, Minge M, Thüring M (2006) Measuring multiple components of emotions in interactive contexts. In: CHI'06: CHI'06 extended abstracts on human factors in computing systems. ACM, New York, pp 1061–1066

Markham S (2004) Learning styles measurement: a cause for concern. Technical report, Computing Educational Research Group

Marr D (1982) Vision – a computational investigation into the human representation and processing of visual information. W. H. Freeman & Company, New York

McAvinue LP, Robertson IH (2007) Measuring visual imagery ability: a review. Imag Cogn Pers 26:191–211

McGrew KS (2009) CHC theory and the human cognitive abilities project: standing on the shoulders of the giants of psychometric intelligence research. Intelligence 37(1):1–10

Messick S (1984) The nature of cognitive styles: problems and promises in educational research. Educ Psychol 19:59–74

Miller G (1956) The magical number seven, plus or minus two: some limits on our capacity for processing information. Psychol Rev 63:81–97

Miller G, Galanter E, Pribram K (1960) Plans and the structure of behavior. Holt, Rinehart, & Winston, New York

Milosevic D, Brkovic M, Debevc M, Krneta R (2007) Adaptive learning by using SCOs metadata. J Knowl Learn Object 3:163–174

Newsome S, Day LA, Catano MV (2000) Assessing the predictive validity of emotional intelligence. Personal Individ Differ 29:1005–1016

Norman D (2004) Emotional design: why we love (or hate) everyday things. Basic Books, New York

Oates JM, Reder LM (2010) Memory for pictures: sometimes a picture is not worth a single word. In: Successful remembering and successful forgetting: a Festschrift in honor of Robert A. Bjork. Psychological Press, New York, pp 447–462

Oatley K (1992) Integrative action of narrative. In: Stein DJ, Young JE (eds) Cognitive science and clinical disorders. Academic Press, San Diego

Oatley K (2001) Emotion in cognition. Elsevier Science Ltd, Hove

Ochsner KN (2000) Are affective events richly recollected or simply familiar? The experience and process of recognizing feelings past. J Exp Psychol Gen 129(2):242–261

Pachana N, Byrne G, Siddle H, Koloski N, Harley E, Arnold E (2007) Development and validation of the Geriatric Anxiety Inventory. Int Psychogeriatr 19:103–114

Paivio A (2006) Mind and its evolution: a dual coding theoretical approach. Lawrence Erlbaum Associates, Mahwah

Paivio A, Csapo K (1973) Picture superiority in free recall: imagery or dual coding? Cogn Psychol 5(2):176–206

Palmer J, Verghese P, Pavel M (2000) The psychophysics of visual search. Vis Res 40:1227–1268

Papanikolaou KA, Grigoriadou M, Kornilakis H, Magoulas GD (2003) Personalising the interaction in a web-based educational hypermedia system: the case of INSPIRE. J User Model User-Adap Inter 13(3):213–267

Peterson MS, Kramer AF, Wnag RF, Irwin DE, McCarley JS (2001) Visual search has memory. Psychol Sci 12:287–292

Peterson E, Deary I, Austin E (2005) A new measure of verbal-imagery cognitive style: VICS. Personal Individ Differ 38:1269–1281

Peterson E, Rayner S, Armstrong S (2009) Researching the psychology of cognitive style and learning style: is there really a future? Learn Individ Differ 19(4):518–523

Picard WR (2000) Affective computing. The MIT Press, Cambridge, MA

Polderman TJC, Stins JF, Posthuma D, Gosso MF, Verhulst FC, Boomsma DI (2006) The phenotypic and genotypic relation between working memory speed and capacity. J Intell 34(6):549–560

Posner MI (1980) Orienting of attention, the VIIth Sir Frederic Barlett lecture. Q J Exp Psychol 32A:3–25

Posner MI, Petersen SE (1990) The attention system of the human brain. Annu Rev Neurosci 13:25–42

Psaltis A, Rizopoulos C, Lekkas Z, Mourlas C (2014) Deducing user states of engagement in real time by using a purpose built unobtrusive physiological measurement device: an empirical study and HCI design challenges. In: Proceedings of the 8th international conference on augmented cognition, HCI 25(2014), pp 55–66

Reder LM, Park H, Kieffaber PD (2009) Memory systems do not divide on consciousness: reinterpreting memory in terms of activation and binding. Psychol Bull 135(1):23–49

Rezaei AR, Katz L (2004) Evaluation of the reliability and validity of the cognitive styles analysis. Personal Individ Differ 26:1317–1327

Riding R (1991) Cognitive styles analysis – research administration. Learning and Training Technology, Birmingham

Riding R, Cheema I (1991) Cognitive styles – an overview and Integration. Educ Psychol 11(3–4):193–215

Robertson EK, Köhler S (2007) Insights from child development on the relationship between episodic and semantic memory. Neuropsychologia 45(14):3178–3189

Russell JA (1980) A circumplex model of affect. J Pers Soc Psychol 39:1161–1178

Sadler-Smith E, Riding R (1999) Cognitive style and instructional preferences. Instr Sci 27(5):355–371

Salovey P, Mayer JD (1990) Emotional intelligence. Imag Cogn Personal Emot Intell 9:185–211

Samoilov A, Goldfried MR (2000) Role of emotion in cognitive-behaviour therapy. Clin Psychol Sci Pract 7(4):373–383

Sapp M (1993) Test anxiety: applied research, assessment, and treatment intervention. University Press of America, Lanham

Sarason G, Sarason BR, Pierce GR (1990) Anxiety, cognitive interference, and performance. J Soc Behav Personal 5:1–18

Schwarzer R (1984) Worry and emotionality as separate components in test anxiety. Int Rev Appl Psychol 33:205–220

Sekuler R, Blake R (2002) Perception, 4th edn. McGraw-Hill, Boston

Shipstead Z, Broadway J (2013) Individual differences in working memory capacity and the Stroop effect: do high spans block the words? J Learn Individ Differ 26:191–195

Smith B, Caputi P (2005) Cognitive interference model of computer anxiety: implications for computer-based assessment. Comput Hum Behav 21:713–728

Spielberger CD (1972) Conceptual and methodological issues in anxiety research. In: Spielberger CD (ed) Anxiety: current trends in theory and research, vol 2. Academic Press, New York

Spielberger CD, Vagg PR (1995) Test anxiety: a transactional process model. In: Spielberger CD, Vagg PR (eds) Test anxiety: theory, assessment, and treatment. Taylor & Francis, Washington, DC, pp 3–14

Spielberger CD, Gorssuch RL, Lushene PR, Vagg PR, Jacobs GA (1983) Manual for the state-trait anxiety inventory (STAI). Consulting Psychologists Press, Palo Alto

Stern LW (1900) Uber Psychologie der individuellen Differenzen (Ideen zu einer "Differen-tiellen Psychologie"). Barth, Leipzig

Sternberg RJ, Grigorenko EL (1997) Are cognitive styles still in style? Am Psychol 52(7):700–712

Stroop JR (1935) Studies of interference in serial verbal reactions. J Exp Psychol 18:643–662

Swindler G (2001) Mental models and hypermedia. EDETC795 Problems/Educational Technology (Hypermedia)

Tennant M (1988) Psychology and adult learning. Routledge, London

Thurstone L (1948) Primary mental capabilities. University of Chicago Press, Chicago

Tolman EC (1948) Cognitive maps in rats and men. Psychol Rev 55(4):189–208

Treisman AM (1988) Features and objects: The fourteenth Bartlett memorial lecture. Q J Exp Psychol 40A:201–237

Treisman AM (1992) Spreading suppression or feature integration? A reply to Duncan and Humphreys (1992). J Exp Psychol Hum Perform Percept 18:589–593

Treisman AM (1993) The perception of features and objects. In: Baddeley A, Weiskrantz L (eds) Attention: selection, awareness, and control. Clarendon Press, Oxford

Treisman AM, Gelade G (1980) A feature integration theory of attention. Cogn Psychol 12:97–136

Treisman AM, Sato S (1990) Conjunction search revisited. J Exp Psychol Hum Percept Perform 16:459–478

Treisman AM, Schmidt H (1982) Illusory conjunctions in the perception of objects. Cogn Psychol 12:107–141

Tsianos N, Germanakos P, Mourlas C (2006) Assessing the importance of cognitive learning styles over performance in multimedia educational environments. In: Proceedings of the 2nd international conference on interdisciplinarity in education (ICIE2006), Athens, 11–13 May 2006, pp 123–130

Tsianos N, Lekkas Z, Germanakos P, Mourlas C, Samaras G (2009) An experimental assessment of the use of cognitive and affective factors in adaptive educational hypermedia. IEEE transactions on learning technologies (TLT), IEEE Computer Society 2(3):249–258, Jul–Sept 2009. doi:10.1109/TLT.2009.29

Tsianos N, Germanakos P, Lekkas Z, Sialarou A, Mourlas C, Samaras G (2010) A preliminary study on learners' physiological measurements in educational hypermedia. In: Proceedings of the 10th IEEE international conference on advanced learning technologies (ICALT 2010), IEEE Computer Society Press, Sousse, Tunisia, 5–7 Jul 2010, pp 61–63

Tsianos N, Germanakos P, Belk M, Lekkas Z, Samaras G, Mourlas C (2012) An individual differences approach in designing ontologies for efficient personalization. In: Anagnostopoulos I, Bielikova M, Mylonas P, Tsapatsoulis N (eds) Semantic hyper/multi-media adaptation: schemes and applications, Studies in computational intelligence. Springer, Berlin Heidelberg

Unsworth N, Spillers G (2010) Working memory capacity: attention control, secondary memory, or both? A direct test of the dual-component model. J Mem Lang 62:392–406

Vecera SP, Cosman JD, Vatterott DB, Roper ZJJ (2014) The control of visual attention: toward a unified account. In Brian H. Ross (ed). Psychol Learn Motiv 60:303–347

Vesterinen E (2001) Affective computing, digital media research seminar, Space Odyssey, Tik-111-590

Villon O, Lisetti C (2007) A user model of psycho-physiological measure of emotion, lecture notes. Artif Intell 4511:319–323

Wang H, Prendinger H, Igarashi T (2004) Communicating emotions in online chat using physiological sensors and animated text. In: CHI'04: CHI '04 extended abstracts on human factors in computing systems. ACM, New York, pp 1171–1174

Ward RD, Marsden PH (2003) Physiological responses to different WEB page designs. Int J Hum Comput Stud 59(1–2):199–212

Wertheimer M (1923) Gestalt psychology, Gestalt theory. Psychol Forsch 3(4):301–350

Whitehouse AJO, Maybery MT, Durkin K (2006) The development of the picture superiority effect. Br J Dev Psychol 24:767–773

Wilfong DJ (2006) Computer anxiety and anger: the impact of computer use, computer experience and self-efficacy beliefs. Comput Hum Behav 22:1001–1011

Winn W, Snyder D (2001) Mental representation. In: The handbook of research for educational communications and technology (Chap. 5). The Association of Educational Communications and Technology, Bloomington

Witkin HA (1962) Psychological differentiation. Studies of development. Wiley, New York

Witkin HA, Oltman P, Raskin E, Karp S (1971) A manual for the embedded figures test. Consulting Psychologists Press, Palo Alto

Witkin HA, Moore CA, Goodenough DR, Cox PW (1977) Field-dependent and field-independent cognitive styles and their educational implications. Rev Educ Res 47(1):1–64

Wolfe JM (1998) Visual search. In: Pashler H (ed) Attention. Psychology Press, Hove

Yantis S, Jonides J (1990) Abrupt visual onsets and selective attention: voluntary versus automatic allocation. J Exp Psychol Hum Percept Perform 16:121–134

Part II
Principles: Web Adaptation and Personalization Processes and Techniques

Chapter 3
User Modeling

Abstract Adaptation and personalization systems build and maintain a user (and data) model throughout the whole human-computer interaction process. A user model is an essential component of any interactive system and entails all the information which is considered important in order to adapt and personalize the user interface (content and navigation) and functionalities to the unique characteristics of a user. Depending on the domain and goals of the system, user models can include different kinds of characteristics about the users (e.g., interests, preferences, traits, etc.) or data with respect to their overall context of use (e.g., environment, time, interaction device type, etc.). Furthermore, this information can be provided explicitly to the system (e.g., with the use of online questionnaires or psychometric tests) by the user or implicitly extracted with the use of computational intelligence algorithms and methods, based on the users' interactions and activities. In this chapter we present the underlying principles of user modeling, including the main factors being modeled in today's adaptation and personalization systems, user data collection methods and user model generation techniques. We also briefly refer to a comprehensive user model composed of intrinsic individual characteristics under a unified representation.

Keywords Modeling factors • Data collection • Model generation • Modeling human factors • Methods

3.1 Introduction

An essential feature of an interactive system is its user model. The user model is a representation of static and dynamic information about an individual that is utilized throughout the whole interaction process aiming to trigger a number of adaptation and personalization effects (i.e., the same system can look different to users with different user models – Brusilovsky and Millán 2007; Frias-Martinez et al. 2005). For example, an information retrieval system may select and prioritize the most relevant items to the user's goals and/or interests. An educational hypermedia system may provide adaptive navigation support by manipulating the links based on the user's knowledge and learning goals. A privacy-preserving mechanism in a

© Springer International Publishing Switzerland 2016
P. Germanakos, M. Belk, *Human-Centred Web Adaptation and Personalization*,
Human–Computer Interaction Series, DOI 10.1007/978-3-319-28050-9_3

commercial Web-based system may adapt the content to the user's level of knowledge towards privacy terms (e.g., provide novice users with personalized privacy information awareness by using simplified terms and additional explanations).

Key technical issues in designing and developing adaptation and personalization systems include how to construct accurate and comprehensive models of each individual user and how these can be used to identify a user and describe the user's behavior in the system. With the advent of new and heterogeneous interaction device types and the globalization of services, user modeling has become a challenging endeavor since today's interactive systems are accessed by different users, with different cognitive and cultural backgrounds and in different contexts of use. In this respect, researchers and practitioners alike have modeled and maintained various factors about the users based on which they provide adaptive and personalized services. Example factors include among others: (i) The user's interest in a particular domain, e.g., E-Commerce systems infer the user's interest towards specific products based on their buying history (Goy et al. 2007); (ii) the user's level of knowledge on a particular learning domain, e.g., E-Learning hypermedia systems model the user's level of knowledge (novice or expert), and accordingly present personalized learning material and content (Brusilovsky and Millán 2007); (iii) the user's individual traits such as personality traits, cognitive processing styles and abilities and accordingly present personalized recommendations of music items (Ferwerda et al. 2015), personalized user authentication tasks (Belk et al. 2014b) or personalized checkout processes in E-Commerce systems (Belk et al. 2014a); and (iv) the user's technology factors such as device type and screen size used and accordingly adapt the interaction and visual design of the system (Herder and van Dijk 2002).

A user model can include static information that rarely or never changes (e.g., demographic information), or dynamic information when it changes frequently over time. Such information is obtained either explicitly, using online Web forms, questionnaires and/or psychometric tests, or implicitly, by dynamically inferring characteristics about the users based on their navigation behavior in the system. For example, such implicit information can be extracted from the total time spent on a particular Web-page by a user, which can be in turn used to understand the interest of the user towards the main subject of that Web-page. Various research works have attempted to investigate the most effective source of information for user modeling (Gauch et al. 2007; Jawaheer et al. 2010; Wærn 2004). Based on Gauch et al. (2007) it is yet not clear-cut whether implicitly created models are more or less accurate than explicitly created models. Nevertheless, since implicit information gathering does not affect the human-computer interaction or the users' cognitive load (Gauch et al. 2007), it seems to be the preferable approach for collecting information about users. On the other hand, this approach is much more complex than explicit user feedback since in most cases the data obtained may be imprecise, incomplete and/ or heterogeneous.

Our main purpose in this chapter is to present the underlying principles of user modeling by presenting the most common user modeling factors for adaptation and personalization, existing explicit and implicit data collection methods for eliciting such factors and state-of-the-art user model generation mechanisms. We conclude the chapter with a high-level comprehensive user model illustrating the main cognitive and emotional attributes incorporated. We believe it is useful for the reader to understand how intrinsic user characteristics (discussed in Chap. 2) can co-exist under a common user modeling schema, and how this can be implemented in an adaptation and personalization architecture as we will see later in Chap. 5.

3.2 User Modeling Factors for Personalization

According to the nature of information that is being modeled, we distinguish models that represent information about the user and about the user's context of use. We next discuss in detail these categories.

3.2.1 User Information

Adaptation decision in adaptation and personalization systems was traditionally based on modeling information that reflects on various aspects about the user. We elaborate our analysis on the five most widely applied characteristics being modeled in such interactive systems: *knowledge*, *interests*, *goals*, *background*, and *individual traits* (Brusilovsky and Millán 2007).

3.2.1.1 Knowledge

Modeling user's knowledge is commonly found in educational hypermedia systems, indicating the level of expertise a user has on a specific subject being taught or the domain represented in a hypermedia system. Adaptation and personalization systems principally adapt content presentation and provide adaptive navigation support based on the user's knowledge model. For example in MetaDoc (Boyle and Encarnacion 1994), expert users are presented with low-level details of a concept and less additional explanations, while novice users are provided with additional support through explanations and less low-level details.

User's knowledge is a dynamic feature since it might change throughout the user's interactions with the system. In this context, an important challenge of adaptation and personalization systems that model the user's knowledge, have to update the user model depending on the changes of the user's knowledge. According to Brusilovsky and Millán (2007), the most common forms of user knowledge modeling are simple scalar models and more complex structural models. *Scalar models* are similar to stereotype models that represent the level of user's overall knowledge on a particular domain based on a quantitative value (e.g., value from 1 to 10) or a qualitative value (e.g., beginner-intermediate-expert). Scalar models are usually generated based on explicit user data collection methods such as self-assessment questionnaires. Although scalar models are easy to implement, they entail an important limitation since they average the user's level of knowledge on the domain, without comprehensively representing the user's level of knowledge on different parts of the domain.

Structural models aim to alleviate this issue by modeling the user's knowledge of different parts of the domain. A widely used structural model is the *overlay model* (Brusilovsky 2001; Hohl et al. 1996) in which each concept of the domain model stores a particular value representing the user's knowledge level on the particular concept (e.g., expert/intermediate/novice). Nevertheless, overlay models are hard to initialize since this requires an extensive interview with the user or a long questionnaire at the very beginning, in order to model all knowledge values of the domain model. Accordingly, several systems combine different solutions to alleviate such problems. For example, Hypadapter (Hohl et al. 1996) uses scalar models in the beginning to classify new users and set initial values, and then utilizes overlay models. Extensions of the overlay model include the *bug model* of Tsiriga and Virvou (2003) that represents misconceptions about a concept. For example, a bug model will include misconceptions of a user's problem solving knowledge which is based on incorrect user behavior (e.g., user typos, calculation errors).

3.2.1.2   Interests

Modeling user's interests has been commonly applied and researched in information retrieval and filtering systems, such as Web recommender systems. Main aim is to model a person's attention or curiosity towards particular domain concepts (e.g., product categories of an E-Commerce system), and accordingly filter and recommend items of that domain concept. Based on the literature, a user model is also known as a user's profile which is a data instance of the user model representing the user's interests or preferences in terms of keywords or concepts (Gauch et al. 2007). In addition, a user profile may include demographic information of the user, like name, age, gender, profession, etc., which is used by the system to refine the personalization process, for example, by presenting personalized male- or female-related products based on gender.

Information for building the user profile can be based on explicit user data collection methods (e.g., user's feedback through registration forms) or based on implicit user data collection methods utilizing the user's navigation behavior. User profiles can be static in which the information remains the same over time (e.g., gender) or dynamic in which the information is modified. Dynamic profiles are further categorized into short-term dynamic profiles that represent the user's current interests and long-term dynamic profiles that represent the user's interests that do not change frequently over time.

The most common approach for representation of user interests is the weighed vector of keywords (Gauch et al. 2007). In this approach, each keyword is associated with a numerical representation (weight), indicating the strength of the user's interest or preference towards that keyword. Each keyword may represent a particular domain concept. The keywords are either explicitly provided by the user (e.g., during registration), or extracted implicitly from Web-pages visited by the user during browsing, bookmarked or saved by the user. The most common technique for assigning weights of interests is based on the widely known *tf*idf* weighting scheme from information retrieval (Salton and McGill 1983). In this technique, each user profile is represented as a weighted vector of keywords, and the Web-pages that are retrieved by the system in response to a search are also converted to a weighted vector of keywords. Then, both vectors are compared using the *cosine* formula, and documents whose vectors are closer to the user's profile are then shown to the user.

A more powerful variation of the keyword-level approach is the concept-level approach for modeling the user's interests through a weighed overlay of a concept-level domain model (e.g., ontologies). The concept-level approach for interest modeling is similar to the overlay modeling approach of user's knowledge. Concept-level models are more powerful and more accurate than keyword-level models since they can separately model different aspects of user interests given a standard definition of entities and their relationships.

The usage of keyword-level models or concept-level models highly depends on the nature of hypermedia content and has led to *closed corpus hypermedia systems* and *open corpus hypermedia systems*. In closed corpus hypermedia systems, such as adaptive museum guides, the content is indexed during system creation, whereas in open corpus hypermedia systems, such as adaptive news systems, new content must be indexed at the time of its insertion in the system (Ardissono et al. 2001). Due to this constraint, adaptive hypermedia systems usually use concept-level models since these have a closed corpus of documents and could be manually indexed during system creation, whereas information retrieval and filtering systems use keyword-level models due to their open corpus nature of content (i.e., new dynamic information is constantly added) requiring them to process documents automatically. Furthermore, research works exist that proposed hybrid solutions combining concept-level models with automatic document processing (Conlan et al. 2006) or combinations of concept-level and keyword-level models (Díaz and Gervás 2005).

3.2.1.3 Goals

Modeling a user's goal or task aims to elicit the user's objective and intention in the system. For example, a search goal in an information retrieval system (e.g., electronic encyclopedia, E-Commerce system), a learning goal/objective in an educational system (e.g., E-Learning system) or a specific task in an application system (e.g., electronic performance support system). Modeling the user's goals is challenging since goals can be dynamic and change within a session of a specific task of the user. Furthermore, another challenging issue is the goal recognition phase. Principally, goal-based modeling systems recognize and mark the current running goal from a predefined list of goals. Different approaches exist for identifying the user's goal. The simplest approach is to let the user explicitly indicate the goal from a predefined list (Garlatti and Iksal 2000).

More sophisticated approaches implicitly infer the goal through user's interaction, for example, by tracking the time a user spends on a topic; the current goal is inferred through a weighted vector of goals (Kaplan et al. 1993). Furthermore, the ADAPTS support system (Brusilovsky and Cooper 2002) utilizes an alternative goal recognition process by determining the current task of the user within a task hierarchy, by following the user's aircraft maintenance operations. Furthermore, given that the goal recognition process may be not be that precise, research works have utilized probabilistic methods (Encarnação 1997; Micarelli and Sciarrone 1996) and data mining technologies (Hollink et al. 2005; Jin et al. 2005) to classify the user's current goal.

Recently, Barua et al. (2014) proposed a goal model that enables users to set, monitor and refine their models over the long term. Barua et al. have evaluated their work with a lab study and field trial providing evidence that the goal interface is usable and aids people in setting their long term goals. In another recent work, Baikadi et al. (2014) proposed an approach for goal recognition that leverages Markov Logic Networks. In particular, the approach utilized a machine learning framework that combined probabilistic inference with first-order logical reasoning aiming to encode relations between problem-solving goals and discovery events, domain-specific representations of user progress in narrative-centred learning environments.

3.2.1.4   Background

Modeling a user's background implies the representation of the user's level of experience on a domain that might be related but is eventually outside the core domain of the system. For example, in a medical information system, the core domain is the hospital, the medical procedures, and terminology. Related but essentially outside the core domain could be the user's profession and experience of work. In this context, the medical information system can distinguish users by their profession (e.g., student, nurse, doctor) which implies the level of knowledge of that person (Brusilovsky and Millán 2007) and accordingly present personalized content to them (complex medical terminology to doctors whereas easier medical terminology to students).

Modeling user background is a subset of knowledge modeling since it is commonly utilized to infer knowledge. Nevertheless, the representation and handling of user's background is much simpler as it is a rather stable feature, provided explicitly to the system and represented as a simple stereotype model, rather than a complex overlay model.

3.2.1.5 Individual Traits

Modeling individual traits aims to elicit characteristics of users that define them as individuals. Popular examples are personality traits (e.g., introvert/extravert), cognitive styles (e.g., imager/verbal), cognitive processing abilities (e.g., working memory) and learning styles. Individual traits are stable user characteristics and are traditionally extracted using psychometric tests or questionnaires.

A considerable amount of research efforts have been undertaken focusing on modeling and utilizing cognitive factors for adaptation and personalization in interactive systems. Several approaches (Germanakos et al. 2008a; Triantafillou et al. 2004; Graf et al. 2009; Papanikolaou et al. 2003; Belk et al. 2013) have distinguished users based on their cognitive styles and learning styles and provided different adaptation effects accordingly. In a study, Germanakos et al. (2008a) have distinguished imager and verbal users, and wholist and analyst users based on Riding's Cognitive Style Analysis (Riding 1991). Each user was provided with adaptive presentation of content and different navigation organization. In a similar approach, Triantafillou et al. (2004) distinguished field dependent and field independent users based on Witkin et al. (1977) and provided different navigation organization, level of user control, and navigation support tools for these groups. Results in both studies indicate that cognitive styles have significant impact in the adaptation and personalization process of Web environments by increasing usability and user satisfaction during navigation and learning performance. On the contrary, various studies concluded that cognitive styles do not have a main effect on users' task performance and preference within hypermedia environments (Brown et al. 2006).

3.2.2 Context Information

Adapting to the user's context of use is commonly related to the user's location, interaction device, physical environment, social context, interaction history, etc. Two major context models that have been proposed in the literature are related to the user's platform and location characteristics which are further discussed in this section, as well as social characteristics that are popular in today's social networks.

3.2.2.1 Platform-Oriented Context Modeling

Platform-oriented context modeling indicates information related to the user's computing environment, such as the device used, its hardware and software, and the available network bandwidth. These platform oriented settings might affect the effectiveness and efficiency of specific tasks as they can influence performance oriented attributes. As an example, low connection bandwidth can cause the replacement of a video based CAPTCHA challenge (Von Ahn et al. 2004) with a static CAPTCHA challenge. Also, if the user's platform cannot show colored pictures or bandwidth is low, the system can convert the pictures to black and white or low resolution (Rist 2001). In another approach a movie could be replaced with a picture in case the user's platform could not show movies due to the absence of a movie player or low bandwidth.

Platform-oriented context modeling is typically described by a set of name-value pairs (e.g., *<screen size, 1024×800>*), which is used in order to provide the most effective available solution according to the user platform oriented context.

3.2.2.2   Location-Oriented Context Modeling

Location-oriented context modeling indicates information related to the user's current physical location. This kind of adaptation is popular in several social activities' contexts such as tourist and gastronomy guides (Cheverst et al. 2000; Panayiotou and Samaras 2004) that present or recommend to the users a subset of nearby objects of interest based on the user's location. In particular, Panayiotou and Samaras (2004) proposed a mobile-based adaptive interactive system that suggests restaurants or fast food stores based on the user's current location and time. For example, the system suggests restaurants that are close to the user's current location in the evening for dinner, or fast food stores in the afternoon. With regard to usable security, a recent study revealed that location information is an important issue which affects user's perception and effectiveness in security oriented tasks (Fidas et al. 2011). In particular, the results of this study suggest providing localized CAPTCHA challenges to the users' location and lingual characteristics aiming to increase usability in CAPTCHA interactions.

3.2.2.3   Social-Oriented Context Modeling

Social-oriented context modeling represents the social activity (e.g., rating of products, participation at social events, etc.) of users. The majority of social context modeling systems recommend items (e.g., products, friends, events, etc.) to users according to the social context model of other users with similar characteristics (e.g., similar interests, same friends, same hobbies, etc.). With the current trend of organizing and sharing digital content through social networks, adaptation and personalization systems could utilize the social activity of users to construct their models based on other users that have similar preferences and settings. A recent study in Kao-Li et al. (2011) proposed a social tag-based method (i.e., sharing of content through user-created metadata) to recognize how users like specific items and further utilize this information for the recommendation of multimedia items to users with similar preferences.

3.3   User Data Collection Methods

The aforementioned user characteristics are principally elicited through a user modeling mechanism utilizing explicit information from the user, i.e., user guided modeling, and/or implicit information, i.e., dynamic user modeling. These two categories are discussed next.

3.3.1   Explicit User Data Collection Methods

Explicit user information collection methodologies rely on personal information provided by the users, typically via registration forms. The data collected usually contain demographic information (i.e., age, gender, and profession), interests and/or preferences. Common techniques for obtaining explicit information that allows specification of the user model include the use of checkboxes, drop-down lists, or text fields where users express freely their opinion. All these techniques have the advantage that the format of the replies are standardized but the main drawback is that the user is aware that the system is storing this information and usually the process may be disrupted due to unwillingness of the user to provide the information, lack of trust or time to participate in the process. Also, the results from these techniques are human-error prone since if the questions are not carefully designed then they might be inaccurate, inconclusive, or at worst, deceptive.

Explicit user data collection approaches are commonly utilized for customizing user interfaces. In this case, a collection of user preferences are used to create a user model and the services provided adapt in order to increase information accessibility. For instance, Google explicitly asks users to provide their personal information which is stored to create user models. The Web-site content is then dynamically organized based on the users' preferences.

An important drawback of customization approaches is that users may not accurately or fully report their preferences and characteristics. Furthermore, most interactive systems utilizing such approaches barely invoke the user to update the information and rarely have intelligent mechanisms behind to identify that something has changed in the users' preferences. Thus, this results to static user models even though the user's interests may change over time. As a consequence, the user model may become highly inaccurate over time.

3.3.2   Implicit User Data Collection Methods

User models could be also dynamically generated based on implicit information, such as the navigation behavior of users. The mechanisms employed for constructing the models are transparent to the user and they do not require any additional effort or interfere in some way, disrupting the interaction process with the system. Kelly and Teevan (2003) provide an overview of the most popular mechanisms for dynamically collecting implicit user information. Gauch et al. (2007) also summarizes different approaches to implicit user information collection.

The most common source of information about users is their browsing history from which the users' interests are extracted. Browsing history of users contains URLs visited by the user and the date/time of the visits. Accordingly, meaningful information could be extracted based on this information, e.g., number of visits to a particular URL and the time spent in that Web-page. Browsing histories could be collected in two ways: Users sharing their browsing caches on a periodic basis (Gauch et al. 2007), or users installing a proxy server that acts as their gateway to the Internet, thereby capturing all Web traffic generated by the user (Trajkova and Gauch 2004). The first technique utilizes the Web browser's cache system that stores the user's Web browsing history. This technique does not require any installation of specific software. However, in order to extract meaningful information from the collected data, the user is required to upload the cache periodically. In the second technique, proxy servers allow easily capturing information without placing any major burden on the user because they only require an initial setup and do not require any software to be maintained or updated afterwards on the user's desktop computer. An important drawback however is that no user model can be created without having a specific proxy enabled by the user.

Another approach to collect implicitly information while the user navigates in an interactive system is through the usage of agents (e.g., Web browser plugins). Browser agents can be installed on the user's desktop computer and are able to capture all of the activities the user performs while browsing. Apart from collecting the user's browsing history (i.e., URLs visited), browser agents accurately collect information about the actions performed on a Web-page, such as bookmarking and downloading to disk. Accordingly, based on this additional information about the user's browsing activity, agents may suggest links on the current page that might be of interest. An important drawback of this approach is that it requires specialized software to be installed.

Enhancements of Web browser agents are desktop agents which are commercial toolbars that include personalized features with the aim to help users organize their browsing activity stored in their desktop caches. Furthermore, navigation activity for desktop agents is not limited to the Web, but also includes access of users on their local computer, e.g., personal folders and documents. Such search tools are implemented in applications like Stuff I've Seen (Dumais et al. 2003).

3.4   User Model Generation

The simplest approach of user model generation is in the case where the information collected by the user is used as-is and remains unprocessed. For example, users might explicitly express their interest on specific topics of a news publishing system which will be further used by simple rule-based mechanisms to adapt the interface by displaying the selected topics on the top of the users' interface. More intelligent approaches for generating user models include cases where the browsing activities of users may be utilized by *data mining* techniques to recognize regularities in user paths and integrate them in a user model.

Data mining is the process of discovering patterns in large data sets. Main aim is to extract information from raw data and transform it into understandable data for further use (Chakrabarti et al. 2006). A thorough literature review on how data mining techniques can be applied to user modeling in the context of adaptation and personalization systems may be found in the works of Eirinaki and Vazirgiannis (2003), Pierrakos et al. (2003) and Mobasher (2007). In this context, the most widely applied and researched approaches for data mining are *clustering*, *classification*, *association discovery* and *sequential pattern mining*. We next provide an overview of each approach.

3.4.1 Clustering

Clustering is an unsupervised process that groups users together sharing common characteristics or similar navigation behaviors (Nasraoui et al. 2008; Castellano and Torsello 2008; Castellano et al. 2007). Nasraoui et al. (2008) perform clustering on user sessions to place users in homogeneous groups based on the similar activities performed and then extract specific user models from each cluster. Clustering techniques are also used in order to divide users into segments containing users with similar navigation behavior. Using a similarity metric, a clustering algorithm groups the most similar users together to form clusters. Because optimal clustering over large data sets is impractical, most applications use various forms of greedy cluster generation. These algorithms typically start with an initial set of segments, which often contain one randomly selected user. Then, they repeatedly match users to the existing segments. Once the algorithm generates the segments, it computes the users' similarity to vectors that summarize each segment, chooses the segment with the strongest similarity and classifies the user accordingly. Some algorithms classify users into multiple segments and describe the strength of each relationship (Perkowitz and Etzioni 2000). The same concept is found within fuzzy clustering techniques, examples of which include the work of Castellano and Torsello (2008) that categorized users based on the evaluation of similarity between fuzzy sets using a relational fuzzy clustering algorithm and Castellano et al. (2007) that derived user models by analyzing user interests. Variations of fuzzy clustering methods include Fuzzy c-medoids, Fuzzy c-trimmed-medoids, relational Fuzzy Clustering-Maximal Density estimator (RFC-MDE) algorithm, hierarchical clustering approaches, which are applied to group user sessions (Fu et al. 1999).

3.4.2 Classification

Classification is a supervised learning process that maps user information (e.g., interaction data) into one of several predetermined classes which usually represent different user models (Wu et al. 2007). Main aim is to understand existing data and predict how new instances might behave. In the context of adaptation and personalization, classification can model the behavior of users based on predefined classes of users. The most common classification methods are *decision tree induction*, *Bayesian classifiers* and *artificial neural networks* (Pierrakos et al. 2003).

Decision tree induction is one of the most popular classification methods (Choa et al. 2002). This method builds a decision tree and then utilizes it to perform classification. A decision tree is a structure that entails a root node which is the topmost node, branches and leaf nodes. Internal non-leaf nodes denote a test on an attribute, each branch denotes the outcome of a test, and each leaf node denotes a class prediction. In the context of adaptation and personalization, decision tree induction has been widely applied in recommender systems (Nikovski and Kulev 2006; Choa et al. 2002).

Bayesian classification is a probabilistic classifier based on applying the Bayes' theorem which enables prediction of future events and provides an embedded scheme for learning (Rett et al. 2008). The Bayesian interpretation of probability can be seen as an extension of logic that enables reasoning with propositions whose truth or falsity is uncertain. To evaluate the probability of a hypothesis, the Bayesian probability specifies some prior probability, which is then updated in the light of new, relevant data. Bayes' formula provides a means to make inferences about an environment of interest described by a state, given an observation. Several research works have utilized Bayesian theory in the context of recommender systems such as early works of Miyahara and Pazzani (2000) that aimed to improve collaborative filtering in recommender systems with simple Bayesian classification and more recent works of Wang and Tan (2011) that similarly aimed to improve collaborative filtering based on a naïve Bayesian method.

Artificial Neural Networks (ANNs) are also used as a powerful technique to dynamically and transparently model human behavior in adaptation and personalization systems. Numerous researchers have attempted to use ANNs in the context of adaptation and personalization systems, primarily for classification of users with the same characteristics and creation of user models with the aim to recommend and adapt content and functionality (Frias-Martinez et al. 2005). For example, Kim et al. (2004) have proposed an ANN-based collaborative filtering method that investigates the possibility of identifying and predicting the correlation between users or items in a Web environment using a Multi-Layer Perceptron (MLP). Chou et al. (2010) aim to identify the users' prior knowledge for specific products in E-Commerce applications by analyzing their navigation patterns through Web mining and constructing a Back-Propagation Network (BPN – Wu et al. 2006) that uses a supervised learning method and a feed-forward architecture, in order to predict the users' potential future needs. Magoulas et al. (2001) use ANNs to learn and fine tune rules and/or membership functions from input-output data to be used in a Fuzzy Inference System (FIS). In particular, they have proposed a classification/recommendation system with the aim to plan the learning content of a course according to the student's level of knowledge.

3.4.3 Association Discovery

Association discovery techniques aim at generating associations and correlations among sets of items (Linden et al. 2003; Su and Khoshgoftaar 2009). Association rules are commonly used in E-Commerce systems to relate different products based on the users' viewing history, e.g., when users view product A and afterwards view product B, then an association rule is created between product A and B indicating a high relationship between the two products (Pierrakos et al. 2003). Accordingly, this information is further utilized by the system to offer recommendations based on the navigation behavior of users.

Early works on adaptation and personalization (Mobasher et al. 1999) proposed association discovery techniques utilizing item sets with the aim to dynamically recommend Web-pages to users. Alternative approaches for discovering associations between items utilize Bayesian networks for defining structured relations between the topics of a Web-site (Schwarzkopf 2001; Ardissono and Torasso 2000).

Nevertheless, association discovery mining techniques have been primarily applied for the prediction and recommendation of the next interesting Web-page and have not been extensively applied in other contexts. According to Pierrakos et al. (2003) the main reason that association discovery mining has not been widely studied in this context is because the prediction of the next best Web-page is best modeled as a sequential prediction task in which association discovery techniques are not appropriate.

3.4.4 Sequential Pattern Mining

Sequential pattern mining aims at finding relevant patterns between data items that are delivered in a sequence (Mabroukeh and Ezeife 2010). Thus, sequential pattern discovery considers time in the discovery process with the aim to identify patterns that frequently occurring. In the context of Web usage mining, this approach can be used to identify the navigational patterns of users. Sequential pattern mining can be categorized in two widely researched methods: *Deterministic methods* that focus on tracking the navigational behavior of users (Spiliopoulou et al. 1999; Paliouras et al. 2000), and *stochastic methods* that represent the users' transitions of Web-pages within a Web-site aiming to predict next visits. A widely used stochastic method is the Markov model to represent the transitions of users in Web-sites (Parka et al. 2008; Cadez et al. 2000; Yang et al. 2003) and they are introduced as a possible indication of which is the next page users might request to visit based on their current location and previous navigation paths. Thus, in the context of a Web-based application, representation schemes, like the ones in Markov chains can be utilized to represent the transition of users between Web-pages, using for example sequence vectors, and thus identify groups of users following same or similar paths.

3.5   Modeling Human Factors in Interactive Systems

Since the early 1990s, applications and services running on the World Wide Web have significantly grown in size and usage. As user interactions in such realms have become an integral part of people's lives, in line with the globalization and sophistication of products and services, the need for personalization strategies for addressing "one-size-fits-all" issues and meeting the users' individual needs and preferences is nowadays even more evident.

As described in this chapter, researchers and practitioners have already identified various characteristics of users and factors that have important roles within specific domains and contexts of use for adapting and personalizing content and functionality of interactive systems. In particular, the factors being modeled for personalization in interactive systems include among others information about the users (e.g., interests, preferences, needs and goals), information about the interaction device (e.g., screen size, input type), and information about the context of use (e.g., physical, social – Brusilovsky and Millán 2007). A number of techniques have been proposed to explicitly extract this information (e.g., through Web forms, questionnaires, etc.) or implicitly based on the users' navigation behavior within the system (Frias-Martinez et al. 2005), as well as through collaborative filtering based on users' common product ratings or buying history (Linden et al. 2003; Karat et al. 2004).

A large number of research studies revealed that modeling the aforementioned factors in specific domains of interaction enable users to demonstrate significant improvement in tasks completion efficiency, effectiveness, comprehension and user experience. For example, personalizing educational hypermedia systems to the students' level of knowledge on particular domains and concepts has shown that raises students' comprehension capabilities. Furthermore, recommending specific products according to the users' interests on particular product categories has shown to improve task completion efficiency and provide a positive user experience. In this context, due to the heterogeneous users' needs and requirements within each domain, modeling these factors could be considered as a successful step towards personalizing human-computer interactions and improving the user experience. Nevertheless, the question remains whether such user models in each domain could be considered complete enough, and whether all the available vital factors of users are taken into account in order to provide a more complete, effective and human-centred result.

In this realm, as specific factors have shown to influence certain domains (e.g., modeling interests in recommender systems, and modeling knowledge in educational hypermedia systems), we believe that individual traits (attributes that define each person as an individual, e.g., cognition, emotions, personality) and their respective values may have an important (even though different in various cases) role in all domains and contexts of use that entail a human interacting with a computing system. For example, emotions might affect students while taking an exam in an educational hypermedia system, or might affect the users' decision for buying a particular product in an E-Commerce system. Furthermore, bearing in mind that human-computer interactions in interactive systems are primarily processed on a cognitive level, e.g., users are required to process and comprehend information, solve problems and take decisions, we suggest that such individual traits should be investigated and integrated in the user interface design process of interactive systems, with the aim to personalize their visual and interaction design accordingly (see Chaps. 6, 7 and 8).

Apparently, modeling individual traits and personalizing content and functionality of interactive systems is a challenging endeavor given the multi-dimensional and complex nature of such human factors. In this respect, individual differences have been widely applied in personalization systems but with mixed outcomes so far. On the one hand, modeling human cognitive factors for personalization systems has shown to improve task completion performance and user experience (Steichen et al. 2014; Belk et al. 2014a, b; Su et al. 2011; Graf et al. 2009; Frias-Martinez et al. 2007; Germanakos et al. 2008a; Papanikolaou et al. 2003; Bull and McCalla 2000). On the contrary, various studies concluded that cognitive processing factors do not have a main influence on users' task performance and preference within adaptive hypermedia environments (Brown et al. 2006; Mitchell et al. 2004). Thus, modeling individual traits and incorporating these in personalization systems still remains an important and challenging issue, and further studies and approaches are yet to be found (Brusilovsky and Millán 2007). In addition, we should not omit to clarify that such a diversity of research findings could be the result of the endogenous multidisciplinary approach of such study designs as follows: (i) The extraction process of intrinsic human factors of users is heavily dependent on the validity and accuracy of the elicitation tools used in the various studies; (ii) the methodology of each study differs based on the scope and objectives of each research work in which also various external factors and different circumstances might influence the results such as environmental parameters, emotions of users, urgency, etc.; and (iii) given the multidimensional nature of intrinsic human factors and overall complexity of conducting such studies, the evaluation should be replicated over time since a single assessment of the influence of such characteristics on user interactions might not fully justify the results.

3.5.1 Identifying Intrinsic Human Factors for Building a Comprehensive User Model

Throughout this book we emphasize on the fact that human-centred adaptation and personalization designs and techniques should be adopted by researchers and practitioners, so to build user interfaces, systems and environments that will have an added value predominantly to the benefit of the end-user. In today's multi-purpose and dynamic technological reality, the starting point for this endeavor is to define a user model that, depending on the scope and the area of application, will incorporate a number of individual characteristics under a common representation schema that will guide the whole adaptation and personalization process. Therefore, building on this premise, we hereafter briefly overview a comprehensive user model (primarily discussed in Germanakos et al. 2008a, b) that consists of a set of human factors which "complete" at some extent the popular and widely used individual character- istics in current personalization systems (the so called, "traditional" user character- istics, e.g., knowledge, interests, goals, background, demographic information, etc., and device/channel characteristics, e.g., device, size, display, connectivity, etc.). This model serves as the main component of the mapU framework (detailed in Chap. 5 – where the reader can have a better insight on more practical issues and implementation challenges), whereas the rationale behind the proposed specific human-centred dimensions has its basis on the discussion in Chap. 2.

3.5.1.1   The User Perceptual Preference Characteristics

As stated earlier in this chapter, one of the key technical issues in developing adap- tation and personalization systems is the problem of how to construct accurate and comprehensive user models and how these can be used to identify significant intrin- sic characteristics of users that describe their behavior. The way people perceive and process information is widely varied on the basis of individual differences that, from a psychological point of view, can explain the significant divergence in the information processing, learning, performance, perception, etc., between them. Henceforth, driven by a cognitive information processing approach to educational psychology (Santrock 2006), and Bloom's (1956) taxonomy (a well-established framework that distinguishes three major domains of a comprehensive method to learning process: Cognitive, affective and psychomotor), we have proposed respec- tively an information processing model in the context of the World Wide Web namely, User Perceptual Preferences Characteristics (UPPC, see Fig. 3.1 – note that psychomotor parameters related to manual or physical skills are currently out of the model's scope).

The proposed model formulates a three-dimensional approach that takes into account cognitive and affective parameters. The first dimension entails users' cogni- tive styles, the second their visual and cognitive processing efficiency, while the third captures their emotional processing during the interaction process with the information space (it has to be mentioned that for the latter dimension, an optimized set of the emotional constructs discussed in Sect. 2.3 was utilized in an effort to reduce at this stage the within complexity generated by the subsequent parameters). Therefore, it refers to "*all the critical factors that influence the visual, mental and emotional processes liable of manipulating the newly information received and building upon prior knowledge, that is different for each user or user group. These characteristics determine the visual attention, cognitive and emotional processing*

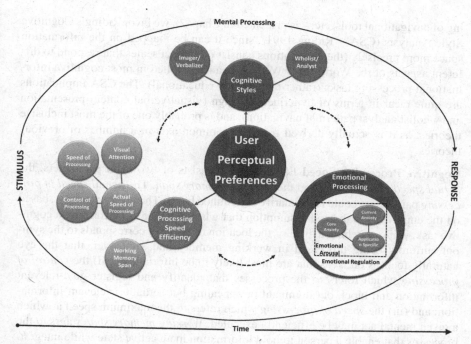

Fig. 3.1 User perceptual preference characteristics – three-dimensional model (Germanakos et al. 2008b)

taking place throughout the whole process of accepting an object of perception (stimulus) until the comprehensive response to it" (Germanakos et al. 2005). The UPPC could be considered as a vital component of the user model since it identifies the aspects of the users that might determine their exact perceptual preferences and lead to a more concrete, accurate and optimized human-centred segmentation (or one-to-one treatment). Its main elements are overviewed below:

Cognitive Styles Cognitive styles reflect the particular set of strengths and preferences that an individual or group of people have in how they perceive and process information; representing typical or habitual modes of problem solving, thinking, perceiving or remembering. By taking into account these preferences and defining specific cognitive, and learning strategies, empirical research has shown that more effective learning and more efficient interactions in Web-based environments can be achieved (Boyle et al. 2003; Wang et al. 2006). In UPPC, we use the construct of cognitive rather than learning style because it is more stable (Sadler-Smith and Riding 1999), and to the extent that there is a correlation with hemispherical preference and EEG measurements (Glass and Riding 1999; McKay et al. 2003), the relationship between cognitive style and actual mode of information processing is strengthened. Amongst the numerous proposed cognitive style theories and typologies (a selection of the most appropriate and technologically feasible ones – those that can be projected to the Web-based content selection and presentation, the tailoring of navigational tools, etc. – is presented in Chap. 2), we favor Riding's Cognitive Style Analysis (CSA – Riding 1991), since it can be mapped on the information space more precisely (the implications consist of distinct scales that respond to different aspects of the World Wide Web) and can be applied in most cognitive informational processing tasks (rather than strictly educational). The CSA implications are quite clear in terms of hypermedia design (visual/verbal content presentation and wholist/analyst pattern of navigation), and is probably one of the most inclusive theories, as it is actually derived from the common axis of a number of previous theories.

Cognitive Processing Speed Efficiency It consists of two main parameters, the *actual speed of processing* and the *working memory span*. The *actual speed of processing* parameters could be primarily determined by: (i) The *visual attention*, based on the empirically validated assumption that when a person is performing a cognitive task, while watching a display, the location of his gaze corresponds to the symbol currently being processed in working memory and, moreover, that the eye naturally focuses on areas that are most likely to be informative; (ii) the *control of processing* which refers to the processes that identify and register goal-relevant information and block out dominant or appealing but actually irrelevant information; and (iii) the *speed of processing* which refers to the maximum speed at which a given mental act may be efficiently executed. *Working memory span* refers to the processes that enable a person to hold information in an active state while integrating it with other information until the current problem is solved (see also Chap. 2 for a more detailed discussion around these constructs and suggestions for further reading).

Emotional Processing The model also contains information on how individuals process and control their emotions and how these interact with other elements of their information processing system. Emotional processing is a pluralistic construct which is comprised of two mechanisms: *Emotional arousal*, which is the capacity of a human being to sense and experience specific emotional situations, and *emotion regulation*, which is the way in which individuals perceive and control their emotions (see Sects. 2.1 and 2.3). These sub-processes manage a number of emotional factors, out of which we have deliberately focused on *anxiety*, as the main indicator of emotional arousal, because it is correlated with learning performance as well as with activities in computer mediated procedures. Therefore, we refer to users' *trait anxiety* (*core*), their *application-specific anxiety*, and their *self-reported state-anxiety* levels. Including these different measurements in the user model, we can extract more precise information about the users' levels of anxiety, which in general is not easily expressed explicitly. The construct of emotional regulation that we used includes the *experiential* level (a person's emotional experience and emotional expression) and the *rational* level (includes emotion recognition, emotional management and emotional motivation). We also refer to *self-efficacy*, as a concept that relates to how we think, feel and behave. By combining the levels of anxiety with the moderating role of emotion regulation, it is possible to examine how affectional responses hamper or promote learning procedures and human-computer interactions. Thus, by personalizing the Web-based content accordingly, we can avoid stressful instances and take full advantage of users' cognitive capacity at any time.

3.6 Summary

Dealing with the information that is more appropriate for the user in a particular context of use and activity step, or how this is acquired, represented and maintained, as well as how this can be extracted and defined in a unified mode, are some of the main challenges that research on user modelling tries to tackle. In this chapter we made an effort to sum up existing knowledge and state-of-the-art works on user modeling in the context of adaptation and personalization systems. In summary, the information being modeled can either be static, when it contains parts that rarely or never change (e.g., demographic information), or dynamic, when the data change frequently. Such information is obtained either explicitly, using online registration forms and questionnaires resulting in static user models, or implicitly, by recording the users' navigation behavior and/or preferences during human-computer interaction. In the latter case, each user can either be regarded as a member of group and take up an aggregate user model or be addressed individually and take up an individual user model.

In this respect, a high number of research works revealed successful personalization approaches that maintain user models which consist of various user characteristics and contextual features depending on their domain of application (most popular ones found in recommender systems and educational hypermedia systems). Yet, the question still remains, when a user model is considered complete? Do designers and developers of interactive systems take into consideration those factors determined by individual differences for providing a more accurate and comprehensive result?

Many times this is not the case. In this respect, towards the end of the chapter we tried to formulate an understanding around the synergy of human factors and user interactions in computing systems and how these can be used in user models in order to drive the adaptation and personalization of content and functionality towards more human-centred results for each end-user. Accordingly, the proposed three-dimensional model seems to cover a wide area of human factors that are proven significant in computer-mediated tasks and interactions, and may provide a basis for meaningful personalization. As we will see in the next chapters of this book, cognitive styles are certainly influencing content presentation and navigation, cognitive processing efficiency and working memory span have an impact on the complexity of Web-based environments and the quantity of information delivered each time, and anxiety (as the main component of emotional processing) can be manipulated for optimization of performance by improving clarity of a Web-page sections' details. There are of course limitations in this approach, mainly due to the nature of the Web content that often limits radically differentiated adaptation, and the psychometric challenges of measuring a wide spectrum of human cognition and emotions. We believe though that the reader will appreciate the importance of such enhancements in user models and will recognize the added value that their practical implications can have in human-computer interactions in various application areas.

References

Ardissono L, Torasso P (2000) Dynamic user modeling in a web store shell. In: Proceedings of the European conference on artificial intelligence, pp 621–625

Ardissono L, Console L, Torre I (2001) An adaptive system for the personalised access to news. AI Commun 14:129–147

Baikadi A, Rowe J, Mott B, Lester J (2014) Generalizability of goal recognition models in narrative-centered learning environments. In: Proceedings of the international conference on user modeling, adaptation, and personalization, pp 278–289

Barua D, Kay J, Kummerfeld B, Paris C (2014) Modelling long term goals. In: Proceedings of the international conference on user modeling, adaptation, and personalization, pp 1–12

Belk M, Papatheocharous E, Germanakos P, Samaras G (2013) Modeling users on the world wide web based on cognitive factors, navigation behaviour and clustering techniques. J Syst Softw 86(12):2995–3012

Belk M, Germanakos P, Asimakopoulos S, Andreou P, Mourlas C, Spanoudis G, Samaras G (2014a) An individual differences approach in adaptive waving of user checkout process in retail eCommerce. In: Proceedings of the international conference on human-computer interaction (HCII 2014), pp 451–460

Belk M, Germanakos P, Fidas C, Samaras G (2014b) A personalisation method based on human factors for improving usability of user authentication tasks. In: Proceedings of the international conference on user modeling, adaptation, and personalization (UMAP 2014), pp 13–24

Bloom BS (1956) Taxonomy of educational objectives. Allyn and Bacon, Boston, Copyright (c) 1984 by Pearson Education

Boyle C, Encarnacion A (1994) MetaDoc: an adaptive hypertext reading system. User Model User-Adap Inter 4(1):1–19

Boyle EA, Duffy T, Dunleavy K (2003) Learning styles and academic outcome: the validity and utility of Vermunt's inventory of learning styles in a British higher education setting. Br J Educ Psychol 73:267–290

Brown E, Brailsford T, Fisher T, Moore A, Ashman H (2006) Reappraising cognitive styles in adaptive web applications. In: Proceedings of the world wide web (2006), pp 327–335

Brusilovsky P (2001) Adaptive hypermedia. User Model User-Adap Inter 11(1,2):87–110

Brusilovsky P, Cooper D (2002). Domain, task, and user models for an adaptive hypermedia performance support system. In: Proceedings of intelligent user interfaces (IUI'02), pp 23–30

Brusilovsky P, Millán E (2007) User models for adaptive hypermedia and adaptive educational systems. In: Brusilovsky P, Kobsa A, Nejdl W (eds) The adaptive web, vol 4321, pp 3–53

Bull S, McCalla G (2000) Modelling cognitive style in a peer help network. Instr Sci 30(6):497–528

Cadez I, Heckerman D, Meek C, Smyth P, White S (2000) Visualization of navigation patterns on a web site using model-based clustering. In: Proceedings of the ACM SIGKDD international conference on knowledge discovery and data mining, pp 280–284

Castellano G, Torsello MA (2008) Categorization of web users by fuzzy clustering. In: Proceedings of international conference on knowledge-based intelligent information and engineering systems. Springer, pp 222–229

Castellano G, Fanelli AM, Mencar C, Torsello MA (2007) Similarity-based fuzzy clustering for user profiling. In: Proceedings of international conference on web intelligence and intelligent agent technology workshop, IEEE/WIC/ACM, pp 75–78

Chakrabarti S, Ester M, Fayyad U, Gehrke J, Han J, Morishita S, Piatetsky-Shapiro G, Wang W (2006) Data mining curriculum: a proposal (version 1.0). ACM knowledge discovery and data mining (SIGKDD)

Cheverst K, Davies N, Mitchell K, Smith P (2000) Providing tailored (context-aware) information to city visitors. In: Proceedings of adaptive hypermedia and adaptive web-based systems (AH'00), vol 1892, pp 73–85

Choa YH, Kim JK, Kim SH (2002) A personalized recommender system based on web usage mining and decision tree induction. Expert Syst Appl 23(3):329–342

Chou P, Li P, Chen K, Wu M (2010) Integrating web mining and neural network for personalized ecommerce automatic service. Expert Syst Appl 37(4):2898–2910

Conlan O, O'Keeffe I, Tallon S (2006) Combining adaptive hypermedia techniques and ontology reasoning to produce dynamic personalized news services. In: Proceedings of adaptive hypermedia and adaptive web-based systems, vol 4018, pp 81–90

Díaz A, Gervás P (2005) Personalisation in news delivery systems: item summarization and multitier item selection using relevance feedback. Web Intelligence Agent Syst 3(3):135–154

Dumais S, Cutrell E, Cadiz J, Jancke G, Sarin R, Robbins D (2003) Stuff I've seen: a system for personal information retrieval and re-use. In: Proceedings of ACM SIGIR conference on research and development in information retrieval, pp 72–79

Eirinaki M, Vazirgiannis M (2003) Web mining for web personalization. ACM Trans Internet Technol 3(1):1–27

Encarnação L (1997) Multi-level user support through adaptive hypermedia: a highly application independent help component. In: Proceedings of intelligent user interfaces (IUI'97), pp 187–194

Ferwerda B, Yang E, Schedl M, Tkalcic M (2015) Personality traits predict music taxonomy preferences. In: Extended abstracts on human factors in computing systems (CHI EA'15), pp 2241–2246

Fidas C, Voyiatzis A, Avouris N (2011) On the necessity of user-friendly CAPTCHA. In: Proceedings of human factors in computing systems (CHI'11), pp 2623–2626

Frias-Martinez E, Magoulas G, Chen S, Macredie R (2005) Modeling human behavior in user-adaptive systems: recent advances using soft computing technique. Expert Syst Appl 29(2):320–329

Frias-Martinez E, Chen S, Macredie R, Liu X (2007) The role of human factors in stereotyping behavior and perception of digital library users: a robust clustering approach. User Model User-Adap Inter 17(3):305–337

Fu Y, Sandhu K, Shih MY (1999) Clustering of web users based on access patterns. In: ACM SIGKDD international conference on knowledge discovery and data mining. Springer

Garlatti S, Iksal S (2000) Context filtering and spacial filtering in an adaptive information system. In: Proceedings of adaptive hypermedia and adaptive web-based systems, vol 1892, pp 315–318

Gauch S, Speretta M, Chandramouli A, Micarelli A (2007) User profiles for personalized information access. In: Brusilovsky P, Kobsa A, Nejdl W (eds) The adaptive web, vol 4321, pp 54–89

Germanakos P, Tsianos N, Mourlas C, Samaras G (2005) New fundamental profiling characteristics for designing adaptive web-based educational systems. In: Proceedings of the IADIS international conference on cognition and exploratory learning in digital age (CELDA2005), Porto, December 14–16, pp 10–17

Germanakos P, Tsianos N, Lekkas Z, Mourlas C, Samaras G (2008a) Capturing essential intrinsic user behaviour values for the design of comprehensive web-based personalized environments. Comput Hum Behav 24(4):1434–1451

Germanakos P, Tsianos N, Lekkas Z, Mourlas C, Samaras G (2008b) Realizing comprehensive user profile as the core element of adaptive and personalized communication environments and systems. Comput J (2009) 52(7):749–770

Glass A, Riding RJ (1999) EEG differences and cognitive style. Biol Psychol 51(1999):23–41

Goy A, Ardissono L, Petrone G (2007) Personalization in e-commerce applications. In: Brusilovsky P, Kobsa A, Nejdl W (eds) The adaptive web, LNCS, vol 4321, pp 485–520

Graf S, Liu T, Kinshuk, Chen N, Yang S (2009) Learning styles and cognitive traits – their relationship and its benefits in web-based educational systems. Comput Hum Behav 25(6):1280–1289

Herder E, van Dijk B (2002) Personalized adaptation to device characteristics. In: De Bra P, Brusilovsky P, Conejo R (eds) Proceedings of the second international conference on adaptive hypermedia and adaptive web-based systems (AH'02), pp 598–602

Hohl H, Böcker H, Gunzenhäuser R (1996) Hypadapter: an adaptive hypertext system for exploratory learning and programming. User Model User-Adap Inter 6:131–156

Hollink V, Someren M, Hage S (2005) Discovering stages in web navigation. In: Proceedings of user modeling conference (UM'05), vol 3538, pp 473–482

Jawaheer G, Szomszor M, Kostkova P (2010) Comparison of implicit and explicit feedback from an online music recommendation service. In: Proceedings of international workshop on information heterogeneity and fusion in recommender systems. ACM Press, pp 47–51

Jin X, Zhou Y, Mobasher B (2005) Task-oriented web user modeling for recommendation. In: Proceedings of user modeling conference (UM'05), vol 3538, pp 109–118

Kao-Li C, Yang T, Lee W (2011) Personalized multimedia recommendation with social tags and context awareness. In: Proceedings of the world congress on engineering (WCE'11), vol 2, pp 1046–1051

Kaplan C, Fenwick J, Chen J (1993) Adaptive hypertext navigation based on user goals and context. User Model User-Adap Inter 3(3):193–220

Karat C, Blom JO, Karat J (2004) Designing personalized user experiences in eCommerce. LNCS, Springer, Netherlands

Kelly D, Teevan J (2003) Implicit feedback for inferring user preference: a bibliography. ACM SIGIR Forum 37(2):18–28

Kim M, Kim E, Ryu J (2004) A collaborative recommendation based on neural networks. In: Proceedings of the conference on database systems for advanced applications (DASFAA'04), vol 2973, pp 425–430

Linden G, Smith B, York J (2003) Amazon.com recommendations: item-to-item collaborative filtering. IEEE Internet Comput 7(1):76–80

Mabroukeh N, Ezeife C (2010) A taxonomy of sequential pattern mining algorithms. ACM Comput Surv 43(1), Article 3, 41 pages

Magoulas GD, Papanikolaou KA, Grigoriadou M (2001) Neuro-fuzzy synergism for planning the content in a web-based course. Informatica 25(1):39–48

McKay MT, Fischler I, Dunn BR (2003) Cognitive style and recall of text: an EEG analysis. Learn Individ Differ 14:1–21

Micarelli A, Sciarrone F (1996) A case-based system for adaptive hypermedia navigation. In: Proceedings of advances in case-based reasoning, pp 266–279

Mitchell T, Chen SY, Macredie R (2004) Adapting hypermedia to cognitive styles: is it necessary? In: Proceedings of workshop on individual differences in adaptive hypermedia, in conjunction with adaptive hypermedia and adaptive web-based system (AH 2004). Springer-Verlag

Miyahara K, Pazzani M (2000) Collaborative filtering with the simple Bayesian classifier. In: Proceedings of the 6th Pacific Rim international conference on artificial intelligence (PRICAI'00), pp 679–689

Mobasher B, Cooley R, Srivastava J (1999) Creating adaptive web sites through usage-based clustering of urls. In: Proceedings of the workshop on knowledge and data engineering exchange (KDEX'99), pp 19

Mobasher B (2007) Data mining for web personalization. In: Brusilovsky P, Kobsa A, Nejdl W (eds) The adaptive web, vol 4321, Lecture notes in computer science. Springer, Berlin/Heidelberg, pp 90–135

Nasraoui O, Soliman M, Saka E, Badia A, Germain R (2008) A web usage mining framework for mining evolving user profiles in dynamic web sites. IEEE Trans Knowl Data Eng 20(2):202–215

Nikovski D, Kulev V (2006) Induction of compact decision trees for personalized recommendation. In: Proceedings of the 2006 ACM symposium on applied computing (SAC 2006), pp 575–581

Paliouras G, Papatheodorou C, Karkaletsis V, Spyropoulos CD (2000) Clustering the users of large web sites into communities. In: Proceedings of the conference on machine learning (ICML'00), pp 719–726

Panayiotou C, Samaras G (2004) mPersona: personalized portals for the wireless user: an agent approach. J ACM Mob Netw Appl (MONET) 9(6):663–677

Papanikolaou K, Grigoriadou M, Kornilakis H, Magoulas G (2003) Personalising the interaction in a web-based educational hypermedia system: the case of INSPIRE. User Model User-Adap Inter 13(3):213–267

Parka S, Sureshb N, Jeonga B (2008) Sequence-based clustering for web usage mining: a new experimental framework and ANN-enhanced K-means algorithm. Data Knowl Eng 65(3):512–543

Perkowitz M, Etzioni O (2000) Adaptive web sites. Commun ACM 43(8):152–158

Pierrakos D, Paliouras G, Papatheodorou C, Spyropoulos C (2003) Web usage mining as a tool for personalization: a survey. User Model User-Adap Inter 13(4):311–372

Rett J, Dias J, Ahuactzin JM (2008) Laban movement analysis using a Bayesian model and perspective projections. Brain Vis AI 4(6):953–978

Riding R (1991) Cognitive style analysis – research administration. Learning and Training Technology, Birmingham, UK

Rist T (2001) A perspective on intelligent information interfaces for mobile users. In: Proceedings of human-computer interaction (HCI'01), vol 1, pp 154–158

Sadler-Smith E, Riding RJ (1999) Cognitive style and instructional preferences. Instr Sci 27(5):355–371

Salton G, McGill M (1983) Introduction to modern information retrieval. McGraw-Hill, New York

Santrock JW (2006) Educational psychology. McGraw-Hill Humanities, New York

Schwarzkopf E (2001) An adaptive web site for the UM2001 conference. In: Proceedings of the user modeling 2001 workshop on machine learning for user modeling, pp 77–86

Spiliopoulou M, Faulstich LC, Wilkler K (1999) A data miner analyzing the navigational behavior of web users. In: Proceedings of the workshop on machine learning in user modeling, 54–64

Steichen B, Wu M, Toker D, Conati C, Carenini G (2014) Te,Te,Hi,Hi: eye gaze sequence analysis for informing user-adaptive information visualizations. In: Proceedings of the international conference on user modeling, adaptation, and personalization (UMAP 2014). Springer-Verlag, pp 183–194

Su X, Khoshgoftaar T (2009) A survey of collaborative filtering techniques. Adv Artif Intell, 2009(4):19

Su J, Tseng S, Lin H, Chen C (2011) A personalized learning content adaptation mechanism to meet diverse user needs in mobile learning environments. User Model User-Adap Inter 21(1–2):5–49

Trajkova J, Gauch S (2004) Improving ontology-based user profiles. In: Proceedings of RIAO 2004, pp 380–389

Triantafillou E, Pomportsis A, Demetriadis S, Georgiadou E (2004) The value of adaptivity based on cognitive style: an empirical study. Br J Educ Technol 35:95–106

Tsiriga V, Virvou M (2003) Modelling the student to individualise tutoring in a web-based ICALL. Int J Cont Eng Educ Lifelong Learn 13(3–4):350–365

Von Ahn L, Blum M, Langford J (2004) Telling humans and computers apart automatically. Commun ACM 47(2):56–60

Wærn A (2004) User involvement in automatic filtering: an experimental study. J User Model User-Adap Inter 14(2-3):201–237

Wang K, Tan Y (2011) A new collaborative filtering recommendation approach based on naive Bayesian method. In: Proceedings of the second international conference on advances in swarm intelligence (ICSI'11), pp 218–227

Wang KH, Wang TH, Wang WL, Huang SC (2006) Learning styles and formative assessment strategy: enhancing student achievement in web-based learning. J Comput Assist Learn 22:207–217, SSCI

Witkin H, Moore C, Goodenough D, Cox P (1977) Field-dependent and field-independent cognitive styles and their educational implications. Rev Educ Res 47:1–64

Wu D, Yang Z, Liang L (2006) Using DEA-neural network approach to evaluate branch efficiency of a large Canadian bank. Expert Syst Appl 31:108–115

Wu X, Kumar V, Quinlan JR, Ghosh J, Yang Q, Motoda H, McLachlan G, Ng A, Liu B, Yu P, Zhou Z, Steinbach M, Hand D, Steinberg D (2007) Top 10 algorithms in data mining. Knowl Inf Syst 14(1):1–37

Yang Q, Huang JZ, Ng M (2003) A data cube model for prediction-based web prefetching. Intell Inf Syst 20(1):11–30

Chapter 4
Personalization Categories and Adaptation Technologies

Abstract Since the early days of the Web, researchers and practitioners studied adaptation and personalization to address comprehension and orientation difficulties presented in "one-size-fits-all" interactive systems. Main aim was to alleviate navigational complications and instead, satisfy the heterogeneous needs and requirements of users. Over time, a number of personalization methods and adaptation technologies and mechanisms have been proposed and applied in interactive systems for personalizing their content and functionality to the users' characteristics. In this chapter we present the underlying principles of adaptation and personalization. Main aim is to provide an overview of state-of-the-art technologies and methods of adaptation and personalization, focusing on the one hand on technical aspects for adapting and personalizing content and functionality, and on the other hand on design aspects for communicating various adaptation effects. Through this chapter the reader will be able to formulate an inclusive theoretical and practical background in the area of adaptation and personalization and understand their differences and commonalities as well as the dynamics that influence their application in various contexts.

Keywords Adaptation and personalization • Categories • Technologies • Adaptation effects • Systems

4.1 Introduction

Engineering interactive systems under the notion of user-centred design approaches does not always intuitively embed features that correspond to the users' characteristics and needs. A challenge met especially in current interactive systems is to dynamically adapt the content presentation and functionality of the system based on explicitly or implicitly retrieved information about the user. In this context, adaptive user interfaces (Schneider-Hufschmidt et al. 1993; Brusilovsky 2001) in interactive systems provide an alternative to the "one-size-fits-all" approach of static user interfaces by adapting the interactive system's structure, terminology, functionalities and presentation of content to users' perceptions, needs and preferences, aiming to increase the usability of the interface and provide a positive user experience.

© Springer International Publishing Switzerland 2016
P. Germanakos, M. Belk, *Human-Centred Web Adaptation and Personalization*,
Human–Computer Interaction Series, DOI 10.1007/978-3-319-28050-9_4

Starting with a few pioneering works on adaptive hypertext in the early 1990s, personalization research now attracts many researchers from different communities such as hypermedia, user modeling, machine learning, natural language generation, information retrieval, intelligent tutoring systems, affective computing, cognitive science, and Web-based education (Brusilovsky and Maybury 2002; Brusilovsky 2003). The most important and most elaborated works on adaptive user interfaces were originally developed in the fields of information retrieval (Korfhage 1997) and intelligent tutoring systems (Sleeman and Brown 1982). Information retrieval and filtering systems attempt to find documents that are most relevant to user interests and then to order them by the perceived relevance. On the other hand, intelligent tutoring systems (ITS), try to select educational activities and deliver individual feedback that is most relevant to the user's level of knowledge.

Various recent research works exist in the literature that propose different approaches for adaptation and personalization, like the work of Reinecke and Bernstein (2011) suggesting an approach for adapting user interfaces based on the cultural preferences of users; Li et al. (2013) proposing an adaptive spellchecker and predictor for people with dyslexia that can adapt its model and interface according to the users' individual behavior; Cheng et al. (2013) recommending an implicit user modeling approach that automatically adapts the layout and position of virtual keyboards based on how and where users are grasping the tablet device; and Matuszyk and Spiliopoulou (2014) emphasizing on a collaborative filtering method for constructing a user's neighborhood by selecting only those users that are reliably similar to the user.

Furthermore, today's major Web information retrieval systems have showed a certain degree of recognition towards this approach, such as Google (2015a), Bing (2015), and Amazon (2015) that offer personalized results and recommendations, by employing adaptation technologies and techniques. These service providers have been offering personalized results and recommendations by employing various intelligent user modeling and adaptation algorithms. Popular approaches for recommendation include collaborative filtering and content-based filtering (Pazzani and Billsus 2007; Konstan and Riedl 2012). Collaborative filtering first collects and analyzes data about the users' interactions with the system or the users' preferences, and then predicts for the rest of the users their future preferences based on the similarity of their interests. Content-based filtering creates a user profile based on a weighted vector of the item features appearing in the content which is more frequently visited by the user. The weights indicate the importance of each feature to the user. Furthermore, various algorithms are employed to recommend new items that are similar to the weighted vector of the user. Various machine learning techniques are used to predict user preference or estimate the probability that users will like particular items, such as cluster analysis, classification, decision trees, and artificial neural networks.

Although the notion of personalization has found its way in users' everyday interactions in Web interactive systems, various research issues are still open with regard to the most influential factors of personalization, such as the behavioral drivers and navigation interaction of users in executing task-oriented reasoning processes. In addition, there is lack of understanding of the relation between individual styles, cognition levels (abilities), emotional processing characteristics and navigation behavior within interactive systems. An interesting example is the case of users' interactions with online content, such as content included in encyclopedia articles. In that case, based on observations of human behavior and preference, the personalization process could influence both the way content is represented as well as the way the content is structured, and thus may have a significant impact on improving the users' experience. Assuming that the content of Web interactive systems can be presented in two ways, either as a visual or a verbal representation of information, illustrating the same content, and users may go through the content in a specific navigation pattern (or navigation behavior), we suggest that individual differences in cognitive styles, which describe the way individuals perceive, process and organize information (Riding and Cheema 1991), might be applied effectively for facilitating the user modeling process of adaptive Web interactive systems (Germanakos et al. 2008). The most widely accredited cognitive style dimensions are the Verbal/Imager dimension, that indicates the habitual approach and preference of users representing information verbally or graphically, and the Wholist/Analyst dimension, which describes the way individuals organize and process information in a holistic or an analytic approach (Peterson et al. 2009; Riding and Cheema 1991).

From a technical point of view, an important challenge for designing an effective adaptation and personalization system is to study and incorporate structures of meta-data (i.e., semantics) at the Web content provider's side, as well as propose the construction of a Web-based adaptation mechanism that will serve as an automatic filter, adapting the distributed Web content based on the user's characteristics. Semantic mark-up can contribute to the whole adaptation process with machine-understandable representation of Web content. In this context, machine-understandable data can be incorporated in the design of Web-based systems to inform the adaptation mechanism of the intention of specific sections and accordingly adapt them based on the user's characteristics and adaptation rules (Belk et al. 2012; Hori et al. 2004).

This chapter presents the underlying principles of adaptation and personalization from a technical and design perspective. From a technical perspective we focus on the main personalization categories and adaptation technologies for adapting content and functionality based on the characteristics of each user. In addition, we refer to how the Semantic Web and the Social Web can contribute for building effective adaptation and personalization systems. From the design perspective we present the main adaptation effects that are communicated to the user interface of adaptation and personalization systems. Finally, we make a reference of selected state-of-the-art adaptation and personalization systems and frameworks starting with recent ones towards early pioneering ones.

4.2 Personalization Categories

Personalization can be split in six categories: *Link personalization, content personalization, personalized search, context personalization, authorized personalization* and *humanized personalization* (Germanakos et al. 2005) and are discussed in detail in the following sub-sections.

4.2.1 Link Personalization

Link personalization involves the adaptation and personalization of the structure and presentation of hyperlinks in an interactive system. This is achieved by selecting the links that are more relevant to the user (e.g., based on interests, preferences), changing the original navigation space by reducing or improving the relationships between nodes, and adapting the presentation of links. Link personalization is used in E-Commerce applications for recommending relevant products to the users based on their buying history and their ratings on specific products or category of products (Rossi et al. 2001). A popular example of applying link personalization in real-life E-Commerce systems is in Amazon (2015) that recommend products to users with relevant to purchased items, new releases, shopping groups, etc. (Rossi et al. 2001; Linden et al. 2003). Link personalization is also widely applied in educational hypermedia systems for adapting the link structure and navigation of particular learning material and concepts (Germanakos et al. 2007a). For example, based on the knowledge model of a user (that represents the knowledge level of the user on particular concepts of a domain), the system may prioritize links pointing to information with easier difficulty level first, in case the student has novice levels of knowledge on the particular concepts, or present links pointing to information with higher difficulty level first in case the student has expert levels of knowledge. Another example may be based on cognitive styles (Wholist/Analyst) for presenting different navigation patterns depending on the student's preferred way of organizing and processing visual information (Germanakos et al. 2007a).

4.2.2 Content Personalization

Content personalization involves adapting and personalizing the content of the user interface. Content personalization can be classified in two categories:

1. Node structure personalization entails filtering the content that is relevant to the users, illustrating sections and information in which the users may be interested. They may explicitly indicate their preferences, or these may be inferred through their static user model or navigation activity. For example, in Apple (2015), users may reorganize and choose a set of "widgets" to be displayed in the initial screen

of their mobile device, and further personalize the content to be displayed based on a specific set of attributes. Automatic personalization may also occur, e.g., a sports news application may present localized information to the users based on their GPS location information.

2. Node content personalization is finer grained than structure personalization and involves adapting the information of the same node to various users. An example can be based on E-Commerce systems that provide users with different discounts by personalizing the price of the same product according to the users' buying history (Rossi et al. 2001).

4.2.3 Personalized Web Search

Personalized Web search (Wen et al. 2009) is the process of tailoring and personalizing the search results to an individual's interests by taking into consideration information about the individual beyond the query provided. Personalized Web search is implemented on the server side as part of a search engine's methods or on the client side on the user's computer (e.g., as a plugin on the Web browser). According to Pitkow et al. (2002), there are two general approaches to personalize the Web search results: (i) By modifying the user's query; and (ii) by re-ranking search results.

In order to provide personalized search results to users, the system models the users' characteristics, interests and preferences on specific concept categories. Specifically, information maintained in the user model may include: (i) Demographic information such as age, gender, language, education; (ii) geolocation information such as, country, address; (iii) interests and preferences; (iv) search history such as prior queries submitted by the user, visited links, downloaded files; (v) browsing behavior such as mouse clicks, mouse movements, scrolling and bookmarking; and (vi) user actions such as bookmarking a Web-page, setting Web-sites as favorites.

According to Wen et al. (2009), modeling users' information for personalized Web search can be achieved through the following techniques: (i) Personalized search based on content analysis in which the system compares and checks the content similarity between Web-pages and user models; (ii) personalized search based on hyperlink analysis in which the system computes the personalized importance of Web documents for each user; and (iii) personalized search based on collaborative approaches in which the system presents similar search results to users with similar user models.

4.2.4 Context Personalization

Context personalization refers to the adaptation of information that is accessed in different contexts of use (Rossi et al. 2001). Context personalization can be based on the user's location, interaction device, physical environment or social context.

For example, a text-recognition CAPTCHA mechanism may localize the text-based challenge by presenting characters personalized to the users' localized information (Fidas et al. 2011).

A high number of research works have focused on personalizing content and functionality of interactive systems based on the user's location. Location-based personalization systems recommend new locations of interest to the users by taking into account their interests and preferences, utilizing content-based or collaborative recommendation techniques (Herder et al. 2014). Herder et al. (2014) has identified four streamlines of research focusing on location-based services: *Human mobility patterns* focusing on people's movements, number of visits, etc.; *predicting next locations* that utilize data mining techniques such as Markov Models and Bayesian Models for predicting the user's next location; *location and social media* aiming to analyze human mobility based on social media data analysis, although research in this area is sparse due to the fact that users rarely share their exact location in the data they share; and *location-based services* that primarily provide location-based recommendations and contextualized search results (Bellotti et al. 2008). Another example is adapting information according to the characteristics of the interaction device and the context of use (Lankhorst et al. 2002). Context personalization can also occur on a combination of contextual parameters such as recommending near-by restaurants to users based on their location and time (e.g., lunch, dinner – Panayiotou and Samaras 2004; Teevan et al. 2011).

4.2.5   Authorized Personalization

Authorized personalization is applied when an interactive system provides different access of information and action permission to users with different roles in the system. The most widely known approach of authorized personalization is role-based access control in which access rights in particular sections of a system are categorized under a role name. In this approach, a many-to-many relationship exists between users-roles-permission in which each user belongs to particular roles, and each role relates to particular permissions. Depending on the status and responsibilities of a user within an interactive system, different roles and thus permissions are given to that user. For example, in a conference paper management system, such as Precision Conference (2015), users have different access rights and action permission depending on their role (authors, reviewers, organizers). In this context, depending on their role in the system, authors may only be able to submit and upload their own paper, whereas the primary reviewer may be able to view and manage multiple papers submitted by the authors.

Role-based access control is highly scalable and hierarchies of roles enables the easy assignment of permissions including the permissions that are associated with one role to another role. An early role-based approach is Role-based Access Control (RBAC – Sandhu 1998) which enhances traditional mandatory and discretionary models for restricting system access to authorized users. Team-based Access Control (TMAC – Thomas 1997) is an access control model that focuses on collaborative team work and incorporates context information (i.e., the members of a team and the object instances) that is associated with collaborative tasks and accordingly applies this context information for access control. Various research works exist that extended the TMAC model with additional factors aiming to model more access policies (Georgiadis et al. 2001; Alotaiby and Chen 2004). For example, in the work of Georgiadis et al. (2001) the TMAC model is enhanced with additional information such as time of access, the location from which access is requested, the location where the object to be accessed resides, transaction-specific values that dictate special access policies, etc.

4.2.6 Humanized Personalization

Humanized personalization aims at creating personalized user interfaces based on intrinsic human factors such emotional factors (anxiety, stress), personality traits, cognitive styles, learning styles, visual attention, elementary cognitive processing abilities, etc. Given the highly complex and multi-dimensional character of these factors, personalizing content and functionality of interactive systems based on such human factors is still at its infancy and not yet widely applied in commercial interactive systems. Furthermore, a practical limitation applying to these factors is related to the fact that the elicitation and user modeling process requires explicit user data collection methods in which users perform a series of psychometric tests, respond to specially designed questionnaires or participate in controlled laboratory studies utilizing external hardware devices such as eye tracking devices for measuring the visual attention and visual search of users, and physiological sensors for measuring blood pressure, heart rate, skin conductance aiming to model the user's anxiety, stress, etc.

Nevertheless, driven by existing research works in psychology suggesting that individuals differ in such human factors, as well as empirical findings that indicate the impact of personalizing content and functionality of interactive systems based on such intrinsic human factors, it is important to further investigate the effects and impact of applying these in adaptation and personalization systems to the benefit of the user. In particular, a high number of research works revealed significant effects of applying several human factors in adaptation and personalization systems in various application domains. For example, Tsianos et al. (2010) conducted a user study aiming to examine learners' emotional arousal variability, and possible correlations of the physiological data with other psychological constructs such as trait and self-reported anxiety. According to the findings, heart rate was significantly correlated with trait and self-reported state anxiety, but not with academic performance in an on-line exam. Skin conductance and blood volume pulse had only marginal variations, perhaps due to the absence of intense stimuli. In a recent work of Steichen et al. (2014), a user study that investigated the effect of elementary human cognitive processes and eye gaze patterns on visual search tasks in information visualization, identified a number of pattern differences that could be leveraged by adaptation and personalization systems aiming to implicitly elicit and consequently adapt to different user characteristics. In the same line, the work of Belk et al. (2014a) revealed that human cognitive differences (i.e., cognitive styles and abilities) could be leveraged for adapting and personalizing security-related tasks such as user authentication mechanisms for improving the task completion performance and effectiveness of such tasks.

4.3 Adaptation Technologies

Adaptation and personalization systems apply specific algorithms that decide what kind of adaptation will be applied to with respect to their content and functionality. Various adaptation technologies have been proposed in the literature during the years. Among those, the most widely applied and researched include *user customization*, *rule-based filtering*, *content-based filtering*, *collaborative filtering*, *Web mining*, *demographic-based filtering*, *agent technologies* and *cluster models*.

4.3.1   User Customization

User customization provides a mechanism that allows users to construct a custom interface representation based on their own preferences. Once the user has entered this information, a matching process is used to find items that meet the specified criteria and display them to the user. The system in this case is not considered adaptive, but rather adaptable because it is explicitly configured by the user how to adapt its content and functionality. Most of today's major service providers provide several user customization mechanisms as part of their services such as Google's (2015b) Gmail that enables users to set the desired display density of the users' emails (i.e., "comfortable" and "cosy" view for larger displays, and "compact" view for smaller displays). Gmail also provides a mechanism for configuring and rearranging email categories (through drag-and-drop functionality of visual tabs) as well as choose a predefined visual theme from which the user can select from and apply different backgrounds on the user interface of his emails. In the same line, other email providers such as Microsoft's (2015) Outlook provide various user customization mechanisms for adapting the display of the online email management system.

4.3.2   Rule-Based Filtering

Rule-based mechanisms refer to the process of producing high-level information from a set of low-level metrics, related to both static and dynamic user context information. Bearing in mind that the dynamic part of the context data model can be updated in real time it becomes obvious that the reasoning capabilities supported provide an added value assisting users in different tasks. Such rules can initiate automated system actions or compare predictive user interaction models with actual user interaction data gathered in real time, providing thus valuable insights related to the current user goals and efficiency of interactions. For example, an online banking system may contain a rule "([USER].*logged=false* and [USER].*loginattempts. count>2*) then [UIOBJECT.*livesupport.show=true*]", which indicates that the system should automatically offer a live customer support option to users who could not succeed to login in the system for several times. Based on another usage scenario such a rule-based mechanism could extremely increase usable security by offering a live customer support option to users whose E-Banking Web accounts are locked due to numerous unsuccessfully login attempts. A detailed analysis and comparison of rule-based mechanisms can be found in (Smyth 2007).

4.3.3 Content-Based Filtering

Content-based filtering suggests labeling of links by analyzing the content of pages. A typical content-based filtering mechanism includes the following steps: (i) Prefetch the content behind the links of the current page; (ii) parse the pre-fetched pages to create a weighted keyword vector of each page; (iii) compare the weighted keyword vector of each page with the user's preferences, that are also usually represented using a weighted keyword vector; and (iv) suggest pages whose keyword vectors are the same with the user's preferences.

This technique is primarily characterized by two weaknesses, content limitations and over-specialization. There are content limitations like information retrieval methods that can only be applied to a few kinds of content, such as text and images, and the extent aspects can only capture certain aspects of the content. On the other hand content-based recommendation systems provide recommendations merely based on user models, therefore, users have no chance of exploring new items that are not similar to those items included in their models and thus leading to over-specialization. A detailed analysis and comparison of content-based filtering mechanisms can be found in (Pazzani and Billsus 2007).

4.3.4 Collaborative Filtering

Collaborative filtering (Schafer et al. 2007) exploits the social process of people to recommend something they have experienced (e.g., read a book, watched a movie, etc.) to other people. Collaborative filtering mechanisms are based on the assumption that if users X and Y rate n items similarly, or have similar behaviors (e.g., buying, watching), hence will have similar interests. Adaptation and personalization systems utilize collaborative filtering mechanisms to provide navigation support by recommending links of interest to the user based on earlier expressed ratings or navigation behavior of similar users.

There are two general classes of collaborative filtering algorithms, *memory-based methods* and *model-based methods* (Eirinaki and Vazirgiannis 2003). Moreover, the goals in a collaborative filtering system are basically focused upon the reduction of computation time, the increase of the extent in which predictions can be computed in parallel, and the increase of prediction accuracy. Collaborative filtering can further refine the process of giving each individual personal recommendations compared to rule-based filtering. It overcomes the drawbacks of the content-based filtering because it typically does not use the actual content of the items for recommendation. It usually works based on assumptions. With this algorithm, the similarity between the users is evaluated based on their ratings of products, and the recommendation is generated considering the items visited by the nearest neighbors of the user. In its original form, the nearest-neighbor algorithm uses a two-dimensional user-item matrix to represent the user models. This original form suffers from three problems: Scalability, scarcity, and synonymy. Some more highlighted drawbacks of collaborative filtering include the following: (i) Collaborative filtering mechanisms are often based on matching in real-time the current user's model against similar records obtained by the system over time from other users. However, it becomes hard to scale collaborative filtering techniques to a large number of items, while maintaining reasonable prediction performance and accuracy. Part of this is due to the increasing scarcity in the data as the number of items increase. One potential solution to this problem is to first cluster user records with similar characteristics, and focus the search for nearest neighbors only in the matching clusters. In the context of adaptation and personalization this task involves clustering user transactions identified in the pre-processing stage; (ii) traditional collaborative filtering does little or no offline computation, and its online computation scales with the number of customers and catalogue items. The algorithm is impractical on large data sets, unless it uses dimensionality reduction, sampling, or partitioning, all of which reduce recommendation quality; (iii) user input may be subjective and prone to bias; (iv) explicit user ratings may not be available; (v) models may be static and can become outdated quickly; (vi) collaborative filtering mechanisms are not able to recommend new items that have not already been rated by other users. An object will become available for recommendation only when many users have seen it and rated it, making it part of their user models first; and (vii) collaborative filtering mechanisms are not satisfactory when dealing with a user that is not similar enough with any of the existing users.

4.3.5   Web Mining

Web mining includes data mining techniques with the aim to identify patterns from Web systems. It is divided in three main categories: (i) *Web content mining* which aims at the extraction and integration of data and knowledge from Web-page content; (ii) *Web-structure mining* which aims at the analysis of node and connection structure of a Web-site; and (iii) *Web usage mining* which aims at extracting useful information from server logs about the interaction activity of users, e.g., discover what users are looking for in a Web-page. Web usage mining is primarily related to adaptation and personalization. This process applies statistical and data mining techniques on server log data, resulting in a set of useful patterns that indicate users' navigational behavior. The data mining methods that are employed are: Association rule mining, sequential pattern discovery, clustering, and classification. Given the site map structure and usage logs, a Web usage miner provides results regarding usage patterns, user behavior, session and user clusters, click stream information, etc. Additional information about the individual users can be obtained by the user profiles (Deshpande and Karypis 2004; Eirinaki and Vazirgiannis 2003; Cingil et al. 2000). The overall process can be divided in two steps: (i) The pre-processing and data preparation step, including data cleaning, filtering, and transaction identification, resulting in a user transaction file; and (ii) the data mining step in which usage patterns are discovered via specific usage mining techniques such as association rule mining, association-rule discovery and usage clustering (Mobasher et al. 2000).

One of the main advantages of Web usage mining are summarized as follows: (i) The models are dynamically obtained from user patterns, and thus the system performance does not degrade over time as the models age; (ii) using content similarly alone as a way to obtain aggregate models may result in missing important relationships among Web objects based on their usage. Thus, Web usage mining will reduce the need for obtaining subjective user ratings or registration-based personal preferences; (iii) models are based on objective information (how users actually use the Web-site); (iv) there is no explicit user rating or interaction with users (saves time and other complications); (v) it supports preservation of user privacy, by making effective use of anonymous data; (vi) the usage data captures relationships missed by content-based approaches; and (vii) it can enhance the effectiveness of collaborative or content-based filtering techniques. Nevertheless, usage-based personalization can be problematic when little usage data is available pertaining to some objects or when the content attributes of a Web-site must be integrated into a Web mining framework and used by the recommendation engine in a uniform manner (Mobasher et al. 2002).

4.3.6 Demographic-Based Filtering

Demographic-based filtering complements other adaptation technologies such as rule-based and collaborative filtering, aiming to refine the personalization result. In particular, demographic information of users (e.g., age, gender, profession, etc.) can be utilized to infer users' interests and accordingly recommend particular objects. This method uses demographic information to identify the types of users that prefer a certain object and to identify one of the several pre-existing clusters to which a user belongs aiming to tailor recommendations based on information about others in this cluster (Pazzani 1999; Basilico and Hofmann 2004).

Early examples of demographic-based filtering approaches include LifeStyle Finder (Krulwich 1997) that aimed to generate user models based on a large-scale database of demographic data. Nevertheless, one of the challenges of demographic-based filtering approaches is that obtaining demographic information can be difficult, and when obtained, the information is usually of poor quality (Mobasher 2007). In LifeStyle Finder, the system provides a dialog to the user to help categorize the user. In an early work of Pazzani (1999), an alternative approach was proposed for obtaining demographic information by leveraging the work users already expended in creating a homepage on their Web browser. Main aim of the approach was to minimize the effort required to obtain demographic-based information.

4.3.7   Agent Technology

Agents are processes that aim at performing tasks for their users, usually with autonomy, playing the role of personal assistants (Delicato et al. 2001; Panayiotou and Samaras 2004). Agents usually solve common problems that users are experiencing on the World Wide Web such as personal history, shortcuts and Web-page watching. Some of the agents' main characteristics could be distinguished according to their abilities used and according to the tasks they execute. The former include characteristics such as intelligence, autonomy, social capacity (inter-agent communication), and mobility, while the latter classify the agents into information filtering agents, information retrieval agents, recommendation agents, agents for electronic market, and agents for network management (Delicato et al. 2001). Pioneer personalization systems implemented with agents are: ARCHIMIDES, Proteus, WBI, BASAR, 1:1 Pro, Haystack, eRACE, mPersona, Fenix system, and SmartClient (Pu and Faltings 2002; Panayiotou and Samaras 2004; Delicato et al. 2001).

4.3.8   Cluster Models

Cluster models are applied mostly in the area of E-Commerce and could be characterized as E-Commerce recommendation algorithms. To find customers who are similar to the user, cluster models divide the customer base into many segments and treat the task as a classification problem. The algorithm's goal is to assign the user to the segment containing the most similar customers. It then uses the purchases and ratings of the customers in the segment to generate recommendations. The segments are typically created using a clustering or other unsupervised learning algorithms, although some applications use manually determined segments. Using a similarity metric, a clustering algorithm groups the most similar customers together to form clusters or segments. Because optimal clustering over large data sets is impractical, most applications use various forms of greedy cluster generation. These algorithms typically start with an initial set of segments, which often contain one randomly selected customer each. Then, these repeatedly match customers to the existing segments, usually with some provision for creating new or merging existing segments. For very large data sets (especially those with high dimensionality) sampling or dimensionality reduction is also necessary. Once the algorithm generates the segments, it computes the user's similarity to vectors that summarize each segment, chooses the segment with the strongest similarity and classifies the user accordingly. Some algorithms classify users into multiple segments and describe the strength of each relationship (Perkowitz and Etzioni 1999). Cluster models have better online scalability and performance than collaborative filtering because they compare the user to a controlled number of segments rather than the entire customer base.

The complex and expensive clustering computation is run offline. However, recommendation quality is relatively poor. To improve it, it is possible to increase the number of segments, but this makes the online user segment classification expensive. Typical examples of E-Commerce systems include amazon.com (Rossi et al. 2001; Linden et al. 2003), dell.com (Eirinaki and Vazirgiannis 2003), and ibm.com (Karat et al. 2003).

4.4 Semantic Web Technologies for Adaptation and Personalization Systems

Apart from studying various user modeling and adaptation mechanisms, in order to build an adaptation and personalization system, it is also necessary to study and design the structure of meta-data (semantics) coming from the provider's side, aiming to feed the adaptation mechanism with semantically enriched, machine-understandable information in order to adapt the hypermedia content based on the users' models. A main prerequisite for the proliferation of personalized Web services is the establishment of a set of standards that will be supported by high profile providers.

In this context, ontologies are widely used to organize and give meaning to information. Ontologies formally define the types, properties and interrelationships of the main entities of an interactive system. Various ontology-based approaches have been proposed in the literature. One such system is OntoSeek (Guarino et al. 1999), which is designed for content-based information retrieval from online yellow pages and product catalogues. OntoSeek uses simple conceptual graphs to represent queries and resource descriptions. The system uses the Sensus ontology (Knight and Luk 1999), which comprises a simple taxonomic structure of about 50,000 nodes. Another similar system developed by Labrou and Finin (1999) uses Yahoo! as an ontology (Yahoo! 2015). The system semantically annotates Web-pages via the use of Yahoo! categories as descriptors of their content. The system uses Telltale

(Chowder and Nicholas 1996; Pearce and Miller 1997) as its classifier. Telltale computes the similarity between documents using *n*-grams as index terms. The ontologies used in the examples above use simple structured links between concepts.

A richer and more powerful representation is provided by SHOE (Heflin et al. 1999; Luke et al. 1997). SHOE is a set of Simple HTML Ontology Extensions that allow Web authors to annotate their pages with semantics expressed in terms of ontologies. SHOE provides the ability to define ontologies, create new ontologies which extend existing ontologies, and classify entities under an "is a" classification scheme. Although many of the aforementioned approaches may refer to their concept hierarchy as an ontology, the only relationship expressed is a parent-child relationship which generally represents an *is-a* and/or *has-a* relationship.

The Semantic Web initiative (Berners-Lee et al. 2001) is focusing on the creation of technologies and ontology languages and use of richer ontologies that can capture a wider variety of relationship types that will facilitate machines to understand the semantics, or meaning, of information on the Web. These ontologies are modeled using ontology representation languages such as SHOE (Heflin et al. 1999), Extensible Markup Language (XML – XML 2015), the Resource Description Framework (RDF: Resource Description 2015), RDF Schema (RDFS 2015), DAML + OIL (DARPA 2015), or the Web Ontology Language (OWL – OWL 2015). Guha et al. (2003) explore the use of these richer ontologies for improved search results. User models based on these richer ontologies may not be far away, however there remain serious roadblocks in the way, primarily due to scalability issues in creating large, diverse ontologies and exploiting them for searching large, distributed document collections. Furthermore, high profile service providers such as Google (2015c) also utilize Semantic Web technologies by using RDFa and Microformats embedded in XHTML (2015), with the aim to support enhanced searching in Web-pages. Google states that the extra (structured) data will be used in order to get results for product reviews (e.g., CNET Reviews), products (e.g., Amazon product pages), and people (e.g., LinkedIn profiles). In a similar semantic approach, Germanakos et al. (2009a) proposed an RDFa vocabulary based on a human factor-based ontology (Germanakos et al. 2009b) for annotating specific divisions of HTML pages of E-Commerce applications. Main aim of this approach was to assist the adaptation process by indicating to the adaptation mechanism (through semantically enriched and machine-understandable content) which visible aspects of the application should be adapted (Belk et al. 2014b).

Finally, Semantic Web technologies also contribute in the "open corpus problem" of adaptive hypermedia (Brusilovksy and Henze 2007). According to Brusilovsky and Henze (2007), *"an open corpus adaptive hypermedia system is an adaptive hypermedia system which operates on a set of documents that is not known at design time, and that can constantly change and expand"*. In contrast, in the case of closed corpus systems, the set of documents, semantics and the relationship between them is known at design time which makes it easier for a provider and author to define which aspects of the system should be adapted and how since the adaptation rules can be set explicitly and beforehand. Apparently, challenges and issues increase in open corpus systems since new information is added dynamically at run time, making it more difficult for the system to adapt and personalize the information to each user model. An approach underpinned in Brusilovsky and Henze (2007) is to utilize ontologies when adding new information to the system by automatically mapping the newly added information to concepts. This way the information will be semantically enriched with machine-understandable information, while the ontology can be used for defining additional models indicating which information should be adapted.

4.5 Leveraging the Social Web for Adaptation and Personalization

With the advent of new technologies and the rise of social networks in the early 2000s, the number of users and information shared on the World Wide Web has significantly increased, posing new possibilities and challenges. In this context, a high number of practitioners and researchers have used social networks as platforms for enhancing existing or proposing new user modeling and personalization techniques. A high number of research works have focused on investigating the effects of personality traits on human behavior in social networks (Amichai-Hamburger and Vinitzky 2010; Caci et al. 2014; Golbeck et al. 2011) or for implicitly eliciting personality traits based on social interaction data (Wald et al. 2012; Ortigosa et al. 2014). Wald et al. (2012) utilized data mining and machine learning techniques to predict users' personality traits based on the Big Five personality model, using demographic and text-based attributes extracted from the users' Facebook profiles. Ortigosa et al. (2014) proposed an automated approach for predicting users' personality traits based on Facebook usage. In particular, the authors have developed a Facebook application which has been used in a large scale study ($N = 20,000$) to collect information about the personality traits of users and their interactions within Facebook. The authors have then trained automatic classifiers using different machine learning techniques aiming to identify interaction patterns (e.g., number of friends, number of wall posts) that relate to (and eventually predict) users' personality traits.

Others have leveraged users' social interaction data to infer users' interests and preferences and accordingly improve recommendations in information retrieval systems (Tyler and Zhang 2008), while others have examined how social interaction data may be used to enrich adaptive educational hypermedia systems (Somyürek 2015 – for a review on recent adaptive educational hypermedia trends). In the latter context, Cristea and Ghali (2011) leveraged social Web technologies in an E-Learning adaptive hypermedia system, e.g., tags, ratings, comments, for providing more personalized and refined recommendations to learners. Research works have also attempted to combine semantic Web technologies and social Web technologies (Jovanović et al. 2009). For example, social Web technologies facilitate the construction process of ontologies through the content tagging of users. In this context, folksonomies and social Web technologies can be utilized to generate open corpus and inter-operable systems (Somyürek 2015).

4.6   Adaptation Effects in User Interfaces

User-centred design approaches are essential in designing complex interactive systems which iteratively involve the user in the whole design and development process. In this respect, aiming to achieve a common understanding between users and interaction designers, a necessary step involves the formalization of the information architecture and the specification of the interaction flow of specific tasks. This requires modeling and analysis of the user actions at an abstract level and identifying the most appropriate content, visual presentation and interaction flow, as depicted in Fig. 4.1.

A key challenge in adaptation and personalization systems is which visible features of the system can be adapted by a particular technique. Based on (Brusilovsky 1996, 2001), there is a number of ways to adapt hypermedia. These are classified under two main classes of adaptation technologies; content-level adaptation, called *adaptive content presentation* and link-level adaptation, called *adaptive navigation support*. Adaptive presentation relates to the adaptation of hypermedia elements inside nodes, and adaptive navigation support relates to the adaptation of links inside nodes, indexes and maps. These are discussed below.

4.6.1   Adaptive Content Presentation

Adaptive content presentation relates to the adaptation of hypermedia elements inside nodes. The idea behind adaptive content presentation is to adapt the information elements (or content) inside a node accessed by a particular user to the needs and preferences of that user. Adapting the presentation of content within a node is most often performed as a manipulation of fragments. Such manipulations aim to provide prerequisite, additional or comparative explanations. For example,

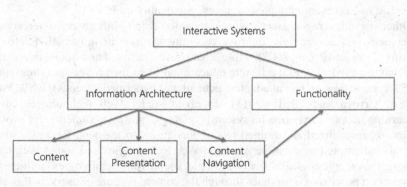

Fig. 4.1 High-level architecture of interactive systems

additional information can be shown for users with a specific state of knowledge to provide missing prerequisite knowledge, additional details, or a comparison with a previously known concept. Techniques that are used to provide adaptive presentation include: (i) Inserting/removing relevant to the user fragments; (ii) expanding/ collapsing content fragments (e.g., expand additional explanations to novice users); (iii) altering content fragments (e.g., present a diagrammatical representation of a concept to an Imager cognitive style user (Germanakos et al. 2009a)); and (iv) sorting content fragments (e.g., some users may prefer to see an example before a definition, while others prefer it the other way around).

In the work of Germanakos et al. (2009a), users with different cognitive typologies (i.e., Verbal, Imager, Intermediate) were provided with different content fragment variations, i.e., users belonging to the Verbal class (that process textual content more efficiently) were presented with more textual content, whereas users belonging to the Imager class (that process graphical content more efficiently) were presented with more graphical content. Furthermore, this study provided adaptive navigation support (described next) based on other cognitive factors (i.e., Wholist-Analyst) that affect navigation behavior of users in interactive systems.

4.6.2 Adaptive Navigation Support

Adaptive navigation support relates to the adaptation of links inside nodes. This kind of adaptation supports user navigation in an interactive system, by adapting to the goals, preferences and knowledge of the individual user. The core idea behind this kind of adaptation is to adapt the presentation of hyperlinks/functionality within a node. Adaptive navigation support can be achieved by: (i) Guiding the user in the system by suggesting a node to visit according to the user's goals, preferences and knowledge. Direct guidance is popular in adaptive educational hypermedia systems where students get suggested nodes based on their level of knowledge on the specific subject (e.g., ELM-ART – Weber and Brusilovsky (2001)); (ii) prioritizing links that are relevant to the user. Link ordering is primarily applied in interactive systems that contain non-contextual hyperlinks such as, adaptive news systems and commercial Web shops. For example, adaptive news systems typically recommend a prioritized list of news articles based on the modeled user's interests and preferences. Similarly, E-Commerce systems recommend a prioritized list of products based on the modeled user's interests and product ratings. Link ordering is typically performed by content-based filtering mechanisms; (iii) hiding, removing or disabling links to restrict navigation space to irrelevant nodes. Link hiding has been very popular in the area of adaptive educational hypermedia systems that aim to protect the users from the complexity of the whole hyperspace and reduce their cognitive overload by hiding irrelevant to them nodes. For example, if the user has novice level of knowledge on a particular concept, the system restricts the user from navigating to it; (iv) augmenting links with additional information about the node behind the link, with some form of annotation. Link annotations are provided with different visual signs, for example different icons, different color and intensity of anchors, or different font sizes. Furthermore, Web technologies such as HTML5 and CSS3 enable adaptive Web systems to annotate hyperlinks with verbal annotations on hyperlink mouse-overs, for example display information on the Web browser's status bar or as a "tooltip" over the hyperlink when the user moves the mouse pointer over the hyperlink; and (v) dynamically generating new, non-authored links based on the user's interests and/or current context (i.e., location) in the system. Link generation is popular in the field of adaptive navigation support systems and Web recommender systems for the dynamic generation of links that are useful within the current context of the user. Web recommender systems attempt to recommend a prioritized list of relevant to the user items, typically based on the user's interests. In this respect, Web recommender systems focus in the underlying technology. On the other hand, adaptive navigation support systems focus on helping users to find their way through hyperspace by adapting links on a page. Link adaptation in adaptive navigation support systems take into account various features of the user, including user's interests, goals, knowledge, and current context (i.e., location in hyperspace). In all cases, navigation support techniques provide guidance that takes into account the user's current location in hyperspace (Brusilovsky 2007). Thus, adaptive navigation support systems focus on the interface.

Accordingly, although the difference between adaptive navigation support systems and Web recommender systems is not clear, an important difference between these two groups is that adaptive navigation support systems primarily focus on the user's current location in hyperspace and aim to guide the user by introducing additional hyperlinks that may be useful in the current context, while Web recommender systems primarily focus to recommend hyperlinks that are related with the user's short- and long-term interests.

4.7 Web Adaptation and Personalization Systems and Frameworks

Given the multidimensional character of user modeling, adaptation and personalization, building a complete adaptive interactive system that will follow an end-to-end process is a challenging endeavor. Thus, the literature reveals a high number of research works that focus and investigate targeted challenges and issues rather than complete personalization systems. For example, incorporating human factors in the design of personalized user authentication mechanisms requires first to investigate whether and which ones affect user interactions in authentication-related tasks. Then, once identified, the observable main effects can be further used to develop adaptation rules and alternatives for personalizing user authentication tasks. Apparently, such an approach requires extensive research efforts by first understanding the users and their behavior in a specific context of use, and accordingly further developing and iteratively evaluating and refining a solution. In this context, this section overviews a representative number of Web adaptation and personalization systems and frameworks that have been designed and developed during the last 20 years.

4.7.1   PAC

PAC (Personalized Authentication and CAPTCHA – Belk et al. 2015) is an extensible personalization framework that adapts and personalizes specific design factors of user authentication and CAPTCHA mechanisms based on a set of human cognitive factors. In particular, the personalization framework follows a two-phase method for adapting and personalizing the user authentication and CAPTCHA task as follows: (i) Adapt the type of the security mechanism (textual or graphical) based on users' cognitive styles (i.e., Verbal/Imager and Wholist/Analyst); and (ii) adapt the complexity level of the security mechanism (number of characters/images) based on users' cognitive processing abilities (i.e., limited/enhanced).

4.7.2   PersonaWeb

PersonaWeb (Germanakos et al. 2015) is an extended and technically enhanced version of Smartag (described next – Belk et al. (2012)) that similarly focuses on adapting and personalizing content and functionality of E-Commerce environments based on human cognitive factors. In the frame of the PersonaWeb system, new adaptation effects have been proposed for adapting the visual and interaction design of E-Commerce product views. An additional sub-system, called PersonaCheck (Constantinides et al. 2015) has been included that is responsible to recommend the "best-fit" checkout process design based on the way individuals process and mentally organize information (holistically or analytically). PersonaWeb further supports the external validity of Smartag since experimental studies have shown that users' task completion efficiency and effectiveness improves when E-Commerce product views and checkout designs are adapted to the users' cognitive characteristics, in contrast to the original, baseline design (Belk et al. 2012).

4.7.3   Hybreed

Hybreed (Hussein et al. 2014) is a software framework for developing complex and hybrid, context-aware recommender systems. Hybreed enables application developers to exploit physical factors based on sensors and user model factors and user interactions, aiming to rapidly develop context-aware applications for generating recommendations for users or user groups. It allows developers to combine and integrate components for defining hybrid recommendation workflows. With Hybreed, developers are not required to specify in advance various user situations for context-adaptation.

4.7.4   Adaptive Notifications in Virtual Communities

In the work of Kleanthous-Loizou and Dimitrova (2013) a framework has been proposed for supporting knowledge sharing in virtual communities through adaptive notifications. It employs a novel computational approach for community-tailored support underpinned by the area of organizational psychology, aiming to facilitate the functioning of the community as a whole entity. The framework makes use of a community model that represents the community based on key processes (i.e., transactive memory, shared mental models and cognitive centrality) aiming to derive knowledge sharing patterns from community log data that are used to generate adaptive notifications.

4.7.5   Smartag

Smartag (Belk et al. 2012) is an adaptation and personalization system that personalizes the visual and interaction design aspects of E-Commerce product views based on individual differences in cognitive processing. The Smartag system consists of three main components: (i) The user modeling component in which explicit and implicit user data collection methods are performed for eliciting the users' cognitive processing factors; (ii) the content management component for creating and managing structured Web content; and (iii) the adaptive user interface that is responsible for performing rule-based mechanisms for deciding and communicating a personalized visual and interaction design according to the users' cognitive characteristics.

4.7.6   PRESYDIUM

PRESYDIUM (Personalized Emergency System for Disabled Humans – Chittaro et al. 2011) is a Web-based adaptive medical information system that provides personalized instructions to nurses and volunteers to better assist persons with disabilities. PRESYDIUM makes use of a user model (called Disabled Person Profile) which maintains the disabilities of an individual. It provides tools and services to nurses and physicians for managing these user models and accordingly communicates tailored instructions dealing with emergencies involving the corresponding disabled persons in the respective user model. Furthermore, disabled persons and their relatives can also access the system through a traditional Web-based and mobile-based user interface for retrieving personalized information about the patients but as well provide useful data to the system.

4.7.7 PERSONAF

PERSONAF (Personalised Pervasive Scrutable Ontological Framework – Niu and Kay 2010) is an abstract framework for pervasive ontological reasoning aiming to address several personalization challenges in the context of pervasive computing such as supporting the ontological reasoning about location, personalization of information about location, and personalization to each user's conceptions of a building. PERSONAF also addresses more practical issues such as the inexpensive creation of ontologies for new buildings as well as usability issues so that users can easily understand and control pervasive applications.

4.7.8 CTRL

CTRL (Collaborative Tutoring Research Lab – Walker et al. 2009) is a framework for providing adaptive collaborative learning support, enabling researchers to combine different types of adaptive support utilizing domain-specific models as input to domain-general components. CTRL also helps researchers to implement conditions for comparison by making it easier to vary single aspects of the adaptive intervention by removing tool or tutor components from a system.

4.7.9 EKPAIDEION

EKPAIDEION (Tsianos et al. 2008) is an adaptive educational hypermedia system that adapts and personalizes the content presentation and navigation support within computer-based educational environments. The system utilizes a human factor based user model that incorporates a combination of human cognitive factors based on a novel, unified theoretical model. The theoretical model entails a set of elementary cognitive processes (visual attention, speed and control of processing, working memory), cognitive styles and emotional factors (anxiety, emotional regulation) and accordingly adapts and personalizes the content presentation, learners' support, navigation menus as well as provides adaptive navigational support during user interactions in E-Learning environments.

4.7.10   AdaptiveWeb

The AdaptiveWeb system (Germanakos et al. 2007b) was one of the early systems of the authors that aimed to personalize content and functionality of interactive systems based on intrinsic human factors. In particular, AdaptiveWeb is a Web-based adaptation and personalization system that is based on a comprehensive user model, incorporating "traditional" user characteristics (i.e., name, age, education, experience, profession, etc.) and intrinsic human factors such as the users' perceptual preference characteristics (visual, cognitive and emotional processing parameters). According to the user model, the system provides adaptive content presentation and adaptive navigation support in the context of an E-Learning environment aiming to assist users during information processing, comprehension and assimilation.

4.7.11   Knowledge Sea II

Knowledge Sea II (Brusilovsky et al. 2006) is a personalized information access system aiming to assist users to effectively organize and maintain Web-based educational resources. It is an extension of Knowledge Sea project that was designed as a mixed corpus C programming resource aiming to bridge the gap between closed corpus materials in the form of lecture notes and open-corpus materials in the form of the set of the links to online resources for C programming. Knowledge Sea II helps users navigate from lectures to relevant online tutorials in a map-based horizontal navigation format. Knowledge Sea II contains a map with hyperlinks pointing to online material and facilitates the navigation by providing traffic and annotation-based social navigation support.

4.7.12   CUMAPH

CUMAPH (Cognitive User Modeling for Adaptive Presentation of Hyper-Documents – Tarpin-Bernard and Habieb-Mammar 2005) is an environment in which the hyper-document presentation is adapted and personalized by selecting the elements that best match the users' cognitive processing characteristics. CUMAPH consists of the following four components: (i) A cognitive-based user model generator for eliciting the users' cognitive characteristics based on a series of psychometric tests; (ii) an authoring tool for building and generating XML-based hyper-documents; (iii) a style sheet generator for building a set of generic style sheets; and (iv) an adaptation engine for building an adapted version of the XML-based hyper-document and the set of available style sheets.

4.7.13 mPERSONA

mPERSONA (Panayiotou and Samaras 2004) is a flexible personalization system for the wireless user that takes into consideration user mobility, the local environment and the user and device model. The system utilizes the various characteristics of mobile agents to support flexibility, scalability, modularity and user mobility. It avoids tying up to specific wireless protocols by using, as much as possible, autonomous and independent components. To achieve a high degree of independence and autonomy mPERSONA is based on mobile agents and mobile computing models such as the "client intercept model".

4.7.14 INSPIRE

INSPIRE (Papanikolaou et al. 2003) is an adaptive educational hypermedia system, which emphasizes the fact that learners perceive and process information in different ways, and integrates ideas from theories of instructional design and learning styles. Its aim is to make a shift towards a more "learning-focused" paradigm of instruction by providing a sequence of authentic and meaningful tasks that matches learners' preferred way of studying. INSPIRE, throughout its interaction with the learner, dynamically generates learner-tailored lessons that gradually lead to the accomplishment of learner's learning goals. It supports several levels of adaptation: From full system-control to full learner-control, and offers learners the option to decide on the level of adaptation of the system by intervening in different stages of the lesson generation process and formulating the lesson contents and presentation. Both the adaptive and adaptable behavior of INSPIRE are guided by the learner model which provides information about the learner, such as knowledge level on the domain concepts and learning style. The learner model is exploited in multiple ways: curriculum sequencing, adaptive navigation support, adaptive content presentation, and supports system's adaptable behavior.

4.7.15 SQL-Tutor

SQL-Tutor (Mitrovic and Martin 2002) is a knowledge-based teaching system which supports students learning SQL. The intention was to provide an easy-to-use system that will adapt to the needs and learning abilities of individual students. The tailoring of instruction is done in two ways: by adapting the level of complexity of problems and by generating informative feedback messages.

4.7.16   Proteus

Proteus (Anderson et al. 2001) is a system that constructs user models using artificial intelligence techniques and adapts the content of a Web-site taking into consideration also characteristics of the wireless connection. The Proteus Web-site *personalizer* performs a search through the space of possible Web-sites. The initial state is the original Web-site of non-adapted pages. The state is transformed by any of a number of adaptation functions, which can create pages, remove pages, add links between pages, etc. The value of the current state (i.e., the value of the Web-site) is measured as the expected utility of the Web-site for the current visitor. The search continues either until no better state can be found, or until computational resources (e.g., time) expire.

4.7.17   WBI

Web Browser Intelligence (WBI, pronounced "WEB-ee" – Maglio and Barret 2000) is a developed system that provides a loosely confederated group of agents on a user's workstation capable of observing user actions, proactively offering assistance, modifying resulting Web documents, and performing new functions. For example, WBI will annotate hyperlinks with network speed information, record pages viewed for later access, and provide shortcut links for common paths. WBI is an architecture in which small programs, or agents, connect to the information stream by registering their trigger conditions and then performing operations on the stream. This structure provides rich opportunities for personalizing the Web experience by joining together personal and global information, as well as enabling collaboration among users.

4.7.18   ARCHIMIDES

ARCHIMIDES (Bogonicolos et al. 1999) personalizes the search results of users according to their interests. The system was based on agent technologies aiming to provide adaptive and personalized navigation to users within Web-based environments. Given a set of keywords that characterize the content on a Web server, ARCHIMIDES retrieves information intelligently and then constructs a personalized version in the form of an index pointing to pages that present some interest to the user.

4.7.19   TANGOW

TANGOW (Carro et al. 1999) is a tool for developing Internet-based courses, accessible through any standard Web browser. Courses are structured by means of teaching tasks and rules which are stored in a database and are the basis of TANGOW guidance ability. In TANGOW a student process is launched for each student connected to the system. Each student process consists of two main modules: A task manager that guides the students in their learning process, and a page generator that generates the HTML pages presented to the student. The student process also maintains information about the actions performed by the student when interacting with the course in the dynamic workspace. This information is used by TANGOW to adapt the course contents to the student's learning progress. TANGOW has also information about student models, which is used to select, at run-time, the contents of each HTML page presented.

4.7.20   AHA!

AHA (De Bra and Calvi 1998) is an open Adaptive Hypermedia Architecture that is suitable for many different applications. This system maintains the user model and filters content pages and link structures accordingly. The engine offers adaptive content through conditional inclusion of fragments. Its adaptive linking can be configured to be either link annotation or link hiding. Link disabling is also achieved through a combination of content and link adaptation.

4.7.21   SKILL

SKILL (Neumann and Zirvas 1998) is a scalable Internet-based teaching and learning system. The primary objective of SKILL is to cope with the different knowledge levels and learning preferences of the students, providing them with a collaborative and adaptive learning environment utilizing new Web technologies. Basic components of SKILL are course material based on concepts organized in an ordinal rating derived from pre-requirements, an annotation facility suited for collaboration work, and a configuration environment for tailoring the system. Topics discussed include: (i) SKILL functionality, including adaptivity/progress control and collaboration through annotations and course extensions; (ii) components, including security, document management, and tutoring components; (iii) implementation issues; and (iv) related work.

4.7.22　ELM-ART II

ELM-ART II (Weber and Specht 1997) is an intelligent interactive textbook to support learning programming in LISP. ELM-ART II demonstrates how interactivity and adaptivity can be implemented in Web-based tutoring systems. The knowledge-based component of the system uses a combination of an overlay model and an episodic user model. It also supports adaptive navigation as individualized diagnosis and helps on problem solving tasks. Adaptive navigation support is achieved by annotating links. Additionally, the system selects the next best step in the curriculum on demand. Results of an empirical study show different effects of these techniques on different types of users during the first lessons of the programming course.

4.7.23　BASAR

BASAR (Building Agents Supporting Adaptive Retrieval – Thomas and Fischer 1997) provides users with assistance when managing their personal information spaces. This assistance is user-specific and is achieved through software agents (called Web assistants) and active views. Users delegate tasks to Web assistants that perform actions on their views of the World Wide Web and on the history of all user actions.

4.7.24　InterBook

InterBook (Brusilovsky et al. 1996, 1998a) is a tool for authoring and delivering adaptive electronic textbooks on the World Wide Web. InterBook provides a technology for developing electronic textbooks from a plain text to a specially annotated HTML. InterBook also provides an HTTP server for adaptive delivery of these electronic textbooks over the World Wide Web. For each registered user, an InterBook server maintains an individual model of user's knowledge and applies this model to provide adaptive guidance, adaptive navigation support, and adaptive help.

4.8　Summary

In this chapter we overviewed the main personalization categories and respective adaptation technologies used for adapting and personalizing content and functionality of interactive systems to the individual user. We also described the main adaptation effects that are communicated to the user interface as a result of the respective mapping rules and adaptation technologies. At the end of this chapter we presented a selected state-of-the-art of adaptation and personalization systems and frameworks.

Traditionally, the aforementioned methods and techniques have been extensively considered from the two overarching research areas of adaptive hypermedia and Web personalization. It is quite clear that these two areas share a number of differences but at the same time many similarities, with the most evident one the fact that they share the same objective. Over time, both research directions have been using interchangeably adaptation technologies and effects for personalizing what is presented to the users, based on their specific needs and preferences. However, one could argue that the application fields are predominantly different, as adaptive hypermedia has found popular use in educational hypermedia and on-line information systems, whereas Web personalization in information retrieval systems (e.g., search engines) in the E-Business/E-Commerce sector (with respect to products and services delivery). In this context, it could be inferred that Web personalization has a more extended scope than adaptive hypermedia and is a relatively new area of research. It explores adaptive content selection and adaptive recommendation based on modeling user interests and interaction behaviors. In fact, the most evident similarity is that they both make use of a user model to achieve their goal. However, the way they maintain the user model is different; adaptive hypermedia requires a regular interaction with the user, while Web personalization employs algorithms that continuously follow the user's navigational behavior without necessarily requesting explicitly an interaction with him. Generally, adaptive hypermedia refers to the manipulation of the link or content structure of an application to achieve adaptation and makes use at a larger extent explicit user modeling, whereas Web personalization refers to the whole process of collecting, classifying and analyzing Web data, and determining based on those the actions that should be performed so that the user is presented with personalized information. Technically, two of the adaptation/personalization techniques they are using are the same: The adaptive navigation support (of Adaptive Hypermedia and else referred to as link-level adaptation) and Link Personalization (of Web Personalization); and adaptive presentation (of Adaptive Hypermedia and else referred to as content-level adaptation) and Content Personalization (of Web Personalization). Last but not least, it is noteworthy to mention that both research fields make use of artificial intelligence techniques.

Nevertheless, although adaptive hypermedia and Web personalization might have been usually applied in different application domains, adapting content and functionality of interactive systems based on different contextual requirements and constraints (and in cases utilizing different technologies), systems in both areas share a common high-level goal; to accurately model the pertinent users' characteristics and accordingly adapt their behavior to meet the unique expectations of users and offer a seamless positive and personalized user experience.

References

Alotaiby FT, Chen JX (2004) A model for team-based access control (TMAC 2004). In: Proceedings of the international conference on information technology: coding and computing (ITCC 2004), pp 450–454

Amazon (2015) Amazon on-line shopping. Available online at http://www.amazon.com. Accessed April 2015

Amichai-Hamburger Y, Vinitzky G (2010) Social network use and personality. Comput Hum Behav 26(6):1289–1295

Anderson C, Domingos P, Weld D (2001) Personalizing web sites for mobile users. In: Proceedings of the 10th international conference on world wide web (WWW '01). ACM, New York, pp 565–575

Apple (2015) Apple iOS 8. Available online at http://www.apple.com/ios/. Accessed August 2015

Basilico J, Hofmann T (2004) Unifying collaborative and content-based filtering. In: Proceedings of the 21st international conference on machine learning, Banff, Canada

Belk M, Germanakos P, Papatheocharous E, Constantinides M, Samaras G (2012) Supporting adaptive interactive systems with semantic markups and human factors. In: Proceedings of the international workshop on semantic and social media adaptation and personalization, pp 126–130

Belk M, Germanakos P, Fidas C, Samaras G (2014a) A personalisation method based on human factors for improving usability of user authentication tasks. In: Proceedings of the 22nd international conference on user modeling, adaptation, and personalization, Springer, Cham, pp 13–24

Belk M, Germanakos P, Papatheocharous E, Andreou P, Samaras G (2014b) Integrating human factors and semantic markups in adaptive interactive systems. Open J Web Technol (OJWT), RonPub UG, 1(1):15–26. ISSN: 2199-188X

Belk M, Germanakos P, Fidas C, Andreou P, Samaras G (2015) The PAC framework: personalized authentication and CAPTCHA mechanisms based on human cognitive factors. Technical report, Department of Computer Science, University of Cyprus, TR-2015-2

Bellotti V, Begole B, Chi E, Ducheneaut N, Fang J, Isaacs E, King T, Newman M, Partridge K, Price B, Rasmussen P, Roberts M, Schiano D, Walendowski A (2008) Activity-based serendipitous recommendations with the magitti mobile leisure guide. In: Proceedings of the ACM conference on human factors in computing systems, pp 1157–1166

Berners-Lee T, Hendler J, Lassila O (2001) The semantic web. Sci Am 284(5):34–43

Bing (2015) Bing search engine. Available online at http://www.bing.com. Accessed April 2015

Bogonicolos N, Fragoudis D, Likothanassis S (1999) ARCHIMIDES: an intelligent agent for adaptive personalized navigation within a web server. In: Proceedings of the 32nd annual Hawaii international conference on system science

Brusilovsky P (1996) Methods and techniques of adaptive hypermedia. User Model User-Adap Inter 6(2–3):87–129

Brusilovsky P (2001) Adaptive hypermedia. User Model User-Adap Inter 11(1–2):87–110

Brusilovsky P (2003) From adaptive hypermedia to the adaptive web. In: Szwillus G, Ziegler J (eds) Mensch & computer 2003: Interaktion in Bewegung, pp 21–24

Brusilovsky P (2007) Adaptive navigation support. In: Brusilovsky P, Kobsa A, Nejdl W (eds) The adaptive web, vol 4321, Lecture notes in computer science. Springer, Berlin/Heidelberg, pp 263–290

Brusilovsky P, Henze N (2007) Open corpus adaptive educational hypermedia. In: Brusilovsky P, Kobsa A, Nejdl W (eds) The adaptive web, LNCS, vol 4321. Springer, Berlin/Heidelberg, pp 671–696

Brusilovsky P, Maybury MT (2002) From adaptive hypermedia to the adaptive web. Commun ACM 45(5):30–33

Brusilovsky P, Schwarz E, Weber G (1996) A tool for developing hypermedia-based ITS on WWW. In: Proceedings of workshop architectures and methods for designing cost-effective and reusable ITSs. In conjunction with the international conference on Intelligent Tutoring Systems (ITS 1996)

Brusilovsky P, Eklund J, Schwarz E (1998a) Web-based education for all: a tool for developing adaptive courseware. Computer Networks and ISDN Systems. In: Proceedings of the 7th international www conference, 14–18 April, 30(1–7), pp 291–300

Brusilovsky P, Kobsa A, Vassileva J (1998b) Adaptive hypertext and hypermedia. Springer, Netherlands, ISBN 978-0-7923-4843-6

Brusilovsky P, Farzan R, Ahn J (2006) Layered evaluation of adaptive search. In: Proceedings of the workshop on evaluating exploratory search systems. At SIGIR 2006

Caci B, Cardaci M, Tabacchi ME, Scrima F (2014) Personality variables as predictors of Facebook usage. Psychol Rep 114(2):528–539

Carro RM, Pulido E, Rodríguez P (1999) TANGOW: task-based adaptive learner guidance on the WWW. Computer Science Report, Eindhoven University of Technology, pp 49–57

Cheng L, Liang H, Wu C, Chen M (2013) iGrasp: grasp-based adaptive keyboard for mobile devices. In: Proceedings of the international conference on human factors in computing systems, pp 3037–3046

Chittaro L, Carchietti E, De Marco L, Zampa A (2011) Personalized emergency medical assistance for disabled people. User Model User-Adap Interact 21(4–5):407–440

Chowder G, Nicholas C (1996) Resource selection in café: an architecture for networked information retrieval. In: Proceedings of workshop on networked information retrieval, pp 1343–1355

Cingil I, Dogac A, Azgin A (2000) A broader approach to personalization. Commun ACM 43(8):136–141

Constantinides A, Belk M, Germanakos P, Samaras G (2015) The PersonaCheck system for personalizing M-commerce checkout processes. Demonstration in the proceedings of the 16th IEEE international conference on Mobile Data Management (MDM 2015), IEEE Computer Society .

Cristea AI, Ghali F (2011) Towards adaptation in e-learning 2.0. New Rev Hypermedia Multimedia 17(2):199–238

DARPA (2015) The DARPA agent markup language. Available online at http://www.daml.org. Accessed April 2015

De Bra P, Calvi L (1998) AHA! An open adaptive hypermedia architecture. The new review of hypermedia and multimedia, 4. Taylor Graham Publishers, London, pp 115–139

Delicato F, Pirmez L, Carmo L (2001) Fenix – personalized information filtering system for WWW pages. Internet Res Electron Netw Appl Policy 11(1):42–48

Deshpande M, Karypis G (2004) Selective Markov models for predicting web page accesses. ACM Transact Internet Technol 4(2):163–184

Eirinaki M, Vazirgiannis M (2003) Web mining for web personalization. ACM Transact Internet Technol 3(1):1–27

Fidas C, Voyiatzis A, Avouris N (2011) On the necessity of user-friendly CAPTCHA. In: Proceedings of human factors in computing systems (CHI'11), pp 2623–2626

Georgiadis C, Mavridis I, Pangalos G, Thomas R (2001) Flexible team-based access control using contexts. In: Proceedings of the ACM symposium on access control models and technologies, pp 21–27

Germanakos P, Mourlas C, Isaia C, Samaras G (2005) An optimized review of adaptive hypermedia and web personalization – sharing the same objective. In: Proceedings of the 1st international workshop on web personalization, recommender systems and intelligent user interfaces (WPRSIUI 2005) of the 2nd international conference on E-business and TElecommunications networks (ICETE2005), pp 43–48

Germanakos P, Tsianos N, Lekkas Z, Mourlas C, Samaras G (2007a) Capturing essential intrinsic user behaviour values for the design of comprehensive web-based personalized environments. Comput Hum Behav J, Spec Issue Integration Hum Factors Netw Comput. doi:10.1016/j.chb.2007.07.010

Germanakos P, Tsianos N, Lekkas Z, Mourlas C, Belk M, Samaras G (2007b) An AdaptiveWeb system for integrating human factors in personalization of web content. Demonstration in the proceedings of the 11th international conference on User Modeling (UM 2007), Corfu, Greece, 25–29 Jun 2007

Germanakos P, Tsianos N, Lekkas Z, Mourlas C, Samaras G (2008) Realizing comprehensive user profile as the core element of adaptive and personalized communication environments and systems. The Comput J 52(7):749–770

Germanakos P, Tsianos N, Lekkas Z, Belk M, Mourlas C, Samaras G (2009a) Proposing web design enhancements based on specific cognitive factors: an empirical evaluation. In: Proceedings of the 2009 IEEE/WIC/ACM international conference on Web Intelligence (WI 2009), pp 602–605

Germanakos P, Belk M, Tsianos N, Lekkas Z, Mourlas C, Samatas G (2009b) Embracing a human factor's ontology in the e-commerce context. In: Proceedings of the 2nd annual EuroMed conference, Salerno, 26–28 Oct 2009, pp 714–725

Germanakos P, Belk M, Constantinides A, Samaras G (2015) The PersonaWeb system: personalizing E-commerce environments based on human factors. Demonstration in extended proceedings of the 23rd international conference on user modeling, adaptation, and personalization (UMAP 2015), CEUR workshop proceedings 1388

Golbeck J, Robles C, Turner K (2011) Predicting personality with social media. In Extended abstracts on human factors in computing systems (CHI 2011), ACM Press, New York, pp 253–262

Google (2015a) Google search engine. Available online at http://www.google.com. Accessed April 2015

Google (2015b) Gmail. Available online at http://www.gmail.com. Accessed May 2015

Google (2015c) About schema.org. Available online at https://developers.google.com/structured-data/schema-org. Accessed August 2015

Guarino N, Masolo C, Vetere G (1999) OntoSeek: content-based access to the web. IEEE Intell Syst 14(3):70–80

Guha R, McCool R, Miller E (2003) Semantic search. In: Proceedings of world wide web, pp 700–709

Heflin J, Hendler J, Luke S (1999) SHOE, a knowledge representation language for internet applications, Technical Report CS-TR-4078. Institute for Advanced Computer Studies: University of Maryland, College Park

Herder E, Siehndel P, Kawase R (2014) Predicting user locations and trajectories. In: Proceedings of the international conference on user modeling, adaptation, and personalization (UMAP 2014), pp 86–97

Hori M, Ono K, Abe M, Koyanagi T (2004) Generating transformational annotation for web document adaptation: tool support and empirical evaluation. J Web Semant Sci Serv Agents World Wide Web 2(1):1–18

Hussein T, Linder T, Gaulke W, Ziegler J (2014) Hybreed: a software framework for developing context-aware hybrid recommender systems. User Model User-Adap Interact 24(1–2):121–174

Jovanović J, Gašević D, Torniai C, Bateman S, Hatala M (2009) The social semantic web in intelligent learning environments: state of the art and future challenges. Interact Learn Environ 17(4):273–309

Karat MC, Brodie C, Karat J, Vergo J, Alpert SR (2003) Personalizing the user experience on ibm. com. IBM Syst J 42(4):686–701

Kleanthous-Loizou S, Dimitrova V (2013) Adaptive notifications to support knowledge sharing in close-knit virtual communities. User Model User-Adap Interact 23(2–3):287–343

Knight K, Luk S (1999) Building a large knowledge base for machine translation. In: Proceedings of the twelfth national conference on artificial intelligence 1:773–778

Konstan J, Riedl J (2012) Recommender systems: from algorithms to user experience. J User Model User-Adap Interact 22(1–2):101–123

Korfhage RR (1997) Information storage and retrieval. Wiley Computer Publishing, New York

Krulwich B (1997) Lifestyle finder: intelligent user profiling using large-scale demographic data. Artif Intell Mag 18(2):37–45

Labrou Y, Finin T (1999) Yahoo! As an ontology-using Yahoo! categories to describe documents. In: Proceedings of the 1999 ACM conference on information and knowledge management, pp 180–187

Lankhorst MM, Kranenburg SA, Peddemors AJH (2002) Enabling technology for personalizing mobile services. In: Proceedings of the 35th annual Hawaii international conference on system sciences (HICSS 2002), pp 1464–1471

Li A, Sbattella L, Tedesco R (2013) PoliSpell: an adaptive spellchecker and predictor for people with Dyslexia. In: Proceedings of the international conference on user modeling, adaptation and personalization, pp 302–309

Linden G, Smith B, York J (2003) Amazon.com recommendations: item-to-item collaborative filtering. IEEE Internet Comput 7(1):76–80

Luke S, Spector L, Rager D, Hendler J (1997) Ontology-based web agents. In: Proceedings of the first international conference on autonomous agents, pp 59–66

Maglio P, Barret R (2000) Intermediaries personalize information streams. Commun ACM 43(8):96–101

Matuszyk P, Spiliopoulou M (2014) Hoeffding-CF: neighbourhood-based recommendations on reliably similar users. In: Proceedings of the international conference in user modeling, adaptation, and personalization, pp 146–157

Microsoft (2015) Outlook free personal e-mail. Available online at. http://www.outlook.com. Accessed June 2015

Mitrovic A, Martin B (2002) Evaluating the effects of open student models on learning. In: Proceedings of the international conference on adaptive hypermedia and adaptive web-based systems, pp 296–305

Mobasher B (2007) Data mining for web personalization. In: Brusilovsky P, Kobsa A, Nejdl W (eds) The adaptive web, vol 4321, Lecture notes in computer science. Springer, Berlin/ Heidelberg, pp 90–135

Mobasher B, Cooley R, Srivastava J (2000) Automatic personalization based on web usage mining. Commun ACM 43(8):142–151

Mobasher B, Dai H, Luo T, Nakagawa M, Wiltshire J (2002) Discovery of aggregate usage profiles for web personalization. Data Min Knowl Disc 6(1):61–82

Neumann G, Zirvas J (1998) SKILL: a scalable internet-based teaching and learning system. In: Proceedings of WebNet 98 world conference of the www, internet & intranet, Orlando, Florida, 7–12 Nov 1998, pp 688–693

Niu W, Kay J (2010) PERSONAF: framework for personalised ontological reasoning in pervasive computing. User Model User-Adap Interact 20(1):1–40

Ortigosa A, Carro RM, Quiroga JI (2014) Predicting user personality by mining social interactions in Facebook. J Comp Sys Sci 80(1):57–71

OWL: Web-Ontology (WebOnt) Working Group (2015) http://www.w3.org/2001/sw/WebOnt. Accessed 12 Apr 2011

Panayiotou C, Samaras G (2004) mPERSONA: personalized portals for the wireless user: an agent approach. Mob Netw Appl 9(6):663–677

Papanikolaou KA, Grigoriadou M, Kornilakis H, Magoulas GD (2003) Personalizing the interaction in a web-based educational hypermedia system: the case of INSPIRE. User-Model User-Adap Interact 13(3):213–267

Pazzani M (1999) A framework for collaborative, content-based and demographic filtering. Artif Intell Rev 13(5–6):393–408

Pazzani M, Billsus D (2007) Content-based recommendation systems. In: Brusilovsky P, Kobsa A, Nejdl W (eds) The adaptive web, vol 4321, Lecture notes in computer science. Springer, Berlin/ Heidelberg, pp 325–341

Pearce C, Miller E (1997) The telltale dynamic hypertext environment: approaches to scalability. Intelligent hypertext: advanced techniques for the world wide web, Lecture notes in computer science, 1326:109–130

Perkowitz M, Etzioni O (1999) Towards adaptive web sites: conceptual framework and case study. Comput Netw 31(11–16):1245–1258

Peterson E, Rayner S, Armstrong S (2009) Researching the psychology of cognitive style and learning style: is there really a future? J Learn Individ Differ 19(4):518–523

Pitkow J, Schütze H, Cass T, Cooley R, Turnbull D, Edmonds A, Adar E, Breuel T (2002) Personalized search. Commun ACM 45(9):50–55

Precision Conference Solutions (2015) PCS paper management system. Available online at http://precisionconference.com. Accessed May 2015

Pu P, Faltings B (2002) Personalized navigation of heterogeneous product spaces using SmartClient. In: Proceedings of the 7th international conference on intelligent user interfaces (IUI 2002). ACM, New York, pp 212–213

RDF: Resource Description Framework (2015) http://www.w3.org/RDF. Accessed 12 Apr 2011

RDFS: Resource Description Framework Schema (2015) http://www.w3.org/TR/rdf-schema. Accessed 12 Apr 2011

Reinecke K, Bernstein A (2011) Improving performance, perceived usability, and aesthetics with culturally adaptive user interfaces. J Transact Comput Hum Interact 18(2), Article 8, 29 p

Riding R, Cheema I (1991) Cognitive styles – an overview and integration. J Educ Psychol 11(3/4):193–215

Rossi G, Schwade D, Guimaraes MR (2001) Designing personalized web applications. In: Proceedings of the 10th international conference on World Wide Web (WWW '01). ACM, New York, pp 275–284

Sandhu R (1998) Role-based access control, Advances in computers, vol 46. Academic Press, New York

Schafer JB, Frankowski D, Herlocker J, Sen S (2007) Collaborative filtering recommender systems. In: Brusilovsky P, Kobsa A, Nejdl W (eds) The adaptive web, vol 4321, Lecture notes in computer science. Springer, Berlin/Heidelberg, pp 291–324

Schneider-Hufschmidt M, Kühme T, Malinowski U (1993) Adaptive user interfaces: principles and practice, human factors in information technology. North-Holland, Amsterdam

Sleeman D, Brown JS (1982) Intelligent tutoring systems, vol 228(4698). Academic Press, London, pp 456–462

Smyth B (2007) Case-based recommendation. In: Brusilovsky P, Kobsa A, Nejdl W (eds) The adaptive web, vol 4321, Lecture notes in computer science. Springer, Berlin/Heidelberg, pp 342–376

Somyürek S (2015) The new trends in adaptive educational hypermedia systems. Int Rev Res Open Distrib Learn 16(1):221–241

Steichen B, Wu M, Toker D, Conati C, Carenini G (2014) Te,Te,Hi,Hi: eye gaze sequence analysis for informing user-adaptive information visualizations. In: Proceedings of the conference on user modeling, adaptation, and personalization (UMAP'14), Springer, Cham, vol 8538, pp 183–194

Tarpin-Bernard F, Habieb-Mammar H (2005) Modeling elementary cognitive abilities for adaptive hypermedia presentation. User Model User-Adap Interact 15(5):459–495

Teevan J, Karlson A, Amini S, Brush AJB, Krumm J (2011) Understanding the importance of location, time, and people in mobile local search behavior. In: Proceedings of the 13th international conference on human computer interaction with mobile devices and services, pp 77–80

Thomas RK (1997) Team-Based Access Control (TMAC): a primitive for applying role-based access controls in collaborative environments. In: Proceedings of the second ACM workshop on role-based access control, Fairfax

Thomas C, Fischer G (1997) Using agents to personalize the web. In: Proceedings of the ACM Intelligent User Interfaces (IUI 1997), pp 53–60

Tsianos N, Germanakos P, Lekkas Z, Mourlas C, Belk M, Christodoulou E, Spanoudis G, Samaras G (2008) Enhancing e-Learning environments with users' cognitive factors: the case of EKPAIDEION. In: Proceedings of the 7th European conference on e-Learning (ECEL 2008), pp 877–889

Tsianos T, Germanakos P, Lekkas Z, Saliarou A, Mourlas C, Samaras G (2010) A preliminary study on learners physiological measurements in educational hypermedia. In: Proceedings of the IEEE international conference on advanced learning, pp 61–63

Tyler S, Zhang Y (2008) Open domain recommendation: social networks and collaborative filtering. Advanced data mining and applications, pp 330–341

Wald R, Khoshgoftaar T, Sumner C (2012) Machine prediction of personality from Facebook profiles. In: International conference on Information Reuse & Integration (IRI), pp 109–115

Walker E, Rummel N, Koedinger K (2009) CTRL: a research framework for providing adaptive collaborative learning support. User Model User-Adap Interact 19(5):387–431

Weber G, Brusilovsky P (2001) ELM-ART: an adaptive versatile system for web-based instruction. Int J Artif Intell Educ 12(4):351–384

Weber G, Specht M (1997) User modeling and adaptive navigation support in www-based tutoring systems. In: Proceedings of user modeling '97, pp 289–300

Wen J, Dou Z, Song R (2009) Personalized web search. Encyclopedia of database systems. Springer, US

XHTML v.1.0: The extensible hypertext markup language (2015), 2nd ed. http://www.w3.org/TR/xhtml1. Accessed 12 Apr 2011

XML: eXtensible Markup Language (2015) http://www.xml.com. Accessed 12 Apr 2015

Yahoo! (2015) Yahoo! directory. Available online at http://www.yahoo.com. Accessed July 2015

Chapter 5
A Generic Human-Centred Personalization Framework: The Case of mapU

Abstract The realization of an adaptation and personalization system entails a number of challenges, from developing appropriate user modeling mechanisms based on explicit and implicit user data collection methods, to implementing adaptation procedures and effects for personalizing the content, behavior and functionality during interaction with the system. In this context, this chapter presents the design of an extensible human-centred personalization framework, namely mapU (Multi-purpose Adaptation and Personalization for the User) for personalizing the visual and interaction design of Web-based interactive systems based on intrinsic human factors. It details its main modules and components, placing special emphasis on the formalization of the user modeling and adaptation procedures. Based on the formalization, we further discuss the design and development of a Web-based adaptive interactive system that makes use of the underlying principles of the framework as well as the respective technologies used for realizing it into a working system prototype. Main objective of this chapter is to serve as a guide of how a number of interdisciplinary elements, attributes and functionalities can co-exist under a unified framework, as well as how these can be implemented into a real-life adaptive interactive system, utilizing current state-of-the-art Web technologies.

Keywords Architecture • Framework • System • Design • Development

5.1 Introduction

The idea of developing adaptation and personalization systems (also referred as adaptive interactive systems) has been mainly supported by arguments focusing on the drawbacks of the "one-size-fits-all" approach (Brusilovsky and Maybury 2002) and essentially the complexity and vagueness of the ever-expanding World Wide Web (De Bra et al. 2004). In parallel, researchers and practitioners in the field of user modeling, adaptation and personalization underline the heterogeneity of the user population, while it is often implied that "static", non-personalized systems fail to satisfy the needs and support the goals of different users (Brusilovsky 2001).

© Springer International Publishing Switzerland 2016
P. Germanakos, M. Belk, *Human-Centred Web Adaptation and Personalization*,
Human–Computer Interaction Series, DOI 10.1007/978-3-319-28050-9_5

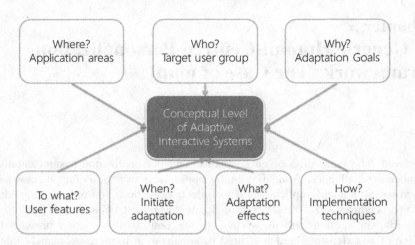

Fig. 5.1 A conceptual frame of reference framework for developing and adaptation and personalization systems

In this realm, since the early days of the World Wide Web, many research works have proposed a number of personalization strategies with the aim to alleviate "one-size-fits-all" issues in interactive systems (Goy et al. 2007; Brusilovsky and Millán 2007). Various factors for personalization have been suggested over time, among others, users' interests, preferences, needs and goals (user information), users' device screen sizes and input types (device information), and users' physical and social factors (contextual information – Goy et al. 2007; Brusilovsky and Millán 2007). In this line, several techniques for modeling such factors were introduced, either based on explicit (e.g., questionnaires) or implicit user data collection methods (e.g., according to users' navigation behavior within the system (Frias-Martinez et al. 2005), or based on collaborative filtering techniques (Linden et al. 2003; Karat et al. 2004)).

However, a rather obvious question is still in the centre of attention: Is it worth to develop extensive personalized services, considering that their technical complexity and requirements far surpass those of static systems (Tsianos et al. 2013)? During the incubation period of adaptive hypermedia, Dieterich et al. (1993) and Brusilovsky (1996) identified certain criteria in order to analyze and document the usefulness of adopting a personalized approach: (i) The area of application; (ii) the goals of the personalized approach; (iii) the target user group; (iv) the characteristics of the users to be taken into account; (v) when should the adaptation process be initiated; (vi) the aspects of the system that can be manipulated and adapted; and finally on a technical level (vii) what techniques should be used for user modeling and adaptation (Fig. 5.1). E-Learning, for instance, qualifies rather easily according to these criteria, since it is a very wide area, the learner population is much diversified (with different goals, needs, and abilities), while the educational content and the instructional methods are highly directive and controllable and can be comparably easily manipulated. However, even in this case, the high cost of designing personalized courses for popular and free to use E-Learning platforms has resulted in a poor exploitation of this kind of solutions outside the research community (Hauger and Köck 2007). Also, Paramythis and Loidl-Reisinger (2004) stress that in many cases adaptive educational hypermedia are not standard compliant. Therefore, the move towards personalized Web applications and services is not expected to be an easy one, especially without the support of high profile service providers.

But, even if this is the case, and in the end personalization is the key to more efficient interactions and a satisfactory experience, still one undeniable issue is when, to what extent and how users would actually benefit? Additional research should focus even more on measuring the added value for the end-users and their unique characteristics, instead of merely developing advanced personalization and user modeling techniques. Individuals are certainly different from each other, but which would be the underlying theories that could guide research endeavors in producing measurable gains? A first approach would be to identify the levels in which individuals demonstrate a considerable divergence, such as demographics, social, mental abilities, personality, goals, needs, and experience, and to build a cohesive user model by including characteristics that could be proven of importance in affecting behavior and performance. Probably, this could be achieved only by conducting extensive empirical work, driven by grounded psychological and sociological theories, and by gradually developing an interdisciplinary framework that would bridge technical possibilities with human factors.

To that end, considering in parallel the main functionalities of adaptive hypermedia, effective personalization of Web content involves two important challenges: (i) Accurately model and represent user information that is deemed as essential and useful for the adaptation process; and (ii) model any hypermedia content in a way that would enable efficient and effective navigation and presentation as a result of the adaptation process. In a more technical view, the challenge is to study and design structures of meta-data (i.e., semantics) at the provider level, aiming to construct a Web-based adaptation mechanism that will serve as an automatic filter adapting the distributed hypermedia content based on the user model. Semantics employ specialized approaches and techniques for alleviating difficulties and constraints imposed by the World Wide Web and contribute to the whole adaptation process with machine-understandable representation of user models and Web content.

In this context, we introduce the notion of individual differences as a core element of the abovementioned research directions, focusing mainly on users' cognitive and emotional characteristics. In particular, human-computer interactions within interactive systems are in principal tasks that embrace perception, recognition, recalling and reasoning. Taken into consideration the diversity of humans in cognitive processing styles and abilities, and the dynamicity of their emotions as seen in Chap. 2 and Sect. 3.5 (Riding and Cheema 1991; Kozhevnikov 2007; Demetriou et al. 2013), when creating adaption and personalization content and functionality of interactive systems, could provide a promising alternative to current state-of-the-art practices. The aim is to support the users' efficiency and effectiveness of processing information as well as decrease cognitive load, and eventually improve the user experience.

The basis of such an approach lies in an initial understanding of how such intrinsic human factors affect user interactions in specific domains and contexts of use and investigate the feasibility and efficacy of incorporating them in the user model and accordingly adapt the content and functionality of the system. In particular, the first steps of any similar approach is to initially design and conduct several stand-alone and targeted user studies that investigate various and different human factors, aiming to recognize and identify which individual characteristics are considered important enough and might affect users' interactions in various application domains (such as E-Learning, E-Commerce and Usable Security as will be extensively discussed in Chaps. 6, 7 and 8). Consequently, depending on the findings of each study, the next step is to interpret and translate the observed main effects into adaptation rules in order to map human factors with design factors of interactive systems. These adaptation rules are further realized and incorporated in an interactive system.

In this respect, based on the theoretical analysis on human factors in Chap. 2 and several targeted user studies that were conducted aiming to understand the impact of human factors on specific design characteristics of interactive systems, we have formalized the main effects and interactions into adaptation rules that unfold this mapping relationship. We have further incorporated those under an extensible personalization framework, namely mapU (Multi-purpose Adaptation and Personalization for the User) that is reported in this chapter. The chapter is organized as follows: We start with a high-level adaptation and personalization architecture and then we present the mapU framework and its main modules for personalizing content and functionality of interactive systems based on specific human factors. Next, following the conceptual design and formalization of the framework, we detail the design and development of a real-life Web-based adaptive interactive system with all the necessary technologies and components. Throughout this chapter we place special emphasis on the user modeling and personalization modules by presenting a formalization of a human factor-based user model (including cognitive styles, speed of processing, control of processing, working memory capacity and emotional processing characteristics), a formalization of an adaptation engine and a set of adaptation rules for personalizing specific design characteristics of interactive systems. We believe that the reader will be able to gain an understanding across the various functionalities and attributes that could work together in order to support a human-centred information flow.

5.2   A High-Level Adaptation and Personalization Architecture

Following the analysis made in Chaps. 3 and 4 that focused on existing state-of-the-art research works in user modeling, adaptation and personalization, we have designed a high-level adaptation and personalization architecture. Figure 5.2 illustrates a generic architecture of an adaptation and personalization system which is conceptually composed of two interconnected modules; the *user modeling* and the

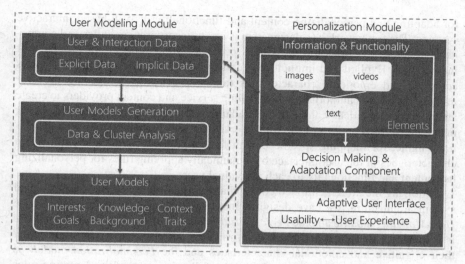

Fig. 5.2 High-level adaptation and personalization system architecture

personalization module. The user modeling module entails data about its users, their interactions and the context in which communication or computation takes place. This information can be provided to the system either explicitly by the users (e.g., through registration forms, questionnaires, psychometric tests, etc.) and/or implicitly retrieved through user's interactions with the system aiming to enrich the user model and to infer information which is considered valuable in order to provide adaptive features (e.g., track how many times the user has logged in the system to extract his level of experience in the system). In this context, various data and cluster analysis techniques are performed on the raw data acquired in order to generate the actual user models which, combined with various decision making and adaptation mechanisms in the personalization module, decide on the adaptation effects to be performed that are further communicated to the adaptive user interface.

To this end, the high-level research goals of adaptation and personalization systems involve accurately modeling the users' characteristics for building comprehensive user models for specific application domains, and effectively adapting content and functionality of interactive systems aiming to provide a personalized and positive user experience.

5.3 Conceptual Design of mapU

Following the technical and design approaches of our previous research works in the context of AdaptiveWeb (2007), EKPAIDEION (2008), Smartag (2012), PersonaWeb (2015) and PAC (2015) (see Sect. 4.7), we have designed at a conceptual level, an extensible human-centred personalization framework, namely mapU for adapting and personalizing content and functionality of Web-based interactive systems. The framework was designed in a way to incorporate modules and components that are essential for the whole personalization process. In particular it includes: (a) Explicit and implicit data collection methods, for eliciting the users cognitive and emotional characteristics (and consequently composing the user model); (b) content authoring tools, enabling service and content providers to create and manage semantically annotated and adaptive content; (c) management tools, for managing various entities of the framework (e.g., user models); and (d) an adaptation engine, for mapping specific human factors of the user models with design characteristics of the user interface by dynamically applying rules for personalizing its content and functionality to each individual user.

Following the aforementioned conceptual frame of reference and the high-level system architecture, we have designed mapU to include two main modules, the *User Modeling module* and the *Personalization module*. The *User Modeling module* is responsible to collect and process information about the users aiming to elicit their cognitive and emotional characteristics and the *Personalization module* is responsible to personalize the user's task by following particular adaptation rules for achieving the appropriate mapping with selected design characteristics. Furthermore, as part of the *Personalization module*, a content management component provides a tool for content providers to create semantically enriched Web-pages. Providers are able to annotate particular divisions of Web-pages, thus indicating which visible aspects of the user interface should be adapted. Figure 5.3 depicts the conceptual design of mapU. We next describe the formalization of the user modeling and personalization modules.

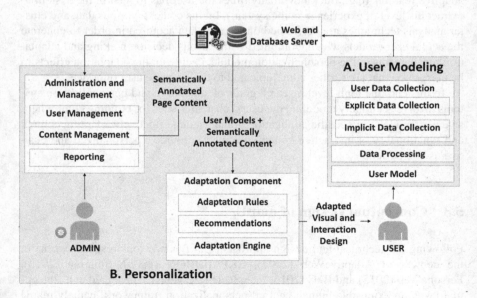

Fig. 5.3 Conceptual design of the mapU framework

5.3.1   Module 1: User Modeling

The user modeling module is responsible to generate the user models of the framework which are necessary for the adaptation behavior of an interactive system. In our case, two cognitive factors are used, *cognitive styles* and *cognitive processing abilities*, and four emotional processing factors, *general anxiety, current anxiety, application specific* and *emotion regulation*, for modeling the users' individual differences. The module supports the management and maintainability of user data collected, enabling the administration and extension of methods and factors of the user model. Explicit and implicit user data collection methods are used for eliciting the user models' characteristics. Explicit user data collection methods include accredited and standardized psychometric tests in which users are required to respond to a series of cognitive aptitude tasks. Depending on the users' responses (accuracy and speed), algorithms are applied for highlighting their cognitive processing characteristics. In particular, the users' Verbal/Imager and Wholist/Analyst cognitive styles are elicited by exploiting two tests of Riding's Cognitive Style Analysis (CSA – Riding 1991; Riding and Cheema 1991) since it is based on a strong theoretical justification and is a widely applied psychometric test for eliciting cognitive styles of users. Although it has been criticized by a number of researchers about its test-retest unreliability, we have improved the psychometric test based on suggestions made by Rezaei and Katz (2004). The users' cognitive processing abilities are elicited by exploiting two Stroop-like tests for extracting the users' speed of processing and control of processing; and two working memory capacity tests as utilized in Demetriou et al. (2013). For eliciting the emotional processing characteristics of users, specially designed questionnaires are employed. For capturing the trait (core) anxiety of users, the Spielberger's State-Trait Anxiety Inventory (STAI) is utilized (Spielberger 1983); self-reported state (current) anxiety is elicited through direct feedback from the user, maintaining a sliding bar on the user interface through of which the users can indicate explicitly how they perceive currently their anxiety levels; application-specific anxiety is elicited through Cassady's Cognitive Test Anxiety (CTA – Cassady and Jonhson 2002), and emotion regulation is extracted through a custom made (and validated) questionnaire that includes items derived from emotional intelligence (Salovey and Mayer 1990), i.e., self-regulation (Halberstadt 2005), and self-efficacy (Bandura 1994) tests.

Given that explicit user data collection methods (e.g., psychometric tests, questionnaires) may decrease the user acceptance of such a personalization approach, we also attempted initially to design several Web interaction metrics for inferring the cognitive styles of users through their interactions with specific divisions in an interactive system. In the next sections we describe both explicit and implicit user data collection methods under a unified formalization.

5.3.1.1 Cognitive Aptitude Tasks

This section describes the cognitive tasks of each psychometric test; Verbal/Imager cognitive style, Wholist/Analyst cognitive style, speed of processing, control of processing, visual working memory and verbal working memory.

Verbal/Imager Cognitive Styles' Task The Verbal/Imager CSA test indicates an individual's tendency to process information verbally or in mental pictures. An individuals' style on the Verbal-Imager dimension is obtained by presenting a series of 48 questions about conceptual category and appearance (i.e., color) to be judged by the users to be true or false. A total of 24 statements require comparing two objects conceptually (e.g., *"Are ski and cricket the same type?"*). The remaining 24 statements require comparing the color of two objects (e.g., *"Are cream and paper the same color?"*). It is assumed that Verbals respond faster than Imagers in the conceptual types of stimuli (verbal-type) because the semantic conceptual category membership is verbally abstract in nature and cannot be represented in visual form (Riding 1991). On the other hand, it is assumed that Imagers respond faster than Verbals in the appearance statements (imager-type) since the objects can be readily represented as mental pictures and the information for the comparison can be obtained directly and rapidly from these images (Riding 1991).

Wholist/Analyst Cognitive Styles' Task The Wholist/Analyst CSA test indicates an individual's tendency to process information as a whole or analytically. An individual's style on the Wholist-Analyst dimension is obtained by presenting a series of 40 questions on judging and comparing geometrical figures made up of three basic geometric shapes (i.e., square, rectangle, and triangle). Twenty of these questions include wholist-type stimuli that require the users to compare whether a pair of figures are identical or not (e.g., *"Is shape X the same as shape Y?"*). As this task involves judgments about the overall similarity of the two figures, it is assumed that Wholists will respond faster than Analysts (Riding 1991).

The remaining 20 questions include analytic-type stimuli that require the users to judge whether a single figure is part of another complex figure (e.g., *"Is shape X contained in shape Y?"* – see Fig. 5.4). This task requires the users to disembed the simple shape from within the complex geometrical figure in order to establish that it is the same as the stimulus shape displayed. It is assumed that Analysts will respond faster in this task (Riding 1991).

Speed of Processing and Control of Processing Task Two Stroop-like tasks are devised to measure reaction time to address speed of processing and control of processing. For measuring speed of processing, users are required to read a number of words denoting a color written in the same or different ink color (e.g., the word "Red" illustrated in red ink color). For measuring control of processing, similarly, a Stroop-like task is devised, but instead of denoting the written word itself, users are required to recognize the ink color of words denoting a color different than the ink (e.g., the word "Red" illustrated in green ink as illustrated in Fig. 5.5). In each test,

Fig. 5.4 Example of an analyst-type stimulus (Riding 1991). In this example, users are required to respond with true/false on whether the *left* simple figure is embedded within the *right* complex figure. It is assumed that Analyst users will solve this challenge faster than Wholists

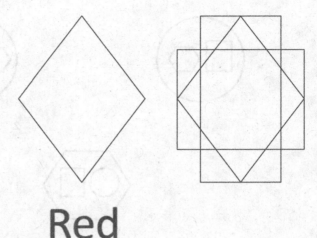

Red

Fig. 5.5 A Stroop-like task. The user is required to recognize the ink color of the word (*green*) which denotes a color different than the ink ("Red")

a total of 18 words are illustrated to the users illustrating the words "Red", "Green" or "Blue" either written in red, green or blue ink color. The users are required to press the R keyboard key for "Red", the G key for "Green" and the B key for "Blue".

Users' Visual Working Memory Capacity Task   This test illustrates a geometric figure on the screen and the user is required to memorize the figure. Thereafter, the figure disappears and five similar figures are illustrated on the screen, numbered from 1 to 5 (Fig. 5.6).

The user is required to provide the number (using the keyboard) of the corresponding figure that was the same as the initial figure. The test consists of 21 figures (seven levels of three trials each). As the user correctly identifies the figures of each trial, the test provides more complex figures as the levels increase indicating an enhanced visual working memory capacity.

Users' Verbal Working Memory Capacity Task   This test illustrates a series of statements and users are required to respond whether they are true or false. In addition, users are required to remember the last word of each sentence and then write the last word of the sentence. The test includes six levels of difficulty, e.g., in level three, users are required to respond true or false on three successive sentences and have to remember and provide the last word of each sentence. For example, for the sentences *"Knives are sharp"*, *"The sun is shining"*, and *"Fish have fur"* the user should respectively respond *true*, *true* and *false*, and then provide the word *"sharp"*, *"shining"* and *"fur"* to the system (Fig. 5.7). The level each user reaches indicates his verbal working memory capacity.

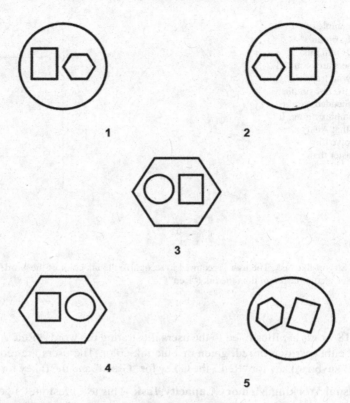

Fig. 5.6 Visual working memory task (Demetriou et al. 2013)

Level 3

Last word of first sentence	sharp	submit
Last word of second sentence	I	submit
Last word of third sentence		submit

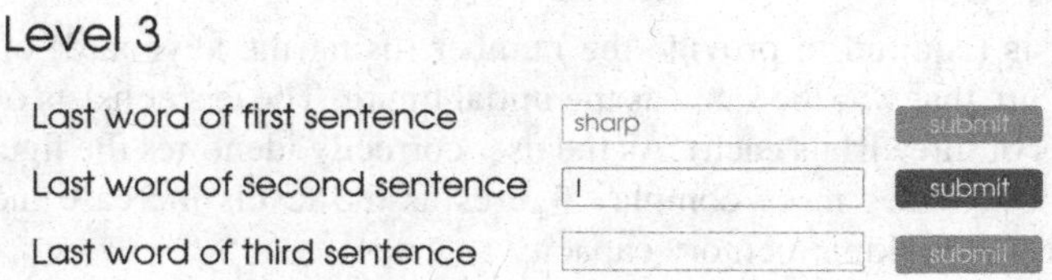

Fig. 5.7 Verbal working memory task (Demetriou et al. 2013)

5.3.1.2　Metrics for Eliciting Emotional Processing Factors

General (Core) Anxiety For eliciting the users' general anxiety we utilize the Spielberger's manual for the State-Trait Anxiety Inventory (STAI – Spielberger 1983). The STAI is an accredited and widely used anxiety inventory which is obtained through a self-report questionnaire aiming to measure the presence and severity of current symptoms of anxiety and a generalized propensity of a person to

Fig. 5.8 Self-reported
current anxiety

be anxious. The questionnaire includes 40 items that measure two sub-scales which are allocated to the State Anxiety Scale (S-Anxiety) and the Trait Anxiety Scale (T-Anxiety). The S-Anxiety measures the current state of anxiety, asking how respondents feel *"right now"* using items that measure subjective feelings of apprehension, tension, nervousness and worry. The T-Anxiety evaluates relatively stable aspects of *"anxiety proneness"* including general states of calmness, confidence, and security. Participants respond for the S-Anxiety by selecting between 4 choices reflecting their current feelings *"at this moment"*: (1) Not at all; (2) somewhat; (3) moderately so; and (4) very much so. Regarding the T-Anxiety, participants respond by selecting between 4 choices aiming to assess the frequency of feelings *"in general"*: (1) Almost never; (2) sometimes; (3) often; and (4) almost always. In the scope of mapU, only the T-Anxiety scale is used. State (current anxiety) is elicited through a self-reported measure described next.

State (Current) Anxiety Current anxiety is elicited through a self-reported measure of state anxiety taken in time slots of 5 min. An "anxiety bar" is used which is a sliding bar on the user interface, in which users position themselves on a scale 1–10 regarding their current anxiety. Figure 5.8 illustrates an example of the sliding bar.

Application-Specific Anxiety Application-specific anxiety is elicited using Cassady's Cognitive Test Anxiety (Cassady and Jonhson 2002) which consists of 27 items and measures the cognitive domain of test anxiety, also referred as worry.

Emotion Regulation For measuring emotion regulation we developed a custom made questionnaire that includes items derived from emotional intelligence (Salovey and Mayer 1990), self-regulation (Halberstadt 2005), and self-efficacy (Bandura 1994) tests; Cronbach's α that indicates reliability reaches 0.718 (Lekkas et. al. 2013).

5.3.1.3 Web Interaction Metrics

The reasoning behind the design of the Web interaction metrics was based on the assumption that cognitive styles may correspond ideally to the structure of Web environments (Germanakos et al. 2009; Tsianos et al. 2013); the content is essentially either visual or verbal and the manipulation of hyperlinks can lead to a more analytic and segmented structure, or to a more holistic and cohesive environment (Germanakos et al. 2009; Tsianos et al. 2013). Thus, differences in cognition are likely to be reflected in users' interactions and navigation with a system. In this respect we reproduced a Web application based on Wikipedia (2015) including additional functionality and content representations. The application monitors the

Web interaction of users on the client-side utilizing a browser-based logging facility to collect the interaction usage data from the hosts accessing the Web application. The following Web interaction data are monitored: (i) Total view time of articles representing content either verbally or graphically; and (ii) the hyperlink interactions. These are described next.

Monitoring Users' Content Representation Preference Given that the Verbal/Imager dimension has implications on the content representation (verbal or visual) of Web environments, we monitored the users' preference towards content representation, by enriching the Web application to include both verbal-based content, i.e., content in textual form without images/visuals (Fig. 5.9A), and image-based content, i.e., content represented with images/visuals and diagrammatical representations of text (Fig. 5.9B). The users have the option to either view the article in its textual version or in its graphical version. The total time spent in each version (viewing time) is recorded during the user's interaction with the system aiming to extract information about their preference towards a particular type of content representation.

Monitoring Users' Hyperlink Navigation Paths For implicitly eliciting the Wholist/Analyst cognitive styles of users, we monitor the users' actual sequences with the hyperlinks of the Web application and accordingly calculate their linearity, i.e., whether a user navigates linearly from one link to the other or in a non-linear manner. For this purpose, as mentioned earlier, we have developed an exact replica of Wikipedia since it is considered a representative example in terms of content structure and hyperlinks that enabled us to track the navigation behavior of users. In particular, given that the structure of Wikipedia articles contains hyperlink anchors that point to specific sections within each article, we measure the actual sequence of visited hyperlinks and the linearity of user interactions with the hyperlinks within each article. Two types of interactions (Fig. 5.10) are considered for monitoring the users' interactions: (i) *Navigation Menu Interactions:* The interactions of users with a navigation menu of each article in which every hyperlink is connected with a particular section in the article; and (ii) *Content Link Interactions:* The interactions of users with hyperlinks within the article that are connected with another article in the system. The reasoning behind this choice is based on the fact that the information behind each hyperlink has close semantic relationship with its previous hyperlink. Accordingly, the usage of the hyperlinks of each interaction type can be used to measure the degree of linear behavior a user has within the Web environment, i.e., whether the user tends to visit successive hyperlinks or not.

We designed a Web navigation metric that calculates the degree of linearity the users follow (linear or non-linear). In this context, in order to represent the users' interactions, all hyperlinks within each article are automatically annotated with an attribute, meaningful to the system. In particular, a browser-based facility was developed that parses a given HTML document and annotates each hyperlink with a unique incremental identifier, in the following format: nav_n_m, in which n identifies the article in which the user currently navigates and m the hyperlink clicked. Each time a user clicks on the annotated hyperlink, the unique identifier, as

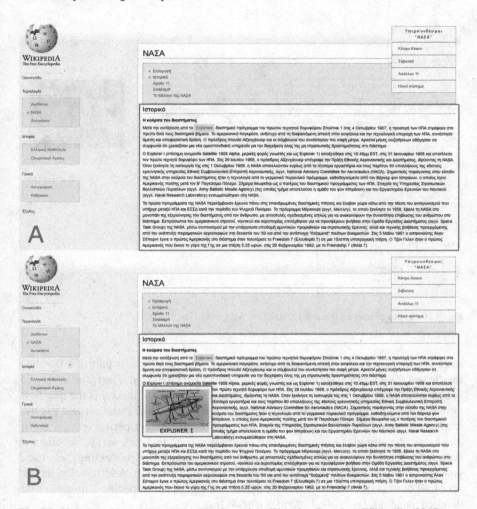

Fig. 5.9 Verbal- and image-based user interface of the Web-site (Based on Wikipedia (2015))

well as the time of hit is sent to the Web server. For example, for article with $ID = 1$ consisting of 4 hyperlinks, the following identifiers are assigned to each hyperlink from top to bottom: nav_1_1, nav_1_2, nav_1_3, nav_1_4.

5.3.1.4   Data Processing

For each stimulus of the aforementioned tasks (e.g., verbal-type or imager-type stimulus), the response time and the provided answer are recorded and processed. In this section, we formalize the user modeling data process. The main symbols and their respective definitions are summarized in Table 5.1. Accordingly, let U denote

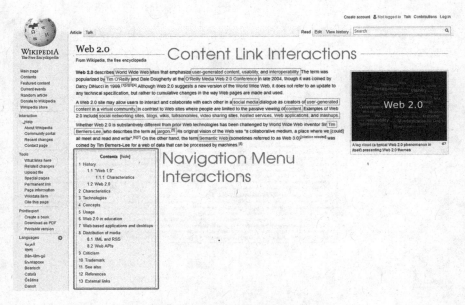

Fig. 5.10 Types of user interactions (Based on Wikipedia (2015))

a set of users $\{u_1, u_2, \ldots, u_n\}$. Let $q_j^{cs}(u_i)$ denote a question j that is part of a psychometric test for a specific stimulus cs and is performed on user u_i. The result of $q_j^{cs}(u_i)$ is a quintuplet of the form (cs, j, u_i, val, t), where cs is the stimulus, j is the question number, u_i is the user, val is the answer (*true* or *false*) to the question and t is the response time ($0 < t \leq timeout$) for some predefined timeout period (e.g., 3 s). In this work, the stimulus cs can be v (i.e., verbal), g (i.e., imager), w (i.e., wholist), a (i.e., analyst), s (i.e., speed of processing), c (i.e., control of processing), ma (i.e., visual working memory) or mb (i.e., verbal working memory). Additionally, let the set of all correct questions (i.e., $val = true$) for user u_i for a specific stimulus cs be denoted as $Q^{cs}(u_i) = \{q_j^{cs}(u_i) : q.val = true, \forall j\}$.

We define the number of correct responses of a specific stimulus cs for user u_i to be:

$$cr^{cs}(u_i) = \left| Q^{cs}(u_i) \right|$$

We define the average number of correct responses (CR) for a psychometric test of a specific stimulus cs for all users to be:

$$CR^{cs} = \frac{\sum_{\forall u_i} cr^{cs}(u_i)}{\left| \{u_i : cr^{cs}(u_i) \geq 0\} \right|}$$

Table 5.1 Table of symbols

Symbol	Description
U	Set of user $\{u_1, u_2, ..., u_n\}$
cs	Set of stimuli $\{v, g, w, a, s, c, ma, mb\}$
t	Response time to answer a question
val	Answer of a question (*true* or *false*)
$q_j^{cs}(u_i)$	Set of answered questions $\{q_1, q_2, ..., q_n\}$ for user u_i of a particular stimulus cs
$Q^{cs}(u_i)$	Set of all correct questions for user u_i of a particular stimulus cs
$cr^{cs}(u_i)$	Number of correct responses of a specific stimulus cs for user u_i
CR^{cs}	Average correct responses for a psychometric test of a specific stimulus cs for all users
DCR^{cs}	Standard deviation of correct responses for a psychometric test of a specific stimulus cs for all users
$rt^{cs}(u_i)$	Average response time for a psychometric test of a specific stimulus cs for user u_i
RT^{cs}	Average response time for a psychometric test of a specific stimulus cs for all users
$\lambda^{v:g}(u_i)$	Verbal/Imager ratio for user u_i
$\lambda^{w:a}(u_i)$	Wholist/Analyst ratio for user u_i
$\mu^{sc}(u_i)$	Average response time of stimulus s and c for user u_i
$z^{ma}(u_i)$	Normalized z-score value of the number of correct responses of stimulus ma for user u_i
$z^{mb}(u_i)$	Normalized z-score value of the number of correct responses of stimulus mb for user u_i
$\mu^{mab}(u_i)$	Average of normalized correct responses of stimulus ma and mb for user u_i
$vt^t(u_i)$	Viewing time in article sections illustrating textual information for user u_i
$vt^g(u_i)$	Viewing time in article sections illustrating graphical information for user u_i
$\lambda^{vt:vg}(u_i)$	Ratio of preferred viewing version for user u_i
$nav^{adl}(u_i)$	The total absolute distance of links for user u_i
$stai^t(u_i)$	The trait anxiety value for user u_i, as extracted based on the STAI manual
$bar^s(u_i)$	The self-reported value of user u_i indicating his current anxiety
$cta(u_i)$	The application-specific anxiety value for user u_i, as extracted based on the CTA manual
$er(u_i)$	The emotion regulation value for user u_i, as extracted based on the questionnaire manual

We define the standard deviation of correct responses (DCR^{cs}) for a psychometric test of a specific stimulus cs for all users to be:

$$DCR^{cs} = \sqrt{\frac{\left(\displaystyle\sum_{\forall u_i} cr^{cs}(u_i) - CR^{cs}\right)^2}{\left(\left|\{u_i : cr^{cs}(u_i) \geq 0\}\right| - 1\right)}}$$

We define the average response time (rt) for a psychometric test of a specific stimulus cs for user u_i to be:

$$rt^{cs}\left(u_i\right) = \frac{\displaystyle\sum_{\forall q_j^{cs}(u_i)\in Q^{cs}(u_i)} q_j^{cs}.t}{cr^{cs}\left(u_i\right)}$$

We define the average response time (RT) for a psychometric test of a specific stimulus cs for all users to be:

$$RT^{cs} = \frac{\displaystyle\sum_{\forall u_i} rt^{cs}\left(u_i\right)}{\left|\left\{u_i : rt^{cs}\left(u_i\right) > 0\right\}\right|}$$

We define the Verbal/Imager Ratio $\lambda^{v:g}$ for user u_i to be:

$$\lambda^{v:g}\left(u_i\right) = \begin{cases} \dfrac{RT^v}{RT^g} & rt^v\left(u_i\right)=0, rt^g\left(u_i\right)=0 \\[2mm] \dfrac{RT^v}{rt^g\left(u_i\right)} & rt^v\left(u_i\right)=0 \\[4mm] \dfrac{rt^v\left(u_i\right)}{RT^g} & rt^g\left(u_i\right)=0 \\[4mm] \dfrac{rt^v\left(u_i\right)}{rt^g\left(u_i\right)} & \text{otherwise} \end{cases}$$

We define the Wholist/Analyst Ratio $\lambda^{w:a}$ for user u_i to be:

$$\lambda^{w:a}\left(u_i\right) = \begin{cases} \dfrac{RT^w}{RT^a} & rt^w\left(u\right)_i=0, rt^a\left(u_i\right)=0 \\[2mm] \dfrac{RT^w}{rt^a\left(u_i\right)} & rt^w\left(u_i\right)=0 \\[4mm] \dfrac{rt^w\left(u_i\right)}{RT^a} & rt^a\left(u_i\right)=0 \\[4mm] \dfrac{rt^w\left(u_i\right)}{rt^a\left(u_i\right)} & \text{otherwise} \end{cases}$$

The cognitive style ratios ($\lambda^{v:g}(u_i)$ and $\lambda^{w:a}(u_i)$) indicate the users' cognitive style on the scales of Verbal-Imager and Wholist-Analyst. Users with a low value of $\lambda^{v:g}$ are considered to respond faster to the verbal types of stimuli, whereas users with a high value of $\lambda^{v:g}$ are considered to respond faster to the imager types of stimuli.

Similarly, users with a low value of $\lambda^{w:a}$ are considered to respond faster to the wholist types of stimuli, whereas users with a high value of $\lambda^{w:a}$ are considered to respond faster to the analyst types of stimuli. The cognitive style ratios of each user are then provided as input for cluster analysis aiming to classify each user to a cognitive style group.

Next we define the cognitive processing efficiency of user u_i as the average response time of stimulus s and c for user u_i to be:

$$\mu^{sc}\left(u_i\right) = \frac{\left(rt^s\left(u_i\right) + rt^c\left(u_i\right)\right)}{2}$$

We define the normalized value (by z-score) of the number of correct responses of stimulus ma for user u_i to be:

$$z^{ma}\left(u_i\right) = \frac{\left(cr^{ma}\left(u_i\right) - CR^{ma}\right)}{DCR^{ma}}$$

We define the normalized value (by z-score) of the number of correct responses of stimulus mb for user u_i to be:

$$z^{mb}\left(u_i\right) = \frac{\left(cr^{mb}\left(u_i\right) - CR^{mb}\right)}{DCR^{mb}}$$

We define the working memory of user u_i as the average of normalized number of correct responses of stimulus ma and mb for user u_i to be:

$$\mu^{mab}\left(u_i\right) = \frac{\left(z^{ma}\left(u_i\right) + z^{mb}\left(u_i\right)\right)}{2}$$

The average response time of stimulus s and $c(\mu^{sc}(u_i)c)$ indicates a user's cognitive processing ability with a low value of μ^{sc} indicating an enhanced cognitive processing ability of that user, and a high value of μ^{sc} indicating a limited cognitive processing ability of that user. The average of normalized number of correct responses of stimulus ma and mb ($\mu^{mab}(u_i)$) indicates a user's working memory capacity with a low value of μ^{mab} indicating a limited working memory capacity of that user, and a high value of μ^{mab} indicating an enhanced working memory capacity of that user.

Finally, we define the users' preferred viewing version as the ratio between the total viewing time of the textual version $vt^t(u_i)$ and the total viewing time of the graphical version $vt^g(u_i)$ for user u_i to be:

$$\lambda^{vt:vg}\left(u_i\right) = \frac{vt^t\left(u_i\right)}{vt^g\left(u_i\right)}$$

The linearity of users' navigation is modeled through the absolute distance of links (*ADL*), which is the total absolute distance between the links visited by a user u_i to be:

$$nav^{adl}\left(u_i\right) = \frac{\left|x_1 - 1\right| + \sum_{i=2}^{N}\left|x_i - x_{i-1}\right|}{N}$$

In the aforementioned equation, x_i represents the identifier of links visited, i.e., $i = 1$ is the first link visited (x_1 is equal to 1), $i = 2$ the second (x_2 is equal to 2) and so on, and N is the number of total links clicked. Thus the distance between sequential links is assumed to be equal to 1.

5.3.1.5   User Classification

For classifying users into specific groups (e.g., Verbal or Imager group), two widely used methods exist in the literature: (i) grouping users based on a predefined threshold value for each psychometric test or questionnaire which is suggested and standardized by the creator of each inventory (e.g., based on the aforementioned processed responses of a user (e.g., Verbal/Imager ratio), the user is grouped in a particular group, given a predefined range of thresholds); and (ii) grouping users based on cluster analysis which aims to divide a set of users into cluster groups that are different from each other and whose members are similar to each other according to each of the aforementioned processed values. In the context of mapU, we classify users based on cluster analysis for the following reasons: (i) the suggested thresholds are standardized and evaluated based on a specific population which might not be representative for different populations under investigation; and (ii) cluster analysis could yield very good results in our case since the data being processed represent a scale with two end points (e.g., low and high values of the Verbal/Imager ratio represent respectively Verbal and Imager users), and thus can effectively separate users from each other depending on the responses to each stimuli (Belk et al. 2013). Apparently, cluster analysis also entails practical limitations, such as initialization issues, i.e., when a limited number of users are registered in the system, making the cluster analysis difficult and ineffective to perform.

In this respect, depending on the aforementioned processed values of each user (i.e., $\lambda^{v:g}(u_i)$, $\lambda^{w:a}(u_i)$, $\mu^{sc}(u_i)$, $\mu^{mab}(u_i)$, $\lambda^{vt:vg}(u_i)$, $nav^{adl}(u_i)$, $stai^t(u_i)$, $bar^s(u_i)$, $cta(u_i)$, $er(u_i)$), users with close distance values will be grouped in the same cluster. Accordingly, the following characteristics for each user are finally elicited based on the cluster the user is assigned: (i) A user is either a Verbal, or an Imager (based on $\lambda^{v:g}(u_i)$ or $\lambda^{vt:vg}(u_i)$); (ii) a user is either a Wholist, or an Analyst (based on $\lambda^{w:a}(u_i)$ or $nav^{adl}(u_i)$); (iii) a user has either limited or enhanced speed and control of processing (cognitive processing efficiency); (iv) a user has either limited or enhanced working memory capacity; (v) a user is in general less or highly anxious in life; (vi) a user is currently highly anxious or less anxious; (vii) a user is less or highly anxious within a specific application domain; and (viii) a user is less able or highly able to regulate his emotions.

For user classification we utilize the k-means clustering algorithm since it is considered one of the most robust and efficient clustering algorithms (Wu et al. 2007). The k-means clustering algorithm is performed as follows: The algorithm initially sets the data point with the smallest value (e.g., Verbal/Imager ratio) as the first cluster centre and the data point with the largest value as the second cluster centre. Given that the desired groups are known in our case (e.g., Verbal and Imager), the algorithm is set to $k=2$. The distance between all other data points and cluster centres are then calculated, and each data point is assigned to the cluster whose distance from the cluster centre is the minimum of all the cluster centres using the Euclidian distance. New cluster centres are recalculated by measuring the mean of all data points of each newly created cluster. Next, the distances between each data point and the newly obtained cluster centres are recalculated in an iterative approach until no data point is reassigned. The respective cluster group that users are assigned represent their cognitive and emotional processing characteristics. For example, all users that are grouped in the "Verbal" cluster are considered to have a verbal type of cognitive style.

5.3.1.6   User Model

The above process results in constructing the final structure of the user model. More specifically, the user model um of a user u_i ($um(u_i)$) is composed of demographics ($category=d$), cognitive characteristics ($category=cc$) and emotional characteristics ($category=em$) and contains triplets of the form (ct, ch, val), where ct represents an information category (e.g., demographics, cognitive characteristics, emotional characteristics, etc.), ch represents a characteristic (e.g., age, gender, verbal/imager cognitive style, wholist/analyst cognitive style, working memory, general anxiety, etc.) and val the value for the specific characteristic. For example, a user u_i may have the following user model:

$$um(u_i) = \{(d,age,25),(cc,v\,/\,i,verbal),(em,anx,high)\}$$

indicating that u_i has an $age=25$ in the demographics (d) information category, he is verbal (v/i) in the cognitive characteristics (cc) category and he is in general highly anxious (anx) in the emotional characteristics (em) category.

5.3.2   Module 2: Personalization

Upon user classification, the Personalization module adapts semantically enriched content at run-time on the client's side. To accomplish this, the Personalization module utilizes: (i) The cognitive and emotional characteristics inside the constructed user model $um(u_i)$ that was described in the previous section; (ii) semantically annotated Web content that can be provided in different formats; and (iii) adaptation rules that decide the "best-fit" visual and interaction design for a specific user u_i according to his user model.

5.3.2.1   Content Management

The framework entails a content management component that enables service providers to create and semantically annotate content that is saved in the database. The semantically enriched content (*SEC*) that is generated by this component can be roughly visualized as a set of triplets of the form $SEC = \{(p_i, s_j, ctype)\}$ where p_i is a unique page identifier, s_j is a unique section identifier (i.e., a specific div tag) inside page p_i and *ctype* is the content type (e.g., title, section) that can be adapted according to the rules incorporated in the Adaptation Engine that is described in the next section.

5.3.2.2   Adaptation Component

The adaptation module is composed of the adaptation rules' pool (*AR*), the recommendations' pool (*R*) and the adaptation engine (*r*). *AR* is the set of all adaptation rules that will be described shortly. *R* is the set of all recommendations in the form of triplets (*category*, *characteristic*, *val*) (e.g., (design, authentication type, textual)). The adaptation engine is responsible for generating a set of recommendations (*R'*) for a user u_i using the user model $um(u_i)$ and a set of adaptation rules (*AR*).

The adaptation engine can be conceptually visualized as the following function:

$$r\big(um(u_i), AR\big) = R', R' \subseteq R$$

An adaptation rule attempts to map particular user model characteristics with specific recommendations. The adaptation rules involve mapping of cognitive factors (e.g., user is Verbal) to design factors of the user interface (e.g., textual or graphical representation). These rules can be extended according to the provider's custom requirements and application domain. An example of an adaptation rule can be *"if user u_i is Verbal (i.e., $(vi, verbal) \in um(u_i)$) then the user authentication type should be text-based"*. This is represented by the following rule:

Example Rule 1: ((*vi*, *verbal*), {(*stype*, *textual*)})

More complex Boolean expressions can of course be expressed by the above format. Additional examples are presented below. Note that there are cases where a set of conditions may result in two or more recommendations (see Example 5), and that is why the recommendations appear as a set.

Example Rule 2: ((*vi, imager*) AND (*wm, limited*), {(*security_type, textual*)})
Example Rule 3: ((*vi, verbal*) OR (*wa, wholist*), {(*security_type, textual*)})
Example Rule 4: ((*vi, imager*) AND (*wa, analyst*) AND (NOT (*wm, limited*)), {(*security_type, graphical*)})
Example Rule 5: ((*vi, imager*) AND (*wm, limited*), {(*security_type, textual*), (*complexity, standard*)})

However, processing complex Boolean expressions is highly inefficient as it introduces parsing and recursive expression recognition and evaluation (e.g., decision trees). In order to alleviate this problem we have introduced a pre-processor step that transforms a Boolean expression into its logically equivalent conjunctive normal form (CNF) using components from the double negative law, De Morgan's laws and the distributive law. It then decomposes the expression into a set of subexpressions (i.e., linked with an *AND* as CNF dictates) that should all evaluate to *true* in order for the rule to be applied. In order to better facilitate our discussion we illustrate the usage of the pre-processor step in the above examples:

Example Rule 1: ({(*vi, verbal*)}, {(*security_type, textual*)})
Example Rule 2: ({(*vi, imager*), (*wm, limited*)}, {(*security_type, textual*)})
Example Rule 3: ({(*vi, verbal*)}, {(*security_type, textual*)}, {(*wa, wholist*), (*security_type*, textual)})
Example Rule 4: ({(*vi, imager*), (*wa, analyst*), (NOT (*wm, limited*))}, {(*security_type, graphical*)})
Example Rule 5: ({(*vi, imager*), (*wm, limited*)}, {(*security_type, textual*), (*complexity, standard*)})

Consequently, the adaptation component stores an adaptation rule $ar_i \in AR$ in the form of a tuple (E, RC), where E is a conjunction of Boolean expressions and $RC \subseteq R$ is a set of recommendations. We have selected to store the Boolean expressions in conjunctive normal form in order to allow for efficient evaluation of each expression in linear time as illustrated in Algorithm #1.

Algorithm #1. Recommendations (*r*)

Input: User model $um(u_i)$ and a set of adaptation rules AR	
Output: Set of recommendations R', $R' \subseteq R$	
1:	**procedure:** $r(um(u_i), AR)$)
2:	// Initialize the recommendations for *user u_i*
3:	$R' = \varnothing$;
4:	// Test every adaptation rule *ar* in the set of adaptation rules AR
5:	**for each** *ar(E, RC)* **in** *AR*
6:	// Assume that the rule *ar* applies
7:	*test = true;*
8:	// Test every expression *e* in the set of Boolean expressions E
9:	**for each** *e* **in** E
10:	// If an expression cannot be found in the user model then *ar* does not apply

(continued)

Algorithm #1 (continued)

11:	**if** ((e is **NOT** && $e \cap um(u_i) \neq \emptyset$) || (! e is **NOT** && $e \cap um(u_i) = \emptyset$)))
12:	$test = false;$
13:	break;
14:	**end if**
15:	**end for**
16:	// If all expressions in ar apply then add the recommendations RC
17:	// to the set of final recommendations R'
18:	**if** ($test == true$)
19:	$R' = R' \cup RC;$
20:	**end if**
21:	**end for**
22:	// return the set of all discovered recommendations
23:	**return** R'
24:	**end procedure**

Based on the aforementioned formalization, we have designed several adaptation rules (AR) that are based on specific design guidelines. A series of design guidelines and adaptation effects will be thoroughly presented in Chaps. 6, 7 and 8.

Next, based on the generated recommendations, the adaptation engine is finally run to adapt the semantically enriched content and functionality according to the cognitive and emotional characteristics inside the user model $um(u_i)$ of a user u_i. More specifically, the adaptation engine can be visualized as a function $ae(um(u_i), R', p_j)$ where $um(u_i)$ is the user model of a user u_i, R' is a set of recommendations generated based on Algorithm #1, and p_j is a unique Web-page identifier. Algorithm #2 depicts the internal mechanisms of the adaptation engine.

Algorithm #2 starts by initializing an empty set of Web-page sections (line #3). Note that at the end of the procedure, this set will contain both adapted and non-adapted content that composes the specific Web-page. Next (line #5), the algorithm retrieves the content of all sections of the Web-page one by one (line #7). For each section, it checks if the specific section has semantically enriched content (line #9). If this is true, then it proceeds with adaptation of the content based on the set of recommendations R' and the cognitive and emotional characteristics that are stored in the user model of user u_i (line #11). If there is no semantically enriched content (i.e., line #9 evaluates to false) then the content is left unchanged. Finally, the adapted or non-adapted content for the specific section is added to the Web-page content set C in line #13 and at the end of the procedure all the Web-page content is returned for display.

Algorithm #2. Adaptation engine (ae)

Input: The user model $um(u_i)$, a set of recommendations R', a semantically enriched Web-page with identifier p_j	
Output: Revised content (C) for the Web-page with adapted sections according to the user model	
1:	**procedure:** $ae(um(u_i), R', p_j))$
2:	// Initialize the content of the revised page
3:	$C = \emptyset;$

(continued)

Algorithm #2   (continued)

4:	// Retrieve all the sections of page with identifier p_j
5:	**for each** s_k **in** sections(p_j)
6:	// Retrieve the original content of the specific section
7:	$C' = $ get_content((p_j, s_k));
8:	// Identify if the specific section is semantically enriched (i.e., it can be adapted). If it's not, do not perform any adaptation
9:	**if** ((p_j, s_k) $\in SEC$)
10:	// adapt the content according to the user's characteristics
11:	$C' = $ adapt($um(u_i)$, R', C');
12:	**end if**
13:	$C = C' \, C'$;
14:	**end for**
15:	**return** C;
16:	**end procedure**

5.4   Design and Development of mapU

The mapU framework has been realized in a two-tier architecture as depicted in Fig. 5.11. It is comprised of the mapU Web server and the mapU Back-end. These are described next in detail.

5.4.1   mapU Web Server

The Web server serves primarily as an interface between the users and the back-end system and consists of three modules: (i) The mapU administration module; (ii) the third-party provider administration module; and (iii) the front-end user modeling module.

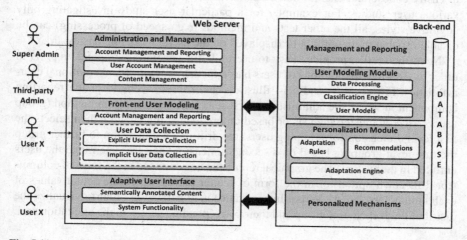

Fig. 5.11 Architectural design of the mapU framework

5.4.1.1 Administration and Management

The administration and management serves as the main front-end system enabling the administrator of mapU to interact with the Back-end system in order to manage various components of the system such as view and manage the actual users' accounts and the third-party providers' accounts. It also enables the administrator to manage the user data collection methods (e.g., psychometric tools) and to adjust the adaptation rules of a particular mechanism.

The third-party provider administration enables any third-party entity who wishes to utilize the user modeling and personalization modules of mapU in their system, to manage their account, plugins and the users that are interacting with their personalized mechanisms. The plugin manager enables the provider to set specific attributes of the plugin (e.g., set new or update the default suggested adaptation rules of mapU). A reporting system is also provided for viewing the users' models, their interactions with the plugins, perform statistical analysis tests, etc.

Account Management and Reporting The account management and reporting component provides a tool to the main administrator of mapU to manage essential information about the system. Managing users is an important component of the administration system in which the administrator creates new users or manages existing user accounts, assigns roles to users (e.g., content provider, simple user) and access rights (e.g., read, write, or both). The administrator is also able to manage the elicitation tools by enabling or disabling specific elicitation tools that are displayed in the front-end user modeling component of the users. Figure 5.12 illustrates the elicitation tools' management component in which all the available elicitation tools of the system are displayed and the administrator is able to activate or deactivate a particular elicitation method by clicking on the corresponding icon of the method.

This component has been developed for enabling researchers and administrators to easily choose and enable the elicitation tools based on the aim and method of various user studies. For example, for a particular user study investigating only cognitive styles, all the other tests and methods (e.g., speed of processing) can be disabled so that these will not be displayed on the users' modeling dashboard.

Next, the system provides easy to use tools for generating graphical reports in order to view the distributions of users based on their cognitive and emotional characteristics. Figures 5.13 and 5.14 illustrate an example scenario of the reporting component in which the administrator first selects the classification method (group users based on cluster analysis or based on predefined thresholds), then selects the first level dimension for grouping users, the drill-down dimension to further group the first-level grouping based on a second dimension, and the date range the users enrolled in the system. The graphical report can be generated in the form of columns (for drill-down option) or in the form of scatter plot in which the actual values of each human factor (e.g., Verbal/Imager ratio) is illustrated in order to visualize the distribution of each user group and their corresponding scores in the elicitation tool.

Name	Is Active Click image to Activate/Deactivate	Is Active For Study Click image to Activate/Deactivate	Date Added
CSA Wholist/Analyst	✓	✓	2013-08-12 20:24:03
Speed of Processing	✓	✓	2013-08-12 20:24:03
Controlled Attention	✓	✓	2013-08-13 16:38:03
Implicit/DPE	✓	✗	2014-04-09 20:19:54
VICS	✗	✗	2013-06-24 16:09:30
GEFT P1	✗	✗	2013-07-12 00:35:15
Visual Working Memory	✓	✓	2013-08-18 16:38:18
Extended CSA	✗	✗	2013-09-02 19:32:38
CSA Verbal/Imager	✓	✓	2013-09-06 13:38:33
Verbal Working Memory	✓	✗	2014-02-05 16:21:12
Personality Test	✓	✓	2014-02-05 16:12:11
Satisfaction Questionnaire	✗	✓	2014-02-05 16:13:07
General Anxiety	✗	✗	2013-08-29 17:25:04
Current Anxiety	✗	✗	2013-08-29 17:25:04
Emotion Regulation	✗	✗	2013-08-29 17:25:04

Fig. 5.12 Enabling/disabling psychometric tests to be displayed in the front-end user modeling dashboard

User Account Management The user account management component provides all the necessary tools and functionalities for managing information that is related to the users of the system. Administrators are able to search for enrolled users based on different keywords and criteria (e.g., name, age range, etc.) and further view information about each user. In particular, the administrator can view information about the users' accounts, their scores on the psychometric tests and Web interaction metrics. Figure 5.15 illustrates an example of listing users based on specific search criteria.

The administrator can further perform specific actions on the user model such as edit basic information about the user and generate new password keys for users that have forgotten their password combination (Fig. 5.16). In the latter case, an email is sent to users with specific steps for resetting their password and creating a new authentication key. An option for deleting the user account and respective model permanently from the database is also available. The system also provides tools for exporting the user's information into different formats for third-party software applications (e.g., MS Excel).

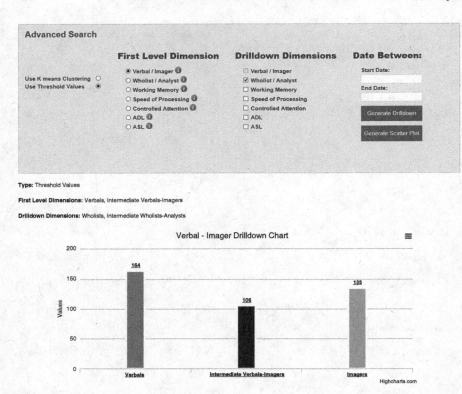

Fig. 5.13 Viewing the total number of users for each cognitive style group (Verbal/Imager) (HighCharts 2015)

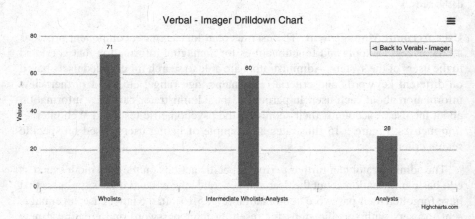

Fig. 5.14 Performing a drill-down action on the Verbal group for viewing the distribution of Verbal users in regards with the Wholist/Analyst cognitive style (HighCharts 2015)

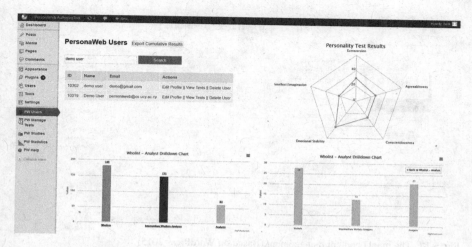

Fig. 5.15 Listing user accounts and viewing information based on a search result (HighCharts 2015)

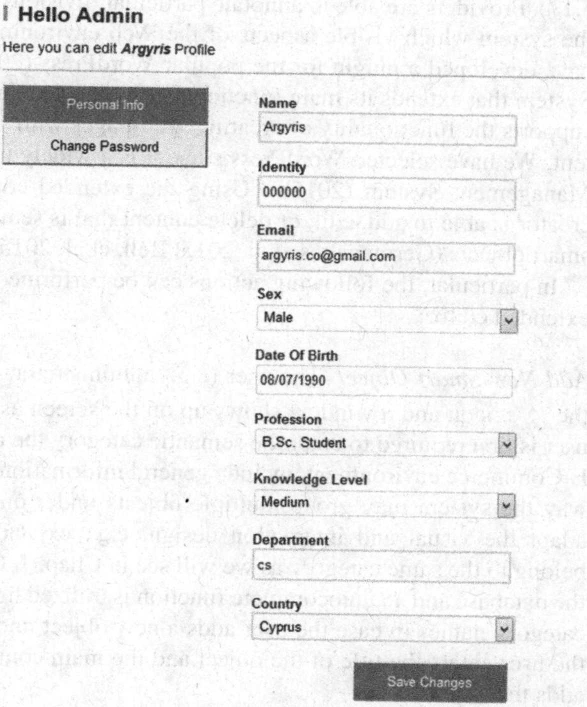

Fig. 5.16 Editing basic information of a selected user

I Hello Admin

Here you can edit *Argyris* Profile

Personal Info
Change Password

Name
Argyris

Identity
000000

Email
argyris.co@gmail.com

Sex
Male

Date Of Birth
08/07/1990

Profession
B.Sc. Student

Knowledge Level
Medium

Department
cs

Country
Cyprus

Save Changes

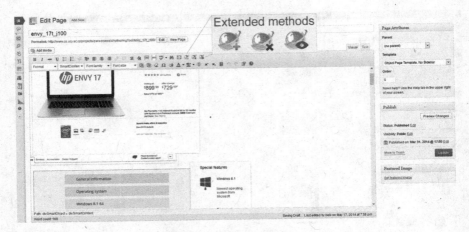

Fig. 5.17   The mapU content management (Based on WordPress 2015)

Content Management The content management component provides an easy to use tool for content providers to create semantically enriched Web-pages (Fig. 5.17). Providers are able to annotate particular divisions of Web-pages indicating to the system which visible aspects of the Web environment should be adapted. We have developed a plugin for the popular WordPress (2015a) Content Management System that extends its main functionality by introducing a Web content editor that supports the functionality of creating Web-pages with semantically annotated content. We have selected WordPress since it is a widely used and accredited Content Management System (2015b). Using the extended editor's methods, the content creator is able to add, edit, or delete content that is semantically annotated through smart objects (Germanakos et al. 2015; Belk et al. 2015).

In particular, the following actions can be performed on the content through the extended editor:

Add New Smart Object The user (e.g., administrator, content provider) clicks on the icon and a window shows up on the screen as illustrated in Fig. 5.18.The user is first required to enter the semantic category the object belongs to (e.g., in an E-Commerce environment, include general information of a laptop computer). This way the system may group multiple objects under one category and accordingly adapt the visual and interaction design, e.g., expanding/collapsing objects that belong to the same category as we will see in Chap. 7. Category names are saved in the database and an autocomplete function is utilized that is recommending existing category names in case the user adds a new object under the same category. Next, the user enters the title of the object and the main content of the object and finally adds the object.

Update Smart Object For updating existing objects, the user selects an existingob-ject as illustrated in Fig. 5.19 and then clicks again on the icon and awindow shows up on the screen entailing the information of that object.

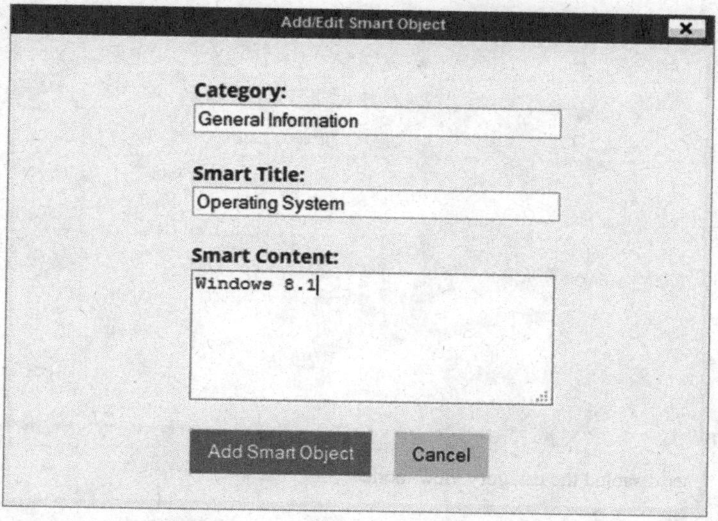

Fig. 5.18 User adds a semantically annotated object

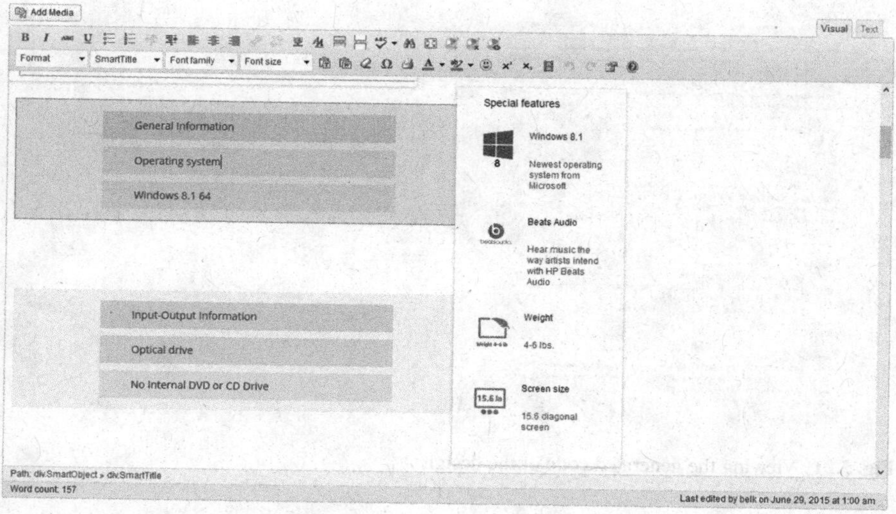

Fig. 5.19 User selects existing objects for update

Delete Smart Object For deleting objects, the user selects an existing object as illustrated in Fig. 5.19 and then clicks on the  icon.

View Main Information of a Smart Object To ease visibility, the user has the option to view the title and content of the objects, with or without the semantic category.

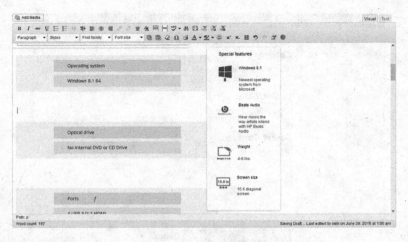

Fig. 5.20 User disabled the category view mode

Fig. 5.21 Viewing the generated code of the design

For changing the view mode the user clicks on the ![icon] icon to switch the viewcategory mode. Figure 5.20 illustrates an example in which no categories are illustrated.

Finally, the extended editor gives full access to the user to manage the HTML code that is generated behind each design as illustrated in Fig. 5.21.

5.4.1.2   Front-End User Modeling

The front-end user modeling is responsible to generate the users' models through explicit and implicit data collection methods. Users initially enroll in the user modeling module, by providing basic account information and their demographics (gender, date of birth, email), and further elicit their cognitive and emotional processing characteristics by running specific human factor elicitation tools or through a controlled implicit user data collection method (as seen in Sects. 5.3.1.1, 5.3.1.2 and 5.3.1.3). Reporting tools are also available for viewing the results of the users' actual responses to the stimuli (i.e., time to respond to the test, whether the answer was correct or not, view the actual result, etc.) but as well compare their user model characteristics with other anonymous user models of the system. Figure 5.22 illustrates the starting page of the front-end user modeling module in which all the user data collection methods (psychometric tests and Web navigation environment) are accessible.

Explicit User Modeling: Psychometric Tests and Questionnaires The primary method for eliciting the users' characteristics is through specially designed psychometric tests and questionnaires. Each psychometric test entails different cognitive aptitude tasks in which users are required to respond to and the system then processes the responses for generating the users' characteristics. A psychometric test initiates by clicking on the "Start" button (Fig. 5.22) which redirects to a page providing instructions to the users for conducting the test. The nature of each psychometric test and stimulus are described in Sect. 5.3.1.1. When the test is completed, the primary results of the test are illustrated in a summative form in the section of the corresponding test (Fig. 5.22). In particular, the section illustrates the following information about each test: Number of times the user conducted the test, the date of the last time the test was conducted, the number of correct responses (where applicable), the mean time or ratio required to answer the stimuli and the user's characteristic extracted.

   An additional option for viewing the analytical results of the tests is also available. The users click on the "Results" button (Fig. 5.22) which redirects to a page with more information about the results of the test. Figure 5.23 illustrates an example of a visual working memory test in which the following information is illustrated to the user: The response time to each stimulus, the validity of the answer (true/false), the user's given answer and the actual correct answer of the stimulus.

Implicit User Modeling: Navigation Behavior An option to elicit the users' cognitive styles is also available through the main dashboard (Fig. 5.22). By initiating the implicit user data collection method the user is redirected to a controlled Web environment which entails a number of reproduced articles from Wikipedia. As described in Sect. 5.3.1.3, the articles' content and hyperlinks have been enhanced with client-side and server-side scripts for recording the users' interactions with the articles.

Send my results

	Session	Date	Correct	Ratio	Style		
✓ **Riding Verbal/Imager CSA Test** *(10 min)* Elicit your cognitive style (Verbal/Imager)	1	June 20, 2015	44/48	1.2	Imager	Start	Result

	Session	Date	Correct	Ratio	Style		
✓ **Riding Wholist/Analyst CSA Test** *(5 min)* Elicit your cognitive style (Wholist/Analyst)	1	June 20, 2015	37/40	0.8	Wholist	Start	Result

	Session	Date	Correct	Ratio	Level		
✓ **Speed of Processing** *(3 min)* Elicit your speed of processing	-					Start	Result

	Session	Date	Correct	Time	Level		
✓ **Controlled Attention** *(3 min)* Elicit your controlled attention	1	June 20, 2015	17/18	1200ms	High	Start	Result

	Session	Date	Correct	Time	Level		
✓ **Visual Working Memory Capacity** *(5 min)* Elicit your visual working memory capacity	1	June 20, 2015	15/21		High	Start	Result

	Session	Date	Difficulty	Time	Level		
✓ **Verbal Working Memory Capacity** *(10 min)* Elicit your verbal working memory capacity	1	June 20, 2015	Medium		Medium	Start	Result

	Session	Date	Navigation	Time	Level		
✓ **Implicit User Modeling** Elicit your cognitive styles by interacting through a Web-based environment	1	June 20, 2015	Linear	17min	Wholist	Start	Result

	Session	Date	Anxiety Level		
✓ **General Anxiety** Elicit your trait anxiety level	1	June 20, 2015	High	Start	Result

	Session	Date	Emotion Regulation Level		
✓ **Emotion Regulation** Elicit your emotion regulation level	1	June 20, 2015	Low	Start	Result

Fig. 5.22 Dashboard of the user modeling module for accessing the explicit and implicit user data collection methods

Date of test	Correct	Level
2015-04-17 15:10:14	17	MEDIUM
2015-04-17 15:14:20	0	LOW
2014-10-09 18:17:42	4	LOW

Question Number	Response Time (ms)	Is Right	Given Answer	Answer
1	1273	Correct	False	False
2	1087	Correct	True	True
3	898	Correct	False	False
4	805	Correct	False	False
5	2079	Correct	False	False
6	1173	Correct	False	False
7	1221	Correct	True	True
8	1189	Correct	True	True
9	879	Correct	False	False
10	1141	Correct	True	True
11	2883	Correct	False	False
12	1685	Correct	False	False
13	5435	Wrong	True	False

Fig. 5.23 Analytical results of a session for eliciting the visual working memory capacity

In particular, in order to track the users' interactions, all hyperlinks (Navigation Menu and Content Hyperlinks) within each article have been automatically annotated with an attribute, meaningful to the system. In particular, a browser-based logging facility was developed that initially parses the HTML document, extracting the Navigation Menu hyperlinks and Content hyperlinks, and further annotates each hyperlink in the following manner: Navigation Menu hyperlinks and Content hyperlinks are respectively annotated with *"nav_x_y"* where x is the unique identifier of the current article and y the unique identifier of the navigation menu hyperlink, and

Contents [hide]	Hyperlink	ID

Contents [hide]
1 History
2 Characteristics
3 Technologies
4 Concepts
5 Usage
6 Web 2.0 in education
7 Web 2.0 and philanthropy
8 Web 2.0 in social work
9 Web-based applications and desktops
10 Distribution of media
  10.1 XML and RSS
  10.2 Web APIs
11 Criticism
12 Trademark
13 Web 3.0
14 See also
15 References
16 External links

Hyperlink	ID
History	nav_1_1
Characteristics	nav_1_2
Technologies	nav_1_3
Concepts	nav_1_4
Usage	nav_1_5
...	nav_x_y

Fig. 5.24 Navigation menu hyperlink semantic annotations

Web 2.0 is a term coined in 1999 to describe web sites that use technology beyond the static pages of earlier web sites. The term is closely associated with Tim O'Reilly because of the O'Reilly Media Web 2.0 conference which was held in late 2004.[1][2] Although web 2.0 suggests a new version of the World Wide Web, it does not refer to an update to any technical specification, but rather to cumulative changes in the ways software developers and end-users use the Web.

A Web 2.0 site may allow users to interact and collaborate with each other in a social media dialogue as creators of user-generated content in a virtual community, in contrast to websites where people are limited to the passive viewing of content. Examples of Web 2.0 include social networking sites, blogs, wikis, video sharing sites, hosted services, web applications, mashups and folksonomies.[3]

Whether Web 2.0 is substantively different from prior web technologies has been challenged by World Wide Web inventor Tim Berners-Lee, who describes the term as jargon.[4] His original vision of the Web was "a collaborative medium, a place where we [could] all meet and read and write".[5]

Hyperlink	ID
Tim O'Reilly	content_1_1
O'Reilly Media	content_1_2
World Wide Web	content_1_3
software developers	content_1_4
end-users	content_1_5
...	content_x_y

Fig. 5.25 Content hyperlink semantic annotations

"content_x_y" where x is the unique identifier of the current article and y the unique identifier of the content hyperlink. In both hyperlink types, y is used to calculate the distance between the hyperlinks visited by the user. The browser-based logging facility is also responsible to store all users' interactions with each annotated hyperlink in the server's database. Figures 5.24 and 5.25 respectively illustrate the annotations made by the browser-based logging facility.

To better explain the metric, we provide an example navigation, e.g., the click stream navigation pattern "nav_2_4 | nav_2_2 | nav_2_3", indicates that the user visited article with ID=2 and then read the content of the fourth, second and third hyperlink of the navigation menu in the system. For this particular navigation, as defined in Sect. 5.3.1.4, the *ADL* metric is then calculated as: $ADL = (|4-1|+|2-4|+|3-2|)/3 = 2$. Accordingly, a high number of the metric indicates that the user followed a non-linear navigation behavior, whereas a small number of the metric indicates a linear navigation behavior.

5.4.1.3   Adaptive User Interface

The adaptive user interface is responsible to communicate adapted and personalized content functionality. Next we provide some examples that correspond to a specific scenario of adapting and personalizing E-Commerce environments. In these scenarios, particular product views were created through the content management component and specific divisions of the page were annotated based on a set of design guidelines and adaptation effects. Similarly, other Web-sites of different domains, e.g., E-Learning environments can be created following the same content creation process and adapted based on a different set of design guidelines and adaptation effects for that particular domain. In this respect, we dedicate Chaps. 6, 7 and 8 for providing a detailed presentation of design guidelines and adaptation effects for three distinct domains (E-Learning, E-Commerce, Usable Security), and the added value of adapting content and functionality in terms of task usability and user experience for each domain.

Figures 5.26, 5.27, 5.28 and 5.29 illustrate different visual and interaction design versions of the same content to users with different cognitive styles and working memory capacity. Accordingly, a user with Verbal-Wholist cognitive style (Fig. 5.26) is provided with textual information, divided in several sections in which the user is able to expand/collapse the content. The expand/collapse functionality was chosen since Wholist users tend to handle information in a holistic manner (in this case by initially viewing the sections of the Web-page – Germanakos et al. 2009) and then proceed to the detail (the content of each section).

In the case of Verbal-Analysts (Fig. 5.27), users are again provided with solely textual illustrations of content but the whole content is available to the users since Analysts tend to move from the parts (content) to the whole (sections) and prefer to have more freedom in their navigation (Germanakos et al. 2009).

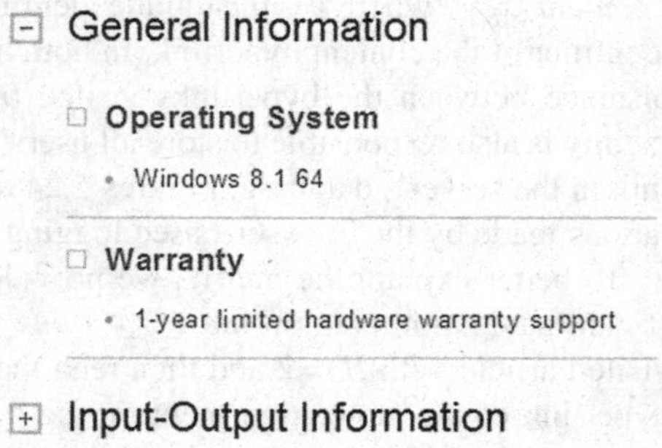

Fig. 5.26 Adaptation effects for Verbal–Wholist–enhanced working memory

☐ **General Information**

   ☐ **Operating System**

      • Windows 8.1 64

   ☐ **Warranty**

      • 1-year limited hardware warranty support

⊞ **Input-Output Information**

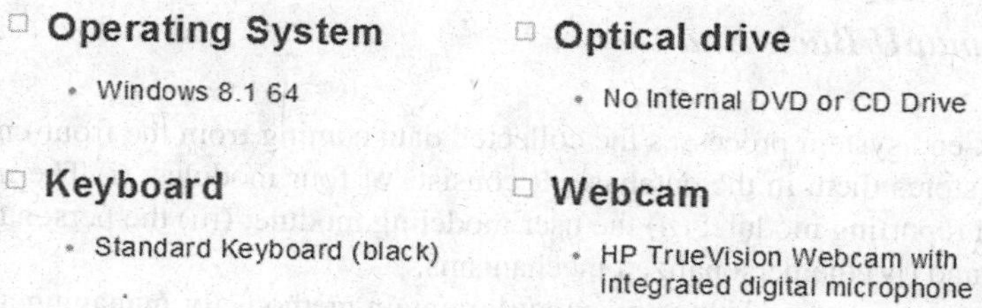

□ **Operating System**   □ **Optical drive**

• Windows 8.1 64   • No Internal DVD or CD Drive

□ **Keyboard**   □ **Webcam**

• Standard Keyboard (black)   • HP TrueVision Webcam with
                                                  integrated digital microphone

Fig. 5.27 Adaptation effects for Verbal – Analyst – enhanced working memory

⊟ General Information

| □ **Operating System** | Windows 8.1 64 |
| □ **Warranty** | 1-year limited hardware warranty support |

⊞ Input-Output Information

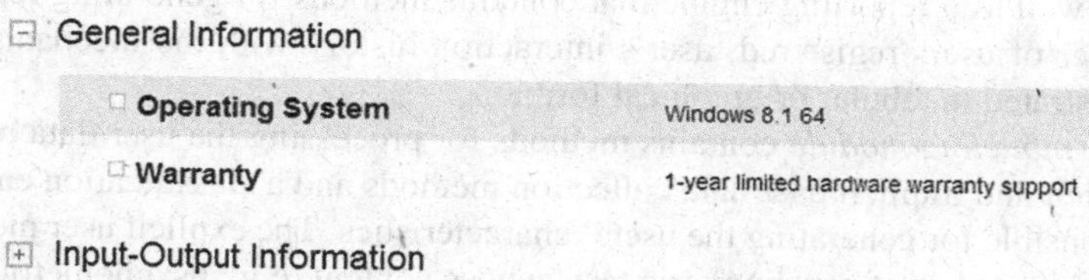

Fig. 5.28 Adaptation effects for Imager–Wholist–enhanced working memory

□ **Operating System**

Windows 8.1 64

□ **Optical drive**

No Internal DVD or CD Drive

Fig. 5.29 Adaptation effects for Imager–Analyst–limited working memory

In the case of Imager-Wholists (Fig. 5.28) and Imager–Analysts (Fig. 5.29), the same logic is applied in regards with the Wholist/Analyst dimension, but instead, the visual design of the content is provided in a colored diagrammatical representation since Imager users do not perform well when exclusively text-based content is provided but rather better with combinations of text and graphical illustrations (Riding and Cheema 1991).

In the case of users having limited working memory capacity, specific visual design enhancements are applied on the content by increasing the size of the text and enhancing the content with additional content indicators or divisors (Fig. 5.29).

5.4.2   mapU Back-End

The back-end system processes the collected data coming from the front-end modules and stores them in the database. It consists of four modules: (i) The management and reporting module; (ii) the user modeling module; (iii) the personalization module; and (iv) the personalized mechanisms.

The *management and reporting module* contain methods for managing and storing information such as the user account of the mapU administrator, the third-party provider administrator and the actual users of the mapU system. It also contains methods for managing the licenses of the plugins and libraries of each third-party provider as well as a reporting engine that contains methods for generating reports (e.g., number of users registered, user's interaction history with the mechanisms) that are illustrated in tabular or graphical format.

The *user modeling module* contains methods for processing the user data based on the explicit and implicit user data collection methods and a classification engine that is responsible for generating the users' characteristics. The explicit user modeling contains a number of psychometric tests whose content (e.g., psychometric test type, questions, figures) is stored in the database and retrieved in a new test occurrence (user session). Each psychometric test and questionnaire corresponds to a particular human factor of the user that is modelled through a value (e.g., cognitive style ratio) that is the result of specific data processing described in Sect. 5.3.1.4. Alternatively, the implicit user modeling contains methods for processing and storing user interaction data coming from a controlled Web environment that tracks the users' navigation behavior (i.e., the sequence of pages a user followed in a Web environment and how long he was reading specific content sections). The users' interaction data are modelled by utilizing specific Web data metrics that indicate a user's tendency to navigate linearly or non-linearly (correlated to the Wholist/Analyst cognitive style dimension) and a user's tendency preferring to read content illustrated in a diagrammatic representation or textual representation (correlated to the Verbal/Imager cognitive style dimension). Furthermore, the resulting values of each user are provided as input to a classification engine that is responsible to classify the user to a particular cognitive factor group that consists of users sharing a similar value of the metric (representing a particular cognitive factor of that user).

The *personalization module* contains an adaptation engine that is responsible to map the elicited human factors with specific design factors (e.g., type of content, complexity of content). In particular, the adaptation engine applies specific adaptation rules and recommendations that are defined by the mapU administrator based on custom requirements.

The *personalized mechanisms* are finally communicated to the user interface based on the recommendation of the personalization module.

5.5   Technologies and Languages for the Design and Development of the mapU System

mapU is a dynamic Web-based adaptation and personalization system. All the information is stored in a database that is essential for eliciting the users' characteristics based on their responses on the online psychometric tests, questionnaires or their navigation behavior in the controlled implicit user modeling component. Accordingly the system adapts the content and functionality of the interactive system. This section will present the main technologies and languages utilized for the design and development of the mapU system. We investigate existing Web languages and technologies (server-side and client-side) and data storage technologies and consequently, we present the ones that have been advanced justifying our decisions.

5.5.1   HTML: HyperText Markup Language

HTML, Hypertext Mark-up Language, is the primary mark-up language for the creation of Web-pages on the World Wide Web. It provides a means to describe the structure of text-based information in a document by annotating certain text as headings, paragraphs, lists, etc., and to supplement that text with interactive forms, embedded images, and other objects. HTML is written in the form of labels, called tags, surrounded by less-than (<) and greater-than signs (>). For example, *<h1> some heading text</h1>* and *<p> some information</p>* denotes that *"some heading text"* and *"some information"* are respectively a heading and a paragraph within the HTML document. HTML tags also contain specific attributes (depending on each tag) that denote further information for that tag. For example, *<img src="images/ logo.png" />* is an image tag that contains the *src* attribute that points to the actual image file that is utilized by the Web browser to illustrate that image in the Web-page. Figure 5.30 illustrates an example HTML code snippet that is embedded within an HTML document.

In this context, the main purpose of HTML is to display and format content, allowing very limited interaction with the Web-page. HTML also describes at some extent the semantics of a document and can include embedded scripting language

```
<p>Age</p>
<select  style="font-size:14px; width:100%" class="m-wrap placeholder-no-fix" name="Age" id="s_age" class="span12 select2">
    <option selected value="">50+</option>
    <option value="1">&lt;20</option>
    <option value="2">20-25</option>
    <option value="3">26-30</option>
    <option value="4">31-35</option>
    <option value="5">36-40</option>
    <option value="6">41-45</option>
    <option value="7">46-50</option>
    <option value="8">50+</option>
</select>
```

Fig. 5.30 An example HTML code snippet

code for manipulating at run-time the HTML elements of a document and the behavior of the Web-page. Since its proposal, HTML has undergone several changes and different versions exist. The following versions of HTML exist:

HTML 1.0 (1989–1994): HTML 1.0 is the first version of HTML and was supported by a non-graphical browser running on UNIX, called Lynx and Mosaic. HTML 1.0 supported inline images and text controls, without further capabilities for styling of content.

HTML 2.0 (1995): HTML 2.0 was specified by the World Wide Web Consortium (W3C) and was supported by more Web browsers. HTML 2.0 was extended to include elements such as tables, text boxes, buttons, and attributes for changing the Web-page background. Since HTML 2.0, Web browsers specified additional features that were not part of the official W3C specification.

HTML 3.2 (1997): HTML 3.2 included support for creating tables, extended options for form elements and cascade style sheets (CSS) as we will see in the next section.

HTML 4.01 (1999): HTML 4.01 further extended cascade style sheets and scripting capabilities. Further support for CSS was included enabling designers and developers to create CSS information in a different file aiming to separate the HTML elements and content structure from the styling information.

HTML 5 (2014): HTML 5 is the latest version of the HTML standard. HTML5 was extended to include new semantic elements (e.g., header, footer, article, section), form control attributes (e.g., number, date, time, calendar, and range), graphic elements (e.g., svg, canvas), multimedia elements (e.g., audio, video), application programming interfaces (e.g., geolocation, drag-and-drop, local storage).

To this end, mapU was implemented utilizing the latest version of HTML5 given its extended capabilities and to conform to the latest standards of today's HTML Web browsers.

5.5.2   CSS (Cascade Style Sheets): Giving Style to HTML

As described above, HTML tags were originally designed to define the content and limited formatting of a document. The content of the document is parsed and its layout and formatting was handled by the Web browser. Given that the two early major browsers; Netscape and Internet Explorer, extended and interpreted differently the HTML tags and attributes (e.g., *<font>* tag and *color* attribute), one major issue of early versions of HTML was how to clearly separate the content from the presentation layout and design. In this context, W3C created a new means for styling HTML documents as part of HTML 4.0. In particular, W3C proposed Cascade Style Sheets (CSS) that provide a means for defining how HTML elements should be displayed, similarly to the font tag and the color attribute in HTML 3.2. CSS are either embedded inline within an HTML document using the *styles* tag or saved in an external text file (with .css file extension) and further embedded within the

HTML document using the *link* tag. The CSS specification entails a high number of styling attributes (e.g., font family, font size, colors, element's positioning, width, height, etc.) that enable Web designers and developers to change the appearance and layout of Web-pages. Since its initial specification by W3C, CSS was released in three different versions. CSS1 was released in 1996, CSS2 was released in 1998, followed by CSS3 in 1999. Each release was extended with additional support for styling Web-pages. In the context of mapU design and development, we utilized the latest version of CSS3 in order to take advantage of current state-of-the-art features for designing high quality user interfaces as well as to conform to the latest W3C Web design standards.

5.5.3 Client-Side Languages

As mentioned previously, HTML defines the layout and formatting of the Web-page, allowing limited interactivity with elements. HTML is initially parsed by the Web browser, interpreted and then displayed within the Web browser. The HTML specification contains a *script* tag in which client-side scripting can be embedded within the document for manipulating the HTML elements and styles that have been loaded by the Web browser. Today's Web-sites typically combine HTML, CSS and client-side scripting for creating interactive navigation menus, highlighting effects, image effects, animation, form field validations, data manipulation and many other actions for manipulating HTML elements and styles for enhancing the users' interactivity with the system.

Since the early versions of HTML, various scripting technologies and languages were proposed including JavaScript, JScript, VBScript and others. JavaScript is currently the dominant and most applied scripting language on the World Wide Web. The most important advantages using JavaScript are: (i) JavaScript is fast because any code functions run immediately once loaded and interpreted by the Web browser; (ii) being a light weight language, it is simple to learn and implement; (iii) it is versatile and can be inserted into any Web-page regardless of the file extension; and (iv) being client-side it reduces the demand on the Web server.

Nevertheless, due to its simplicity and due to the fact that it is a light-weight scripting language, building highly complex interactive systems on the client-side can be a challenging endeavor. In this context, over the past years, a JavaScript library called JQuery (2015) has been developed that enables an easy and effective way for building more complex scripts. JQuery's syntax is designed to simplify the development of client-side scripting by making it easier to navigate an HTML document, select elements, create animations, handle events, and develop AJAX (Asynchronous JavaScript and XML) applications. JQuery enables developers to create abstractions for low-level interaction and advanced effects.

Considering the aforementioned analysis, we have decided to use JavaScript, based on JQuery library as the main client-side scripting language for our system.

The need for implementing the mapU system with JavaScript rose for multiple reasons:

1. *User Modeling:* The users' response time is of critical importance for eliciting their cognitive characteristics since the user classification highly depends on the actual time users respond to a cognitive stimulus. In addition, the implicit user data collection method tracks the users' interactions with the hyperlinks, and these interactions must be stored in the system's database asynchronously without affecting the users' interaction with the system (without reloading the Web-page). In this context, we utilized JQuery with AJAX for processing all the required information (e.g., response time) and asynchronously communicating the data to the system's database.

2. *Content Authoring and Adaptation:* Adapting content and functionality requires pre-processing the semantically annotated content (before displaying it in the Web browser) and further applying different style sheets on the HTML elements for matching each user's cognitive characteristics.

3. *Management and Reporting:* Several JavaScript plugins have been utilized for managing and reporting the data stored in the database. For example, HighCharts (2015) reporting plugin has been utilized for generating graphical reports in the management and administration component.

5.5.4 Server-Side Languages and Frameworks

Server-side scripting is a technique for Web development in which a script is created and run on a Web server which generates a customized response for each user's request to the Web-site. Server-side scripting enables the development of dynamic Web applications since the content presented in the Web-site can be different for different users. Server-side scripting is primarily used for content management in which the main content of the Web-site is stored in a database and retrieved and presented to each user on request. The main operations include the client user requesting data from the Web server, e.g., information retrieved from the database, and the client user sending information to the Web server, e.g., storing user information in the database.

Web-based adaptation and personalization systems are by definition dynamic Web applications since the user models need to be stored on a Web server (e.g., in a relational database), and retrieved for adapting and personalizing the content and functionality of the system to each request made by the client user. Similarly, in the context of mapU, we developed a number of methods both for the user modeling and personalization module. The following main methods were developed as server-side scripts:

1. *User Modeling:* the users' response time to the psychometric tests, questionnaires and Web interaction metrics were processed and stored in a relational database on the Web server.

2. *Content Authoring:* the content of each Web-site is created on the client side and further stored in a relational database on the Web server.
3. *Management and Reporting:* all the content stored on the Web server is requested by the client user, in which the stored information is retrieved from the database, processed and sent back to the client user in HTML form.
4. *Adaptation and Personalization:* the content of each Web-site requested by the client user is retrieved from database, processed and sent to the user.

Among the most popular server-side technologies today (like Servlet Technology, JSP, PHP, ASP, etc.), which are used to pre-process pages and output HTML that is sent to the client user, we focus predominantly on PHP and ASP that have been respectively utilized in the development of mapU, and earlier prototype systems (e.g., AdaptiveWeb 2007).

5.5.4.1 PHP–PHP: Hypertext Pre-processor

PHP is an open-source and cross-platform server-side scripting language for creating dynamic Web-pages. PHP code is embedded in regular HTML documents (with .php extension) through PHP tags (.). When a user requests a PHP Web-page, the Web server initially processes the PHP code snippets (which are essentially code commands) and then sends the results in HTML format back to the user's Web browser. PHP runs on Apache Web server under Windows NT or UNIX. PHP language syntax is similar to C and Perl, however is more light-weight. For example in PHP, developers are not required to declare variables before use.

PHP entails a number of advantages and disadvantages. Its main advantages are: (i) It is fast, stable and easy to use; (ii) it is free, open source and cross-platform; (iii) it is easy to understand and learn; and (iv) it provides connective abilities with many databases and interface with a variety of libraries. The main disadvantages are: (i) It has security flaws given its open-source nature, anyone can see the source code, so any weaknesses can be revealed more easily; (ii) it is hard to maintain due to its lack of modularity; and (iii) it is difficult to implement complex Web applications since presentation of content (HTML and CSS) and PHP code is embedded in the same file.

5.5.4.2 ASP: Active Server Pages

Active Server Pages (ASP) is a technology proposed by Microsoft that enables the implementation of dynamic Web-sites. ASP uses server-side scripting to dynamically generate Web-pages. ASP pages have the extension .asp(x) instead of .html. When an ASP Web-page is requested by a Web browser, the Web server interprets any ASP code contained within the Web-page, processes and compiles the code and further produces HTML that is sent back to the client user's Web browser. Accordingly, ASP is only processed on the Web server and does not run on the Web server as in the case of JavaScript which is a client-side scripting language.

ASP runs on Internet Information Services (IIS) which is an extensible Web server created by Microsoft for use with Windows NT family. The latest version of ASP is ASP.NET which entails several enhancements over the old ASP such as, better language support, programmable controls, event-driven programming, XML-based components, user authentication, higher scalability, increased performance and easier configuration and deployment.

ASP.NET separates the page presentation from code through the *code-behind* feature which enables developers to separate the code run on the server-side out of an ASP.NET page and put it in a separate file. ASP.NET makes use of two popular code-behind languages; Visual Basic .NET and C# .NET. Essentially, the two coding languages have a different syntax and grammar, however, due to the Common Language Runtime (CLR), high-level codes written in Visual Basic or C# are compiled into MSIL (Microsoft Intermediate Language) code. Then at runtime, the CLR's just-in-time compiler (JIT compiler) converts the MSIL code into code native to the operating system.

ASP has advantages and disadvantages. The main advantages are: (i) it provides powerful database-driven functionality, enabling developers to implement Web applications that easily interface with a database; (ii) through Microsoft's Visual Studio (Microsoft's main Integrated Development Environment (IDE) it provides a set of developer tools that allow faster development and more functionality; (iii) it provides a good tradeoff between efficiency, security and robustness; (iv) it effectively handles memory leak and crash protection; (v) it supports coding in multiple language under a common development environment; and (vi) it supports reusability of existing mechanisms and solutions. The main disadvantages of ASP are: (i) ASP requires to be hosted on a Microsoft Web server, and thus does not provide flexibility; (ii) Web-pages containing ASP code snippets cannot be run by opening the Web-page in a Web browser, but instead the Web-page must be requested through a Web server that supports ASP. Nevertheless, this is a general disadvantage of any server-side languages and does not only concern ASP.

5.5.4.3   Server-Side Language and Framework Used for the mapU System

A direct comparison between PHP and ASP.NET cannot be made since PHP is a programming language (like C#) whereas ASP.NET is a Web framework. Both are currently widely used for developing dynamic Web-pages. Given the popularity in use and improvements made on both PHP and ASP.NET since their specification, choosing the one or the other would be in our opinion a rather good development choice. From our perspective the key factors for choosing either PHP or ASP.NET to develop dynamic Web applications are the following: (i) Costs: One might choose PHP since the costs for hosting ASP.NET applications are usually higher than PHP because PHP is open-source and free to use as opposed to ASP.NET; (ii) hosting options: PHP is cross-platform and can be run on both Windows NT and UNIX, whereas ASP.NET primarily requires running on a Windows NT Web server; (iii) programming preferences: some developers might choose PHP or ASP.NET due to its multiple language support; and (iv) development environment: developers might choose ASP.NET due to the functionalities provided in Visual Studio IDE, or PHP for developing Web applications in other development environments.

In this context, taking into account both languages; their advantages and disadvantages, we opted to develop mapU with PHP. Although developing the mapU system with ASP.NET would as well be a good development alternative, the rationale behind this choice was driven by the fact that, at this point in time, given that mapU is a proof of concept and research-oriented Web-based adaptation and personalization system, we decided to leverage the main advantages of PHP, being an open-source, cross-platform and free to use language.

5.5.5 Storing and Retrieving Data

In mapU, the database is an integral component. It forms the core of the application, holding all of the system's information and data: user models, Web-page content (Web objects) and functionality. The database is an essential and an active component, with a high throughput of data. The database has thus been designed in a way to provide the facility to efficiently store the information as well as quickly retrieve it.

We used a relational database management system to store all the information and SQL computer language to effectively manage (create, retrieve, update and delete) the data. MySQL was used since PHP provides easy connectivity and interfaces for calling and retrieving data from MySQL databases.

Furthermore, an important concern is to ensure openness and interoperability within and between the system's components. In case an external component aims to access the user's models, either for adaptation, for historic or statistic calculations, the system must be able to support extraction of the user's model. In order to achieve this, the user's model must be easily extendible and easy to handle. Using JSON (JavaScript Object Notation) for communicating the characteristics of the user's model seems to be the best way to achieve this since it provides the extendibility we need and enhances interoperability and integration among systems' components. JSON is s a lightweight data-interchange format which is easy for humans to read and write and easy for machines to parse and generate. In this context, we have designed a Web service (a software system designed to support interoperable machine-to-machine interaction over a network) for retrieving the users' model. Depending on the needs of a third-party system that interacts with our system through this middleware; calculations are made and are finally exported in JSON format.

5.6 Summary

The science behind adaptation and personalization systems has undergone tremendous changes in recent years and due to the multidimensional nature of such systems, a concrete definition has not been given to date. Yet, the basic goal of all systems remains the same: To transparently adapt and personalize content and functionality of interactive systems to the unique preferences and needs of users. Based on various definitions given to date (Brusilovsky 2001; Mulvenna et al. 2000; De Bra et al. 2004; Perkowitz and Etzioni 2000; Cingil et al. 2000; Blom 2000; Frias-Martinez et al. 2005), we conclude that any adaptation and personalization system employs mechanisms that automatically or semi-automatically adapt its content, behavior and functionality according to user data (e.g., user's interaction with the system or the context of use) that have been extracted either implicitly or explicitly. The utter goal is to increase the functionality of a system and improve the users' experiences by providing personalized and bootstrapped functionalities.

In this context, this chapter presented an effort towards designing an open and extensible personalization framework for building comprehensive user models including intrinsic human factors, and accordingly adapt and personalize the content and functionality of any Web-based interactive system. The chapter presented the main modules and components of the framework, placing special emphasis on the formalization of a human factor-based user model (including cognitive and emotional processing characteristics of users), and the adaptation procedures and algorithms for communicating a personalized result to the user interface. Following the conceptual design and formalization of the framework, we further presented the design and implementation of a real-life Web-based adaptive interactive system, considering current technological features of Web interactive systems.

We envision that this chapter will serve as a guide for researchers and practitioners on how a number of interdisciplinary elements, attributes and functionalities can co-exist under a unified framework, and enhance usability, satisfaction, and user experience delivered via its intelligent user interface to a number of heterogeneous contexts of interaction.

References

AdaptiveWeb (2007) An AdaptiveWeb system for integrating human factors in personalization of web content. Available online at http://adaptiveweb.cs.ucy.ac.cy. Accessed August 2015

Bandura A (1994) Self-efficacy. In: Ramachaudran VS (ed) Encyclopedia of human behaviour, vol 4. Academic, New York, pp 71–81

Belk M, Papatheocharous E, Germanakos P, Samaras G (2013) Modeling users on the world wide web based on cognitive factors, navigation behaviour and clustering techniques. J Syst Softw 86(12):2995–3012

Belk M, Germanakos P, Andreou P, Samaras G (2015) Towards a human-centered e-commerce personalization framework. In: Proceedings of the 2015 IEEE/WIC/ACM international conference on web intelligence (WI 2015). IEEE Computer Society Press (in press)

Blom J (2000) Personalization: a taxonomy. In: Proceedings of extended abstracts on human factors in computing systems (CHI'00), ACM Press, New York, 313–314

Brusilovsky P (1996) Methods and techniques of adaptive hypermedia. User Model User-Adap Inter 6(2–3):87–129

Brusilovsky P (2001) Adaptive hypermedia. User Model User-Adap Inter 11(1–2):87–110

Brusilovsky P, Maybury MT (2002) From adaptive hypermedia to the adaptive web. Commun ACM 45(5):30–33

Brusilovsky P, Millán E (2007) User models for adaptive hypermedia and adaptive educational systems. In: Brusilovsky P, Kobsa A, Nejdl W (eds) The adaptive web: methods and strategies of web personalization, LNCS 4321. Springer, Berlin/Heidelberg, pp 3–53

Cassady JC, Jonhson RE (2002) Cognitive test anxiety and academic performance. Contemp Educ Psychol 27(2):270–295

Cingil I, Dogac A, Azgin A (2000) A broader approach to personalization. Commun ACM 43(8):136–141

De Bra P, Aroyo L, Chepegin V (2004) The next big thing: adaptive web-based systems. J Digit Inf 5(1), Article 247

Demetriou A, Spanoudis G, Shayer M (2013) Developmental intelligence: from empirical to hidden constructs. Intelligence 41:744–749

Dieterich H, Malinowski U, Kühme T, Schneider-Hufschmidt M (1993) State of the art in adaptive user interfaces. In: Schneider-Hufschmidt M, Kühme T, Malinowski U (eds) Adaptive user interfaces: principles and practice. North-Holland, Amsterdam

Ekpaideion (2008) Adapting e-learning environments based on human factors. Available online at http://www3.cs.ucy.ac.cy/ekpaideion. Accessed August 2015

Frias-Martinez E, Magoulas GD, Chen SY, Macredie RD (2005) Modeling human behavior in user-adaptive systems: recent advances using soft computing technique. J Expert Syst Appl 29(2):320–329

Germanakos P, Tsianos N, Lekkas Z, Belk M, Mourlas C, Samaras G (2009) Proposing web design enhancements based on specific cognitive factors: an empirical evaluation. In: Conference on web intelligence. IEEE Computer Society, Washington, DC, pp 602–605

Germanakos P, Belk M, Constantinides A, Samaras G (2015) The PersonaWeb system: personalizing e-commerce environments based on human factors. Demonstration in extended proceedings of the international conference on user modeling, adaptation, and personalization (UMAP 2015), CEUR workshop proceedings 1388, Dublin, 29 Jun 29–3 Jul 2015

Goy A, Ardissono L, Petrone G (2007) Personalization in e-commerce applications. In: Brusilovsky P, Kobsa A, Nejdl W (eds) The adaptive web: methods and strategies of web personalization. LNCS 4321. Springer, Berlin/Heidelberg, pp 485–520

Halberstadt AG (2005) Emotional experience and expression: an issue overview. J Nonverbal Behav 17(3):139–143

Hauger D, Köck M (2007) State of the art of adaptivity in e-learning platforms. In: Proceedings of the 15th workshop on adaptivity and user modeling in interactive systems, Halle, pp 355–360

HighCharts (2015) Interactive JavaScript charts for web-pages. Available online at http://www.highcharts.com. Accessed July 2015

JQuery (2015) The write less, do more, JavaScript library. Available online at https://jquery.com. Accessed July 2015

Karat C, Blom JO, Karat J (2004) Designing personalized user experiences in eCommerce, LNCS. Springer, Dordrecht

Kozhevnikov M (2007) Cognitive styles in the context of modern psychology: toward an integrated framework of cognitive style. Psychol Bull 133(3):464–481

Mulvenna M, Anand S, Boechner A (2000) Personalization on the net using web mining: introduction. Commun ACM 43(8):122–125

Lekkas Z, Germanakos P, Tsianos N, Mourlas C, Samaras G (2013) Personality and emotion as determinants of the learning experience: how affective behavior interacts with various components of the learning process. In: Proceedings of the 15th international conference on human-computer interaction – HCI international 2013 (HCI 2013), Las Vegas, 21–26 Jul 2013, LNCS 8005. Springer, Berlin/Heidelberg, pp 418–427

Linden G, Smith B, York J (2003) Amazon.com recommendations: item-to-item collaborative filtering. IEEE Internet Comput 7(1):76–80

PAC (2015) Personalized authentication and CAPTCHA. Available online at http://pac.cs.ucy.ac.cy. Accessed August 2015

Paramythis A, Loidl-Reisinger S (2004) Adaptive learning environments and eLearning standards. Electron J e-Learn 2(1):181–194

Perkowitz M, Etzioni O (2000) Adaptive web sites. Commun ACM 43(8):152–158

PersonaWeb (2015) Personalizing generic web environments. Available online at http://personaweb.cs.ucy.ac.cy, http://adaptiveweb.cs.ucy.ac.cy/. Accessed August 2015

Rezaei AR, Katz L (2004) Evaluation of the reliability and validity of the cognitive styles analysis. Personal Individ Differ 26:1317–1327

Riding R (1991) Cognitive styles analysis. Learning and Training Technology, Birmingham

Riding R, Cheema I (1991) Cognitive styles – an overview and integration. J Educ Psychol 11(3–4):193–215

Salovey P, Mayer JD (1990) Emotional intelligence. Imagin Cogn Pers 9:185–211

Smartag (2012) Intelligent authoring of smart web objects for personalizing e-services. Available online at http://smartag.cs.ucy.ac.cy. Accessed August 2015

Spielberger CD (1983) Manual for the state-trait anxiety inventory (STAI). Consulting Psychologists Press, Palo Alto

Tsianos N, Germanakos P, Belk M, Lekkas Z, Samaras G, Mourlas C (2013) An individual differences approach in designing ontologies for efficient personalization. In: Anagnostopoulos I, Bielikova M, Mylonas P, Tsapatsoulis N (eds) Springer series studies in computational intelligence, edited volume Semantic hyper/multi-media adaptation: schemes and applications. Springer, Berlin/Heidelberg, pp 3–21

Wikipedia (2015) Available online at http://www.wikipedia.org. Accessed May 2015

WordPress (2015a) Free content management system. Available online at http://www.wordpress. org. Accessed July 2015

WordPress (2015b) Wordpress statistics. Available online at https://wordpress.com/activity. Accessed July 2015

Wu X, Kumar V, Quinlan J, Ghosh J, Yang Q, Motoda H, McLachlan G, Ng A, Liu B, Yu P, Zhou Z, Steinbach M, Hand D, Steinberg D (2007) Top 10 algorithms in data mining. Knowl Inf Syst 14(1):1–37

Part III
Practice: A Practical Guide and Empirical Evaluation in Three Distinct Application Areas

Chapter 6
The E-Learning Case

Abstract Over recent years, the use of computer-based (and Web-based) learning has become increasingly popular. Various E-Learning systems have been developed to provide users with the opportunity to access large quantities of data, often remotely, be part of electronic courses and enjoy facilitations that once could only be part of a traditional classroom, such as communication with other students, or the teacher. However, in many cases, the information in those systems is uniformly presented to all learners, neglecting any potential particularities driven by their human nature like cognitive abilities, learning style, perceptions and affective states. In this respect, research has concentrated on creating E-Learning environments that would integrate existing theories regarding individual differences in such a way as to maximize learning performance through adaptive presentation and navigation support. The personalization factor acts as a barometer to the design quality of such systems and interfaces that positively influence the learning process, academic performance, and satisfaction of learners. In this chapter, we propose a number of human-centred design guidelines for adaptive E-Learning systems that could be considered by researchers and educators in order to create more effective and efficient personalization methods and adaptivity rules to increase the students' learning experience and comprehension capabilities while interacting with a system.

Keywords E-Learning • M-Learning • Design • Guidelines • User study

6.1 Introduction

Computer-based learning has become an increasingly applied phenomenon in recent years. As technology and, more specifically, Internet continue to develop and spread out, a whole new world of potentials is open for the field of education. E-Learning, which once could be described as a fleeting trend, has nowadays given new dimensions to the field of teaching and learning. It finds its full application in distance learning, where a wide range of taught courses are uploaded entirely on dedicated Web spaces, accompanied by a huge number of resources. However, the massive amounts of content and information, delivered through a uniform approach does not necessarily mean that can generate the same levels of knowledge to

© Springer International Publishing Switzerland 2016
P. Germanakos, M. Belk, *Human-Centred Web Adaptation and Personalization*,
Human–Computer Interaction Series, DOI 10.1007/978-3-319-28050-9_6

learners, equally meeting their expectations and capabilities. In fact, it could act as a barrier for students' learning performance, as they likely share a variety of different characteristics in terms of information processing and learning abilities.

One possible way of responding to the different needs, preferences and characteristics of each student is to apply a different approach to the educational process and adapt teaching in accordance to their needs and particular modalities (Brusilovsky 2007; De Bra 2006; Aragon et al. 2002; Miskelly 1998). Several studies (Curtis et al. 1999; Riding and Grimley 1999; Gilbert and Han 1999) have supported this perspective, demonstrating that the accomplishment of learning goals is facilitated when teaching meets the specific learning needs of each student. In other words, when the learning environment is compatible or in line with the individual differences, learning becomes easier (Germanakos et al. 2008). In this respect, over the years, several attempts have been made to design and develop hypermedia systems and environments to satisfy the heterogeneous needs of the various users maximizing their information assimilation and satisfaction. Adaptive educational hypermedia systems are particularly popular since they provide students with the ability to control their access to information. Their educational value is strengthened given their enhanced functionality that enables the personalization of hypermedia in regards to the presentation and sequencing of learning material. At this stage, the objective is to make optimum use of learners' characteristics through completing the traditional user models (which are usually limited to personal data) and introduce the personalization factor in E-Learning environments in order to facilitate the learning process. Given that, failing to address learners' needs may potentially lead to reduced learning efficiency.

Moreover, with the adoption of wireless technologies, the use of mobile, portable, and handheld devices is gradually embraced across every sector of education. M-Learning, together with E-Learning, has also a growing visibility by offering tools and alternative support to the pedagogical approaches, the presentation of the educational material, the teaching strategies, and the interaction of learners with the learning material, for enhancing the learnability process and satisfaction of individuals.

For the sake of completeness, we have to clarify that today's pervasive and ubiquitous digital reality enables learners to stay connected 24/7 through their devices whether they are on the move, at work, or at home. In this respect, the E-Learning and M-Learning concepts are vaguely and interchangeably used, with their main differences to focus upon their learning objectives (apart from the technological-driven ones). For *E-Learning* there is a specific goal to learn something acquiring the particular knowledge or skills in a structured and formal manner; while for *M-Learning*, learning becomes more informal and opportunistic and it is based on more unstructured data and/or content (Traxler 2007). In order to give a broader perspective to the reader with respect to this application area's surrounding characteristics, constraints, and opportunities, we consider in this book E- and M-Learning as two highly interconnected research disciplines. Their differentiation is determined mostly from the device/ mobile technologies in use and the specialized services offered (such as SMS), that may impact the design of user interfaces and interactions. Therefore, we consider M-Learning as a "sub-set" of E-Learning that shares virtues, properties, and/or qualities.

In E-Learning, users are able to learn at any time, anyhow and at any location by using their devices. As a result, the different learning contexts that an individual is found each time create a dynamic learning setting in the E-Learning environment. In many cases the development of E-Learning context-aware applications and systems constitutes an interdisciplinary academic subject, and most approaches derive from the fields of Computer Science and/or Psychology, as a result of combined efforts to improve the effectiveness of Web-based education. The context of learners may consist of time, place, and activity-based patterns during interaction and learning processes, as well as from intrinsic and psychological characteristics, such as learner's information processing abilities and state-like cognitive and affective parameters. Considering these issues and concerns in their approaches, researchers could benefit for the design of robust E-Learning environments that are driven from diversified requirements for the provision of personalized, consistent and effective E-Learning content.

6.1.1 Potential, Limitations and a High-Level Classification of E-Learning Systems

Today's consensus that computers, portable devices and the Internet are broadening the scope and potentials of administration, organization and support of educational methodologies (i.e., affordable, effective, ease of use), has created new opportunities of content delivery in terms of representation and speed, organization and interconnection of learning objects, teaching tools, and teaching approaches/ strategies (Stanchev 1993; Gavrilova et al. 1999). Some of the main benefits are summarized as: (i) Learners can interact with each other and with their practitioners more efficiently in a common collaborative and personalized learning environment, exchanging notes and assignments in a real time mode (benefited by the technological advancements, such as wireless networks), increasing decision making in a given learning task; (ii) mobile devices are much easier to be installed in a classroom setting than desktop computers (i.e., the approved governmental funding schemes and attempts recently to install iPad devices in various schools in the United States, substituting the old PCs); (iii) PDAs and/or tablets are more convenient to hold notes and E-Books are lighter than textbooks, files or even laptops; (iv) handwriting with stylus pen is more intuitive than using keyboard and mouse; (v) mobile devices are independent of space and time, as well as can be personalized given the needs, requirements and perceptions of a user, increasing the familiarization and engagement during the learning process; while last but not least; (vi) these technologies may contribute to the digital equality, as these are generally cheaper than desktop computers.

However, even though there are various potentials and opportunities, the concerns and hindrances for ubiquitous, transparent and secure development of E-Learning applications and systems are still numerous. Building intelligent applications and smart solutions (i.e., promote reflection on individuals' evolving knowledge and misconceptions, and to increase their understanding of the learning process more generally – Cheverst et al. 2003), mostly on portable devices, could be considered as not an easy task, but rather as a time consuming and conflicting procedure. This realization could be generally perceived by various conceptual and technological constraints (Germanakos 2011). On one hand there is the challenge of developing consistent interdisciplinary user-centred models based on the unique individual/learner needs, psychological (cognitive and affective) intrinsic characteristics, and the conventional pedagogical models and teaching approaches; and on the other hand there are technological constraints still in place. These include: the non-reliable connections, due to uneven coverage of the wide areas (or fluctuations on the bandwidth capacity based on usage); the limited screen size of such devices, making it difficult to design user interfaces that provide the range of functionality needed to support users in their tasks (as in conventional desktop screens); the limited storage capabilities (i.e., to keep the demanding multimedia objects used in E-Learning environments nowadays); the limited life-time and variability of the batteries (may lead to disruptions in the learning process and/or loss of content, if there is a malfunction or there is not the possibility of immediate re-charging); the lower computational power may restrict the use of complex models and representation content schemes, such as moving graphics (although 3G and 4G technologies eventually allow to overcome this problem); and the reduced robustness of such devices, compared to desktop computers, may restrict the implementation of complex algorithms and secure routines (especially when building adaptive E-Learning environments where the resources and processes are more demanding).

Nevertheless, the wide range of technologies and devices in use allow the classification of E-Learning systems based on various characteristics. The most common classifications are related to Information Communication Technology (ICT) and educational technologies described next.

6.1.1.1 Classification Based on ICT

According to ICT, the systems are classified by the type of mobile devices and the type of wireless communication technologies that are supported. One of the technical classifications described in the literature (Naismith et al. 2004) employs two indicators – the portability of the devices and the personal use ability. The systems that are accessed through devices such as mobile phones and laptops can be classified as personal, since they support a single user, and as portable since they can be available in different locations. Some other technologies, less portable than mobile phones and PDAs, can still offer personal interactions with learning experiences. Classroom response systems consist of individual student devices that are used to respond anonymously to multiple choice questions administered by a teacher on a central server. This technology is static in the sense that it can only be used in one location, but remains personal because of its small size and allocation to one single user. There are also technologies that can provide learning experiences to users on the move, but the devices themselves are not physically movable. For example, interactive museum displays offer pervasive access to information and learning experiences, but it is the learner who is portable, not the delivery technology. Such systems are typically seen as being less personal, and are likely to be shared between multiple users. These are shared portable technologies.

Furthermore, according to Bull et al. (2003), in many cases mobile and desktop devices could be used in combination to provide hybrid E-Learning solutions. When the user is moving or has limited time, mobile devices could be employed to enable the learning process. However, when users do not face these constraints, and a desktop PC can be used, users might prefer a desktop PC for searching learning material. Therefore, various systems split the learning environments for two different types of devices (e.g., C-POLMILE, MoreMaths – Bull and McEvoy 2003). Combining desktop/ mobile environments raises a lot of issues because of the heterogeneous platforms, capabilities and devices as well as the difference in their monitors' size. In particular, is it better to use a unified method of presentation that can be applied in both types of devices (i.e., responsive), or use a method that applies specifically in each type of device? Also, how do we integrate mobile learning into a learning management system? How can we ensure the constant update and maintenance of the learning model across these kinds of developments? How do we determine whether a mobile device is the right tool for a particular objective/ activity? We can therefore understand that the challenges researchers still have to confront with in E-Learning are many and in different levels and dimensions. In this regards, a major challenge is to design dynamic personalized interfaces and software (Vassileva and Deters 1998) enabling easy access to information while being sufficiently flexible to handle changes in a user's context, activities and available resources.

6.1.1.2   Classification Based on Educational Technologies

With regard to educational technologies the proposed classification is based on the support of synchronous and/or asynchronous education, E-Learning standards, location of the users and the access to learning materials and/or administrative services. By examining each indicator separately we can create groups of classifications based on the corresponding attribute. Given the amount of time teachers and students share information with each other, the E-Learning systems can be classified as follows: (a) Systems which support *synchronous* education. These systems enable communication between students as well as among students and teachers in a real time environment. Often, voice communication and chat are employed for this purpose; (b) systems which support *asynchronous* education. Using these systems, students cannot communicate in real time with teachers and other students. Usually asynchronous communication is supported, exchanging information via emails and/or SMS; and (c) systems which support *synchronous and asynchronous* education.

The second group that uses as a classification indicator the support of *E-Learning standards* divides systems in: (a) E-Learning systems which don't support E-Learning specifications and standards; and (b) E-Learning systems which support E-Learning specifications and standards. To this group, E-Learning platforms which have a module for M-Learning (like Blackboard) can be added.

Based on Horstmanshof (2004) and Stratmann (2004), the systems are classified with respect to the ability to support *on-line* and/or *off-line (location based) access* to educational resources. Based on this attribute we have three kinds of systems: (a) On-campus systems, which can be accessed inside universities, schools and companies. The typical access to such systems is by using laptop computers or tablet PCs and via the wireless networks of the educational institutions; (b) off-campus systems, which can be accessed outside of universities, schools and companies. The access to these systems is realized by pocket size computers (PDA), cell phones or smart phones as these devices support long distance wireless communications and offer mobility at a larger extent than laptop computers and tablet PCs; and (c) systems which can be accessed both inside and outside of educational institutions (like Mobile ELDIT – Trifonova et al. 2004).

Depending on the *access to learning materials and/or administrative services*, existing systems can be divided into the following three groups: (a) E-Learning systems which support access to the educational content – materials, tests, dictionaries. This group includes systems like MobiLP (Chan et al. 2003); (b) E-Learning systems which support access to the educational administrative services. An example of such systems is Mobile Quest (Leverage 2009); and (c) E-Learning systems which support access to the learning materials as well as to an educational organization's administrative services. A system of this type is WELCOME (Lehner et al. 2003).

6.1.2 Context-Aware and Activity-Based Considerations in E-Learning Environments

Context-aware E-Learning has become critical in an effort to identify the contextual parameters of mobile environments and to adapt on the changing context during a student's learning process. A pioneering psychologist in the field of learning theories, Vygotsky argues that the environment plays an important role in the process of learning, which is produced through the interaction of social and personal factors (Schunk 2000). According to Dey (2001), *"context is any information that can be used to characterize the situation of an entity. An entity is a person, place, or object that is considered relevant to the interaction between a user and an application, including the user and applications themselves"*; Schmidt et al. (1999) depict context as a three dimensional construct, including the dimension of self (device state, physiological, and cognitive). There are a number of context-aware challenges identified for E-Learning. Schmidt (2005) and Yau and Joy (2006) refer to three challenges associated with context-awareness: (a) Context is difficult to identify – there is not a defined set of elicitation methods for obtaining contextual factors; (b) context is difficult to acquire – the challenge lies within the question of how to obtain the actual information about the user, once the relevant context features have been identified; and (c) context is difficult to make use of – if and how learning efficiency can be improved with context-awareness is not known. Context-aware learning support requires pedagogical theories and methodologies as its foundation.

Furthermore, given the dynamic change of learners' context, the identification of the appropriate learning activity at each stage of the learning process and task engagement is considered of increasing importance in order for the E-Learning systems to react and support individuals' accordingly. Activity-centred literature reveal seven broad theory-based categories of activity (considering new practices – Naismith et al. 2004): (a) *Behaviourist* – activities that promote learning as a change in learners' observable actions. The learning should invoke a stimulus and a response. In the case of E-learning, a message or notification, for example, invokes a stimulus which may lead to an action as a response; (b) *constructivist* – activities that enable learners to construct knowledge as a result of the point of view they formulate based on the conversion they do on the receiving information. The emphasis is on the participation of the learner in the process of learning and the aim is active and reflective knowledge. Constructivist teaching practices are related to the process of knowledge building and are primarily focused on the learner and the environment where learning happens. The applications of this theory in the field of educational technology aim for the development of authentic digital environments, which will provide the context within which the user will construct their knowledge instead of mere information collection. Taking into account the overall concept of the theory, E-Learning environments according to Boyle (1997) should provide chances for knowledge construction, give opportunities for experiencing a range of perspectives, integrate learning in authentic contexts which are directly related to the real world, encourage the expression of learners' views in the learning process, give learning a social perspective, encourage the use of multiple forms for representing reality, and encourage self-consciousness during the process of knowledge construction; (c) *meaningful learning* – has a Piagetian nuance and refers to activities that support the learning of ideas, concepts and principles through the linking of new information with prior knowledge (Ally 2004; Ausubel 1977). In this case, learning can be described as meaningful when new information has a systematic connection to relevant concepts stored in long-term memory (Schunk 2000). This can be achieved through the process of "assimilation" (use of existing cognitive structures to deal with new information) and "accommodation" (modification of existing cognitive structures to better meet the new requirements). The balance between these two complementary processes is known as "adaptation" and differs from one learner to another (Piaget 1969); (d) *situated* – activities that promote learning within an authentic context and culture. Situated learning posits that learning can be enhanced by ensuring that it takes place in an authentic context. With the use of mobile devices E-Learning applications are available in different contexts, and so can draw on those contexts to enhance the learning activity; (e) *collaborative* – activities that promote learning through social interaction. Computer supported collaborative learning is a relatively new term used in the field of educational technology. It combines the collaborative method of learning with the benefits that new technologies may offer. More specifically, it is the interaction that takes place in teamwork and the facilitation of which is offered by the use of new technologies during the distribution of knowledge and experiences within a learning community (Lipponen 2002). This interaction can be achieved not only between a user and a computer, but also between multiple users and one computer or multiple users and multiple computers and can be either synchronous or asynchronous (Scott et al. 2002). For example, mobile devices can support computer supported collaborative learning by providing another means of coordination without attempting to replace any human-human interactions. Alternative interaction ways are the online discussion boards which are provided from a number of M-Learning systems (Zurita et al. 2003); (f) *informal and lifelong* – activities that support learning outside a dedicated learning environment and formal curriculum. Research on informal and lifelong learning recognizes that learning happens continuously and is influenced both by our environment and the particular situations we are faced with. Informal learning may be intentional, for example, through intensive, significant and deliberate learning "projects", or it may be accidental, by acquiring information through conversations, TV and newspapers. Such a broad view of learning occurs outside the classroom and, by default, embeds learning in everyday life, thus emphasizing the value of mobile technologies in supporting it; and (g) *learning and teaching support* – activities that assist in the coordination of learners and resources for learning activities. Education as a process relies on a great deal of coordination of learners and resources. Mobile devices can be used by teachers for attendance reporting, reviewing students' marks, general access of central school data, and managing their schedules more effectively (Holme and Sharples 2002).

Adapting and personalizing to context and activity during human-computer interaction could help to improve usability of devices that are mounted with smaller screens and user interfaces (Brusilovsky 2001), especially when users are undertaking complex or specialized learning tasks. Again user types and characteristics, individual differences, tasks, location, etc., are issues relevant in supporting adaptive access to information, where different user modeling and adaptation techniques may be suitable in different contexts.

6.1.3   The Importance of Adapting and Personalizing E-Learning Environments

The use of hypermedia for educational purposes takes advantage of their ability to support the student in the process of collecting and using information, their potential to provide alternative teaching approaches to support different learning styles and, finally, their ability to support multiple representations of complex and insufficiently structured fields (Spiro et al. 1987). However, in practice, and given that the design of an educational system aims beyond usability, to achieve learning as well in a hypermedia environment various problems arise, such as: (i) It is doubtful whether all students are able to follow their own path regarding the course material (Jonassen et al. 1993); (ii) the level of knowledge of students on the subject matter differs significantly and can be developed differently through random interactions with the system (Hammond and Allinson 1989); (iii) learners tend to be lost in a state of unrestricted navigation (lost in hyperspace – Conklin 1987), especially when the field is wide and/or the students are beginners in the subject area (leading to cognitive overload – Gygi 1991); (iv) students during their navigation, may fail to gain an overview of the provided material and its structure (Hammond and Allinson 1989) and; (v) lack of adequate information, which would help students to formulate goals and find the material needed, may cause disorientation and ineffective teaching (Hammond and Allinson 1989; Romiszowski 1990).

The adaptivity of an educational system aims to support the learners during their study, by giving the system the ability to be adjusted dynamically according to learners and their progress. In recent years, many research works exist that focus on E-Learning content adaptation and personalization techniques and methods, trying to provide guided and efficient learning engagement through intelligent hypermedia environments (Brusilovsky 2001; Germanakos et al. 2010). These systems aim to improve the usability of content and navigation towards the various learning objectives. For example, they may adjust the content of the course to the choices, the knowledge and the preferences of the student or they may suggest to the learner the most relevant to their level and preferences, links (McCalla 1992). In general, these systems are classified according to their adaptation techniques: Adaptation based on the device's characteristics, on the context, and on the user.

- Adaptation based on device characteristics; is a device-centred approach that uses for example portable device's specific characteristics (i.e., smart phones, tablets, notebooks), like resolution analysis, data entry methods and the type of search engine. Before content presentation and based on the device's characteristics, part of the content is altered in order to match with the device. The most common technique of this approach is to access the database and use the most applicable content (or learning objects) based on the needs of a device (Huang et al. 2012), e.g., selecting image types (.jpeg, .gif) and their sizes.
- Context-awareness; throughout the learning procedure, context-aware systems monitor and sense the environment altering the content accordingly. An example is the R-CCANS system, a RFID-based campus context-aware notification system that conveys real-time messages and updates to students while they are moving around in the campus (Haron et al. 2010).
- User-centred adaptation systems; are systems that take into consideration users' personal and perceptual characteristics (Tretiakov and Kinshuk 2008; Kinshuk and Lin 2004; Brusilovsky 2001; Germanakos et al. 2007), like learning and cognitive styles and/or affective factors. These values are stored in user models

which are created either dynamically – the system analyzes users' navigation patterns while they browse over the information space and based on various techniques and methods, their models are dynamically constructed; or statically – users' explicitly define their characteristics, for example through on-line questionnaires.

In addition to the generic classification above, a thorough review from Somyürek (2015) revealed six new technological trends and approaches with respect to adaptive educational hypermedia systems namely, standardization, semantic Web technologies, the modular approach, data mining, machine learning techniques, and the social Web.

When it comes to learning, the audience of a class is usually mixed skill regarding prior knowledge, pace of learning, perceptual preferences and level of familiarity with new technologies. Therefore, an important issue in adaptive educational hypermedia systems is to investigate the characteristics of the learner, to which the educational process should be adapted (Wang and Kobsa 2007). The goals of the learner, but also their background (Brusilovsky and Millán 2007; Harackiewicz et al. 2002), knowledge level (Henze and Nejdl 1999), experience and learning style (Surjono and Maltby 2003; Brusilovsky 1996) are perceived as characteristics that differentiate the users of a system and are considered very important regarding the influence they may have on the learning process. User perceptual preferences (characteristics which influence visual, cognitive and emotional processes which take place throughout the entire process of accepting a stimulus until the final response to it – Germanakos et al. 2005) and learning/cognitive styles, in particular, received special attention from several researchers in the field of adaptive hypermedia, who share the belief that personalization will help students to learn more effectively. Thus, they began to explore those dimensions for a more accurate modeling. In addition to that, learners' preferences regarding the presentation of the educational material along with their need for navigation support are also aspects, which are taken into account for the design of adaptive educational hypermedia systems.

Nevertheless, one of the main issues that adaptive educational hypermedia systems face at some extent still today, is that they do not (or vaguely) consider the individual differences, i.e., intrinsic cognitive and emotional characteristics of students (such as learning and cognitive style, cognitive processing, working memory capacity, anxiety levels, etc.), in the representation of their content, providing the same learning material, links and resources to all users (or group of users), resulting in many cases to disorientation difficulties or cognitive overload during the learning process (Moallem 2007; Chen 2002; Brusilovsky 2003). In other words, these points raise the notion of human-centred adaptation and personalization that positively influence the design quality of E-Leaning environments and methods. The function of adaptation allows the meaningful use of activity and context-related information with respect to individual differences and may as well be considered as a level of intelligence embedded in an E-Learning system, regardless of whether users' or interface/technical characteristics are involved. A certain form of mapping rules and corresponding implications on the information space are required, in order for a system to alter visible to the user aspects of the environment regarding content presentation and navigation. Therefore, a collection and analysis of multi-level user requirements, human factors and behaviors need to be documented, taking into consideration adaptation and personalization design guidelines that suggest solutions based on the interdisciplinary theoretical user aspects in combination with the practical technological concepts and attributes.

6.2 Design Considerations and Constraints

The design and development of E-Learning systems, especially from a pedagogical perspective, presupposes the consideration and evaluation of multiple factors based on principles and practices, which support and facilitate the learning process. In this respect, several studies (Buendia and Hervas 2006; Colace et al. 2003) have outlined various criteria for designing E-Learning platforms until today. However, these criteria present some weaknesses, constituting either a collection of technical specifications for standardization purposes or they are not formulated based on a strong theoretical background, and therefore, do not consider any pedagogical principles and practices in the first place (Hsu et al. 2009). E-learning design requires a comprehensive and holistic approach, which includes all the key parameters. A selective evaluation which takes only a couple of major factors into account, although it may satisfy some needs, is by default fragmentary.

Recent studies suggest that a sound E-Learning environment design, apart from any technological specifications, should also take into account aspects which relate to learning theories and pedagogical principles (Papanikolaou et al. 2006; Bielaczyc 2006; Dagger et al. 2004; Chen and You 2001). Many researchers have outlined that effective online learning design should consider criteria such as instructional design, learning styles, learning content, multimedia application, etc. (Siragusa et al. 2010; Ally 2004; McGreal 1998; Swisher 1994). For example, Ally (2004) refers to nine aspects which should be taken into account for designing effective E-Learning environments including learners' motivation, individual differences, meaningful learning, learners' interaction and support. Khan and Vega (1997) point out that instructional goal(s) content quality and interactive design are the most important criteria for evaluating online course effectiveness. In the same vein, Siragusa (2005), based on Reeves and Reeves' model (1997), addresses nine main aspects for designing quality E-Learning environments. Specifically, she groups 24 recommendations in 9 main sections and argues about factors such as instructional strategies, the educator's role, subject content, knowledge and preferences of learners.

In general, some aspects such as interface, content quality and graphical environment, which are considered key factors for the design of E-Learning systems, are influenced by a combination of learning and activity approaches (e.g., constructivist learning, meaningful learning, teaching and learning support), as discussed earlier, and in their majority are met in a number of "checklists". A summary of the most frequently reported factors with their characteristics is given below:

Interface It is an integral component of a system and refers to the part where the interaction between a user and computer takes place. The effectiveness of the interface is one of the most important features of a system (Dumas and Redish 1999). This process shapes the level of control that users may have on their interaction with the system. The issue of users' control level regarding their interactions is essential from both educational and social perspectives. The ability, which is provided to the students in order to control their learning process, can create favorable conditions that promote self-activity and autonomy in learning.

Usability The significance of interface as a parameter also raises usability issues. The usability of an educational hypermedia system refers to the optimization of its interface in order to achieve maximum utilization of both the capabilities of the system itself, and the learning capabilities of the user. The concept of usability also includes the ability for quick learning and easy handling of the system by the user and, additionally, the system's potential of adaptation to user's needs and not vice versa (Nielsen and Molich 1990; Preece 1994).

Navigation Design It is also an important parameter that determines the educational value of an E-Learning environment. The appropriate and unambiguous grouping of the several options and functions can increase the usability and functionality of the system and consequently have a positive effect on the learning outcome (Melguizo et al. 2008; Kirk and Kennedy 2001).

Graphical Environment Symbols, icons, images and other elements of the graphical environment are aspects, which have to be taken into account during the design process (Kirk and Kennedy 2001). All these should be characterized by "intuitiveness" and to not require extensive thinking on the part of the user regarding their meaning, but, rather, should be easily understood by their effect (Squires and Preece 1999). The overall picture of the system must be user friendly and give the impression that the system works as it is defined by its graphical environment.

Learning Material and Instructional Design To produce effective online learning and teaching requires a comprehension of the processes by which students learn and interact with technology. The development of E-Learning resources, as well as the instructional approaches used, are considered two of the basic aspects which significantly influence the level of successful online learning. Initially, the quality of learning material in terms of accuracy (Hsu et al. 2009), appropriateness, consistency, structure and organizational clarity are classified among the most important parameters, which determine course content effectiveness. In addition, instructional design and, more specifically, the learning/teaching strategies used to support the learning material are also key factors in the process of learning (Turker et al. 2006).

Instructional design refers to the teaching methods and approaches that may be adopted in order to create pedagogically efficient and effective learning environments (Knowlton and Thomeczek 2007). A major issue during this process is the successful exposure of the learning goal to the learners, along with the effective integration of learners' past experience to new knowledge (see constructivist and meaningful learning in Sect. 6.1.2).

Cater to Individual Needs/Preferences It is important for the pedagogical design of an E-Learning environment to consider the system's capabilities to cater to individual differences, to process information in multiple ways and its ability to be adapted to the learning preferences, pace and control of each student (Siragusa 2005; Ally 2004; Sampson et al. 2002). This possibility occurs particularly in systems supported by adaptive hypermedia technologies and aim to adapt the system to the needs and characteristics of different users.

Friendliness Finally, a system should be characterized by friendliness and simplicity on a design and interaction level. It is important to generate a positive and enjoyable mood into users so that they will be motivated to use it again. The interest for learning is related to the way in which the environment encourages the user to continue using it and whether it strengthens their confidence to deal with the learning subject supported by the system.

Adaptive educational hypermedia systems have the ability to follow certain rules through which try to satisfy the abovementioned design criteria in order to provide personalized learning to users, at presentation – content-level (adaptive content presentation) and navigation – link-level (adaptive navigation support – Brusilovsky 1996) as discussed in Chap. 4. The design of such systems extents across techniques and methods capable of capturing the needs and intrinsic characteristics of an individual and then apply rules that can meet those in a given environment. Therefore, these systems may present different information to different learners and withhold information deemed unnecessary or unsuitable at a particular time. An important issue in the design of an adaptive educational system is the kind of adaptivity to be applied, and, more specifically, the features of the system, which may differentiate according to the learner. Several technologies that support personalized learning have been developed. These vary and may be applied from the adaptation of the actual content as it occurs through the interaction between the students and the system or to simply support and advise the learners during their study.

6.3   Human-Centred Design Guidelines

Considering all the appropriate theoretical and practical implications discussed so far, in this section we elaborate on a set of human-centred design guidelines and adaptation effects for personalizing E-Learning and M-Learning environments

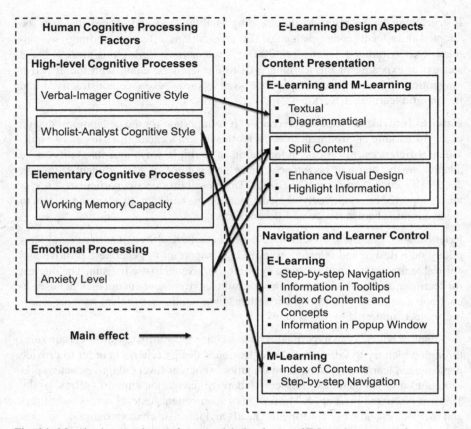

Fig. 6.1 Mapping between human factors and design factors of E-Learning systems

(such a distinction at this stage is deemed necessary in order to approach the subject to the level of detail that corresponds to a design perspective). In this respect, driven by a selected number of human factors (see Fig. 6.1), a high-level mapping between those and related design characteristics with regard to E-Learning systems is taking place.

The particular mapping is based on specific rules that are consistent to the respective psychological theories, in order to filter the raw content and deliver the most personalized Web-based result to the user. Accordingly, the cognitive styles dimension has been used for adapting the content presentation, structure and navigation support of E-Learning environments, since this dimension applies to a greater number of information processing circumstances, and deals rather with the broader construct of cognitive, than learning style. In line with the theory behind, for example, the number of images (few or many) to be displayed each time has a primary implication on Imagers, while the text (more concise or abstract) has a secondary implication. The analytic or holistic preference has a main effect on the links (learner control and navigation support). Working memory capacity primarily affects information quantity while emotional processing primarily affects the provision of aesthetics and highlighting important information as well as affects information quantity.

A practical example of the mapping could be as follows: A user might be identified that is: Verbal – Wholist with regard to cognitive styles, has a fair working memory capacity (weighting 5/7) and has high levels of anxiety. The design factors affected, according to the mapping for this particular instance are the: *images* (few images displayed), *text* (any text could be delivered), *info quantity* (less info since working memory capacity is limited), *links and learner control* (less learner control because the user is Wholist, *additional navigation support* (significant because the user has high levels of anxiety), and *high aesthetics* (to give more structured and well defined information, with more colors, larger fonts, more bold text, since the user has high levels of anxiety).

At this point it should be mentioned that in case of internal correlation conflicts, primary implications take over secondary ones. Additionally, since emotional processing is the most dynamic parameter compared to the others, any changes occurring at any given time are directly affecting the yielded value of the adaptation and personalization rules and henceforth the format of the content delivered. Furthermore, Table 6.1 summarizes the main criteria in order to analyze and document the usefulness of adopting a personalized approach in E-Learning environments.

In the following sections we describe in detail each guideline of Table 6.1 and their corresponding adaptation effects and human factors. For each guideline we also provide a visual illustration of the respective design and the triggered mapping of human factors and design characteristics for both E-Learning and M-Learning environments. Please note that the following design guidelines illustrate content in the Greek language since these have been applied and evaluated in a university setting in which the lectures are taught in the Greek language, ensuring therefore the control over the main principles under investigation and avoiding any side-effects driven by language barriers. Nonetheless, since the suggested guidelines and adaptation effects are communicated on a visual and interaction design level, these are not affected by the raw content of the setting.

6.3.1 Guidelines for E-Learning Environments

E-Learning environments are adapted and personalized on a content presentation, structure, navigation and learner support level. For creating the respective design guidelines and adaptation effects, we have initially developed an E-Learning content for a university lecture on the subject of algorithms. This environment includes a course named "Introduction to Algorithms" and is a first year E-Learning course environment that aims to provide students with systematic thinking and top-down methodology techniques for further development of constructive solutions to given problems. Figure 6.2 illustrates the original design of the lecture indicating

Table 6.1 Guidelines for personalizing E-Learning environments according to human cognitive and emotional processing factors

Where	Why	What	How	Guideline
E-Learning	Improve learning performance Assist comprehension Assist information processing Prevent cognitive load Improve task completion time Improve task effectiveness Improve user experience	Verbal Wholist Enhanced WMC	Textual Guidance Present information in tooltips	1 (Fig. 6.3)
		Verbal Analyst Enhanced WMC	Textual Learner control Index of contents and concepts Present information in popup windows	2 (Fig. 6.4)
		Imager Wholist Enhanced WMC	Graphical Guidance Present information in tooltips	3 (Fig. 6.5)
		Imager Analyst Enhanced WMC	Graphical Learner control Index of contents and concepts Present information in popup windows	4 (Fig. 6.6)
		Limited working memory capacity	Split content	5 (Fig. 6.7)
		Medium-high anxiety	Highlight information Make text large and bold Split content	6 (Fig. 6.8)
M-Learning		Verbal Wholist Enhanced WMC	Textual guidance	7 (Fig. 6.10)
		Verbal Analyst Enhanced WMC	Textual Index of contents and concepts	8 (Fig. 6.11)
		Imager Wholist Enhanced WMC	Graphical Guidance	9 (Fig. 6.12)
		Imager Analyst Enhanced WMC	Graphical Index of contents and concepts	10 (Fig. 6.13)
		Limited working memory capacity	Split content	11 (Fig. 6.14)

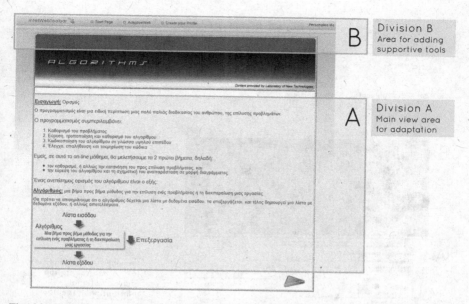

Fig. 6.2 Original design of the "Introduction to Algorithms" university lecture. Division A and B indicate the area in which the guidelines and adaptation effects will be applied

additionally two divisions in the layout in which the guidelines and adaptations effects will be applied; *Division A* which is the main view area in which adaptive content presentation will be applied, and *Division B* which is the main area for adding supportive tools (e.g., assisting the learner during navigation).

6.3.1.1   Guideline #1: Textual Representation with a Guided, Holistic Structure and Support Tools

Guideline #1 entails communicating the learning content in a textual representation that follows a holistic structure as well as additional navigation support tools. Figure 6.3 illustrates the design of this guideline. Accordingly, this guideline suggests illustrating content in a textual representation since the users in this case are Verbals and thus aiming to assist the cognitive processing of textual information (see Sect. 2.2.6). The user is provided with less learner control but instead the design is communicated in a way to guide the users from one page to the other since the users are Wholists and thus need more guidance during navigation. Their navigational path is essentially sequential, but they can visit previously seen Web-pages, which are annotated on the navigational panel (Division B). To further support their learning

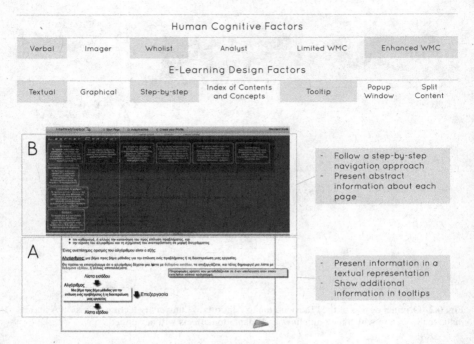

Fig. 6.3 Guideline #1: Textual representation with a guided, holistic structure and support tools

process we present abstract information about each page as a form of external guidance and framing of the course. Also, additional concepts are presented in the form of tooltips which are viewed by hovering over each concept, maximizing the coherence of each section and minimizing the possibility of disorientation.

6.3.1.2   Guideline #2: Textual Representation with Analytic Structure and Learner Control

Guideline #2 entails communicating learning content in a textual representation that follows an analytic structure and provides extended learner control (Fig. 6.4). Similarly to Guideline #1, this guideline suggests illustrating content in a textual representation since the user in this case is Verbal. Given also that he has an analytic cognitive style, the user is provided with extended learner control since it is suggested based on theory that Analyst users need more control and freedom during navigation and learning due to their analytic approach in information processing and content representation. In this respect, users are provided with a linked index of content and concepts that redirect them to any Web-page of the learning environment providing full control in their navigation. This enables Analysts to form an understanding of the course according to their own mode of information processing,

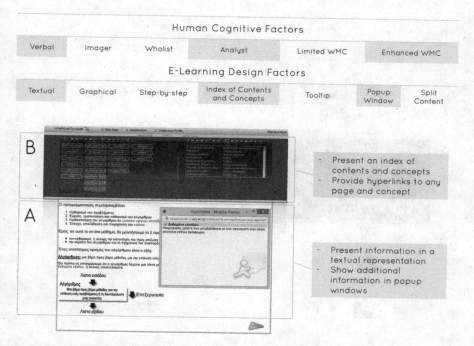

Fig. 6.4 Guideline #2: Textual representation with analytic structure and learner control

increasing their level of control over the course. Additional concepts are presented in the form of popup windows (instead of tooltips) aiming to give full control to manage and rearrange the concepts throughout the learning process. The links that are clicked (as in the linked index) should be highlighted with a different color, helping users to monitor their path.

6.3.1.3 Guideline #3: Graphical Content with a Guided, Holistic Structure and Support Tools

Guideline #3 entails communicating learning content with more graphical content that follows a holistic structure as well as additional navigation support tools. Figure 6.5 illustrates the design of this guideline. The reasoning behind this guideline is the same as Guideline #1 from the Wholist/ Analyst cognitive style perspective. The major change in this guideline is in the way content is presented. In particular, given that in this case the user is an Imager, more graphical information, i.e., diagrammatical representation, or flow chart visualizations should be used as illustrated in Fig. 6.5 aiming to assist the preferred and habitual way Imagers process information.

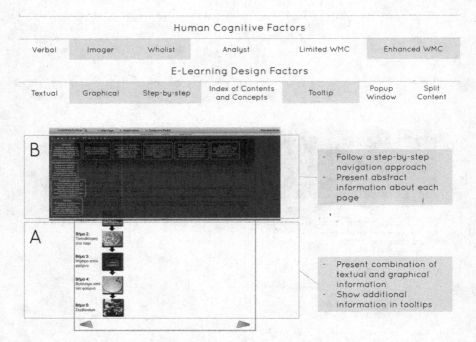

Fig. 6.5 Guideline #3: Graphical content with a guided, holistic structure and support tools

6.3.1.4   Guideline #4: Graphical Content with Analytic Structure and Learner Control

Similar to Guideline #3 previously, the new Guideline #4 entails communicating more graphical content rather than textual content since the user is an Imager (Fig. 6.6). Furthermore, regarding the structure, learner control and navigation support follows the same guideline as Guideline #2 in which specific tools and functionality is provided, enabling an analytic approach for Analyst users to have full control and navigate freely in the environment.

6.3.1.5   Guideline #5: Support for Users with Limited Working Memory Capacity

Guideline #5 provides support for users with limited working memory capacity. Figure 6.7 illustrates an example of this case. Given that users with limited working memory capacity cannot process and keep active high volumes of data for a short period of time during information processing, the design guideline suggests splitting the content of a particular Web-page. The main idea is to alleviate the possibility of cognitive overload, and is based on the notion that information processing is not sequential but parallel – therefore, the segmentation in clear-cut proportional

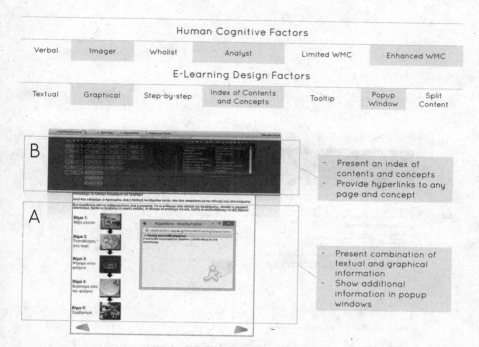

Fig. 6.6 Guideline #4: Graphical content with analytic structure and learner control

chunks may assist users' with low working memory capacity. Specifically, the Web-pages should be divided in logically coherent sections (from top to bottom), and users with low working memory capacity are able to click on a link in order for the rest of the content to be presented.

6.3.1.6 Guideline #6: Support for Users with High Levels of Anxiety

Guideline #6 provides support for users with high levels of anxiety. Figure 6.8 illustrates such an example. The elicitation process is through explicit feedback in which the users indicate their current anxiety levels through a horizontal sliding bar (on a scale of low-high – as a reminder the construct of anxiety is determined by subsequent processes with respect to current/self-reported anxiety, trait anxiety, application-specific anxiety and emotion regulation – see Sects. 2.1 and 2.3 and Chap. 5). Accordingly, in case the user has medium to higher levels of anxiety the design guideline and adaptation effect suggests enhancing the visual design with additional aesthetics, highlight important information, make text more visible by changing the size and font weight. Additional functionality for splitting content is also provided as in the case of users with limited working memory capacity, since users with high levels of anxiety might get confused and overwhelmed with large quantity of information.

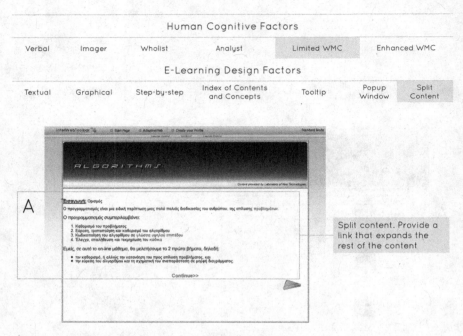

Fig. 6.7 Guideline #5: Support for users with limited working memory capacity

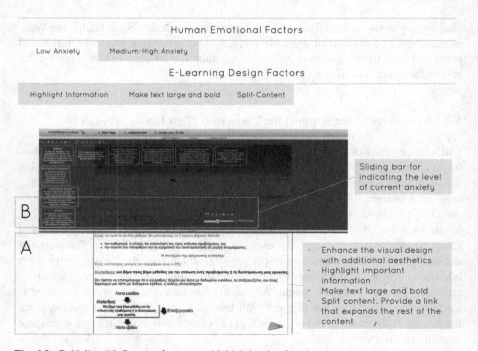

Fig. 6.8 Guideline #6: Support for users with high levels of anxiety

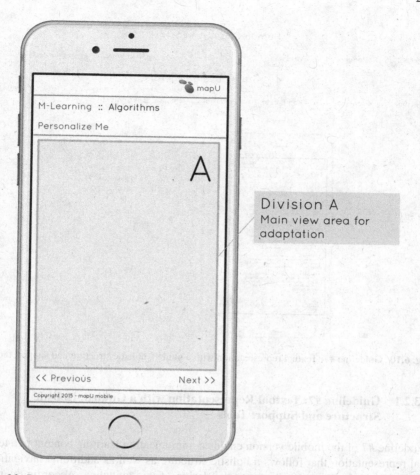

Fig. 6.9 Baseline design of the mobile version of the "Introduction to Algorithms" university lecture. Division A indicates the area in which the guidelines and adaptation effects will be applied

6.3.2 Guidelines for M-Learning Environments

Similar to the E-Learning setting, M-Learning environments are adapted and personalized on a content presentation, Web-site structure and navigation and learner support level. Accordingly, we have designed and developed a mobile version of the same university E-Learning content ("Introduction to Algorithms"). Figure 6.9 illustrates the baseline design of the lecture indicating the main division in the layout in which the guidelines and adaptations effects will be applied.

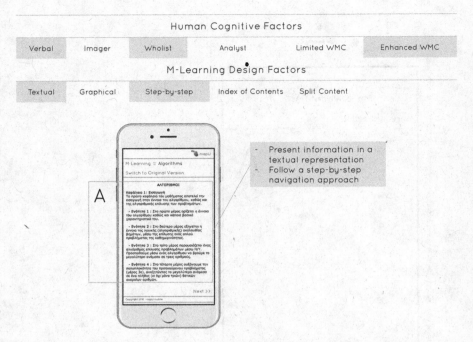

Fig. 6.10 Guideline #7: Textual representation with a guided, holistic structure and support tools

6.3.2.1 Guideline #7: Textual Representation with a Guided, Holistic Structure and Support Tools

Guideline #7 of the mobile version entails communicating learning content in a textual representation that follows a holistic structure as well as additional navigation support tools. Figure 6.10 illustrates the design of this guideline. Accordingly, the prominent representation of information is textual since the user is Verbal, and images are used when required, accompanying and not replacing texts. Furthermore, in the Wholist condition learners navigate through the environment in an externally guided way, which provides prefixed linkage and descriptions of the sequentially interconnected information, i.e., users navigate from one page to the other through "next" and "previous" link buttons. The organization of the distinct parts of the course is strict and outlined in a clear way. Users have access to previously acquired information, but they do not have access to links that lead to information of chapters not visited.

6.3.2.2 Guideline #8: Textual Representation with Analytic Structure and Learner Control

Guideline #8 entails communicating learning content in a textual representation that follows an analytic structure and provides extended learner control (Fig. 6.11). Similar to Guideline #7, this guideline suggests illustrating content in a textual

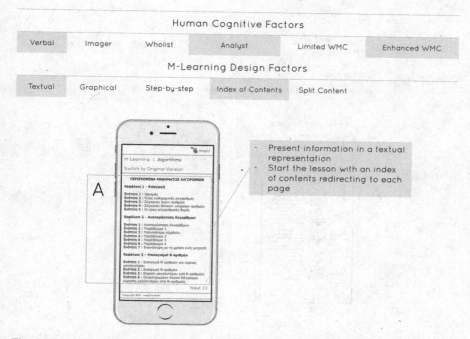

Fig. 6.11 Guideline #8: Textual representation with analytic structure and learner control

representation since the user in this case is Verbal. In the analytic condition, learners are free to navigate through the educational environment. They are not required to be guided externally, and may choose to follow a linear suggested path. They have also access to separate index of contents in order to follow an analytic path (maybe more scattered) in accessing information and forming knowledge. The information is extensively interconnected since hypertext is used at a greater extent and users can access at the same time different parts of the educational content.

6.3.2.3   Guideline #9: Graphical Content with a Guided, Holistic Structure and Support Tools

Guideline #9 entails communicating learning content with more graphical content that follows a holistic structure as well as additional navigation support tools. Figure 6.12 illustrates the design of this guideline. The reasoning behind this guideline is the same as Guideline #7 from the Wholist/ Analyst cognitive style perspective. The major change in this guideline is in the way content is presented. In particular, given that the user has an Imager cognitive style, images, diagrams and schemes are used, when possible for the representation of information. Specifically, instead of lengthy verbal descriptions, a schematic approach is suggested as an equally important

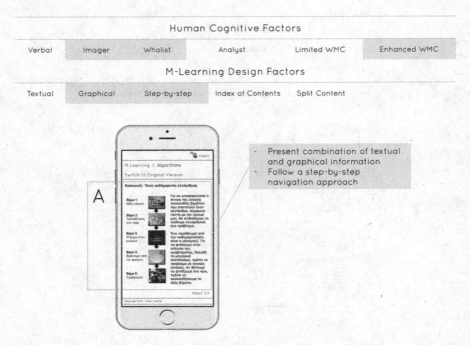

Fig. 6.12 Guideline #9: Graphical content with a guided, holistic structure and support tools

mean of instruction. Text is also used, but is reduced by approximately 40 % in comparison to Verbal learners.

6.3.2.4 Guideline #10: Graphical Content with Analytic Structure and Learner Control

Similar to previous Guideline #9, the new Guideline #10 entails communicating more graphical content rather than textual content since the user is an Imager (Fig. 6.13). Furthermore, in regards to structure, learner control and navigation support follow the same logic as in Guideline #8 in which extended learner control is provided due to the analytic approach of the users as well as the required freedom and control during navigation and learning process.

6.3.2.5 Guideline #11: Support for Users with Limited Working Memory Capacity

Guideline #11 provides support for users with limited working memory capacity (an example is depicted in Fig. 6.14). Since a large amount of information, especially when presented through a small screen device, may impair learners'

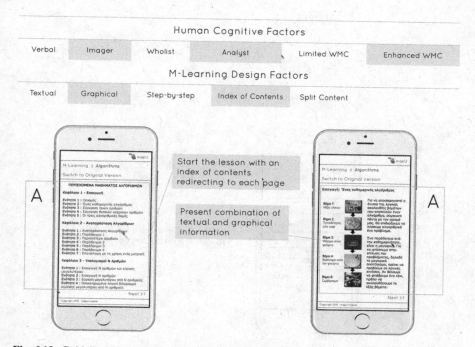

Fig. 6.13 Guideline #10: Graphical content with analytic structure and learner control

comprehension and readability, the guideline suggests presenting less information in a consecutive way, allowing users to devote more reading time to each resource and manually progress when they feel ready. Learning objects are accessible through a button link in which the user may activate to view more information.

6.3.3 Adaptation Paradigm in mapU Based on Guidelines

In this section we present an adaptation paradigm in mapU based on the aforementioned guidelines (considering as examples Guidelines #1 and #6). The aim is to illustrate and make more clear to the reader how the guidelines and adaptation effects (from a user interface design level) can be realized and applied at an implementation and technical level based on the formalizations and algorithms of the mapU framework (see Chap. 5). We hereafter present how the E-Learning content (based on "Introduction to Algorithms") is personalized based on a particular user model, using the aforementioned design guidelines and adaptation effects. According to Fig. 6.15, the adaptation paradigm follows a four step process as follows: (1) the user's model characteristics are initially retrieved from the database; (2) specific rules are applied and adaptation decisions are taken based on the pool of available adaptation rules (e.g., whether extensive learner control should be

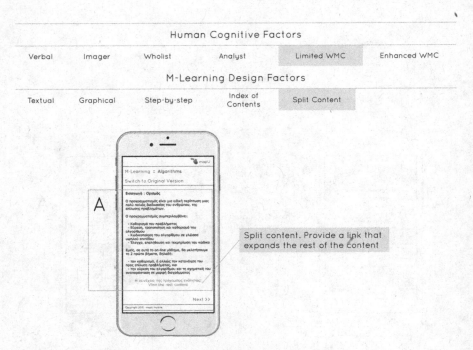

Fig. 6.14 Guideline #11: Support for users with limited working memory capacity

provided or more guidance); (3) retrieve the content, tools and functionalities from the database; and (4) extract the semantically annotated divisions from the Web-page content and then, based on the generated set of adaptation decisions, a client-side rule-based mechanism is run in which CSS design styles and client-side scripts are applied to the extracted content and finally communicated in a personalized format to the user's Web browser.

More specifically, in Step 1 the user model characteristics are retrieved through a client-side script that calls the Web server's database. In this particular example, the user is interacting on a desktop computer, the user is a Verbal and Wholist with regard to cognitive styles, has limited working memory capacity (weighting 2/7), and has medium-high levels of anxiety. In Step 2, given the retrieved user model, a set of recommendations and decisions are generated by calling the adaptation engine r which is responsible to generate a set of recommendations (R') for a user u_i using the user model um(u_i) and a set of adaptation rules (AR) which are based on the abovementioned design guidelines. In this case, it is suggested to apply and combine the designs of Guideline #1 and Guideline #6 that communicate content in a textual representation since the user is Verbal and is provided with more guidance during navigation. In addition, abstract information about each page is provided and additional concepts are presented in the form of tooltips. Furthermore, the content is split to prevent possible cognitive overload, and it is enhanced with additional visual aesthetics given his high levels of anxiety. In Step 3, a client-side script

1. User Model

$$um(u_i) = \{ \\ (d, age, 22), \\ (cc, vi, verbal), (cc, wa, wholist), \\ (cc, wmc, limited), (em, anxiety, medium - high) \\ \}$$

Client-side call to get user model

```
$.ajax({
    type: "GET",
    dataType: "json",
    url: "um.php",
    success: function (response) {
        um = JSON.parse(response);
    },
    error: function (jqXHR, textStatus, errorThrown){
        console.log(jqXHR.status);
    } });
```

2. Recommendations

$$r(um(u_i), AR) = R', R' \subseteq R$$

$$AR = \begin{cases} [(vi, verbal), \{(content, textual)\}] \\ [(vi, image), \{(content, graphical)\}] \\ [(wa, wholist), \{(learner\_control, guided)\}] \\ [(wa, analyst), \{(learner\_control, index\_of\_concepts)\}] \\ ... \end{cases}$$

$$R' = \begin{cases} \{(content, textual) \\ (learner\_control, guided) \\ (content\_quantity, split) \\ (aesthetics, enhanced)\} \end{cases}$$ *Guideline #1 and #6*

Client-side call to get recommendations

```
$.ajax({
    type: "GET",
    dataType: "json",
    Data: um,
    url: "recommendations.php",
    success: function (response) {
        rec = JSON.parse(response);
    },
    error: function (jqXHR, textStatus, errorThrown){
        console.log(jqXHR.status);
    }
});
```

3. Retrieve Content from Database

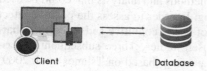

Client   Database

Client-side call to retrieve the content from the database

```
// Get main content objects
$.ajax({
    type: "GET",
    data: rec
    url: "GetContent.php",
    success: function (response) {
        var content = JSON.parse(response);
    },
    error: function (jqXHR, textStatus, errorThrown){
        console.log(jqXHR.status);
    } })
```

4. Adaptation and Personalization

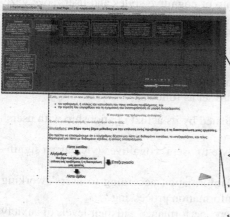

Extract *SmartObjects* and adapt the content

```
// Extract information inside the division
$(".SmartObject").each(function(index){
    CategoryArr.push($(this).find(".Category").text());
    TitleArr.push($(this).find(".SmartTitle").text());
    ContentArr.push($(this).find(".SmartContent").text());
});

$(this).find(".aesthetics").addClass("aesthetics");

// Create learner control
$.ajax({
    type: "GET",
    Data: rec
    url: "GetLearnerControl.php",
    success: function (response) {
        $("#divLearnerControl").html(response);
    },
    error: function (jqXHR, textStatus, errorThrown){
        console.log(jqXHR.status);
    }});
```

```
<div class="SmartObject">
    <div class="Category">Εισαγωγή</div>
    <div class="SmartTitle">Εισαγωγή: Ορισμός</div>
    <div class="SmartContent">
    <div>
        Ο προγραμματισμός είναι μια ειδική περίπτωση μιας πολύ παλιάς διαδικασίας
        του ανθρώπου, της επίλυσης <span id='con1' class='concept'>προβλημάτων</span>.
    </div>
    <div>
        <span class='aesthetics'>Ο προγραμματισμός συμπεριλαμβάνει:</span>
        .........
    </div>
</div>
</div>
.........
```

Fig. 6.15 Adaptation paradigm of the E-Learning environment

performs a call to the database to retrieve the content of the particular Web-page. Finally, in Step 4, the semantically annotated divisions (that entail the CSS class name *Category*, *SmartTitle*, and *SmartContent*) are extracted from the whole Web-page content. Then the generated recommendations R' (retrieved as a JSON object) are applied on these divisions. In particular, the set of recommendations entails predefined CSS class names which are applied on the content divisions. In this particular example, the user is provided with content illustrated in textual information (which is already retrieved from the database given the suggested recommendations) and provided with less learner control and rather more guidance given that he is a Wholist. Since the user has high levels of anxiety, specific predefined CSS classes are applied on semantically annotated divisions for emphasizing these and making them more visible to the user. The learner control toolbar is created on the server side based on the suggested recommendation and further embedded on the user interface through a client-side script.

6.4   Evaluation

This section aims to support the abovementioned guidelines and to make the reader more familiar with experimental validation methods and analysis that could be used in the context of E-Learning and M-Learning. In order to assess the positive effect and validity of personalization on the basis of users' cognitive and emotional characteristics, we next present four selected user studies. Three subsequent experiments were conducted in the context of E-Learning (based on Tsianos et al. 2009) and one experiment in the context of M-Learning (based on Germanakos et al. 2010).

The first study explores the relationship of cognitive styles and users' eye gaze behavior as to validate this specific psychological construct in the context of educational hypermedia. The second and third studies present the effect of a set of human factors (cognitive styles, visual working memory and anxiety) in an adaptive educational environment. The last experiment aims to elucidate whether personalization on working memory capacity may promote more efficient learning in the context of mobile devices. Our research questions are set as follows:

- Is the construct of cognitive style validated by its actual relationship with users' eye gaze patterns?
- Does matching online instructional style to users' cognitive style have a significant effect on their performance?
- Does providing the right amount of information according to users' working memory capacity promote effective information processing?
- Is there any correlation between learners' performance and their levels of anxiety and emotional regulation? In that case, is the aesthetic enhancement of the environment supportive?
- Does providing the right amount of information on small screen sizes (mobile devices) according to users' working memory capacity promote effective information processing?

6.4.1 Method of Study 1: Eye-Tracking Study

The methodology of the eye-tracking study did not involve any personalization processes. It should be clarified that only the Verbal/Imager axis was examined, because this dimension focuses on the preference for textual or visual information, which consequently can be mapped as learning objects in an adaptive system. In contrast, the Wholist/Analyst dimension describes a rather intrinsic organization of information that is rather inappropriate, in our opinion, to measure with such an experimental method.

The experimental design was between participants. Each individual took the cognitive style elicitation test for the assessment of the Imager/Verbal axis of cognitive style, and afterwards participated in an on-line learning course ("Introduction to Algorithms"). The number of participants was 21 (12 female and 9 male) and were all undergraduate students. Their mean age was 23, ranging from 20 to 26. It turned out that they were roughly equally distributed in groups according to their cognitive style: 7 Imagers, 8 Verbals and 6 Intermediates (users that do not belong to either of the two extremes of the cognitive style scale).

During the on-line course, an eye-tracker system recorded learners' eye fixations and tracking on the educational content. The procedure took place in a controlled environment, a computer lab, and each participant was alone during the experiment. It should be noted that the learning content consisted of a balanced (to the extent that would allow the delivery of the necessary information) number of visual and textual objects.

The *Video Eyetracker Toolbox* by Cambridge Research Systems Ltd. was used. It consists of a 50Hz camera, an adjustable tower that stabilizes the head of the participant during the measurements. A calibration procedure for each participant was required in order to increase accuracy by minimizing errors and deviations. The manufacturer provided a library of Matlab instructions, the CRS (Cambridge Research Systems) Toolbox for Matlab, which was used for signal processing and data exporting.

The dependent variables of our analysis were the calculated ratios of eye: (i) Fixations; and (ii) tracking. Fixation is defined as the focus on learning objects (eye gaze pause). In a sense, each visual or textual object may be considered as an Area of Interest (AOI), though it was not technically possible to measure the depth of focus on each object. Tracking refers to search patterns on the screen without focusing on specific areas.

The ratio in both cases is an images-to-text ratio on a scale of 1–10, with higher positioning on the scale implying a preference for images. For example, a ratio value of 10 (though realistically not possible) would mean that the user fixated exclusively on images (fixation ratio) or that he/she tracked only visual objects on the screen, avoiding anything else (tracking ratio). The positioning on these ratio scales displays a tendency that would ideally represent users' style preference.

The ratios were calculated from the raw data exported by the system. These data included: (i) Eye scanpaths on the x-y axises (tracking); and (ii) number and duration of fixations and pupil dilations (fixations), all in relation to the visual and textual objects on screen (or areas). Also, fixations and tracking on the navigation menu of the learning environments were measured, though proven to be insignificant in this experiment. The reason for converting fixations and tracking data to images to text ratios was that the cognitive style elicitation test is based on exactly such a ratio (see Chap. 5); thus, this conversion would allow the comparison of user behavior according to their style. The duration (ms) of the experiment was measured, but only for a number of participants, due to an internal technical error. It should be noted that users were free to allocate as much time as they wanted to each Web-page of the lesson.

The component that gathers and presents the eye-tracking data was developed within and integrated in the mapU system. Figures 6.16 and 6.17 respectively illustrate how an Imager differs in his/her eye-tracking patterns from a Verbal.

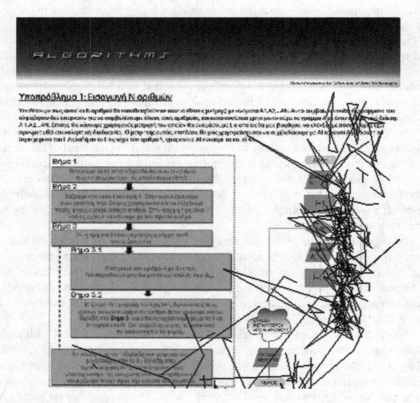

Fig. 6.16 Eye-tracking of an Imager

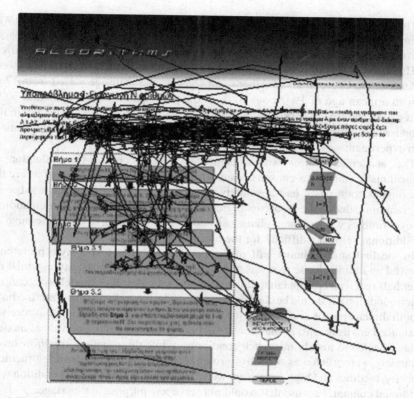

Fig. 6.17 Eye-tracking of a Verbal

6.4.2 Method of Study 2: Personalized E-Learning Study

The experimental design of the two subsequent personalization studies in E-Learning was a between participants memory test. In the first study, the effect of personalization on cognitive style was examined. The second study involved personalization on working memory capacity and anxiety.

The procedure in both experiments was the same: users created their user models through a series of psychometric tests, logged into the system, took the online course, and afterwards participated in an on-line exam assessing their level of comprehension. The order of the psychometric tests was not predetermined, since users were free to choose which test to take by clicking on the corresponding links. As soon as they created their user models by taking all tests, they were navigated to the on-line course, and upon the completion of the lesson, they clicked on a link that initiated a multiple choice exam on the subject they were taught.

The dependent variable was users' score on the memory test. The procedure was an in-class simultaneous learning activity, with students divided in groups of approximately 15 participants, and took place in computer labs of two universities.

The total number of participants in these experiments was 219; all of them were students in the Universities of Athens and Cyprus, and their age varied from 17 to 22 with a mean age of 19. About 70 % of the participants were female and 30 % were male. The first experiment took place at the University of Cyprus, while the second was conducted at the University of Athens. The number of participants in each experiment was 138 and 81 respectively.

The academic subject was a computer science course ("Introduction to Algorithms"), which was chosen because the students of the departments where the experiments took place had absolutely no experience or previous knowledge on programming, due to the theoretical orientation of their curriculum. Participation in the experiments was voluntary, but most students were willing to take the course, as an additional help on a difficult for them academic subject.

In the first study, almost half of the participants who had a style preference received an online course that was personalized on their cognitive style, whilst the other half received a course that didn't coincide with their user models (match/mismatch condition). It should be clarified that those who were classified as Intermediates in both dimensions of cognitive styles were treated as a control group that received a balanced environment; in the second study only users with high levels of anxiety were allocated to match/ mismatch conditions, while those with normal/low levels of anxiety were treated as a control group. Also, in the case of working memory capacity, medium and high span users were not placed in a mismatch condition with additional content, because that would not serve any purpose at this stage.

The allocation to the match/mismatch condition was quasi-random; each user that logged in was placed in the opposite from the previous user group, with the exception of Intermediates as a control group. In the second experiment, a user could as well be in a matched condition regarding working memory capacity, but in a mismatched condition as it concerns anxiety. Thus, all combinations were possible, and correspondingly considered in the statistical analysis.

Figures 6.18 and 6.19 respectively show the same Web-page of the on-line course, albeit differentiated (personalized) according to user preferences. Figure 6.18 is addressed to an Analyst/ Verbal user. Thus, the navigation menu on top allows free navigation and includes an index of concepts, and on the main area of the page the information is verbal. On the contrary, the screenshot in Fig. 6.19 is provided to a Wholist/Imager, with high levels of anxiety. The navigation menu is sequential, with short overviews of each section, framing more coherently the entire course. In this page, information is conveyed through visual representations. Moreover, the popup window provides additional support, and though it is not visible in this screenshot, the above text is aesthetically enhanced. In the case of low working memory capacity, the page is segmented, and is presented in distinct phases, by clicking of the user.

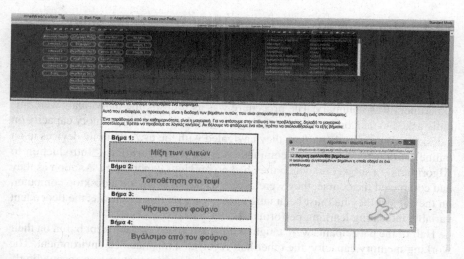

Fig. 6.18 Personalized environment for a Verbal-Analyst

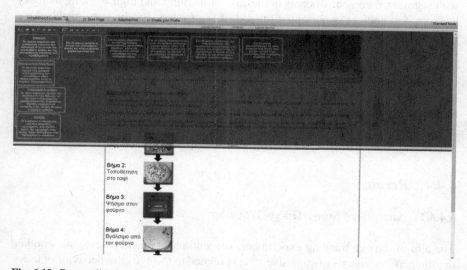

Fig. 6.19 Personalized environment for an Imager-Wholist

6.4.3 Method of Study 3: Personalized M-Learning Study

The design of this study was based on a between-participants approach. The number of participants was 49, with a mean age of 22.4; they were all students from the University of Cyprus, 60 % female and 40 % male and the participation in the experiment was voluntary. The procedure was as follows: the individuals were initially asked to take online user modeling tests to elicit working memory capacity on a desktop computer; thereupon, they navigated with the use of mobile devices in an online introductory course on computer science and algorithms ("Introduction to Algorithms", a subject on which they had no previous experience). As soon as they had completed the course, they were asked to take an exam, on a desktop computer, on the subject they had just been taught; the score on this exam was the dependent variable indicating learning performance.

Half of the participants were taught within a matched environment based on their working memory capacity; the other half received a mismatched environment. The characteristics of each distinct aspect of the environment that was correspondingly altered are described in the respective guidelines of this chapter. Figure 6.20 illustrates an example personalized environment for users with limited working memory capacity. Accordingly, learners with low working memory capacity are presented with segmented content whereas in the case of medium and high working memory learners, full content is presented instead of segmented. By the term matched we refer to the condition in which the presentation and structure of the environment is consistent to each individual's working memory capacity; on the contrary, in the mismatched condition the attributes of the environment do not coincide with an individual's abilities, and thus are the opposite. The purpose of this approach was to examine at a first level whether it is possible to positively affect learners' performance; if personalization on working memory is of any significance, then learners in the matched condition would outperform those in the mismatched.

6.4.4 Results

6.4.4.1 Analysis of Study 1: Eye-Tracking

The aim of the eye-tracking experiment, as mentioned, was to investigate whether the Imager/ Verbal axis of cognitive style is related to the eye gaze behavior of users in a hypermedia environment. This would provide additional validity to the concept of using cognitive style as a personalization parameter in adaptive systems: If users indeed behave according to their style preference, then content selection should accordingly be affected.

Since the variance of users' ratios of images to text fixations was homogeneous (Levene's statistic $(2,17)=0.845$, $p=0.446$), one way analysis of variance was performed on the data. Indeed, there was a linear differentiation in users' fixations with

Fig. 6.20 Personalized environment for a user with low working memory capacity. In this example, the content is proportionally segmented and enhanced with a button for further expanding and reading the rest of the content of this particular page

respect to their cognitive style; Imagers focused more on images, Verbals on texts, and Intermediates were placed in the middle. This difference is statistical significant: $F(2,18)=6.074$, $p=0.01$. The actual differences in the calculated images to text ratio are shown in Fig. 6.21.

Exactly the same applies with the calculated ratio of images to text tracking (Imagers: 5.82, Intermediates: 4.80, Verbals: 4.27), albeit with even greater statistical effect and significance: $F(2,18)=10.411$, $p=0.001$. Fixation and tracking on the menus of the user interface is more or less the same among categories with no differences observed.

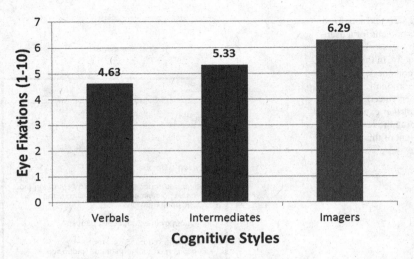

Fig. 6.21 Calculated images to text ratios of eye fixations on a scale from 1 to 10 (textual to visual preference)

Table 6.2 Differences in participants' allocation of time to the on-line course

Dependent variable: duration (ms)				
	(I) style	(J) style	Mean difference (I-J)	Sig.
Tukey HSD	Verbal	Imager	−209285[a]	.030
		Intermediate	−207172[a]	.021
	Imager	Intermediate	2113	.978

[a]The mean difference is significant at the .05 level

As it concerns the time that users allocated to the entire course, which was available only for 12 out of 21 participants due an internal technical error, there was also an effect of cognitive style: Imagers and Intermediates devoted about the same amount of time, while Verbals spent considerably less amount of time. Post hoc analysis of variance has shown that this difference on behalf of Verbals is statistical significant compared to both Imagers and Verbals (see Table 6.2).

The explanation of this finding is not as clear cut as with the aforementioned results. It could be argued that the processing of visual stimuli and the interpretation of the meanings that are conveyed is a more time consuming cognitive process; since Verbals have a clear preference towards text, they allocate less time in the processing of text. However, according to Riding's theory, Imagers also focus on textual resources, while the reverse is not observed; therefore, more time is consumed. With the case of Intermediates on the other hand, it makes much sense that equal processing of all objects would require further allocation of time.

Therefore, it is rather clearly indicated that the visual behavior of users in a Web environment, according to the eye-tracker measurements, depends on their cognitive style. These results also provide a form of validation for the effect of style in information processing within the context of hypermedia. This is of course a preliminary study conducted with a small number of participants, and it has to be replicated. Still, since the results are statistically robust, we believe that style could be considered as an important personalization factor in system design.

6.4.4.2 Analysis of Study 2A: Personalization in E-Learning

The first personalization experiment focused only on the construct of cognitive style as a personalization factor. Besides users' cognitive style, their working memory capacity was also included in their user model as a control variable. Participants had either a cognitive style preference or were classified as Intermediates (no cognitive style preference). The latter were treated as a control group that has no need for a personalized environment, and received the intermediate balanced course. The remaining users were randomly allocated to a "matched" or "mismatched" group of learners. If cognitive style is of any importance, these two groups should have statistically significant different scores.

A 3X3 analysis of variance was performed (three groups of cognitive style and three groups of working memory capacity), since the variance of the dependent variable was homogeneous, in order not only to assess the effect of matching the environment to users' style, but also to control for the effect of working memory capacity. Indeed, learners that received a matched environment ($n = 53$) outperformed mismatched learners ($n = 61$): $F(2, 137) = 4.395, p = 0.014$. There was no main effect of working memory capacity, or interaction with cognitive style.

The group scores were 66.53 % in the matched condition and 57.79 % in the mismatched. Intermediates had a mean score of 58.58 %. Post hoc analysis (see Table 6.3) has demonstrated that a difference actually exists only between matched and mismatched learners; Intermediates ($n = 24$) do not seem to vary from the former groups, and they are more dispersed. Perhaps in the absence of a cognitive style preference, other factors may have a stronger effect on learners' performance in a hypermedia environment (such as those involved in the next experiment).

In sum, the argument that personalization on the basis of cognitive style may improve learners' information processing in a hypermedia environment can be supported; those who demonstrate cognitive style preference are indeed benefited. The mean difference of approximately 9 points should also be evaluated in relation to the small variation of participants' scores.

6.4.4.3 Analysis of Study 2B: Personalization in E-Learning

By controlling the cognitive style parameter (environment matched to this preference), users received either matched or mismatched environment in regards to each separate factor of our model (working memory capacity and level of anxiety). In order to distinguish the effects of matching/ mismatching each factor, since the distribution of the sample was homogenous, a 2X2X3 analysis of variance was

Table 6.3 Post hoc analysis of learners' scores in all three conditions

Dependent variable: score %

Tukey HSD

(I) Matched environment	(J) Matched environment	Mean difference (I-J)	Sig.
Matched	Mismatched	8.74[a]	.034
Intermediate	Matched	−7.94	.189
	Mismatched	.80	.982

Based on observed means
[a]The mean difference is significant at the .05 level

Table 6.4 Differences of mean scores in the matched and mismatched condition with regards to users' levels of anxiety

Dependent variable: score %

Matched emotion	Mean	Std. error	95 % Confidence interval	
			Lower bound	Upper bound
Matched	56.250	3.905	48.461	64.039
Mismatched	43.107	3.667	35.792	50.421
Control	51.826	4.567	42.716	60.936

performed; there were three groups of learners in the emotional categorization, since users with low levels of anxiety were treated as a control group. There was a significant main effect of matching the instructional style to users' working memory capacity ($F(1,80)=4.501$, $p=0.037$), and to their levels of anxiety ($F(2,80)=3.128$, $p=0.05$). Cognitive processing efficiency was not found to have a main effect on score or interaction with the other parameters. The differences in mean scores are demonstrated in Tables 6.4 and 6.5.

Post hoc analysis of the differences between the three anxiety groups has demonstrated that the difference is statistically significant between matched and mismatched anxious users, with the control group scoring in between.

The relatively moderate sample of the second experiment necessary limits the level of analysis that can be applied. However, it is certainly encouraging the fact that there were found significant differences in learners' scores that can be attributed to the importance of taking into account factors such as those included in our approach; it seems that designing educational hypermedia with such factors left at chance may hamper the performance of users.

The finding that cognitive processing efficiency didn't affect users' performance may be explained by the fact that there were no real-time tasks involved in our online course; therefore, it would be difficult for this kind of individual differences to be revealed. It is also possible that a different approach to the personalization process or the experimental design could have provided different results.

Our methodology in this endeavor to investigate the role of these human factors is of course not exhaustive. Working memory capacity has been proven to be of importance as a parameter, and a certain effect of aesthetics has been demonstrated, but further empirical research is undoubtedly required.

Table 6.5 Differences of mean scores in the matched and mismatched condition with regards to users' working memory capacity

Dependent variable: score %

Matched working memory	Mean	Std. error	95 % Confidence interval	
			Lower bound	Upper bound
Matched	55.372	2.016	51.351	59.393
Mismatched	45.417	4.237	36.963	53.780

Table 6.6 Mean scores in each condition

Condition	N	Mean score	Standard deviation
Low WMC matched	6	70.67	16.990
Low WMC mismatched	6	51.00	16.852
Medium WMC matched	11	79.82	17.730
Medium WMC mismatched	7	80.14	14.938
High WMC matched	8	79.75	11.260
High WMC mismatched	11	78.36	22.357
Total	49	74.88	19.119

Table 6.7 Post hoc analysis of variance between learner groups

(I) Condition	(J) Condition	Mean difference (I-J)	Sig.
Low WMC matched	Low WMC mismatched	19.667*	**0.050**
Low WMC mismatched	Medium WMC matched	−28.818*	**0.002**
	Medium WMC mismatched	−29.143*	**0.005**
	High WMC matched	−28.750*	**0.004**
	High WMC mismatched	−27.364*	**0.004**

*The mean difference is significant at the .05 level

6.4.4.4 Analysis of Study 3: Personalization in M-Learning

The analysis aimed to investigate whether working memory capacity of users has an effect on their academic performance (score achieved on the test) regarding the matched and mismatched conditions of the M-Learning environment. A one-way analysis of variance on the data has shown that there are differences in the learning performance between the different user groups: $F(5,43) = 2.803$, $p = 0.028$. Based on Table 6.6, it is evident that learners with low working memory were benefited in the matched/ personalized condition.

Correspondingly, Table 6.7 presents the statistical significant score differences between all learner groups (LSD post-hoc analysis of variance).

Therefore, according to these initial findings, it seems that working memory capacity is a catalytic factor in the learning performance of mobile users in this experiment, since: (i) The differences in performance are highly related to differences in working memory capacity; and (ii) the corresponding personalization techniques were proven effective only on the low working memory capacity group of learners.

6.5   Benefits, Impact and Limitations

Adaptive educational hypermedia systems are among the most popular application areas of personalization research. Since the early days of adaptive hypermedia, research has been primarily focused on assisting students during their learning process by adapting and personalizing content and functionality of E-Learning environments according to their level of knowledge on specific subjects, their current goal in the system and their background. Research works also attempted to model more intrinsic parameters that define them as individuals such as learning and cognitive styles and cognitive processing abilities, with mixed outcomes so far (Brusilovsky and Millán 2007). On the one hand, results have shown that personalizing E-Learning environments according to human cognitive and learning factors improve the learning process, comprehension and information assimilation, while other works did not find significant improvements in learning. In any case, we believe that such a phenomenon does not reflect a single source of truth due to the multidimensional and complex character of these approaches (as described in Sect. 3.5). Accordingly, a challenging task is to extensively study existing theories on human factors and accurately identifying those that by matching their subsequent attributes with certain design aspects of E-Learning environments could have a practical value for the learner.

In this context, given that any task during learning is processed on a cognitive level with an evident influence of emotionality throughout the progress of learning activities, we believe that incorporating intrinsic user values and features in the personalization process of E-Learning environments (i.e., adapting content and functionality to users' abilities and preferences) is an important step towards alleviating learning and navigational difficulties, imposed by one-size-fits-all learning approaches. Henceforth, the suggested human-centred design guidelines and adaptation effects driven by a comprehensive user model that incorporates a selected number of cognitive and emotional human factors seem to have a strong impact in the adaptation and personalization of E-Learning settings. In particular, the evaluation results of various studies (a sample of which is presented also in this chapter) may provide a good argument towards that direction, since: (i) Users' eye gaze patterns are indeed related to their cognitive style; (ii) matching the instructional style to users' cognitive style promotes learning performance and effectiveness; (iii) segmenting the simultaneously presented information (in both E-Learning and M-Learning settings) according to learners' working memory capacity benefits information processing; and (iv) the aesthetical enhancement of the environment is correlated to the increase of academic performance of learners with high levels of anxiety.

More specifically, the eye-tracker study provided support for research on the construct of cognitive style in the context of adaptive hypermedia. The choice of the specific theory, its application in the hypermedia environment and the validation process with the use of an external measure, establish a relationship with individuals' actual behavior when interacting with digital learning content. As it concerns the personalization experiments in the E-Learning setting, the findings are quite consistent with the psychological theories that are referred in our framework and it seems that the difficult task of interpreting these theories into adaptation rules was at some extent successful. The differences in scores are not extreme, but an aggregation of this increase in performance may as well imply a far more efficient learning procedure. In regards to the M-Learning evaluation, according to the analysis, visual working memory was found to have a significant impact on learners' performance leveraging at some extent the inherent constraints imposed by the nature of mobile devices during interaction, e.g., the screen size.

Therefore, we could say that primarily the benefit of the human-centred design guidelines in E-Learning settings is two-fold. At first, they directly or indirectly reveal that enriching current user models with individual differences is a feasible approach; which now more than ever is considered necessary given the users' different cognitive abilities, emotional characteristics and contexts of use in combination with the alternative methods of content generation (driven from the heterogeneous infrastructures, devices and data representations). Secondly, there is an added value at an implementation level where the practical implications conveyed through the case-dependent content reconstruction, the proposed navigation designs, the aesthetic interventions and the supportive tools positively influence the overall design quality of E-Learning systems, as perceived by the users in most of the evaluation cases (the personalized conditions overruled the non-personalized ones). Thus, researchers and educators should consider optimizing the design of their learning material and their instructional strategies by bringing the learner into the centre and exploiting more effective and efficient personalization methods and adaptivity rules respectively. This way they could increase the students' learning performance, usability, satisfaction, and motivation, and decrease cognitive loads and unnecessary interaction steps that lead to confusion and disappointment.

At this point we should mention that as expected there are several limitations in this kind of approaches that entail the interpretation of theory into practice. In most cases, the participants selected for the purpose of a study, seemed to address the research questions satisfactorily, allowing for the extraction of conclusions regarding the subject under examination. However, external validity upon which generalizability depends could potentially be increased by a larger sample given the high complexity of the theoretical models and the scales of the subsequent constructs and attributes. In regards to the methodology, the unequal distribution of learners in some of the groups is also an issue of consideration, and a more elaborated sampling procedure is necessary in replicating and further confirming the results. Moreover, these studies were conducted using a specific adaptive hypermedia content which has been regulated based on the objectives and the related control factors of each experiment. To further test the viability of these theories and personalization interventions, an extended evaluation in different E-Learning settings and procedures should take place aiming to increase the sustainability of the findings. Lastly, supplementary control groups and conditions should be incorporated in the design of future experiments, additionally examining and fine tuning the effect of the numerous parameters involved in our information processing model (see Sect. 3.5.1). For example, an emerging research direction could combine and shift the focus towards pedagogical methods and models. A big challenge is to understand how the human-centred personalization factors could be optimally utilized in developing pedagogically efficient E-Learning environments and potentially lead to the development of pedagogical evaluation criteria for adaptive hypermedia systems, which will ensure both learners' satisfaction and enhance academic performance.

6.6   Summary

There is a growing body of empirical evidence to suggest that users tend to make poor decisions in traditional Web-based educational environments as the 'same next page of content' and navigational freedom given to the user leads to comprehension and orientation difficulties in the sense that users may become spatially disoriented, lose sight of educational objectives, skip important content, choose not to answer questions, look for stimulating rather than informative material or simply use the navigational features unwisely. Since the user population is relatively diverse, such traditional static hypermedia applications suffer from an inability to satisfy the heterogeneous needs of the many users. Moreover, the growth of mobile and wireless communication allowed content providers (i.e. teachers) to develop new ways of interactions for users delivered through a variety of channels and devices, but developing also more demanding requirements, inconsistent designs and complex educational settings; driven most of the times by their own preferences and what they think should be offered to them.

To this end, adaptive educational hypermedia systems tend to support students during the learning process through friendlier user interfaces and interactions by adapting the content presentation and navigation to their goals, needs and characteristics. More specifically, they enable active involvement of the students during information acquisition, they provide them with additional information or comparative explanations, they pass over the control and conditionally show, hide, highlight or dim fragments on a page, and they provide students with easier means of orientation and guidance by e.g. adaptively selecting and prioritizing the most relevant items to their searches. Nevertheless, adding to the challenges of classic adaptive educational hypermedia applications other characteristics like the user perceptual preference characteristics must be taken into consideration in order to deliver a more inclusive adapted result. It is true that nowadays, there are not many researches that move towards the consideration of comprehensive user models, based on intrinsic human factors, that could provide more holistic adaptive approaches to the users.

In this chapter, we have tried to bridge this gap by proposing a set of human-centred design guidelines, for the adaptation and personalization of E-Learning environments, which are primarily driven by specific cognitive and emotional factors. More specifically, we have shown how researchers can evaluate their impact onto the information space and how they can interpret their theoretical nature into a more tangible understanding that can be used in a form of mapping rules in order to give students the expected adaptive result.

References

Ally M (2004) Foundations of educational theory for online learning. In: Anderson T, Elloumi F (eds) Theory and practice of online learning. Athabasca University, Athabasca, pp 3–31

Aragon S, Johnson S, Shaik N (2002) The influence of learning style preferences on student success in online versus face-to-face environments. Am J Dist Educ 16(4):227–244

Ausubel DP (1977) Education psychology: a cognitive view. Holt, Rinehart and Winston, New York

Bielaczyc K (2006) Designing social infrastructure: critical issues in creating learning environments with technology. J Learn Sci 15(3):301–329

Boyle T (1997) Design for multimedia learning. Prentice Hall, London

Brusilovsky P (1996) Methods and techniques of adaptive hypermedia. User Model User-Adap Inter 6(2-3):87–129

Brusilovsky P (2001) Adaptive hypermedia. User Model User-Adap Inter 11(1-2):87–110

Brusilovsky P (2003) Adaptive navigation support in educational hypermedia: the role of student knowledge level and the case for meta-adaptation. Br J Educ Technol 34(4):487–497

Brusilovsky P (2007) Adaptive navigation support. In: Brusilovsky P, Kobsa A, Neidl W (eds) The adaptive web: methods and strategies of web personalisation. Springer-Verlag, New York, pp 263–290

Brusilovsky P, Millán E (2007) User models for adaptive hypermedia and adaptive educational systems. In: Brusilovsky P, Kobsa A, Neidl W (eds) The adaptive web: methods and strategies of web personalisation. Springer-Verlag, New York, pp 3–53

Buendia F, Hervas A (2006) An evaluation framework for e-learning platforms based on educational standard specifications. In: Proceedings of the 6th IEEE international conference on advanced learning technologies, 5–6 Jul 2006, IEEE Computer Society, Washington, pp 184–186

Bull S, McEvoy A (2003) An intelligent learning environment with an open learner model for the desktop PC and pocket PC. In: Proceedings of international conference on artificial intelligence in education, IOS Press, Amsterdam, pp 389–391

Bull S, McEvoy A, Reid E (2003) Learner models to promote reflection in combined desktop PC/mobile intelligent learning environments. In: Proceedings of workshop on learner modelling for reflection, international conference on artificial intelligence in education, IOS Press, Amsterdam, pp 199–208

Chan Y, Leung H, Wu A, Chan S (2003) MobiLP: a mobile learning platform for enhancing lifewide learning. In: Proceedings of the 3rd international conference on advanced learning technologies, Athens, Greece, pp 457–457

Chen SY (2002) A cognitive model for non-linear learning in hypermedia programs. Br J Educ Technol 33(4):449–460

Chen W, You M (2001) Internet mediated design course: the construction of the internet to assist design course. Design Res 2:109–115

Cheverst K, de Carolis N, Krueger A (2003) Workshop: user modeling in ubiquitous computing (preface). In: The 9th international conference on user modeling, Johnstown

Colace F, De Santo M, Vento M (2003) Evaluating on-line learning platforms: a case study. In: Proceedings of the 36th Hawaii international conference on system sciences (HICSS'03), IEEE Computer Society, Washington

Conklin J (1987) Hypertext: an introduction and survey. IEEE Comput 20(9):17–41

Curtis A, Carver J, Howard R, Lane W (1999) Enhancing student learning through hypermedia courseware and incorporation of student learning styles. IEEE Trans Educ 42(1):33–38

Dagger D, Wade V, Conlan O (2004) Developing active learning experiences for adaptive person-alised eLearning. In: Proceedings of the 3rd international conference on adaptive hypermedia and adaptive web-based systems. Eindhoven, pp 55–64

De Bra P (2006) Web-based educational hypermedia. In: Romero C, Ventura S (eds) Data mining in e-learning. WIT Press, Spain, pp 3–17

Dey AK (2001) Understanding and using context. Pers Ubiquit Comput 5(1):4–7

Dumas J, Redish J (1999) A practical guide to usability testing. Intellect Books, Oregon

Gavrilova TA, Voinov AV, Lescheva IA (1999) Learner-model approach to multi-agent intelligent distance learning system for program testing. In: The 12th international conference on indus-trial & engineering applications of artificial intelligence & expert systems (IEA/AIE-99), Cairo, 31 May–3 Jun 1999

Germanakos P (2011) Framing the theoretical and technological context of mLearning environ-ments – issues and concerns. In: Proceedings of the 6th mediterranean conference on informa-tion systems (MCIS 2011), Limassol, 3–5 Sept 2011, paper 36

Germanakos P, Tsianos N, Mourlas C, Samaras G (2005) New fundamental profiling characteris-tics for designing adaptive web-based educational systems. In: Proceeding of the IADIS international conference on cognition and exploratory learning in sigital age (CELDA2005), Porto, 14–16 Dec 2005, pp 10–17

Germanakos P, Tsianos N, Lekkas Z, Mourlas C, Samaras G (2007) Capturing essential intrinsic user behaviour values for the design of comprehensive web-based personalised environments. Comput Hum Behav J, Special Issue on Integration of Human Factors in Networked Computing, Elsevier Science Publishers B. V. Amsterdam, The Netherlands, 24(4): 1434–1451. doi:10.1016/j.chb.2007.07.010

Germanakos P, Tsianos N, Lekkas Z, Mourlas C, Samaras G (2008) Realizing comprehensive user profiling as the core element of adaptive and personalized communication environments and systems. Comput J, Special Issue on Profiling Expertise and Behaviour, Oxford University Press, Oxford, UK, 52(7), 749–770. doi:10.1016/j.chb.2007.07.010

Germanakos P, Belk M, Tsianos N, Lekkas Z, Mourlas C, Kleanthous G, Samaras G (2010) Adapting mLearning environments on learners' cognitive styles and visual working memory span. In: Proceedings of the 5th mediterranean conference on information systems (MCIS 2010), Tel-Aviv-Yaffo, p 38

Gilbert JE, Han CY (1999) Adapting instruction in search of 'a significant difference. J Netw Comput Appl 22(3):149–160

Gygi K (1991) Recognizing the symptoms of hypertext and what to do about it. In: Laurel B (ed) The art of human computer interface design. Addison-Wesley, Reading

Hammond NV, Allinson LJ (1989) Extending hypertext for learning: an investigation of access and guidance tools. In: Sutcliffe A, Macaulay L (eds) People and computers. Cambridge University Press, Cambridge, pp 293–304

Harackiewicz J, Barron K, Taurer J, Elliot A (2002) Predicting success in collage: a longitudinal study of achievement goals and ability measures as predictors of interest and performance from freshman year through graduation. J Educ Psychol 94(3):562–575

Haron NS, Saleem NS, Hasan MH, Mazeyanti MA, Aziz IA (2010) A RFID-based campus context-aware notification system. J Comput 2(3), pp 122–129, ISSN 2151–9617

Henze N, Nejdl MW (1999) Student modeling in an active learning environment using Bayesian network. In: 2nd workshop on user modeling and adaptive systems on the WWW, Toronto, May 1999

Holme O, Sharples M (2002) Implementing a student learning organizer on the pocket PC plat-form. In: Proceedings of MLEARN 2002: European workshop on mobile and contextual learn-ing, Birmingham, pp 41–44

Horstmanshof L (2004) Using SMS as a way of providing connection and community for first year students. In: Proceedings of the 21st ASCILITE conference, Perth, Australia, pp 423–427

Hsu C, Yeh Y, Yen J (2009) Development of design criteria and evaluation scale for web-based learning platforms. Int J Ind Ergon 39(1):90–95

Huang HC, Wang T, Hsieh FM (2012) Constructing an adaptive mobile learning system for the support of personalized learning and device adaptation. Procedia - Social and Behavioral Sciences, 64(9): 332–341, ISSN 1877-0428

Jonassen D, Mayes T, McAleese R (1993) A manifesto for a constructivist approach to users of technology in higher education. In: Duffy T, Lowyck J, Jonassen D (eds) Designing environments for constructivist learning. Springer-Verlag, Berlin, pp 232–247

Khan BH, Vega R (1997) Factors to consider when evaluating a web-based instruction course: a survey. In: Khan BH (ed) Web-based instruction. Educational Technology Publication, Englewood Cliffs, pp 375–378

Kinshuk T, Lin T (2004) Application of learning styles adaptivity in mobile learning environments. Third Pan Commonwealth Forum on Open Learning, pp 4–8

Kirk J, Kennedy G (2001) Adding value to educational multimedia: the role of graphic design. In: Proceedings of the 18th annual conference of Australasian society for computers in learning in tertiary education. ASCILITE, Melbourne, pp 93–96

Knowlton DS, Thomeczek MA (2007) Heuristic-guided instructional strategy development for peripheral learners in the online classroom. Quart Rev Dist Educ 8(3):233–249

Lehner F, Nösekabel H, Lechmann H (2003) Wireless e-learning and communication environment: WELCOME at the University of Regensburg. e-Service J 2(3):23–41

Leverage the power of an e-learning solution (2009) http://www.knowledgeanywhere.com/mobile.htm

Lipponen L (2002) Exploring foundations for computer-supported collaborative learning. In: Stahl G (ed) Computer support for collaborative learning: foundations for a CSCL community. Lawrence Erlbaum Associates, Hillsdale, pp 72–78

McCalla G (1992) The search for adaptability, flexibility and individualization: approaches to curriculum in ITS. In: Jones M, Winne P (eds) Adaptive learning environments: foundations and frontiers. Springer-Verlag, Berlin, pp 91–122

McGreal R (1998) Integrated distributed learning environments (idles) on the internet: a survey. Educ Technol Rev 9:25–31

Melguizo M, Madrid R, Van Oostendorp H (2008) The importance of navigation support and reading order on hypertext learning and cognitive load. In: Proceedings of the 8th international conference for the learning sciences, Utrecht, June 2008

Miskelly T (1998) Interactive student modeling. In: Proceedings of the annual southeast regional conference (ACM-SE 36), ACM Press, New York, pp 88–94

Moallem M (2007) Accommodating individual differences in the design of online learning environments: a comparative study. J Res Technol Educ 40(2):217–245

Naismith L, Lonsdale P, Giasemi V, Sharples M (2004) Literature review in mobile technologies and learning. NESTA Futurelab, Bristol

Nielsen J, Molich R (1990) Heuristic evaluation of user interfaces. In: Proceedings of the SIGCHI conference on human factors in computing systems: empowering people, Seattle, April 1990

Papanikolaou KA, Mabbott A, Bull S, Grigoriadou M (2006) Designing personalised educational interactions based on learning/cognitive style and learner behaviour. Interact Comput 18(3):356–384

Piaget J (1969) The mechanisms of perception. Rutledge & Kegan Paul, London

Preece J (1994) Human-computer interaction. Addison-Wesley, New York

Reeves T, Reeves P (1997) Effective dimensions of interactive learning on the World Wide Web. In: Khan BH (ed) Web-based instruction. Educational Technologies Publications, Englewood Cliffs

Riding R, Grimley M (1999) Cognitive style and learning from multimedia materials in 11-year children. Br J Educ Technol 30(1):43–59

Romiszowski AJ (1990) The hypertext/hypermedia solution-but what exactly is the problem? In: Jonassen D, Mandl H (eds) Designing hypermedia for learning. Springer-Verlag, Berlin, pp 321–354

Sampson D, Karagiannidis C, Kinshuk (2002) Personalised learning: educational, technological and standardisation perspective. Interact Educ Multimedia, Special Issue on Adaptive Educational Multimedia 4:24–39

Schmidt A (2005) Potentials and challenges of context-awareness for learning solutions. In the workshop of the SIG adaptivity and user modelling in interactive systems

Schmidt A, Aidoo KA, Takaluoma A, Tuomela U, Van Laerhoven K, Van de Velde W (1999) Advanced interaction in context. In: Proceedings of the 1st international symposium on hand-held and ubiquitous computing, Karlsruhe, 27–29 Sept 1999, Springer-Verlag London, pp 89–101

Schunk D (2000) Learning theories: an educational perspective, 3rd edn. Prentice-Hall, Upper Saddle river

Scott SD, Mandryk RL, Inkpen KM (2002) Understanding children's interactions in synchronous shared environments. In: Stahl G (ed) Computer support for collaborative learning: foundations for a CSCL community. Lawrence Erlbaum Associates, Hillsdale, pp 333–341

Siragusa L (2005) Identification of effective instructional design principles and learning strategies for students studying in Web-based learning environments in higher education. PhD thesis. Curtin University of Technology, Perth, Australia

Siragusa L, Dixon CK, Dixon R (2010) Designing quality e-learning environments in higher education. Educ Res 1(6):186–197

Spiro RJ, Vispoel W, Scmitz J, Samarapungavan A, Boerger A (1987) Knowledge acquisition for application: cognitive flexibility and transfer in complex content domains. In: Britton BC, Glynn S (eds) Executive control processes in reading. Erlbaum, Hillsdale

Squires D, Preece J (1999) Predicting quality in educational software: evaluating for learning, usability and the synergy between them. Interact Comput 11(50):467–483

Stanchev I (1993) From decision support systems to computer supported cooperative work, computer mediated education of information technology: professionals and advanced users (A-35), In: Barta BZ, Eccleston J, Hambusch R (eds). Elsevier Science Publishers B. V, North-Holland, pp 287–295

Stratmann J (2004) From virtual university to mobile learning on the digital campus: experiences from implementing a notebook-university. In: The international conference on education and information systems, technologies and applications (EISTA 2004), Orlando

Surjono H, Maltby J (2003) Adaptive educational hypermedia based on multiple student characteristics. In: Zhou W, Nicholson P, Corbitt B, Fong J (eds) Proceedings of the 2nd international conference on web-based learning. Springer, Berlin, pp 18–20

Swisher K (1994) American Indian learning styles survey: an assessment of teacher knowledge. The J Educ Issues Learn Minor Stud 13:59–77

Traxler J (2007) Defining, discussing, and evaluating mobile learning: the moving finger writes and having writ. Int Rev Res Open Dist Learn 8(2):1–12

Tretiakov A, Kinshuk (2008) Towards designing m-learning systems for maximal likelihood of acceptance. Int J Eng Educ 24(1):79–83

Trifonova A, Knapp J, Ronchetti M, Gamper J (2004) Mobile ELDIT: challenges in the transition from an e-learning to an m-learning system. In: Proceedings of the world conference on educational multimedia, hypermedia and telecommunications (ED-MEDIA 2004), Lugano, ISBN: 1-880094-53-3, 21–26 Jun 2004, pp 188–193

Tsianos N, Lekkas Z, Germanakos P, Mourlas C, Samaras G (2009) An experimental assessment of the use of cognitive and affective factors in adaptive educational hypermedia. IEEE Trans Learn Technol, IEEE Computer Society 2(3):249–258

Turker A, Gorgun I, Conlan O (2006) The challenge of content creation to facilitate personalised e-learning experiences. Int J E-Learning 5(1):1–17

Vassileva J, Deters R (1998) Dynamic courseware generation on the WWW. Br J Educ Technol 29(1):5–14

Wang Y, Kobsa A (2007) Respecting users' individual privacy constraints in web personalisation. In: Conati C, McCoy K, Paliouras G (eds) Proceedings of the 11th international conference on user modeling, Corfu, pp 157–166

Yau J, Joy M (2006) Context-aware and adaptive learning schedule for mobile learning. In: The international workshop on mobile and ubiquitous learning environments (MULE) at the international conference on computers in education (ICCE 2006), Beijing, 30 Nov–4 Dec 2006

Zurita G, Nussbaum M, Sharples M (2003) Encouraging face-to-face collaborative learning through the use of hand-held computers in the classroom. In: Proceedings of Mobile HCI 2003. Springer-Verlag, Udine, pp 193–208

Chapter 7
The E-Commerce Case

Abstract Ensuring that the design of E-Commerce environments is in-line with the task at hand, providing satisfactory guidance and user experience to customers is critical for a company's success. Despite the popularity of online shopping, especially due to the increasing use of mobile channels and platforms, research reveals that astonishingly between 60 % and 70 % of online users terminate their purchasing process, abandoning their shopping carts. The most important reasons appear to be that users do not have a clear understanding or direction through the purchasing process, or they have difficulties on locating and collecting the respective information for their targeted items or services. Current personalization approaches try to solve at some extent these problems, but still most of them fail to provide solutions aligned to the unique capabilities and characteristics of the end-users. Hence, taking into consideration that human-computer interactions within E-Commerce settings are in principal cognitive tasks, it is vital to follow human-centred adaptation and personalization design guidelines to model and develop such user interactions. This way, we will be able to more inclusively tackle the customers' needs, requirements and perceptions, while at the same time companies will benefit from more sustainable buying behaviors. Among the numerous dimensions of individual differences in cognitive processing found in the literature, this chapter proposes design guidelines driven by high-level cognitive factors and elementary cognitive processes of the human mind, discussing how researchers and professionals could integrate them in the user interface design of E-Commerce environments.

Keywords E-Commerce • Design • Guidelines • Checkout • User study

7.1 Introduction

The Internet has been adopted by the mass market more quickly than any other technology over the past century and currently provides an electronic connection between progressive businesses and millions of customers (and potential customers). With the growing maturity and diffusion of ICT-based applications, infrastructures and methodologies, the challenge for companies to do business electronically (E-Business) is now more evident than ever. Doing business electronically, which is

© Springer International Publishing Switzerland 2016
P. Germanakos, M. Belk, *Human-Centred Web Adaptation and Personalization*,
Human–Computer Interaction Series, DOI 10.1007/978-3-319-28050-9_7

the automation of business processes both intra- and inter-firm over computer mediated networks, implies a primary focus on commercial transactions and services delivery between companies and their customers/consumers (B2C) or other companies, processes within a company and between companies (B2B), as well as processes between the consumer and the business (C2B) or among the consumers (C2C). Although the prefix 'E-' in E-Business becomes a 'must' for companies to stay competitive, the underlying concepts are still changing fast, which translates into a constant 'adopt and adapt' for many of them. In the E-Business sector, companies deliver digital technology products and services as a significant part of their core business or use digital technologies as their primary channel to market. The term E-Business is many times used interchangeably with E-Commerce, which refers to the purchase and sale of goods and/or services via electronic channels such as the Internet. Those two concepts include a number of functions, processes and transactions that at some extent determine their different philosophy and scope of application. E-Commerce deals mostly with "external" processes that reach the customers, suppliers, partners or other stakeholders, while E-Business extends, at the same time, beyond that scope covering internal processes such as products development and management, risk management, inventory control, etc.

Most of the discussion in this chapter concentrates around the area of E-Commerce, while for the sake of simplicity we will regard the terms of 'goods/products' and 'services' as two complementary concepts that refer to the same high-level understanding. The terms 'goods/products' and 'services' are closely related in today's digital reality since the line of distinction is relatively fuzzy. Strictly speaking, a product is something tangible that is produced by a company and can be evaluated while a service refers to some more intangible benefits which are less concrete or easily measured. However, in many cases, those two terms are closely associated since a product includes the concept of service.

The World Wide Web has brought E-Commerce to an entirely new era by aiding the trade, distribution and sales between organizations and consumers (Corbitt et al. 2003). It is fairly often described as a company's gateway to global business and markets, exploiting the opportunities provided by ICT to improve performance and revenue. To be able though to gain a better understanding of the impact of ICT and the actions to be undertaken, the related trends and opportunities embedded in the internal mechanisms and operational procedures of the various enterprises have to be realized. In the new digital economy, this approach presupposes the shift of the focus on strategies which result from substantial structural organizational changes, competitive scenarios, interventions, policies, etc. In more practical terms, in the ever changing business environment, companies face opportunities that mainly focus on the development of multi-channel (especially mobile) and broadband solutions; to provide more interactive business services that match their customers' needs in terms of ease-of-use, personalized functionalities, timely and on demand delivery, etc. Especially current computer and network infrastructures stimulate the use of the Internet and enable the usage of rich applications and services, improving their functionality and performance. In this respect, two different strategies for enterprises' improvement are identified (Germanakos et al. 2005a): *Process inte-*

gration (back-end) and *service delivery* (front-end). The first one refers to the degree to which a service is re-engineered in the transformation from of an off-line service to E-Service, while the second refers to the channel and distribution strategies in the provision of business services. Relevant channel and distribution strategies are critical for the future advancement of services to achieve accessible, customer-focused and responsive competences. Following the growing user demands and requirements as well as the rapid development of the technological advancements and infrastructure capabilities, the development of services should not only focus on making the service available on the Internet, but also examine the different delivery platforms and interaction alternatives through it. A multi-channel (Web, SMS, Cloud, IoT, Satellite etc.) and a multi-device (PC, mobile phones, PDA, tablet PC, interactive digital television, satellite handset, etc.) access mix improves the accessibility to the services offered, since these are available anytime, anywhere and anyhow through a single point of access entry. This increases productivity at a lower cost and time while at the same time enhances the business services' sustainability. Indisputably, this is the vision of an interoperable, transparent and secure business continent whereby multi-channel service integration and delivery over seamless personalized interfaces is considered fundamental.

To be able to meet this vision, customers must not be spatially disoriented but they should be able to have continuous and adapted access on the requested information and services. Providers must take into consideration their customers' requirements, and needs (e.g., the ability to have direct interaction with a service provider when this is needed, the services provided to be of certain quality, findable, usable, and affordable, and delivered efficiently in terms of response time), and provide adjustable service information and interactions in terms of activity, context and time. Having these in mind, business analysts and practitioners should offer quality on demand multi-channel services delivery by developing intelligent user interfaces and processes that are based on adaptive presentation and navigation techniques targeting their customers' individual characteristics and perceptions (Germanakos et al. 2007). In such a case, they will be able to retain their customers and gain the competitive advantage in their market segment.

7.1.1 Potential and Limitations of Multi-channel E-Commerce Products and Services Delivery

The plethora of networked devices and platforms that continuously come to light, as well as the emergence of alternative ways to access the Internet have increased the demand for multi-channel access to applications, products and services. The faster and cheaper W4 (Wireless World Wide Web), the fourth generation (4G) wireless networks, the cloud technologies as well as the more sophisticated mobile devices are currently establishing mobile broadband services as the future trend. Nowadays, products and services can be delivered through a wide variety of channels (the term 'channels' is often used as a concept that includes 'channel type', 'technology', 'platform', 'media', 'device' and 'touch point'), while the interaction with any one of those is capable to change the customers' perception of a product or service per se. When customers have free choice between different channels to access a service, they will choose the channel that realizes the highest relative value for them, by means of high quality, usability, cost-efficiency and effectiveness. In that sense, in order for providers to increase the value of their services should have their processes and delivery channels more integrated and coordinated based on solid business and architectural models, liable to accept any change or additions deemed necessary (then the introduction of a new channel is not merely an additional channel but a new opportunity to improve products and services delivery). With regard to the customer, this integration of channels means more accessible and more flexible service delivery which leads to better services. On the other hand, separate development of different channels for a single service can lead to inconsistencies such as different data formats and/or interfaces.

To avoid this, common data that are used by the front-office applications should be stored centrally so that they can be shared by the applications. Storing data centrally means that they need to be collected only once and that they can be accessed by back-office applications. When data are stored centrally, users can also access the services they want from the location(s) and medium they want (desktop or mobile), as all the relevant information retrieval is taking place from the same databases. When back-office processes are also integrated, full service integration becomes possible, which raises the quality and number of services significantly. Unquestionably, this can be an overwhelmingly difficult and costly task for companies, since many of them are currently found in a transitional period trying to co-op with the dynamicity of their market. They might face difficulties with the volume of data (millions of records stored for a single stand-alone application), data redundancies, or inherent technical difficulties that derive when building and maintaining business applications for access by heterogeneous platforms.

Nevertheless, apart from the technological constraints or limitations of the various channels such as the size, data entry, storage, etc. (see Sect. 6.1.1), the mobility emergence creates tremendous opportunities for most companies allowing them to innovate and promote their products and services effectively and efficiently, by cutting the cost, increasing productivity and addressing return on investment on their applications and services. At the same time, it enables them to increase customer retention, by establishing valuable direct links and strengthening important relationships through "anyhow, anytime, and anywhere" interaction achieving the competitive difference. Moreover, mobile technologies and interactions could be considered as a new kind of front-end access to smart applications and services with specific capabilities of delivering on demand real time personalized information, orders, products, and payments adapted to the individual customer. Below we present a related high-level overview of a number of potentials/requirements that have been identified (Germanakos et al. 2005b):

- *Flexibility: anyhow, anytime, anywhere.* (a) The technological developments have introduced a wide variety of new channels over which different forms of contact and interaction could take place (i.e. consuming services by means of self-service on a 24×7 basis irrespective of location); and (b) many service delivery processes should consist of two or more interaction alternative sessions between the customer and the provider (i.e., if the organization is flexible in terms of its service delivery, it will allow the user to choose the channel or location for the interaction processes, and allow him to switch between channels at any preferable time).
- *Accessibility.* (a) Customers should be able to locate the required services (awareness); (b) customers should be able to identify the channels that they can use to access the service they need; (c) once a service is located and accessed, customers should be able to consume the information provided by the service; (d) the legal basis of E-Commerce services stipulates that they must be accessible for all potential users; and (e) a pricing policy for services should guarantee that the intended target groups can afford the services.
- *Quality.* (a) There are many situations in which a customer needs more than just one service to deal with a particular activity. In a one-stop shop approach, a single interaction should be able to address all requirements, thus saving the customer's amount of time considerably; (b) E-Commerce services are usually regulated by means of strictly defined specifications. In this respect, quality could be described as satisfactory if the service is provided in conformance with the relevant specifications; (c) in a user-centred approach, services must be offered pro-actively in a personalized manner. A timely service is a service that is offered at the moment a customer may need it, even though he may not yet be aware of it; and (d) quality comes at a price (i.e., faster delivery of a service may involve more costs than delivery at a regular speed).
- *Security.* (a) A trusted exchange of information depends on an assured security level. If a channel is not secure, or if customers do not trust its security, the channel will not be used for services that involve sensitive information; (b) security is not only a technical matter, it is also one of perception. Due to a lack of trust in security matters, relatively large segments of the user population are less inclined to use channels and services that they do not fully trust, especially when payment is involved (as we discuss in the next section).

Hence, companies have to analyze thoroughly the abovementioned challenges, optimize their production and delivery cycles and improve the interaction with their services. This means that they have to balance the efficiency of the (re-) design and (re-) development process with their organizational priorities and resources aiming always at the unique end-user. A key to success is the supply of uninterrupted sustainable online services through adaptive and personalized user interfaces and techniques.

7.1.2   Why to Adapt and Personalize E-Commerce Environments

Over the past years, the world has faced tremendous advancements in the field of digital communication, and the execution of online commercial transactions has become a fairly common and frequent task for users. Such transactions include activities like browsing over products' characteristics, collection of information, comparison of features and prices, purchasing, etc. Especially, the checkout process during the actual purchasing process has become widely known over the years in online commercial environments, and making purchases on the World Wide Web is a fairly standard activity, with relative clear steps and expected outcomes (Nielsen 2014). The checkout process is one of the basic components of any commercial Web-site whose purpose is to gather the customer's personal, shipping and payment information for performing an online purchase. In this respect, we consider it as an integrated part/activity of a service provided over an E-Commerce Web-site, liable to influence the acceptability and satisfaction of a consumer during the interaction process (Belk et al. 2014a, 2015b). Ensuring that the checkout process design in an E-Commerce retail environment is in alignment with the task at hand and providing satisfactory user experience (UX) is critical to business success.

Despite its popularity, research reveals that astonishingly between 60 % and 70 % of online users abandon shopping carts (Kukar-Kinney and Close 2010; Close and Kukar-Kinney 2010), while a recent study by Appleseed and Holst (2013), investigating the top 100 E-Commerce checkout processes showed that 82 % have usability issues. Kukar-Kinney and Close (2010) argue that despite placing items in virtual shopping carts, online shoppers frequently abandon them; an issue that perplexes online retailers and has yet to be explained by scholars. Shopping cart abandonment occurs when a potential customer initiates an order by starting the checkout process, but exits the Web-site before the purchase is made. The most important reason for shopping cart abandonment appears to be that users are not given a clear direction through the process (Appleseed and Holst 2013) or it seems that there is a considerable influence of psychological factors on this phenomenon (Cho et al. 2006; Moore and Matthews 2006; Rajamma et al. 2009).

In more generic terms, research has shown that although there is a growing number of people that use the World Wide Web to search and compare product information, the number of actual online purchases remain still relatively small (Moe and Fader 2004; Storto 2013). A significant number of users abandon E-Commerce Web-sites due to a high number of usability issues, in combination to technology-related constraints as for example the small screen displays in mobile devices (Shim et al. 2002). Several studies examined the relationship between navigational decisions and online purchase behavior (Sismeiro and Bucklin 2004; Moe and Fader 2004; Van den Poel and Buckinx 2005), supporting in many cases the view that what looks beautiful, or pleasurable, does not necessarily mean it is usable (Ilmberger et al. 2008). Recent findings by industry analysts revealed that consumers are impatient, easily dissatisfied and are likely to abandon their online shopping activity and move to a different retailer if a Web-site's features fail to meet their expectations (Forrester Consulting 2009). This work reports that attributes such as fast loading of pages, ease of navigation, efficient search and detailed product content are some of the features that online consumers expect from retail Web-sites and decrease the likelihood that consumers will leave Web-sites without making purchases. Moreover, Moore and Matthews (2006) found that besides immediate purchase intention, online shopping carts are also used for hedonic purposes such as securing price promotions, organizing items and as a 'wish list' for future purchases. This can be explained by the fact that, similarly to traditional retail shoppers, consumers shop online with utilitarian (e.g., goal-directed, task based) and/or hedonic (e.g., enjoyment gained by the shopping experience) motivations (Arnold and Reynolds 2003; Bridges and Florsheim 2008). Perceived risk related to privacy issues (e.g., sharing personal information with third parties), security aspects (e.g., non-delivery of products, transaction), and perceived waiting time (loading time), were found to mainly influence the online shopping process abandonment (Kukar-Kinney and Close 2010; Rajamma et al. 2009) as well as other contextual factors (e.g., time pressure, uncertain need) and consumer characteristics (e.g., attitude toward online shopping – Moore and Matthews 2006). Thirumalai and Sinha (2011) investigated the customization of the online purchase process of 422 electronic retailers relevant to the two constituent sub-processes in the online purchase process: (i) Decision customization, the customization of the information content delivered to users to help them in the decision-making sub-process; and (ii) transaction customization, the customization of the purchase transaction sub-process for each user. The results indicated that decision customization that provides choice assistance by way of personalized product recommendations is positively associated with user satisfaction; and transaction customization, oriented towards making the transaction sub-process personal, convenient, and interactive is positively associated with user satisfaction with the purchase transaction sub-process. Additionally, the results indicate that both decision customization and transaction customization are associated with overall customer satisfaction with the online purchase process of electronic retailers. A recent research by Li and Meshkova (2013) compared static displays with two rich media presentation formats (product videos and virtual product experience) and their impact on purchase intentions and willingness to pay in online stores. The results confirmed that the rich media displays enhanced the feeling of informedness about the examined products and increased excitement regarding the shopping experience. Virtual product experience had a direct positive effect on consumer purchase intentions, suggesting that virtual product experience-focused tools have the potential to outperform passive videos. Nevertheless, although in the last years many scholars have provided frameworks, metrics, guidelines and a number of methods to evaluate E-Commerce Web-sites (Boyd 2002; Merwe and Bekker 2003), there is generally a lack of consensus on the multi-faceted dimensions of the online buying process and theoretical justifications of the frameworks and evaluation criteria they adopt.

In this realm, personalization strategies have been embraced by researchers and practitioners aiming to improve the user experience and tackle "one-size-fits-all" issues in E-Commerce systems by providing personalized products, content presentation and functionality, bootstrapped on the needs and characteristics of each user. The factors being modeled for personalization in E-Commerce systems include, among others, information about the users (e.g., interests, preferences, needs and goals), information about the interaction device (e.g., screen size, input type), and information about the context of use (e.g., physical, social – Goy et al. 2007; Brusilovsky and Millán 2007). A number of techniques have been proposed to extract explicitly this information (e.g., through Web forms, questionnaires, etc.) or implicitly by discovering the users' navigation behavior within the system (e.g. focusing upon users' common product ratings or buying history – Frias-Martinez et al. 2005), through collaborative filtering and/or recommender algorithms (Schafer et al. 2007; Linden et al. 2003; Karat et al. 2004 – see Chaps. 3 and 4). This is primarily achieved through customer segmentation; which is extensively used by large companies nowadays (e.g. Amazon, eBay, etc. – see also Sects. 3.4.1 and 4.3.8). It figures as a technique that enables a faster and easier way towards one-to-one service provision; which however, still remains a functionality of the distant future. Customer segmentation means that the customers are subdivided (ideally per service or group of related services), into more or less homogeneous, mutually exclusive subsets of customers who share an interest in the service. The subdivisions are based on one or more customers' characteristics: Demographic characteristics (i.e., age, gender, urban or rural based, region), socio-economic characteristics (i.e., income, class, sector, number of employees, volume of business, channel access), psychographic characteristics (i.e., life style, values, sensitivity to new trends), or broader customer physical and psychological characteristics (i.e., disabilities, attitude, loyalty).

However, although research in other disciplines revealed that intrinsic human factors correlate with users' task performance, preference, comprehension and learning (Steichen et al. 2014; Belk et al. 2014b; Tsianos et al. 2010) in hypermedia systems, not many personalization approaches in E-Commerce environments include into their user models intrinsic users' perceptual characteristics that define them as individuals (e.g., cognitive processing abilities). Since users' behavior is changing profoundly – particularly due to the ways that technology is now being used as part of the shopping process – there is lack of capturing and/or effectively modeling those human factors that determine how users might inherently perceive the quality of the Web-sites that they are experiencing. In this respect, bearing in mind that human-computer interactions in E-Commerce systems are processed on a cognitive level (users are required to process and comprehend information and take decisions – Zhang and von Dran 2000), we suggest that individual differences in cognitive processing (with respect to high-level cognitive factors and elementary cognitive processes – see Chap. 2) should be investigated and integrated in the user interface design process of E-Commerce systems and the adaptation and personalization mechanisms they employ respectively, with the aim to personalize the visual and interaction design of such environments to the individuals' preferred cognitive processing styles and abilities (see Sect. 7.3).

7.2 Design Considerations and Constraints

An important prerequisite for the success of E-Commerce Web-sites is to ensure that the customers' experience related to their user interface interaction satisfies their needs, preferences, perceptions and reactions. For example, studies have shown that user interface features, such as page and content design, are key determinants of sales in online stores (Bellman et al. 1999). Predominantly, the methodology and design principles followed by companies nowadays for developing E-Commerce Web-sites are more or less similar to those that have been suggested and applied to Web-sites whose purpose and functionality might differ. The main concern is to provide users with usable hypermedia environments, to enhance user satisfaction, and to support a seamless user experience as those expressed through specific guidelines proposed during the years by a number of white reports, researchers and professionals alike, such as Gould and Lewis (1985); Nielsen (2000), 2014; Norman (2007, 2013); Hassenzahl (2014) and others (the reader can use these as a reference point to obtain more detailed information on the know-how; design principles, methods and techniques). Of course, the alternatives and variations of the respective factors and models are inevitable for a rather subjective and domain-specific matter as the one under investigation. Many organizations, depending on their industry and context of the markets they are functioning in (e.g., software, clothes, games, books, etc.), have adopted different approaches and developed specific design guidelines based on their strategies and policies (e.g., SAP 2015; Apple 2015; Google 2015; IBM 2015), in an attempt to excel and gain the competitive advantage. Nevertheless, on their back-bone, these organizations share the same high-level philosophy, that concentrates on: Information acquisition (support active involvement), system controllability (give the customers the control), navigation (provide easy means for navigation and orientation), versatility (support alternate interaction techniques), errors (tolerate customer's errors and support error system-based and context-oriented correction of customer's errors), personalization (on multimedia and multimodal user interfaces to particular user's needs), iteration (identify problems and refine designs based on feedback; trial and error), dynamic feedback (based on users activities and behaviors; support users' navigation and maintain controllability), consistency (across designs and applications), to mention but a few. For a related theoretical background please also refer to Chap. 1.

In principle, some characteristics that designers and developers of E-Commerce environments should have in mind are as follows: By nature these settings are based on more lose data structures and scope as compared for example to E-Learning systems (where learning objectives are clear, and the learning process could be easier modelled to meet students' expectations); users have more flexibility to move across different online environments driven at a large extent by dispersed motivations, interests and goals; they are directly linked to generation of revenue (with designs that mainly focus on how to sell more, e.g., providing suggestions to customers what else to buy based on their current choice or similar purchases of others with similar user profiles and/or characteristics); while last but not least, they contain as an integral part of their design the shopping cart and check out page which is a determinant factor of an online shop's success.

In this respect, analysts and interaction designers are trying to come up with intuitive solutions and interactions that overcome popular problems driven mostly by the diversification of population, expertise, technology familiarization, knowledge, multi-objective business processes, etc. Again, recognizing these factors in E-Learning, for designing and building hypermedia systems, we could say that constitute a much more straightforward activity since these dimensions are more or less known a priori and can be easier defined in this context by an instructor who can in turn provide the necessary controllability to his students during the interaction with the learning material. In the E-Commerce domain though this task might not be that simple, since this kind of information is usually difficult to collect and analyze to the needed detail (due to practical or legal reasons), while on the other hand the requirements of the population that might visit an E-Commerce Web-site might vary significantly.

For example, elderly people might have different requirements or follow a different process than teenagers when buying a product. Younger people usually undergo through a more extensive research beforehand over the Web and they select the online shop to do their shopping based on the best price, availability, trust, payment options, etc. In contrast, elderly are more loyal to a specific seller/brand and need all the information in one place before they decide. Another case for consideration with respect to designing E-Commerce Web-sites would be for example the filtering options of products and/or specifications, e.g., whether they are locally or globally set, or to what level of detail and for which product categories they should apply, in order to satisfy the various purchasing behaviors (for example, a customer might prefer to undertake a more broader search over the product categories before he narrows down to his main choices, while another might follow a more targeted activity over the detailed characteristics of an item that he knows already that he wants to purchase).

Furthermore, an E-Commerce environment should provide the necessary searching and configuration capabilities, e.g., in fashion online shops, customers should be able to select color, size, material, brand, etc., or in an electronics online store, they should be able to set up their own PC or laptop from the provided parts. Concerning the shopping cart and the checkout page during the purchasing process, these should primarily guarantee a usable interaction which is based on simplicity (e.g., the process of loading items into the shopping basket as well as the tasks for checking-out should be very "light" and easy, and to offer all the usual payment and delivery options).

Today, this need is further intensified given that potential customers are using more often the online shops on their smartphones or tablets, where the corresponding mental models they have already created for a specific task when navigating on their laptops or PCs might not apply anymore in this context of use (e.g., specific options might not be shown in the same location, or they are not visible at all, as expected, or controls might behave differently as experienced in the past), or they need to go through a comparably painful process (for many) of entering data using virtual keyboards. So, it is crucial to keep the designs to the minimum providing always meaningful feedback, e.g., clearly indicating if an item has been added successfully into the basket (the shopping basket is in most of the cases located at the top right corner of the screen and flashes, or the popup opens, after the user clicked on the "add to cart button"). Also, a good practice for companies would be to develop E-Commerce mobile native applications (M-Commerce) in order to take advantage of the portable devices' specific features, in order to improve the mobile user experience (such as location-based services, indicating the consumers which is the closest to their location physical store so to pick-up their product; or to make use of the camera, so to be able to search for the code or the availability of a desired item in a store by just sharing a snapshot of it). But, also when considering desktop users, simplicity might be the key to success, given the strong competition of the online stores, where many of them offer the same products for the same price (or even cheaper). The final decision might be dependent on how fast someone can locate and obtain the related information of the items he is interested in as well as how easy he can complete the respective purchasing process. As an example, many online shops today offer automatic favorites for some checkout steps, e.g., preselected shipping and billing address as well as favorite payment method to improve the user experience. These settings are either provided explicitly by the user, or the shop suggests the most used ones.

The design that is able to offer alternative dynamic views of a given content based on the device at hand (in other words switching easily between various screen sizes no matter if the device is desktop or mobile) is called *Responsive Web Design* (RWD – Marcotte 2011). There is lately an on-going debate with respect to the main differences of RWD and Adaptive Web Design (AWD – Gustafson 2013), triggered mainly by the excessive usage of mobile devices in recent years. Their distinction lies mostly at a more technical level and the way the design layouts are developed and delivered. RWD employs CSS3 media queries and fluid grids (based on percentages) composing a flexible framework that enables the responsive design to adapt its layout to the target device and screen. On the contrary, AWD uses predefined static layouts (usually through CSS3, rich semantic HTML5 markups and JavaScript) based on the targeted devices' screen sizes. Once the system detects the current device it loads the respective layout. Even though it seems that with RWD someone has more flexibility than with AWD (which might be limited for example to the six most common screen sizes), it can be eventually proved a far more complex approach given the necessary development with the media queries, which might cause in turn performance and loading problems, if not properly addressed. Additionally, with AWD it is more difficult and complex to accommodate any changes and updates rather than with RWD which is easier to re-organize and shuffle the content on demand. Moreover, it is considered an easier method for development even for inexperienced designers, offering many libraries and themes, and that is the reason why it is vastly used today by most companies to increase the user experience.

Nevertheless, no matter the design/development method of the layouts and routines, the bottom line always lies on what kind and how the content will be presented to the users and to what extent the interaction design offers adequate navigation support to their tasks. A consistent optimized design approach should consider all the positive and negative outcome viewpoints and ideally follow guidelines that enable a sufficient alignment with the unique customer. To get customers the right information at the right time and the right place is not an easy task. At the same time the user population (customers) is not homogeneous, nor should be treated as such. In this respect, we suggest that, to be able to deliver quality products and services, E-Commerce strategies and action plans should adhere to human-centred design and development guidelines tailored to the needs of individual customers, providing them with personalized and adaptive information upon request.

7.3   Human-Centred Design Guidelines

An important aspect for designing an adaptive interactive system is which of its visual aspects and functionalities can be adapted and personalized and why. In the context of E-Commerce systems, we undertook a thorough review of popular E-Commerce Web-sites and research works (Appleseed and Holst 2013) and concluded that the following aspects can be tailored to the unique characteristics of a user: (i) The *product presentation views* in which the system illustrates features and characteristics of products. Accordingly, an adaptation and personalization system can present different visual and interaction designs of product views to users with particular characteristics; (ii) the *checkout process* which is an essential process of any E-Commerce system that aims to gather the customer's personal, shipping and payment information for performing an online purchase; and (iii) the *product search and recommendations* in which different products are retrieved given a specific query of the user or automatically recommended to different users according to their interests and preferences. In the scope of this chapter we primarily focus on adapting and personalizing product presentation views and checkout processes based on human cognitive factors. Product search and recommendations are not considered in this chapter since these are primarily affected by users' interests and preferences rather than cognitive traits.

Following the theory behind cognitive styles and working memory capacity (WMC), individuals that are placed towards the edges of each axis have a strong preference for a specific method of information structure (Wholist/Analyst), presentation (Verbal/Imager) as well as a particular ability with regards to their cognitive capacity to control and process information (limited/enhanced working memory capacity – see Table 7.1). Consequently, when individuals are required to process information in an E-Commerce environment, it is most likely that the matching of their preference to the hypermedia structure and method of presentation of the Web-site would lead to better understanding, efficiency and satisfaction.

In this context, the first step to ground the need for personalization in regards to cognitive styles and working memory would be a preliminary inspection of the design direction and philosophy that major E-Commerce Web-sites at some extend

Table 7.1 Preferences of individuals according to cognitive characteristics

Cognitive factors	Preference
Analyst	Internal (self-)guidance, non-linearity, index of interconnected concepts, view of situations in parts
Wholist	External guidance, linearity, defined framework, view of situations as a whole
Imager	Images, diagrams, schemes, better comprehension through visual representations
Verbal	Predominance of text, better comprehension through verbal representations
Working memory	Level of information quantity, provide more or less content accordingly

follow today respectively. For that reason, we selected five very deeply elaborated Web-sites of major commercial companies in the field of computers: www.dell. com, www.ibm.com, www.sony.com, www.apple.com, and www.hp.com. Due to the extended content categories and the high volume of diverse messages delivered from these Web-sites, our analysis was limited to information related to the characteristics of computers that these companies offer. The assumption is that this kind of information is factual and visitors are expected to understand and retain these data for further processing that could lead to commercial decisions.

Based on the analysis, the following common patterns were observed: (a) The lack of sequential organization and the extreme segmentation of the content (require that the users should adopt an analytic path); (b) external guidance is missing; (c) a general framework that would benefit Wholists is absent; (d) important information is available only through additional clicking and navigation; (e) the amount of links and information is rather exhaustive; (f) the lack of a coherent pattern or even better an adaptive mechanism that would adjust the availability of information to users' capabilities and could as well reduce the efficiency of navigation through the Web-site; and (g) the majority of Web-sites utilized two broad checkout designs; a single one-page checkout process that contains all the necessary information for performing the purchase in a single page, and a guided step-by-step checkout process in which users have to fill out their information in multiple steps, usually across multiple pages.

In our opinion, the Web-sites that were inspected are not exactly biased towards specific preferences. At each instance, a mode of information presentation predominates, but this is not stable; it may as well change, for example when an actual product is shown. Still, it is of high interest that when users successfully navigate to a specific product, the presentation is rather sequential, since information is provided without interconnections and links to concepts that would allow Analysts to form a deeper understanding; Wholists on the other hand would find this simplicity more to their liking. It could as well be supported that this is not an intermediate approach, with all aspects of information processing being equally taken into account, but a mixed-mode that at instances may serve users' preferences in a random way. Of course, this is expected since these Web-sites are not built around a framework of analysis that involves individual differences at its core.

As it concerns the Verbal/Imager dimension, while all Web-sites are aesthetically very pleasant with the inclusion of photos and banners, all significant (task related) information is mostly conveyed through text. The idea of schematically presenting important details is not actualized in any case, although, these Web-sites accompany many texts with relevant images that provide a somehow visual description of the information, as long as users are slightly experienced with computers. To that end, it could be supported that these Web-sites are heavily suitable for Verbal users.

With regard to the construct of working memory capacity in all five Web-sites, the amount of links and information is rather exhaustive. Especially at the first levels of the navigational structure, there are many links to information resources that could burden users with low working memory capacity. There is also lack of an adaptive mechanism for keeping active relevant information to users with limited working memory capacity. In this context, the most demanding task is to keep track of the paths that lead to different resources in order to avoid disorientation; it seems that, according to existing research studies, this task requires a satisfactory level of working memory capacity.

Henceforth, in this chapter we are exploiting the possibilities of whether we could dynamically alter specific design aspects of an E-Commerce Web-site (the computer section in this case) by personalizing the content and the structure to specific users' cognitive characteristics. This can be achieved by enriching the existing Web structures with further design enhancements and specific content transformations based on the adaptation mapping rules derived from selected cognitive factors. In the event that this would be proven successful and meaningful, individuals would acquire better the information that is important to them.

Following prior targeted and stand-alone research studies that have shown several interaction effects between cognitive factors and design characteristics of E-Commerce environments (Germanakos et al. 2009, 2010; Belk et al. 2014a, 2015a, b), we depict below a high-level correlation amongst them: (i) Map the Verbal/Imager cognitive style to content representation of product views; (ii) map the Wholist/Analyst cognitive style to the content structure and interaction design of product views and checkout designs; and (iii) map the users' working memory capacity to supportive tools for assisting the information process during navigation and keeping active specific information throughout the user's interactions. Figure 7.1 illustrates the proposed mapping between the main factors of the user model.

Accordingly, we will next present a set of human-centred design guidelines for personalizing E-Commerce product views and checkout processes based on users' cognitive styles and working memory capacity. Table 7.2 summarizes the main criteria in order to analyze and document the usefulness of adopting a personalized approach in E-Commerce environments.

In the following sections we describe in detail each guideline of Table 7.2 and their corresponding adaptation effects and human cognitive factors. For each guideline we also provide a visual illustration of the respective task and the triggered

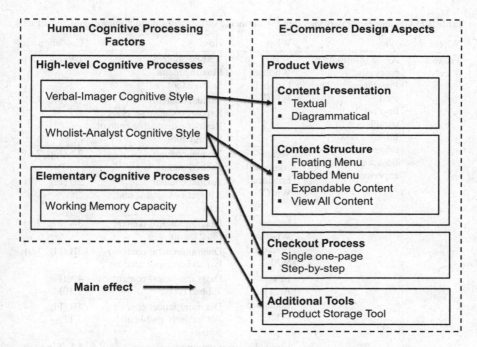

Fig. 7.1 Mapping between human factors and design factors of E-Commerce systems

mapping of human cognitive factors and design characteristics for both product views and checkout processes.

7.3.1   Guidelines for E-Commerce Product Views

Personalized product views are communicated to the user. We have used two different product view designs based on the existing E-Commerce Web-sites of Sony (2015) and HP (2015). We indicatively chose those two Web-sites since the visual and interaction design of their content in terms of presentation and navigation fits into the short analysis and challenges identified earlier and provide the grounds for further investigation towards that direction. Figures 7.2 and 7.3 illustrate respectively product view examples of the original design of Sony and HP.

The figures also indicate two divisions in the layout in which the guidelines and adaptations effects will be applied; *Division A* which is the main product view area and *Division B* which is the area for adding supportive tools. In the guidelines that follow we illustrate and describe two alternative designs and adaptation effects for a particular set of human factors, applying theory into practice consistently and equally effective but differently, given the context and design principles originally followed by the providers.

Table 7.2 Guidelines for personalizing E-Commerce tasks according to human cognitive factors

Where	Why	What	How	Guideline
Product Views	Assist information processing Prevent cognitive load Improve task completion time Improve task effectiveness Improve user experience	Verbal Wholist Limited WMC	Textual content Floating menu Storage tool	1A (Fig. 7.4)
			Textual content Expand/collapse sections Restrict expandable content Storage tool	1B (Fig. 7.5)
		Verbal Analyst Enhanced WMC	Textual content Tabbed menu	2A (Fig. 7.6)
			Textual content All sections visible and active	2B (Fig. 7.7)
		Imager Wholist Enhanced WMC	Diagrammatical content Float menu	3A (Fig. 7.8)
			Diagrammatical content Expand/collapse sections	3B (Fig. 7.9)
		Imager Analyst Enhanced WMC	Diagrammatical content Tabbed menu	4A (Fig. 7.10)
			Diagrammatical content All sections visible and active	4B (Fig. 7.11)
		Limited WMC	Storage tool	5A (Fig. 7.12)
		Verbal Analyst Limited WMC	Textual content All sections visible and active Storage tool Increase visibility	5B (Fig. 7.13)
Checkout process		Analyst	One-page checkout	6 (Fig. 7.14)
		Wholist	Step-by-step checkout	7 (Fig. 7.15)

7.3.1.1   Guideline #1: Textual Representation with Holistic Structure and Additional Navigation Support Tools

Guideline #1 entails communicating product views in a textual representation that follow a holistic structure as well as additional navigation support tools. Figures 7.4 and 7.5 show two alternative designs of these guidelines. Both guidelines illustrate content in a textual representation since the users in this case are Verbals and thus the aim is to assist the cognitive processing of textual information (see Sect. 2.2.6). In Guideline #1A, an additional floating menu is provided that includes hyperlinks that are linked to the corresponding section of the product. Each visited link stays

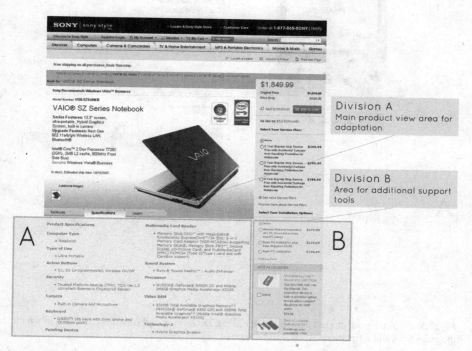

Fig. 7.2 Original product view design of Sony (2015). Division A and B indicate the area in which the guidelines and adaptation effects will be applied

highlighted with a different color as constant reminder of the areas the user has already navigated. The reasoning behind this choice is based on existing theory on cognitive styles and prior studies that have shown that Wholists need more guidance during navigation within an interactive system in order to maintain the control. Furthermore, in case a user has limited working memory capacity (as in this case), he needs to keep active, relative to the task, important chunks of information, e.g., from a particular Web-page, in order to make a decision. Thus, we provide him with a supportive tool (buffer) for storing those temporarily for future reference; assisting him throughout his current session/activity process (refer to Guideline #5 for a more focused description on the storage tool).

In Guideline #1B, a user with Verbal-Wholist cognitive style is provided with textual information, divided in several sections in which the user is able to expand/collapse the content. The expand/collapse functionality was chosen since Wholist users tend to handle information in a holistic manner – retaining a global or overall view of information (Chen and Liu 2008 – in this case by initially viewing the sections of the Web-page) and then proceeding to the detail (the content of each section). Since the user has limited working memory capacity, specific visual design enhancements are applied on the content by increasing the size of the text and

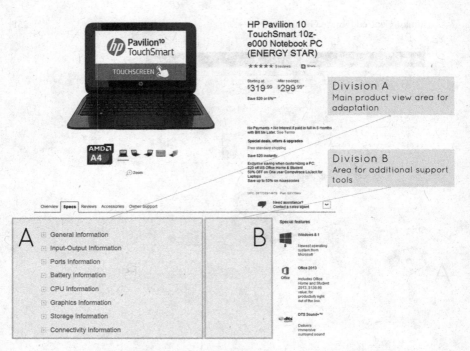

Fig. 7.3 Original product view design of HP (2015). Division A and B indicate the area in which the guidelines and adaptation effects will be applied

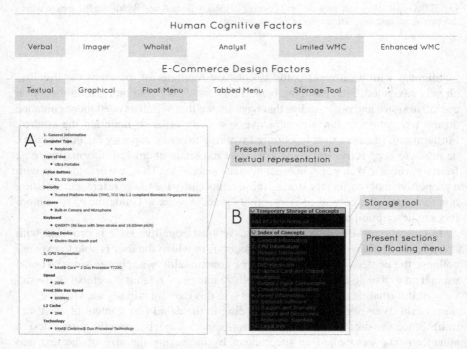

Fig. 7.4 Guideline #1A: Textual representation with holistic structure and additional navigation support tools (Based on Sony design)

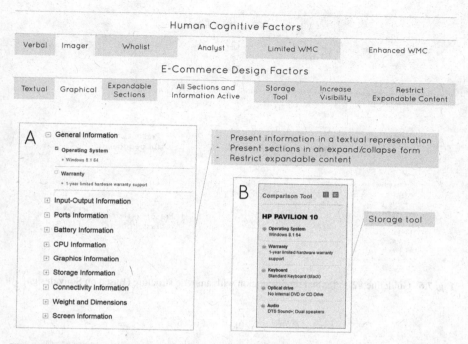

Fig. 7.5 Guideline #1B: Textual representation with holistic structure and additional navigation support tools (Based on HP design)

enhancing the content with additional content indicators or divisors. In addition, the expand/collapse functionality restricts the user to expand multiple sections of content at the same time avoiding to generate any excessive levels of cognitive load. Similar to Guideline #1A, the user is provided with a supportive tool for storing important information from a particular Web-page (refer to Guideline #5 for a more focused description on the storage tool).

7.3.1.2   Guideline #2: Textual Representation with Analytic Structure

Guideline #2 suggests illustrating product views in a textual representation with an analytic content structure. Figures 7.6 and 7.7 illustrate two alternative designs of these guidelines. Similar to Guideline #1, in both Guideline #2A and Guideline #2B, content is illustrated in a textual representation since the user in this case has Verbal cognitive style, meaning the user processes more efficiently textual information and represents information in words. In Guideline #2A, information is presented in horizontal tabbed menus that serve as a hyperlink to specific sections of information that the user can unrestrictedly visit. The reasoning behind this design guideline is based on the fact that the user has an analytic approach to information representation and structure, and thus prefers to have a full view of all the main

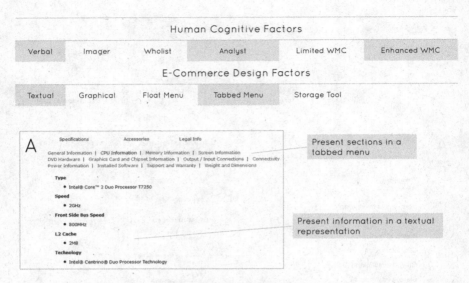

Fig. 7.6 Guideline #2A: Textual representation with analytic structure (Based on Sony design)

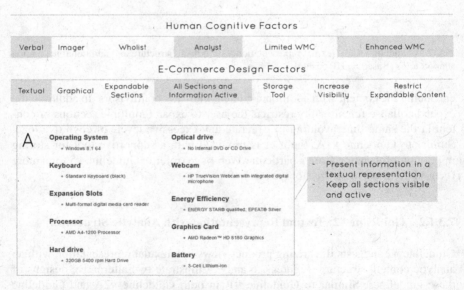

Fig. 7.7 Guideline #2B: Textual representation with analytic structure (Based on HP design)

information at hand navigating freely to the respective segments of interest (information component parts) in order to construct the desired concepts.

In Guideline #2B, users are again provided with solely textual illustrations of content since they are Verbals, and they navigate freely to the whole online material, as Analysts tend to move from the parts (content) to the whole (sections) and prefer to have more freedom in their navigation (Chen and Liu 2008).

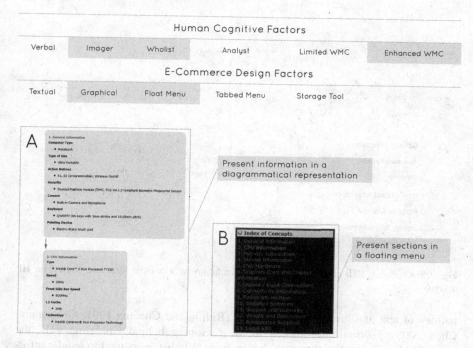

Fig. 7.8 Guideline #3A: Diagrammatical representation with holistic structure (Based on Sony design)

7.3.1.3   Guideline #3: Diagrammatical Representation with Holistic Structure

Guideline #3 illustrates product views in a diagrammatical representation with a holistic structure of content. Figures 7.8 and 7.9 illustrate two alternative designs of these guidelines. In both guidelines, content is illustrated in a diagrammatical representation since users are Imagers and thus are more efficient in processing graphical information as well as prefer and tend to structure information in pictures. In Guideline #3A, all the content is presented with a top-down approach with guided illustrations from one section to the other (using top-to-down visual arrows). The Web-page is further enhanced with a floating menu that guides the user to the corresponding section he wishes to visit. The reasoning behind this design was based on the fact that the user is Wholist and based on existing theory and research work, Wholists need more guidance during navigation (hence the use of visual indicators and floating menu – see Sect. 2.2.6).

In Guideline #3B, a user with Imager-Wholist cognitive style is provided with diagrammatical illustrations of information, divided in several sections in which the user is able to expand/collapse the content. The visual design of the content is provided in a colored diagrammatical representation since Imager users do not perform well when exclusively text-based content is provided but rather better with combi-

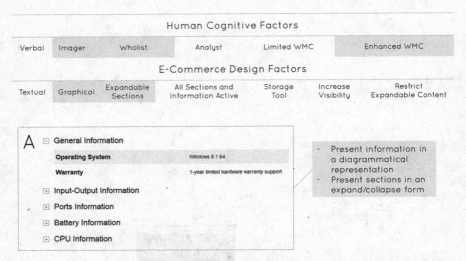

Fig. 7.9 Guideline #3B: Diagrammatical representation with holistic structure (Based on HP design)

nations of text and graphical illustrations (Riding and Cheema 1991; Ghinea and Chen 2008). Furthermore, similar to the reasoning behind Guideline #1B, the expand/collapse functionality was chosen since Wholist users tend to handle information in a holistic manner (in this case by initially viewing the sections of the Web-page) and then proceed to the detail (the content of each section).

7.3.1.4   Guideline #4: Diagrammatical Representation with Analytic Structure

Guideline #4 suggests providing a diagrammatical representation of product views with an analytic content structure. Figures 7.10 and 7.11 illustrate two alternative designs of these guidelines. In both guidelines the user is an Imager and thus the information is presented diagrammatically. Furthermore, in Guideline #4A, the user has an analytic approach in information representation and structuring and consequently the sections of the Web-page are illustrated in a tabbed menu over which the user can freely navigate. Each time the user clicks on a link of the tabbed menu, he is guided to the corresponding data of the section item.

In Guideline #4B, since the user is an Imager-Analyst, the visual design of the content is provided in a colored diagrammatical representation and the whole content is available to the users since Analysts tend to move from the parts (content) to the whole (sections).

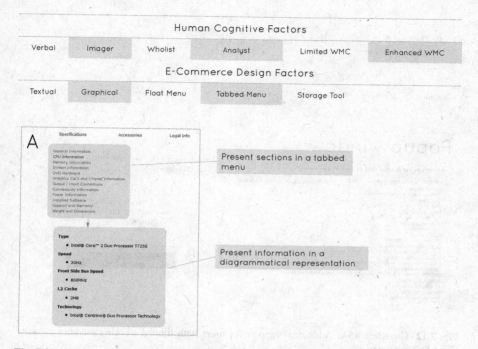

Fig. 7.10 Guideline #4A: Diagrammatical representation with analytic structure (Based on Sony design)

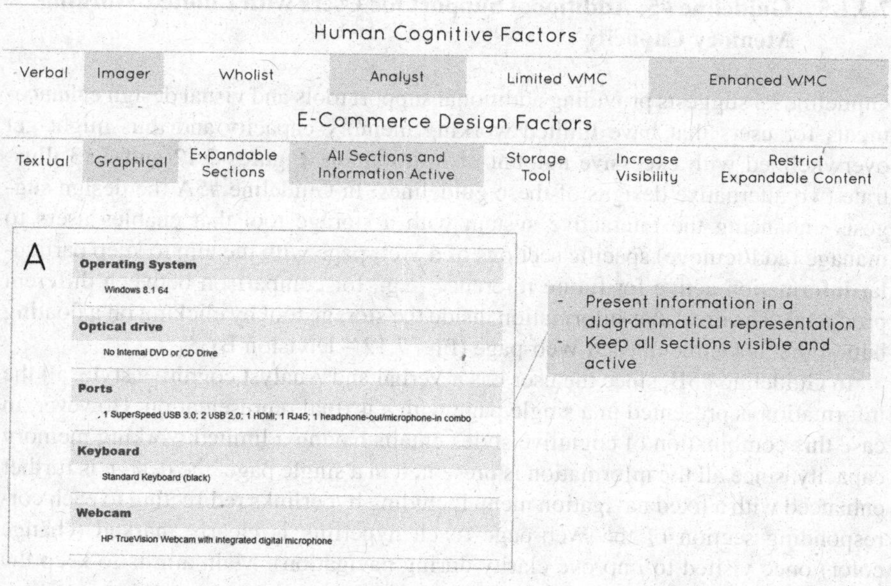

Fig. 7.11 Guideline #4B: Diagrammatical representation with analytic structure (Based on HP design)

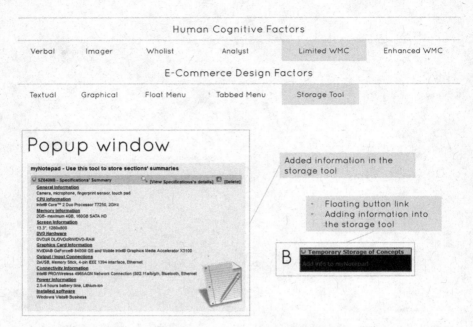

Fig. 7.12 Guideline #5A: Additional support for users with limited working memory capacity (Based on Sony design)

7.3.1.5   Guideline #5: Additional Support for Users with Limited Working Memory Capacity

Guideline #5 suggests providing additional support tools and visual design enhancements for users that have limited working memory capacity and thus might get overwhelmed with excessive amount of information. Figures 7.12 and 7.13 illustrate two alternative designs of these guidelines. In Guideline #5A the design suggests enhancing the interactive system with a storage tool that enables users to manage (add/remove) specific sections of a Web-page with the aim to keep particular information active for future reference (e.g., for comparison between different products). The user adds information inside the storage tool by clicking on a floating button that is visible in each Web-page (Fig. 7.12 – Division B).

In Guideline #5B, since the user has a Verbal and Analyst cognitive style, all the information is presented in a single page with a textual representation. However, in case this combination of cognitive styles entails having a limited working memory capacity, since all the information is presented in a single page, the design is further enhanced with a fixed navigation menu including hyperlinks redirecting to each corresponding section of the Web-page (each hyperlink is clearly marked (change color) once visited to improve clarity during navigation). Main aim is to keep the

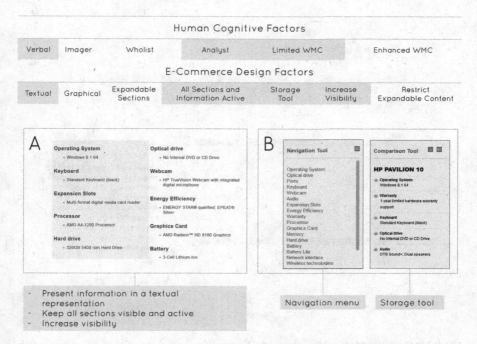

Fig. 7.13 Guideline #5B: Additional support for users with limited working memory capacity (Based on HP design)

suggested design seamlessly across all Verbal-Analyst users, but since users might get overwhelmed by the high quantity of information, we included the additional navigation support tool to assist the navigation and information process. In addition, content is visually enhanced by increasing the text and highlighting vertically the sections to make these more visible. Finally, a storage tool like in Guideline #5A is included enabling the user keeping specific sections of the Web-page active for future reference.

7.3.2   Guidelines for E-Commerce Checkout Process

As discussed earlier, the checkout process is an activity step with distinctive functionality that differentiates the scope of E-Commerce Web-sites from others. In the end, the whole usability and acceptability of an online shop might be influenced at most by this factor; whether a consumer managed to purchase his items easily and within the expected timeframe. Henceforth, in this section we present two design guidelines and adaptation effects for E-Commerce checkout processes that tend to simplify this interaction to the benefit of the end-user.

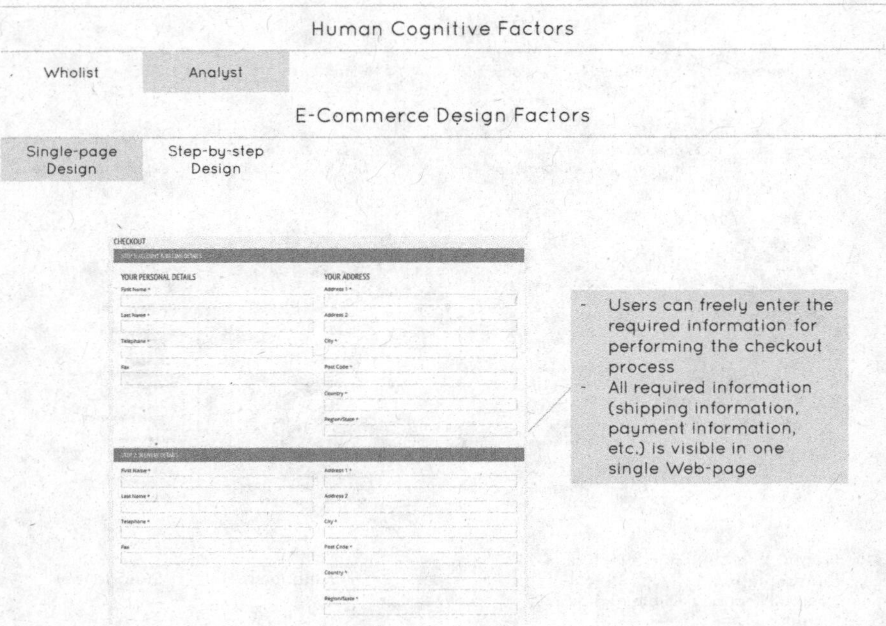

Human Cognitive Factors

Wholist	Analyst

E-Commerce Design Factors

Single-page Design	Step-by-step Design

- Users can freely enter the required information for performing the checkout process
- All required information (shipping information, payment information, etc.) is visible in one single Web-page

Fig. 7.14 Guideline #6: Single one-page checkout design

7.3.2.1   Guideline #6: Single One-Page Checkout Design

Guideline #6 entails communicating a single one-page checkout design (Fig. 7.14). This particular checkout design follows a simple top-down navigation style in which users can freely enter the required information for performing the checkout process. All required information (shipping information, payment information, etc.) is visible in one single Web-page. This one-page design should be communicated to Analyst users since according to theory it satisfies some of their basic characteristics regarding information assimilation and navigation; in this case, by enabling free access to all sections of the checkout process on a single page.

7.3.2.2   Guideline #7: Step-by-Step Checkout Design

Guideline #2 entails communicating a step-by-step checkout design (Fig. 7.15). This particular checkout design illustrates content in a guided horizontal step-by-step navigation style in which users can only enter information in a particular section, and only then to proceed to the next one. The step-by-step checkout design should be communicated to Wholist users since based on the theory of cognitive styles, they expect to interact with a content given in a constrained and guided environment.

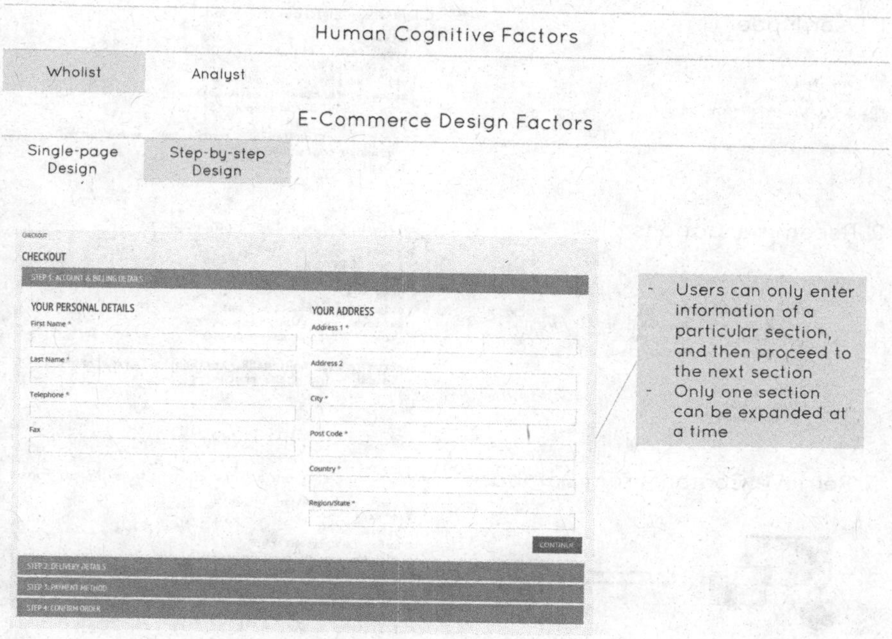

Fig. 7.15 Guideline #7: Guided step-by-step checkout design

7.3.3 Adaptation Paradigm in mapU Based on Guidelines

In this section we present an adaptation paradigm at an implementation level, following Guideline #1B, with the aim to illustrate and make more clear to the reader how the guidelines and adaptation effects (from a user interface design level) can be realized and applied to a more technical perspective using the respective algorithms and formalizations in the mapU framework (see Chap. 5). According to Fig. 7.16, the adaptation paradigm follows a four step process as follows: (1) the user's model characteristics are initially retrieved from the database; (2) depending on the pool of available adaptation rules, specific rules are applied and adaptation decisions are taken (e.g., whether the content should be illustrated in a textual or graphical representation); (3) retrieve the content from the database; and (4) extract the semantically annotated divisions from the Web-page content and then, based on the generated set of adaptation decisions, a client-side rule-based mechanism is run in which CSS design styles and client-side scripts are applied to the extracted content and finally communicated in a personalized format to the user's Web browser.

More specifically, in Step 1 a client-side script calls the Web server for retrieving the user model characteristics of the user. In this particular example the user is 60 years old, has Verbal and Wholist cognitive styles and has limited working memory capacity. In Step 2, the system calls the adaptation engine r which is responsible to generate a set of recommendations (R') for a user u_i using the user model um(u_i) and

1. User Model

$$um(u_i) = \{ \\
\quad (d, age, 60), \\
\quad (cc, vi, verbal), (cc, wa, wholist), \\
\quad (cc, cpe, limited) \\
\}$$

Client-side call to get user model

```
$.ajax({
    type: "GET",
    dataType: "json",
    url: "um.php",
    success: function (response) {
        um = JSON.parse(response);
    },
    error: function (jqXHR, textStatus, errorThrown){
        console.log(jqXHR.status);
    } });
```

2. Recommendations

$$r(um(u_i), AR) = R', R' \subseteq R$$

$$AR = \begin{cases}
\{(vi, verbal), \{(content, textual)\}\} \\
\{(vi, image), \{(content, graphical)\}\} \\
\{(wa, wholist), \{(structure, expandable)\}\} \\
\{(wa, analyst), \{(structure, active\_sections)\}\} \\
...
\end{cases}$$

$$R' = \begin{cases}
\{(content, textual) \\
(structure, expandable) \\
(use\_storage\_tool, true) \\
(restrict\_expansions, true)\}
\end{cases}$$

Guideline #1B

Client-side call to get recommendations

```
$.ajax({
    type: "GET",
    dataType: "json",
    Data: um,
    url: "recommendations.php",
    success: function (response) {
        rec = JSON.parse(response);
    },
    error: function (jqXHR, textStatus, errorThrown){
        console.log(jqXHR.status);
    }
});
```

3. Retrieve Content from Database

Client-side call to retrieve the content from the database

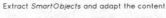

```
// Get main content objects
$.ajax({
    type: "GET",
    url: "GetContent.php",
    success: function (response) {
        var content = JSON.parse(response);
    },
    error: function (jqXHR, textStatus, errorThrown){
        console.log(jqXHR.status);
    } })
```

Client   Database

4. Adaptation and Personalization

Extract *SmartObjects* and adapt the content

HP Pavilion 10
TouchSmart 10z-
e000 Notebook PC
(ENERGY STAR)

★★★★★ 3 reviews

Starting at   After savings:
$319.⁹⁹ $299.⁹⁹

Save $20 or 6%**

```
// Extract information inside the division
$(".SmartObject").each(function(index){
    CategoryArr.push($(this).find(".Category").text());
    TitleArr.push($(this).find(".SmartTitle").text());
    ContentArr.push($(this).find(".SmartContent").text());
});

$(".SmartObject").addClass(rec.design);
$(".SmartObject").addClass(rec.interaction);

// Get content for the storage tool
$.ajax({
    type: "GET",
    url: "GetStorageTool.php",
    success: function (response){
        var obj = JSON.parse(response);
        for(var i = 0; i < obj.results.length; i++) {
            Title = obj.results[i].Title;
            Content = obj.results[i].Content;
            // Include title and content in each div
            stringResult = '<div>...</div>';
            $('#innerComparison').append(stringResult);
        }
    },
    error: function (jqXHR, textStatus, errorThrown){
        console.log(jqXHR.status);
    }});
```

JSON Data
{"storagetool_data":[
    {"Title":"Operating System", "Content":"Windows 8.1 64"},
    {"Title":"Optical Drive", "Content":"No internal DVD or CD Drive"},
    {"Title":"Keyboard", "Content":"Standard Keyboard (black)"},
...
]}

```
<div class="SmartObject">
    <div class="Category">General Information</div>
    <div class="SmartTitle">Warranty</div>
    <div class="SmartContent">1-year limited...</div>
</div>
...
```

```
<div class="SmartObject">
    <div class="Category">General Information</div>
    <div class="SmartTitle">Operating System</div>
    <div class="SmartContent">Windows 8.1 64</div>
</div>
...
```

Fig. 7.16 An adaptation paradigm based on Guideline #1B

a set of adaptation rules (AR) which are based on the abovementioned design guidelines. According to the set of all available recommendations R in the system, a subset R' is retrieved for that particular user. In this case, Guideline #1B is chosen and applied which entails communicating content in a textual representation with a holistic structure and additional navigation support tools. In Step 3, a client-side script performs a call to the database to retrieve the content of the particular Web-page. Finally, in Step 4, the semantically annotated divisions are extracted from the whole Web-page content, i.e., divisions that entail the CSS class name *Category*, *SmartTitle*, and *SmartContent*. Then the generated recommendations R' (retrieved as a JSON object) are applied on these divisions. In particular, the set of recommendations entails predefined CSS class names which are applied on the content divisions. In this particular example, the user is provided with information illustrated in textual format, divided into several sections in which the user is able to expand/collapse the content. However, the user is restricted to expand multiple sections of content at the same time given his limited working memory capacity. Furthermore, since the user has limited working memory capacity, specific visual design enhancements are applied on the content by increasing the size of the text and enhancing the content with additional content indicators and divisors. In addition, a supportive tool for storing important information from a particular Web-page is created and loaded on the user interface. The information illustrated in the storage tool is retrieved in JSON format, parsed and then HTML5 snippets are produced and applied in the Web-page.

7.4 Evaluation of Product Views Personalization (Based on Sony Design)

This section presents a user study with the aim to support and practically recognize the added value of the abovementioned guidelines in the context of E-Commerce, as well as to make the reader more familiar with experimental validation methods and analyses for evaluating the impact of human cognitive factors in E-Commerce environments. Specifically, a within participants experiment based on a match-mismatch approach (personalized vs. non-personalized version) was conducted using the Sony environment, seeking out to explore if the personalized condition serves users better at finding information more accurately and fast. The experimental evaluation focuses on three parameters: (i) The users' task completion performance, for the personalized condition compared to the original condition; (ii) the users' task accuracy, for the personalized condition compared to the original condition; and (iii) the users' satisfaction, for the personalized design and navigation enhancements compared to the original condition. The reader may also refer to Germanakos et al. (2009) for a similar user study evaluating the impact of the suggested guidelines in the Sony environment.

7.4.1 Methodology

The study was carried out at the University of Cyprus and the National and Kapodistrian University of Athens. Our sample included 70 participants. All participants were students from both universities and their age varied from 18 to 21, with a mean age of 19. They accessed the system using personal computers located at the laboratories of the universities, divided in groups of approximately 20 participants. Each session lasted about 40 min; 20 min were required for the user modeling process, while the remaining time was devoted to navigate in a Web-site specifically designed for the experiment.

During the user modeling process, students provided their demographic characteristics (i.e., name, age, education, etc.) and performed a number of interactive tests using attention and cognitive processing efficiency grabbing psychometric tools (described in Chap. 5) in order to quantify the cognitive characteristics of the students.

Furthermore, the students were asked to navigate in a replica of an existing E-Commerce Web-site (Sony 2015) that we developed for the purpose of the experiment. The Web-site's content was about a series of laptop computers; general description, technical specifications and additional information were available for each model. The students first navigated through the original content (Fig. 7.17) and then through the personalized content (Fig. 7.18) that was adapted based on their user models' characteristics.

We consider that the original version of the Web-site was designed without any consideration towards cognitive style preferences, and the amount of information was so high and randomly allocated that could increase the possibility of cognitive load. The personalized condition addressed these issues by introducing as personalization factors both cognitive style and working memory capacity. In each condition (original or personalized), students were asked to fulfill three tasks; they had to find the necessary information to answer three sequential multiple choice questions that were given to them while navigating. All six questions (three per condition) were about determining which laptop excelled with respect to the prerequisites that were set by each question. There was certainly only one correct answer that was possible to be found relatively easy, in the sense that the students were not required to have hardware related knowledge or understanding.

As soon as users finished answering all questions in both conditions, they were presented with a comparative satisfaction questionnaire; they were asked to choose which environment was better (1–5 scale, where 1 means strong preference for environment A and 5 for environment B), regarding usability and user friendliness factors.

The dependent variables that were considered as indicators of differences between the two environments were: (i) Task completion time; task accuracy (number of correct answers); and (iii) user satisfaction. Furthermore, with the aim to increase the internal validity of the study we did not inform the users about which was the personalized condition to avoid bias effects, nor were they encouraged to use any additional features. In addition, to avoid training effects, half of the users

Fig. 7.17 Web-site screenshot (original condition) (Sony 2015)

received the original condition first (considered as environment A), whilst the other half started the procedure with the personalized (again considered as environment A). To avoid the effect of differences in difficulty of each set of three questions (equal level of difficulty for all questions), users were alternated in both environments. The within participants design allowed the control of differences and confiding variables amongst users.

7.4.2 Results

In order to assess the significance and impact of cognitive factors in personalizing E-Commerce systems we performed three analyses. In the first and second analysis, we respectively explored if the personalized condition serves users better at finding

Fig. 7.18 Web-site screenshot (personalized condition) (Based on Sony (2015))

information faster and more accurately. In the third analysis, we compared users' satisfaction of the personalized environment to the original (non-personalized) environment. We separated users into different groups according to their cognitive styles and working memory capacity as follows: (i) Verbal, Intermediate or Imager; (ii) Wholist, Intermediate or Analyst; and (iii) low, medium or high working memory capacity. Each combination of cognitive factors (e.g., a user being Verbal-Wholist-low WMC) was assigned a particular adaptation effect based on the suggested design guidelines above. For the purpose of this analysis and to minimize complexity, users that were classified as Intermediates (for both Verbal/Imager and Wholist/Analyst cognitive styles) received the personalized condition that corresponds to the one or the other extreme (e.g., Verbal or Imager), depending where their actual value, extracted from the psychometric tests, was leaning upon. For example, an Intermediate user with a tendency closer to the Verbal class received the same personalized version as Verbal users.

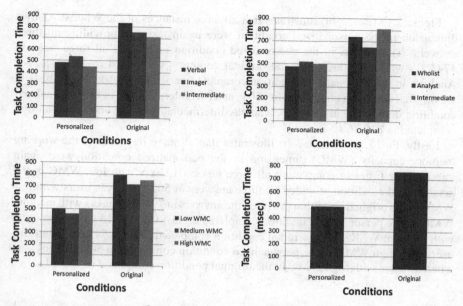

Fig. 7.19 Task completion performance for personalized and original condition

7.4.2.1 Task Completion Performance

In the first analysis, we compared the users' task completion performance (time for completing all three tasks) of the personalized condition to the original condition. In Fig. 7.19 (top-left, top-right, bottom-left) we illustrate the task completion performance based on each one of our model's dimensions (i.e., Verbal/Imager dimension, Wholist/Analyst dimension, and working memory capacity dimension, respectively). Figure 7.19 (bottom-right) demonstrates the overall performance results of the users for all three dimensions. Based on these results, we note that equally interesting is the fact that users in the personalized condition were significantly faster at task completion. The mean aggregated time of answering all three questions was 758.28 s in the original condition, and 488 in the personalized. A paired samples t-test was performed ($t(69)=5.501$, $p<0.001$) demonstrating significance at zero level of confidence.

More specifically, Fig. 7.19 (top-left) illustrates that all three instances of the Verbal/Imager dimension in the personalized condition were significantly faster at task completion: (i) Imagers in the personalized condition answered all three questions in 482.10 s, while the mean aggregated time for answering all three questions by Imagers in the original condition rose to 831.57 s; (ii) Verbals in the personalized condition completed the tasks in 536 s whereas Verbals in the original condition completed the tasks in 751.2 s; and (iii) Intermediates in the personalized condition completed the tasks in 446.15 s whereas Intermediates in the original condition completed the tasks in 711.53 s.

Figure 7.19 (top-right) illustrates that all three instances of the Wholist/Analyst dimension in the personalized condition were again faster in providing all three answers: (i) Wholists in the personalized condition completed all three tasks in 474.73 s whereas Wholists in the original condition completed in 739.47 s; (ii) Analysts in the personalized condition completed in 516.66 s whereas Analysts in the original condition completed in 650 s; and (iii) Intermediates in the personalized condition completed in 500.76 s whereas Intermediates in the original condition completed in 810.76 s.

Lastly, Fig. 7.19 (bottom-left) illustrates that all three instances of the working memory capacity (WMC) dimension in the personalized condition were again interestingly faster in completing all three tasks: (i) Users with low WMC in the personalized condition provided all three answers in 502 s whereas users with low WMC in the original condition provided the answers in 794 s; (ii) users with medium WMC in the personalized condition completed all tasks in 459.13 s whereas users with medium WMC in the original condition completed them in 715.65 s; and (iii) users with high WMC in the personalized condition completed in 502.35 s answers whereas users with high WMC in the original condition completed in 752.94 s.

7.4.2.2   Task Completion Accuracy

In the second analysis, we compared the users' task completion accuracy (number of correct answers) of the personalized condition to the original condition. In Fig. 7.20 (top-left, top-right, bottom-left) we illustrate the task completion accuracy based on each of our model's dimensions (i.e., Verbal/Imager dimension, Wholist/Analyst dimension, and working memory capacity dimension, respectively). Figure 7.20 (bottom-right) demonstrates the overall accuracy results of the users for all dimensions. All users in the personalized condition were more accurate in providing the correct answer for each task. The same user in the original condition had a mean of 0.87 correct answers, while in the personalized condition the mean rose to 2.22. Since the distribution was not normal and the paired samples t-test assumptions were not met, Wilcoxon Signed Ranks Test was performed, showing that this difference is statistically significant at zero level of confidence ($Z = -5.861$, $p < 0.001$).

More specifically, Fig. 7.20 (top-left) illustrates that all three instances of the Verbal/Imager dimension in the personalized condition were more accurate in providing correct answers for each task: (i) Imagers in the personalized condition answered 2.36 correct answers whereas Imagers in the original condition answered 0.68; (ii) Verbals in the personalized condition answered 2.2 correct answers whereas Verbals in the original condition answered 0.84; and (iii) Intermediates in the personalized condition answered 2.15 correct answers whereas Intermediates in the original condition answered 1.03.

Figure 7.20 (top-right) illustrates that all three instances of the Wholist/Analyst dimension in the personalized condition were again more accurate in providing correct answers for each task: (i) Wholists in the personalized condition answered 2.15 correct answers whereas Wholists in the original condition answered 0.81; (ii)

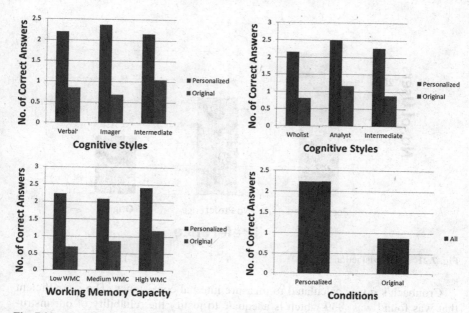

Fig. 7.20 Task completion accuracy for personalized and original condition

Analysts in the personalized condition answered 2.5 correct answers whereas Analysts in the original condition answered 1.16; and (iii) Intermediates in the personalized condition answered 2.26 correct answers whereas Intermediates in the original condition answered 0.88.

Finally, Fig. 7.20 (bottom-left) illustrates that all three instances of the working memory capacity (WMC) dimension in the personalized condition were again more accurate in providing correct answers for each task: (i) Users with low WMC in the personalized condition answered 2.23 correct answers whereas users with low WMC in the original condition answered 0.7; (ii) users with medium WMC in the personalized condition answered 2.08 correct answers whereas users with medium WMC in the original condition answered 0.86; and (iii) users with high WMC in the personalized condition answered 2.41 correct answers whereas users with high WMC in the original condition answered 1.17.

7.4.2.3   User Satisfaction

In the third analysis we studied the satisfaction levels of all users comparing the personalized version of the environment to the original. For this study we used a satisfaction questionnaire with 12 items. Two sub-scales were included to measure usability (control and efficiency during navigation) and user friendliness. A total of 70 questionnaires were completed and returned. 18 of them were half completed or had double answers and were omitted from the sample. Our final sample included 52 participants' questionnaires.

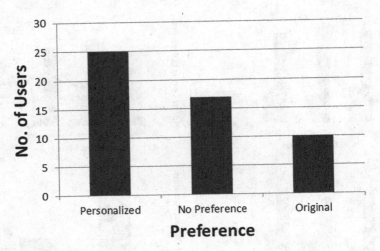

Fig. 7.21 User satisfaction results

Cronbach's *a* was calculated to measure internal consistency. The *a* coefficient that was found was .839 which is adequate to justify the reliability of our instrument. Although there are no standard guidelines available on appropriate magnitude for the coefficient, in practice, an alpha greater than .60 is considered reasonable in psychological research.

Based on the satisfaction questionnaire (Fig. 7.21), 25 users leaned towards the personalized environment, 17 had no preference while 10 preferred the original. A *chi square* goodness of fit test was performed to investigate whether our categories were populated because of our conditioning or because of random effects. Chi square is useful for analyzing whether a frequency distribution for a categorical or nominal variable is consistent with expectations or not. The results clearly indicate that users showed a preference to the personalized version of our Web-site in a degree higher than that of expected frequency due to randomness. Chi square has shown significance at the .05 level of .039.

This statistical analysis is merely indicative of whether participants would consciously observe any positive or negative effects of the personalized condition. A considerable percentage leaned towards that condition (or at least users did not seem somehow annoyed by such a restructuring), but overall it cannot be supported that they were fully aware of their increase in performance.

7.5 Evaluation of Product Views Personalization (Based on HP Design)

Following a similar approach as in Sect. 7.4, we present two subsequent user studies to further support and practically recognize the added value of the guidelines related to the HP design. A within-subjects study design was followed based on a

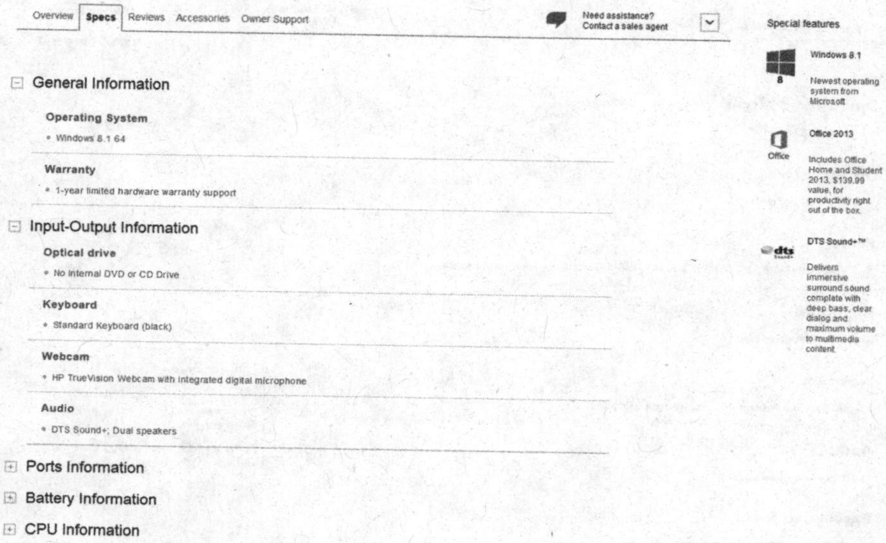

Fig. 7.22 User interface of the original design (HP 2015)

match-mismatch approach (personalized vs. non-personalized version) using the HP environment aiming to assess the added value of applying the suggested guidelines and adaptation effects in terms of users' task efficiency, effectiveness and users' perceived usability. The reader may also refer to Belk et al. (2015b) for a similar user study evaluating the impact of the suggested guidelines in the HP environment.

7.5.1   Methodology

Two user studies were conducted in which a total of 135 participants (62 in Study #1 and 73 in Study #2) volunteered and consented to participate. Participants were recruited primarily at university laboratories, and they accessed a Web-based experimental E-Commerce environment which presented content based on an exact replica of the HP online shop (HP 2015). Each session lasted approximately 45 min; where users spent 25 min on the user modeling process, and the remaining time to navigate in two different versions of the commercial Web-site environment (the original HP design (Fig. 7.22) and the personalized design based on the suggested adaptation effects (Fig. 7.23)).

Participants began the study by indicating their demographic information (e.g., age, gender, education level, online shopping experience) and cognitive characteristics via a set of specifically designed psychometric tests. After completing the user modeling process, participants were asked to navigate in the two different versions of the E-Commerce environment.

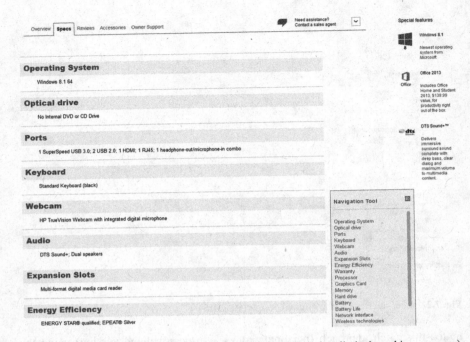

Fig. 7.23 User interface of a personalized design (Imager-Analyst-limited working memory) (Based on HP (2015))

A within-subjects study design was followed; all users navigated sequentially in both versions of the same environment. The sequence of the two versions was randomly provided to the participants with the aim to avoid any familiarity or learnability effects. Based on a specific scenario, each user was required to navigate and answer three task-based questions in each design version (six in total) whose answers could be found in the Web content. The task-based questions were carefully designed to ensure the same level of complexity and understanding among them. As soon users completed answering the questions they were presented with a comparative, 5-scale Likert questionnaire based on WAMMI (Kirakowski and Cierlik 1998); users were asked to choose which environment was more usable.

7.5.2   *Results*

Based on the within-subjects study design, several paired samples *t*-test analyses were run to determine differences in terms of time to complete the task and success rate between user interactions with the original vs. the personalized design.

Table 7.3 Descriptive statistics of the processed values for each cognitive-based cluster

Cognitive factor	Clusters	Sig.	Mean	SD	N
Verbal/Imager	Verbal	<.001*	.85	.14	73
	Imager		1.27	.60	62
Wholist/Analyst	Wholist	<.001	.89	.27	102
	Analyst		1.5	.46	33
Working memory	Limited	<.001*	2.34	2.34	59
	Enhanced		16.79	3.76	74

*The mean difference is significant at the .05 level

Table 7.4 Task efficiency and effectiveness of Study #1

Outcome	Original		Personalized			
	M	SD	M	SD	n	t
Efficiency	56.19	58.38	32.82	30.50	62	3.38**
Effectiveness	21.50	24.95	42.47	34.93	62	−4.67**

**The mean difference is significant at the .05 level

7.5.2.1 User Modeling

The participants' scores on each psychometric test were processed and fed to the clustering mechanism in order to generate groups of users for each cognitive factor (see Chap. 5). The cluster analysis of the user modeling mechanism separated users into clusters based on their processed scores of the psychometric tests (Table 7.3).

Several independent-samples t-tests were conducted to determine mean differences on the processed values (e.g., cognitive style ratios) between the generated cluster groups (e.g., Verbal and Imager group). Homogeneity of variances was violated in the cases of Verbal/Imager cognitive style values and working memory values, as assessed by Levene's test for equality of variances (Table 7.3). In these cases a Welch t-test was conducted for unequal variances of data. Results indicate that there were significant differences among the processed values between all the clusters, indicating that the user modeling procedure grouped effectively the users into different clusters, and could be thus safely used in the main data analysis.

7.5.2.2 Task Performance Between Original and Personalized Design

A paired samples t-test was run on the sample to determine whether there is a statistically significant difference in task completion efficiency and effectiveness when participants used the personalized design compared to the original design.

The results of Study #1 are displayed in Table 7.4. Accordingly, there are statistically significant differences, at the .01 significance level, in original to personalized designs' scores for both task efficiency and effectiveness. More specifically, when users navigated in the original design, they completed the three tasks in a mean time of 56.19 s, in contrast to 32.82 s which were required to complete the tasks in the

Table 7.5 Task efficiency and effectiveness of Study #2

Outcome	Original		Personalized		n	t
	M	SD	M	SD		
Efficiency	106.57	79.39	58.70	41.69	73	5.62**
Effectiveness	25.57	23.90	32.87	29.12	73	−1.77*

*The mean difference is significant at the .05 level
**The mean difference is significant at the .01 level

personalized design. In terms of effectiveness, results indicate that users had a task success rate of 21.50 % in the original design as opposed to a 42.47 % success rate in the personalized design.

Table 7.5 presents the results of Study #2, further indicating significant differences at the .01 (for task efficiency) and .05 (for task effectiveness) levels between original and personalized designs. Similarly, users navigating in the personalized design were able to complete the tasks much faster (58.70 s) as compared to the original design (106.57 s). In the same line, there was a noticeable difference in the task success rate between personalized and original designs (32.87 % and 25.57 % respectively).

To this end, the two studies revealed that users spent considerably less total time to complete the study's tasks and their success rate of answering the questions has been improved significantly when they were navigating in the personalized condition as opposed to the original design. Overall, the results suggest that the personalized interface design embedding the suggested guidelines and adaptation effects which are based on users' cognitive styles and working memory characteristics enables them to process, comprehend and complete the information task requirements more efficiently and effectively.

7.5.2.3   Users' Perceived Usability

At the end of the study, focus group sessions were conducted aiming to validate findings of the quantitative analysis. The focus groups followed a semi-structured process based on predetermined questions that lasted approximately 15 min and investigated the following factors: (i) perceived task efficiency (e.g., "Which environment enables the faster completion of your tasks?"); (ii) perceived task effectiveness (e.g., "Which environment is easier to find the needed information?"); and (iii) user preference in regards with the content structure of the two E-Commerce versions (e.g., "Which environment is better visually structured?").

In general, most of the users' responses showed a positive tendency towards the personalized E-Commerce environment. In particular, users found the visual and interaction design enhancements appealing and supportive during their navigation with the system. They were able to understand faster the concepts and the terms presented as well as to compare the features of each product easily without unnecessary steps during their task execution. In this respect, it seems that the storage tools that were provided for enhancing their memorability did not hinder the process but in contrast helped them to keep the related to the questions information active in order to give their answers. Furthermore, they perceived the personalized condition as more straightforward and easy to use compared to the normal one, mentioning that they found the functionalities consistent and well integrated. They felt that they completed the tasks faster and more effectively when they were interacting with the personalized version (even though they were not aware each time which of the two versions was enabled).

Such observations can be promising since the users perceived the personalized environment as more usable and the suggested adaptation effects as a positive intervention. This can be further supported through the quantitative analysis which revealed significant improvements in task completion time and accuracy in the personalized version.

7.6 Evaluation of Checkout Process Personalization

In this section we present a user study to support the benefit of the guidelines related to the checkout processes. The reader may also refer to Belk et al. (2014a, 2015a) for a detailed version of this study. Main aim of this evaluation is to investigate whether individual differences in cognitive processing styles (Wholist/Analyst) affect user preference and task performance in different checkout designs that are deployed on alternative interaction device types (standard desktop vs. touch-based devices). In this respect, this evaluation investigates the following research questions:

- Do users with different cognitive processing styles prefer a particular visual and interaction design of checkout processes?
- Do users with different cognitive processing styles perform differently in terms of task completion efficiency in different visual and interaction designs of checkout processes?
- Is there an observable interaction effect between cognitive processing styles of users and device type towards user preference and task performance of different checkout designs?

For the purpose of this study, we utilized different checkout designs of two existing commercial Web-sites: nordstrom.com (Nordstrom) and amazon.com (Amazon). Nordstrom checkout design follows a simple top-down navigation style in which users can freely enter the required information for performing the checkout process (Fig. 7.24). All required information (shipping information, payment information, etc.) is visible in one single Web-page. Amazon illustrates content in a guided horizontal step-by-step navigation style in which users can only enter information of a particular section, and then proceed to the next section (Fig. 7.25). In the desktop version, a horizontal menu is utilized illustrating the active section of the checkout process.

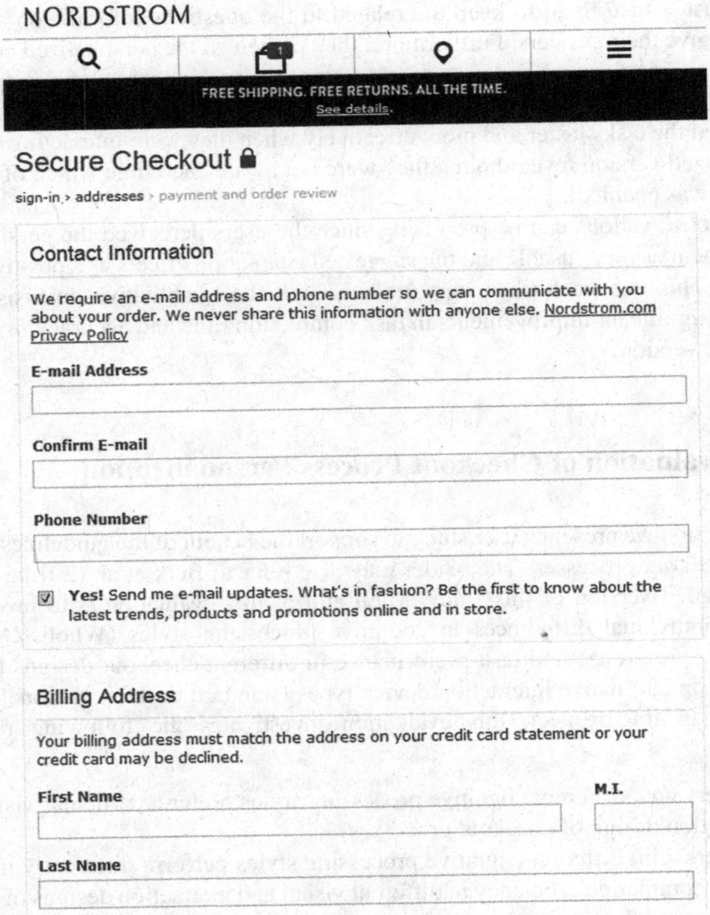
NORDSTROM
FREE SHIPPING. FREE RETURNS. ALL THE TIME.
See details.
Secure Checkout
sign-in > addresses > payment and order review
Contact Information
We require an e-mail address and phone number so we can communicate with you about your order. We never share this information with anyone else. Nordstrom.com Privacy Policy
E-mail Address
Confirm E-mail
Phone Number
Yes! Send me e-mail updates. What's in fashion? Be the first to know about the latest trends, products and promotions online and in store.
Billing Address
Your billing address must match the address on your credit card statement or your credit card may be declined.
First Name
M.I.
Last Name

Fig. 7.24 Nordstrom checkout process design (Nordstrom 2015)

7.6.1 *Methodology*

A total of 38 undergraduate Computer Science students (18 female and 20 male, age 20–25) participated voluntarily in a controlled user study held at the laboratory of the researchers. Controlled laboratory sessions were conducted with a maximum of two participants in each session and were held at times convenient to the students. Participants initially interacted with a psychometric instrument aiming to classify each user to the Wholist or Analyst cognitive style class. Depending on the cognitive style classification of each participant, a mixed design (within-subjects and between-subjects) was followed in which all participants navigated in two different commercial Web-sites; Nordstrom and Amazon, and were assigned to complete an

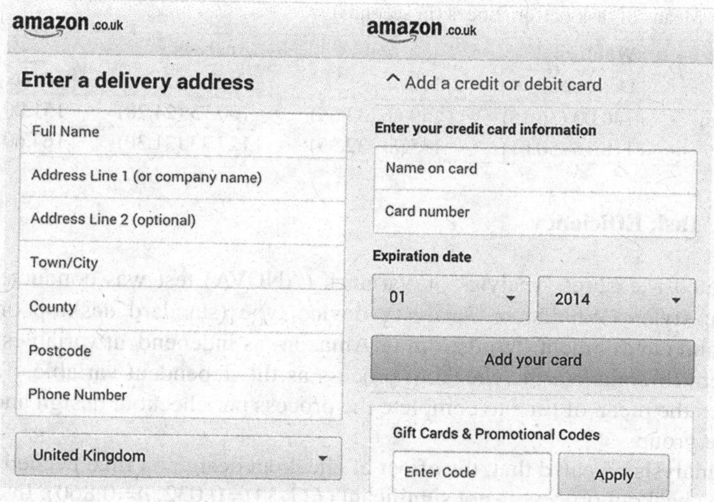

Fig. 7.25 Amazon checkout process design (Amazon 2015)

online purchase in each checkout setting (within-subjects). Half of the participants interacted with standard input/output (IO) devices (keyboard and mouse) on desktop computers (IBM Thinkcentre M73, 21″ monitor), and the other half interacted with mobile touch-based devices (Apple iPad 3) (between-subjects). The allocation of checkout designs' sequence as well as the device types used for interaction was balanced across users depending on their cognitive styles' classification.

The instructions provided to the participants for both navigation scenarios were as follows: i) select a product of their choice and add it to the shopping basket of the system; and ii) start the checkout process until buying the product with a virtual credit card that was provided to them at the beginning of the study. A client-side logging tool measured the total time spent for completing the checkout process, aiming to compare the usability of each checkout process in terms of task efficiency. At the end of the study, focus group sessions were conducted and questionnaires were provided in order to elicit the users' subjective preference and perception of each design.

7.6.2   Results

Users were grouped as follows based on their responses to the psychometric test: Wholists ($N=21, f=55\%$), Analysts ($N=17, f=45\%$).

Table 7.6 Means of task performances (in seconds)

	Wholists		Analysts	
	Desktop	Touch	Desktop	Touch
Nordstrom	140.00 (36.15)	159.66 (57.39)	100.75 (24.28)	151.00 (18.74)
Amazon	118.16 (50.81)	135.73 (32.99)	127.33 (31.30)	164.60 (14.53)

7.6.2.1 Task Efficiency

A Repeated Measures Analysis of Variance (ANOVA) test was conducted using cognitive styles (Wholist or Analyst), device type (standard desktop or touch-based), and environment (Nordstrom or Amazon) as independent variables and the time spent to complete the checkout process as the dependent variable. Table 7.6 illustrates the mean of time to complete the process per checkout design and cognitive style group.

The analysis revealed that, the effect of checkout design on time needed to complete the checkout process is not significant ($F(1,34)=0.032$, $p=0.860$). In contrast, there was a statistically significant interaction between cognitive styles and checkout design on the time to complete the checkout process ($F(1,34)=7.525$, $p=0.01$, partial $eta^2=0.181$). Furthermore, there was no interaction effect between cognitive styles and device type on the time to complete the checkout process ($F(1,34)=0.232$, $p=0.633$, partial $eta^2=0.007$). Pairwise comparisons between checkout designs for each cognitive styles group and device type revealed that Analysts were significantly more efficient in completing the single page checkout design (Nordstrom) when this was deployed on desktop computers ($MD=-26.583$, $SE=12.583$; $F(1,34)=4.463$, $p=0.042$). Furthermore, when the interaction was performed on touch-based devices, again, Analysts were faster in completing the single page checkout process but with no statistical significant differences ($MD=-13.600$, $SE=19.494$; $F(1,34)=0.487$, $p=0.490$). On the other hand, Wholists were significantly more efficient in completing the guided step-by-step checkout process (Amazon) when this was deployed on touch-based devices ($MD=23.933$, $SE=11.255$; $F(1,34)=4.522$, $p=0.042$), whereas no significant differences where observed when the interaction took place on desktop computers ($MD=21.833$, $SE=17.795$; $F(1,34)=1.505$, $p=0.288$). Furthermore, a comparison between the two cognitive style groups revealed that Analysts were significantly faster than Wholists when interacting in Nordstrom ($F(1,38)=7.056$, $p=0.012$). On the other hand, no significant differences were observed between Wholists and Analysts in Amazon ($F(1,38)=0.422$, $p=0.520$).

7.6.2.2 User Preference

Focus group sessions were concentrated around the participants' subjective preference and perception of the different checkout designs. The focus groups followed a semi-structured process based on predetermined questions that lasted approximately

Table 7.7 User preference of checkout design

	Wholists		Analysts	
	Desktop	Touch	Desktop	Touch
Nordstrom	2	7	8	6
Amazon	7	5	2	1

15 min. The participants were asked to rank the checkout designs based on their preference. In particular, participants ranked the checkout designs with 1 and 2 to represent their first and second choice. Table 7.7 lists the number of participants who chose a specific design as their first choice.

A Chi square test revealed that there is statistical significant association between cognitive styles and checkout design preference in desktop computers (*Chi square value* = 6.343, *df* = 1, *p* = 0.012). For interactions that took place on desktop computers, Analyst users significantly preferred the single one page design, whereas Wholists preferred the guided step-by-step approach. On the contrary, in cases where users interacted with touch-based devices, no significant association between cognitive styles and checkout design has been revealed (*Chi square value* = 1.534, *df* = 1, *p* = 0.216) since the majority of participants preferred the single page checkout design (Nordstrom). Based on comments, this might be based on the fact that users preferred to have all information in a single page due to size and interaction limitations. In the case of Wholists, although the task efficiency analysis revealed that they were significantly faster when interacting in a guided step-by-step checkout design (Amazon), they preferred the other type of checkout given the limitations of the touch-based device.

7.7   Benefits, Impact and Limitations

Adaptation and personalization methods and techniques received great attention lately for the design and development of any E-Commerce Web-site that has a significant number of products or services to offer. Traditionally, the focus when deploying these kind of environments was upon the creation of a hypermedia space where all items of a store or a service's organization could be available online; for the consumers to access them faster, easier and at a lower cost. The tendency was mostly towards services' marketing models that emphasized on "one-size-fits-all" paradigms. However, the rapid technological evolution created new means of communication and channels to share the digital content that companies had to consider and thereupon to align their strategies accordingly to stay competitive. This requirement has been further intensified by the rising demands of the consumers who want and feel the need to be the main actors in the whole purchasing process. Inevitably, this reality generated new opportunities for providers to target the unique user with smart and hybrid but simple solutions. The focal strategic point now is the analysis and composition of user interfaces and functionalities that will more accurately and efficiently present the optimal content and navigation to the end-user. Main attempt is to create sustainable solutions that will increase user experience and satisfaction investing in long-term benefits for both sides.

Adaptation and personalization seems to be the philosophy that encapsulates this need, providing the grounds to implement theoretical decisions into ubiquitous environments emphasizing not only to 'what' content should be available online but also 'how' this will be presented, so to match the context, intrinsic characteristics and capabilities of users. However, how can one reconcile these seeming benefits of adaptive and personalized designs with respect to individual differences in order to improve the quality of the E-Commerce Web-sites? The selection of the psychologically-appropriate human cognitive characteristics and models that have a direct impact on the information space becomes critical. The big question though still remains which ones of those are more suitable in order to enrich the user models that consequently will determine best-fit design approaches with respect to content generation and delivery? In such a way, that they can provide tangible guidance for the presentation of the content, e.g., visual or textual, or to suggest which particular navigational strategies are appropriate depending on the unique characteristics of the users and the specification of products and services.

In this chapter we have suggested a number of cognitive factors and we have seen that the practical impact that drives the respective designs bring an added value to E-Commerce Web-sites. The findings of the aforementioned evaluation studies provide initial evidence for the utilization of the proposed human-centred design guidelines and adaptation effects towards that direction. According to those, personalizing E-Commerce tasks based on intrinsic cognitive characteristics could support the users in terms of usability and improve their buying experience, while on the other hand benefit the providers since the interaction with personalized tasks improve the user acceptance of their services. More specifically, the personalized user interface designs substantially increased users' ability to choose the correct answers regarding specific products as well as to complete their tasks faster (both during product viewing and checkout process), since users exhibited significant differences in their tasks' accuracy and execution time using the personalized versions of the environments, as opposed to the non-personalized ones. In the latter cases, the findings raised the possibility that users spent a considerable amount of time interacting with the Web-sites probably because they needed to understand the product features before making their selection. In the case of low working memory users, this was even more evident since without the support of the auxiliary tools (provided in the personalization conditions) the users had to navigate back and forth in order to recall or to make available the related to the task information. Furthermore, the adaptation of visual and textual format according to the cognitive differences of users figured as an effective online shopping intervention, since it has indicated a positive user engagement when users interacted with the personalized environments. These kind of adaptive designs are especially critical in the context of E-Commerce Web-sites, where understanding the relationship between cognitive interaction strategies and the generated purchasing decision output can help consumers to have predictable and efficient interactions. With further support of the qualitative evaluation (using the usability evaluation questionnaires and focus groups) we can observe that users perceive the personalized conditions of the two Web-sites positively in terms of their design functionality, aesthetics, usability and satisfaction. One of the most common feedback statements, was drawn upon the utilization of the storage tool which helped them to keep a snapshot summary of the products active for their current task, increasing their involvement, and enabling them to more effectively complete specific tasks (e.g., comparing product features) and take decisions.

Nonetheless, the practical feasibility of such an approach entails a number of issues and challenges that need closer attention. An important challenge relates to the prior knowledge required by an E-Commerce system, about the users' cognitive characteristics in order to provide personalized designs without engaging users in any psychometric tests. Given the complexity of cognitive styles' research, their implicit elicitation methods without engaging users in a psychometric test is still at its infancy. However, existing noteworthy works could be used as a starting point, for implicitly extracting the users' cognitive styles based on their navigation behavior (Chen and Liu 2008; Belk et al. 2013). In this line of reasoning, given the challenging task of implicitly modeling cognitive characteristics of users, another point relates to practitioners adopting the cognitive style elicitation process in their business processes and methods. Such an approach not only would increase development and maintenance costs for the implicit user modeling mechanisms but also would have to comply with confidentiality agreements with users (customers) which is considered a sensitive issue from a legal perspective. With respect to the current studies, the limitations relate to the rather small sample size (in relation to the number and complexity of the cognitive dimensions) and to non-varying user models (e.g., age, experience) used, mostly due to practical reasons. Furthermore, although the studies show in a clear way that users performed better within the personalized environment, it could be argued that there is no way to be fully aware if information processing was more efficient at a deeper level, or users simply found the personalized condition more of their liking, thus devoting more conscious cognitive effort.

On the other hand, the overall feedback and the studies evaluation, provides support for the further development and adoption of the suggested, and any, human-centred design guidelines. In view of a long-term goal of personalizing product and services views and checkout tasks on individual differences, current findings build on the promise that human cognitive factors could offer an alternative perspective to the "one-size-fits-all" paradigm of E-Commerce Web-sites helping a company to gain the competitive advantage. Lastly, considering the social dimension of the current interactions over the World Wide Web, further research could explore the value of presenting information or recommending products liked by people who belong to the same or similar cognitive characteristics. The idea behind a 'buying path visualization' (e.g., featuring as an additional intelligent tool that illustrates the related information in a form of an aggregated visual chart) is to leverage users with identical/similar cognitive styles or abilities, demographics and/or content/navigation behaviors when searching for particular products.

7.8 Summary

The World Wide Web has dramatically changed the way consumers collect information, compare products and purchase goods and services, and the way companies conduct their business. Although the number of users in recent years that visit E-Commerce Web-sites for their shopping is increasing steadily, the actual purchases over dedicated online shops remain relatively small. Research has shown that this observation lies mostly to the multi-level usability issues (with regard to content presentation and navigation, checkout processes, etc.) that these environments still face today, hindering at a large extent the users' shopping experience. These hitches become even more obvious with the extensive use of mobile devices where, apart from the inherent limitations of the various channels of communication (e.g., screen size, data entry methods, etc.), it is difficult for users to create a respective conceptual understanding of the various design layouts and functionality, expecting always the same. Customers want to find quickly what they are looking for, be presented with the required transparency, and conclude their purchasing process with the expected simplicity that will not cause them any additional cognitive load or frustration.

In this respect, personalization techniques have become a necessity for any E-Commerce site that aim to maintain its loyalty with their customers and to stay competitive in the market. However, most of the current personalization approaches primarily focused on user models that include information about the users' preference, interests, tasks, goals, etc., without emphasizing on more intrinsic cognitive abilities that could add even more value during an interaction and purchasing process.

Indeed, information processing and cognition are central activities when consumers interact with Web-sites (Zhang and von Dran 2000), and should be analyzed into more detail by designers and practitioners before deciding on particular design strategies and implementation methods. Taken into consideration that users do not necessarily share common cognitive backgrounds in which online purchase decisions are required to be taken, main efforts should concentrate on answering fundamental questions, such as whether individual differences in cognitive processing styles and abilities affect customers' behavior and decisions, with respect to preference, task performance and accuracy, on different visual and interaction designs that are deployed on multiple devices (i.e., standard desktop and touch-based devices).

Thereupon, we have suggested a number of human-centred adaptation and personalization design guidelines and practices with the aim to improve the overall user experience of E-Commerce environments. We have shown how specific theoretical dimensions and human factors can be interpreted into design patterns and adaptation rules that can benefit the end-user. We believe that this attempt, even though found at early stages, is at the right direction, positively influencing users' buying behavior and at the same time helping companies to gain long term sustainability. Such findings are expected to provide useful insights to researchers and professionals to further work on and enrich or suggest alternative design guidelines driven by the unique user and his individual values.

References

Amazon (2015) Amazon E-Commerce web-site. Available online at http://www.amazon.com/. Accessed December 2013

Apple (2015) Designing for Yosemite. Available online at https://developer.apple.com/library/mac/documentation/UserExperience/Conceptual/OSXHIGuidelines/. Accessed July 2015

Appleseed J, Holst C (2013) E-commerce checkout usability: exploring the customer's checkout experience. Baymard Institute, Copenhagen

Arnold M, Reynolds K (2003) Hedonic shopping motivations. J Retail 79(2):77–95

Belk M, Papatheocharous E, Germanakos P, Samaras G (2013) Modeling users on the world wide web based on cognitive factors, navigation behavior and clustering techniques. Syst Softw 86(12):2995–3012

Belk M, Germanakos P, Asimakopoulos S, Andreou P, Mourlas C, Spanoudis G, Samaras G (2014a) An individual differences approach in adaptive waving of user checkout process in retail e-commerce. In: Proceedings of the 16th international conference on human-computer interaction – HCI international 2014 (HCI 2014), Heraklion, Crete. Springer, Berlin/Heidelberg, pp 451–460, 22–27 Jul 2014

Belk M, Germanakos P, Fidas C, Samaras G (2014b) A personalisation method based on human factors for improving usability of user authentication tasks. In: Conference on user modeling, adaptation, and personalization, Springer, Switzerland, pp 13–24

Belk M, Germanakos P, Constantinides A, Samaras G (2015a) A human cognitive processing perspective in designing E-commerce checkout processes. In: Proceedings of the 15th IFIP TC13 conference on human-computer interaction (INTERACT 2015), Bamberg, LNCS. Springer, Berlin/Heidelberg, INTERACT (1):523–530, 14–18 Sept 2015

Belk M, Germanakos P, Andreou P, Samaras G (2015b) Towards a human-centered E-commerce personalization framework. In: Proceedings of the 2015 IEEE/WIC/ACM international conference on web intelligence (WI 2015), IEEE Computer Society Press (in press)

Bellman S, Lohse GL, Johnson EJ (1999) Predictors of online buying behavior. Commun ACM 42(12):32–38

Boyd A (2002) The goals, questions, indicators, measures (GQIM) approach to the measurement of customer satisfaction with e-commerce web sites. Aslib 54(3):177e–187e

Bridges E, Florsheim R (2008) Hedonic and utilitarian shopping goals: the online experience. J Bus Res 61(4):309–314

Brusilovsky P, Millán E (2007) User models for adaptive hypermedia and adaptive educational systems. In: Brusilovsky P, Kobsa A, Nejdl W (eds) The adaptive web, Springer, Berlin/Heidelberg, 4321, pp 3–53

Chen S, Liu X (2008) An integrated approach for modeling learning patterns of students in web-based instruction: a cognitive style perspective. ACM Trans Comput-Hum Interact 15(1), Article 1, 28 pages

Cho CH, Kang J, Cheon HJ (2006) Online shopping hesitation. Cyber Psychol Behavior 9(3):261–274

Close GA, Kukar-Kinney M (2010) Beyond buying: motivations behind consumers' online shopping cart use. J Bus Res 63:986–992

Corbitt BJ, Thanasankit T, Yi H (2003) Trust and E-commerce: a study of consumer perceptions. Sel Pap Pac Asia Conf Inf Syst 2(3):203–215

Forrester Consulting (2009) E-commerce web site performance today: an updated look at consumer reaction to a poor online shopping experience, White Paper. Available online at http://www4.akamai.com/dl/whitepapers/ecommerce_website_perf_wp.pdf. Accessed Jul 2015

Frias-Martinez E, Magoulas GD, Chen SY, Macredie RD (2005) Modeling human behavior in user-adaptive systems: recent advances using soft computing technique. J Expert Syst Appl 29(2):320–329

Germanakos P, Mourlas C, Isaia C, Samaras G (2005a) Web personalized intelligent user interfaces and processes – an enabler of multi-channel e-business services sustainability. In:

Proceedings of the 2nd international conference on E-business and Telecommunications networks (ICETE2005), Reading, pp 177–180, 3–7 Oct 2005

Germanakos P, Mourlas C, Samaras G (2005b) Considering the new user requirements for apt mobile internet services delivery. In: Proceedings of the IADIS international conference on WWW/Internet 2005, Lisbon, pp 148–152, 19–22 Oct 2005

Germanakos P, Tsianos N, Lekkas Z, Mourlas C, Samaras G (2007) Improving M-commerce services effectiveness with the use of user-centric content delivery. eCommerce Organ J, Spec Issue Mob Context Aware eCommerce 6(1):1–18

Germanakos P, Tsianos N, Lekkas Z, Belk M, Mourlas C, Samaras G (2009) Proposing web design enhancements based on specific cognitive factors: an empirical evaluation. In: Proceedings of the 2009 IEEE/WIC/ACM international conference on web intelligence (WI 2009), IEEE Computer Society Press, pp 602–605

Germanakos P, Belk M, Tsianos N, Lekkas Z, Mourlas C, Samaras G (2010) Adapting mLearning environments on learners' cognitive styles and visual working memory span. In: Proceedings of the 5th mediterranean conference on information systems (MCIS 2010)

Ghinea G, Chen S (2008) Measuring quality of perception in distributed multimedia: verbals vs imagers. Comput Hum Behav 24(4):1317–1329

Google (2015) Google design guidelines. Available online at https://www.google.com/design/spec/material-design/introduction.html. Accessed July 2015

Gould JD, Lewis CH (1985) Designing for usability: key principles and what designers think. Commun ACM 28(3):300–311

Goy A, Ardissono L, Petrone G (2007) Personalization in E-Commerce applications. In: Brusilovsky P, Kobsa A, Nejdl W (eds) The adaptive web, Springer, Berlin/Heidelberg, 4321, pp 485–520

Gustafson A (2013) Adaptive web design: crafting rich experiences with progressive enhancement, Easy Readers, LLC, ISBN-13: 978–0983589501

Hassenzahl M (2014) User experience and experience design. In: Soegaard M, Dam RF (eds) The encyclopedia of human-computer interaction, 2nd ed. The Interaction Design Foundation, Aarhus. Available online at https://www.interaction-design.org/encyclopedia/user_experience_and_experience_design.html. Accessed July 2015

HP (2015) Hewlett Packard E-commerce web-site. Available online at http://store.hp.com/. Accessed September 2013

IBM (2015) Guidelines to design global solutions. Available online at www.ibm.com/software/globalization/guidelines/. Accessed July 2015

Ilmberger W, Schrepp M, Held T (2008) Cognitive processes causing the relationship between aesthetics and usability. Springer, Berlin/Heidelberg

Karat C, Blom JO, Karat J (2004) Designing personalized user experiences in e-commerce. LNCS, Springer, Dordrecht

Kirakowski J, Cierlik B (1998) Measuring the usability of web site. In: Human factors and Ergonomics society annual meeting, Santa Monica, CA 42(4):424–428

Kukar-Kinney M, Close AG (2010) The determinants of consumers' online shopping cart abandonment. J Acad Mark Sci 38(2):240–250

Li T, Meshkova Z (2013) Examining the impact of rich media on consumer willingness to pay in online stores. Electron Commer Res Appl 12(6):449–461

Linden G, Smith B, York J (2003) Amazon.com recommendations: item-to-item collaborative filtering. IEEE Internet Comput 7(1):76–80

Marcotte E (2011) Responsive web design. A Book Apart, New York. ISBN-13: 978–0984442577

Merwe R, Bekker J (2003) A framework and methodology for evaluating e-commerce web sites. Internet Res Electron Netw Appl Policy 13(5):330–341

Moe WW, Fader PS (2004) Capturing evolving visit behavior in clickstream data. J Interact Mark 18(1):5e–19e

Moore S, Matthews S (2006) An exploration of the online shopping cart abandonment syndrome: a matter of risk and reputation. J Website Promot 2:71–88

Nielsen J (2000) Designing web usability. New Riders Press, Indianapolis

Nielsen J (2014) E-commerce usability. NNGroup

Nordstrom (2015) Nordstrom E-commerce web-site. Available online at http://www.nordstrom.com/. Accessed December 2013

Norman D (2007) The design of future things. Basic Books, New York

Norman D (2013) The design of everyday things. Basic Books, New York

Rajamma RK, Paswan AK, Hossain MM (2009) Why do shoppers abandon shopping cart? Perceived waiting time, risk, and transaction inconvenience. J Prod Brand Manag 18:188–197

Riding R, Cheema I (1991) Cognitive styles – an overview and integration. J Educ Psychol 11(3–4):193–215

SAP SE (2015) The SAP Fiori design guidelines. Available online at http://experience.sap.com/fiori-design/. Accessed July 2015

Schafer JB, Frankowski D, Herlocker J, Sen S (2007) Collaborative filtering recommender systems. In: Brusilovsky P, Kobsa A, Nejdl W (eds) The adaptive web, vol 4321, Lecture notes in computer science. Springer, Berlin/Heidelberg, pp 291–324

Shim JP, Bekkering E, Hall L (2002) Empirical findings on perceived value of mobile commerce as a distributed channel. In: Proceedings of the information systems, 1835–1837

Sismeiro C, Bucklin RE (2004) Modeling purchase behavior at an E-commerce web site: a task-completion approach. J Mark Res 41:306–323

Sony (2015) Sony style E-Commerce web-site. Available online at http://store.sony.com/. Accessed November 2007

Steichen B, Wu M, Toker D, Conati C, Carenini G (2014) Te, Te, Hi, Hi: eye gaze sequence analysis for informing user-adaptive information visualizations. In: Conference on user modeling, adaptation, and personalization, Springer, pp 183–194

Storto C (2013) Evaluating ecommerce websites cognitive efficiency: an integrative framework based on data envelopment analysis. Appl Ergon 44:1004e–1014e

Thirumalai S, Sinha KK (2011) Customization of the online purchase process in electronic retailing and customer satisfaction: an online field study. J Oper Manag 29:477–487

Tsianos N, Germanakos P, Lekkas Z, Mourlas C, Samaras G (2010) Working memory span and E-learning: the effect of personalization techniques on learners' performance. In: Conference on user modeling, adaptation, and personalization, Springer, pp 64–74

Van den Poel D, Buckinx W (2005) Predicting online purchasing behaviour. Eur J Oper Res 166(2):557–575

Zhang P, von Dran GM (2000) Satisfactor and dissatisfactors: a two-factor model for website design and evaluation. J Am Soc Inf Sci 51(4):1253e–1268e

Chapter 8
The Usable Security Case

Abstract Security mechanisms are of critical importance in today's interactive systems. While the primary goal of such mechanisms is to preserve security of information and premises, researchers and practitioners have come to understand the critical importance of usable security which is an area focusing on how to design and develop security mechanisms that respect human performance and their goals within an interactive system. Motivated by recent research works that underpinned the necessity of usability in security mechanisms, in this chapter we present an alternative approach to current state-of-the-art practices with the aim to achieve a balance between usability and security of two widely deployed and critical security mechanisms. In particular, we propose a set of human-centred design guidelines for adapting and personalizing user authentication and CAPTCHA mechanisms. Our intention is to provide the most optimized condition, in terms of design type and complexity level, based on specific human cognitive factors. The reader can further realize the adaptation effects and added value of this approach through a user study that investigated user interactions on given security tasks. According to these, the personalized condition of the user security tasks significantly improved task completion performance compared to the non-personalized one. Results of a post-study qualitative survey analysis also revealed that users perceived the improved usability of the personalized condition.

Keywords User authentication • CAPTCHA • Design • Guidelines • User study

8.1 Introduction

Nowadays, a high number of security mechanisms exist in which users play an important role in the security process. For example, users setup and make use of passwords for accessing a system, while they have to comply with security certificates and share information that highly affect the security of a system. Furthermore, security mechanisms are deployed on the World Wide Web in which many users are required to interact as secondary tasks in order to proceed with their primary one. For example, they are required to solve a CAPTCHA challenge to prove that they are

© Springer International Publishing Switzerland 2016
P. Germanakos, M. Belk, *Human-Centred Web Adaptation and Personalization*,
Human–Computer Interaction Series, DOI 10.1007/978-3-319-28050-9_8

humans in order to proceed with their main task (e.g., posting a comment in an online blog). Such practices have shown to significantly decrease the experience of users while interacting with the system (Florencio and Herley 2007; Fidas et al. 2011).

In this realm, the research community has come to an understanding regarding the critical importance of *usable security* which is an area that focuses on how to design and develop security mechanisms that respect users' performance and their goals within an interactive system (Cranor and Garfinkel 2005; Kobsa et al. 2013; Fidas et al. 2015; Shay et al. 2012; Inglesant and Sasse 2010; Bursztein et al. 2014; Albert et al. 2010). There is a growing demand and interest to enhance both the security and the usability aspects of such mechanisms aiming to meet the security requirements of the system but at the same time to provide interaction transparency to actual users (Inglesant and Sasse 2010; Fidas et al. 2011; Biddle et al. 2012). However, usable security is still an open and challenging research area mainly due to the lack of in depth understanding of user security tasks and their intuitive integration in the user interface design process by following user-centred design approaches (Fidas et al. 2010). User-centred design approaches focus on interacting iteratively with the end-users, especially for identifying and validating user requirements, designing system prototypes as well as for evaluating them. The aim is to investigate thoroughly what users require from a system design and how the system can support them in accomplishing specific tasks effectively, efficiently, and with a certain degree of user satisfaction. An important aspect of this process is to model a user's interaction with a user interface. A good design practice aims to establish a common ground among designers and users related to aspects of the user-system interaction by formalizing the information architecture of the respective interactive system and specify the interaction flow for accomplishing specific tasks.

User security interactions over the World Wide Web are commonly related with: (a) user authentication; (b) human interaction proof mechanisms (e.g., CAPTCHA challenges (von Ahn et al. 2004)); (c) installation and usage of data encryption software tools, especially for secure e-mail communication; and (d) installation of certificates for authorization issues, etc. In this respect, research on usable security entails a high number of challenges and issues due to the multidimensional and complex character of each security mechanism. The two areas that receive significant attention from the research community (and that we also focus in this chapter) are those of user authentication and CAPTCHA challenges. Both security mechanisms are currently widely deployed in online services and are of critical importance for the security of today's interactive systems. User authentication on the one hand aims to verify that the identity of a user is genuine, whereas CAPTCHA challenges aim to prove that the entity interacting with a service is human and not malicious software. These tasks are currently performed by millions of users as part of their daily activities, thus having a usability flaw in such human-computer interaction cycles could eventually decrease the overall user experience and user acceptance of an interactive system.

In this context, the overarching design goal of these security mechanisms is to simultaneously increase usability, without sacrificing the level of provided security. Such a design goal however is inevitably compromised by service providers due to the increasing computing power of today's systems that are more powerful and more capable in attacking systems, thus forcing them to decrease the task usability in an attempt to preserve security. For example, current password mechanisms are becoming increasingly less usable and memorable through strict password policies that require users to memorize an ever-increasing number of alphanumeric and special characters (Proctor et al. 2002; Komanduri et al. 2011; Inglesant and Sasse 2010). In addition, with the increasing capabilities of Optical Character Recognition systems (OCR), current CAPTCHA mechanisms require users to recognize highly distorted text-based challenges (Yan and El Ahmad 2008; Baecher et al. 2011).

In the rest of this chapter we will first make a brief overview of user authentication and CAPTCHA mechanisms and the need for adaptation and personalization, following the design and security considerations and constraints of each mechanism. Next we thoroughly present a set of human-centred design guidelines for adapting and personalizing design aspects of user authentication and CAPTCHA mechanisms based on specific human cognitive factors. Consequently we present an experimental evaluation in which the design guidelines and adaptation effects have been applied in a real-life setting aiming to investigate the added value of adapting and personalizing such user security tasks. The results of the experimental evaluation are further analyzed and discussed. Finally the chapter concludes with the impact and limitations of the reported work.

8.1.1 User Authentication

User authentication is the process of verifying the physical identity of a person and is a vital component of any security infrastructure of today's interactive systems. During an authentication task, users are required to provide specific secret information in order to prove their identity. Depending on the factor used for authentication, researchers and practitioners promote different mechanisms; *knowledge-based authentication mechanisms* that require from users to either memorize and provide a sequence of characters (e.g., password, personal identification number (PIN)) or a sequence of images; *token-based authentication mechanisms* that require a specific object from users such as a credit card; or *biometric-based authentication mechanisms* that require biometric information from users such as fingerprint information. In this chapter we primarily focus on knowledge-based authentication mechanisms (that principally require users' cognitive processing) with the aim to assist users during such cognitive tasks by providing personalized user authentication tasks bootstrapped on their preferred cognitive processing styles and abilities. Figure 8.1 illustrates examples of knowledge-based user authentication mechanisms, and Fig. 8.2 illustrates examples of token-based, biometric-based and multi-factor user authentication mechanisms.

In the context of knowledge-based authentication mechanisms, the literature reveals many proposals for improving the usability and user experience of text-based password authentication and graphical authentication mechanisms. Text-based

A. Alphanumeric Password

Copyright: Mozilla Firefox

B. Pin-based Authentication
SwiPIN

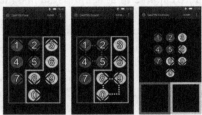

Copyright: Von Zezschwitz et al.

C. Graphical Authentication
Passfaces

Copyright: Passfaces

D. Graphical Authentication
Deja Vu

Copyright: Dhamija R. and Perrig A.

Fig. 8.1 Knowledge-based user authentication mechanisms. (**a**) Alphanumeric Password; (**b**) pin-based authentication with SwiPIN (Von Zezschwitz et al. 2015); (**c**) recognition-based graphical authentication with Passfaces (Passfaces 2009); (**d**) recognition-based graphical authentication with Déjà vu (Dhamija and Perrig 2000)

password mechanisms principally require from users to memorize a sequence of alphanumeric characters to gain access to a resource. Accordingly, research works have focused on providing guidance and feedback during password creation (Shay et al. 2015), and assisting users to create memorable passwords, e.g., through image-based mnemonic techniques (Nelson and Vu 2010), text-recognition techniques (Wright et al. 2012) and password policies (Komanduri et al. 2011; Inglesant and Sasse 2010; Vu et al. 2007). Graphical authentication mechanisms require from users either to solely remember information and reproduce a secret drawing on a static image (recall-based) (Jermyn et al. 1999; Gao et al. 2008; Tao and Adams 2008; Wiedenbeck et al. 2005; Biddle et al. 2012; Chiasson et al. 2008) or create an authentication key by selecting and memorizing specific images, and then recognize the images among decoys to authenticate (recognition-based) (Passfaces 2009; Mihajlov and Jerman-Blazic 2011; Nicholson et al. 2012).

A. Biometric-based Authentication
Android Face Unlock

Copyright: Google

B. Biometric-based Authentication
Apple Touch ID

Copyright: Apple

C. Multi-factor Authentication
Glass Unlock

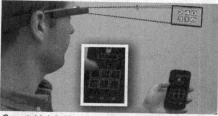

Copyright: Winkler et al.

D. Token-based Authentication
WebTicket

(a) Front

(b) Back

Copyright: Hayashi et al.

Fig. 8.2 Token-, biometric- and multi-factor user authentication mechanisms. (**a**) Biometric-based authentication with Android Face Unlock (Google); (**b**) biometric-based authentication with Apple Touch ID (Apple); (**c**) multi-factor authentication with Glass Unlock (Winkler et al. 2015); (**d**) token-based authentication with WebTicket (Hayashi et al. 2012)

8.1.2 Human Interaction Proofs (CAPTCHA)

Human Interaction Proofs (HIP) are security defense mechanisms aiming to prove that the entity interacting with a system is a human being and not a malicious software (Chellapilla et al. 2005). A Completely Automated Public Turing test to tell Computers and Humans Apart (CAPTCHA – von Ahn et al. 2004) is an example HIP mechanism which is widely used today by service providers to protect their systems against automated software attacks (e.g., denial of service attacks, password dictionary attacks, etc.). CAPTCHA challenges typically require from legitimate users to solve visual cognitive-based challenges before performing the primary task of interaction in a system. For example, systems require from users to recognize distorted alphanumeric characters or solve image puzzle problems before commenting on a Web-site. Main aim of this process is to prevent a possible automated software attack that could automatically generate and send thousands of comments in the system that would decrease the quality of services. These challenges are based on the assumption that they can be easily solved by humans but present significant difficulty for computing systems (e.g., Optical Character Recognition (OCR) or other image-recognition systems).

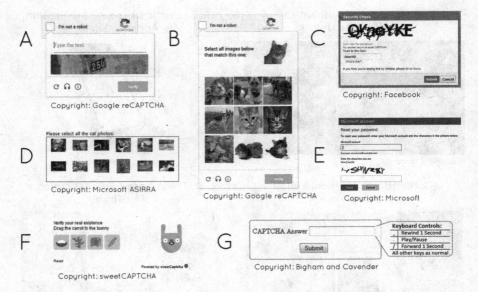

Fig. 8.3 Selected CAPTCHA schemes. (**a**) NoCAPTCHA reCAPTCHA (text-recognition); (**b**) NoCAPTCHA reCAPTCHA (mobile friendly image-recognition); (**c**) Facebook CAPTCHA (text-recognition); (**d**) Microsoft ASIRRA (image-recognition) (Elson et al. 2007); (**e**) Microsoft CAPTCHA (text-recognition); (**f**) sweetCAPTCHA (drag-and-drop interaction); (**g**) non-visual access CAPTCHA (speech-recognition) (Bigham and Cavender 2009)

Recent research works underpinned the necessity for designing usable CAPTCHA challenges since studies have shown that current CAPTCHA schemes are difficult to solve and frustrate users (Fidas et al. 2011; Bursztein et al. 2010). In this context, researchers and practitioners promote different types of challenges aiming to address usability issues of CAPTCHA, without compromising security. Depending on the type of challenge, current CAPTCHA implementations are classified in the following three categories: (i) *text-recognition challenges* require from a legitimate user to type alphanumeric characters based on a distorted image that appears on the screen (von Ahn et al. 2008; Bursztein et al. 2014; Chew and Baird 2003); (ii) *image-recognition challenges* require from users to solve image puzzle problems and annotate static or animated images (e.g., select images of a particular theme – Elson et al. 2007; Vikram et al. 2011; Gossweiler et al. 2009); and (iii) *speech-recognition challenges* that require users to listen and recognize a recording of simple words and numbers which entails disturbance and noise (Bigham and Cavender 2009; Holman et al. 2007; Gao et al. 2010). Figure 8.3 illustrates selected CAPTCHA mechanisms of each category.

8.1.3   Why to Adapt and Personalize Security-Related Tasks

A number of research works investigated the impact of several factors (human, technology and design related) on both user authentication and CAPTCHA mechanisms, aiming to understand human-computer interactions in such realms and further apply that knowledge in designing and developing usable security mechanisms (Biddle et al. 2012; Bursztein et al. 2014; Shirali-Shahreza et al. 2013). Yet, a common practice with regard to the design of existing user authentication and CAPTCHA schemes is that they do not primarily take into consideration intrinsic individual characteristics of users but rather follow a "one-size-fits-all" paradigm, i.e., the visual and interaction design of the security task is rarely personalized to the intrinsic characteristics of users which define them as individuals (e.g., individual traits). The majority of today's systems utilize the same text-based passwords and text-recognition CAPTCHA as their sole means for security (Herley and van Oorschot 2012; Bursztein et al. 2014). Although, recent research revealed that human factors (e.g., age differences, cognitive differences), technology factors (e.g., device) and design factors (e.g., text vs. images) have a main effect on task performance and user preference of both user authentication and CAPTCHA (Ma et al. 2013; Forget et al. 2014; Belk et al. 2013a; Fidas et al. 2011; von Zezschwitz et al. 2014; Reynaga and Chiasson 2013). According to the aforementioned research works, findings suggest that modeling these factors and applying them in user-adaptive and personalized security mechanisms could improve the user experience and eventually the users' acceptance (Belk et al. 2014a, b).

In this context, human-computer interactions with regards to user authentication and CAPTCHA mechanisms are in principal cognitive tasks that embrace perception, recognition, recalling and reasoning. Taken into consideration the diversity of humans in cognitive processing styles and abilities (Riding and Cheema 1991; Kozhevnikov 2007; Demetriou et al. 2013), this research work builds on the promise that adapting and personalizing user authentication and CAPTCHA tasks, bootstrapped on the users' cognitive processing characteristics, could provide a promising alternative to current state-of-the-art practices, aiming to support the users' efficiency and effectiveness of processing information as well as decrease cognitive load, and eventually improve the user experience and user acceptance of user authentication and CAPTCHA mechanisms.

In order to investigate the feasibility and efficacy of such an approach, we initially designed and conducted several standalone and targeted user studies that investigated various and different human cognitive processing factors, aiming to understand and identify which individual characteristics are considered important enough and might affect users' interactions in user authentication and CAPTCHA mechanisms (Belk et al. 2014b, 2015). Findings of these studies have shown several interaction effects between specific human cognitive factors and user authentication and CAPTCHA design factors in terms of task completion performance and user preference. For example, results have shown that users with Verbal cognitive styles (users that process textual information more efficiently than graphical information) prefer and perform faster in text-based password mechanisms than graphical authentication mechanisms (Belk et al. 2014b), suggesting that Verbal users should be provided with text-based passwords in order to improve the usability of the authentication task. The aforementioned studies aimed to guide and contribute to the design of personalized user authentication and CAPTCHA mechanisms that take into consideration such intrinsic human factors.

Consequently, we have interpreted and translated the observed main effects into adaptation rules in order to map human cognitive factors with design factors of user authentication and CAPTCHA mechanisms. These adaptation rules have been formalized and applied in mapU (described in Chap. 5) in which the user authentication and CAPTCHA tasks are personalized based on a two-phase method as follows: (i) adapt the type of the security mechanism (textual or graphical) based on users' cognitive styles (i.e., Verbal/Imager and Wholist/Analyst); and (ii) adapt the complexity level of the security mechanism (number of characters/images) based on users' cognitive processing abilities (i.e., limited/enhanced).

8.2   Design Considerations and Constraints

An important challenge of any adaptation and personalization system is to identify which aspects of the system can be adapted and why, with the aim to improve the usability and experience of user interactions. Accordingly, we identify and present the design and security considerations of knowledge-based user authentication and CAPTCHA mechanisms.

8.2.1   Design Considerations in Knowledge-Based User Authentication

Knowledge-based authentication mechanisms (*"what the user knows"*) require from the user to memorize specific information (e.g., password, passphrase, PIN code, sequence of images, etc.). Text-based passwords are the dominant means for authentication and are currently utilized in the majority of computing systems worldwide since they are familiar to most of the users, and easy and inexpensive to implement (Herley and van Oorschot 2012; Herley et al. 2009). Nevertheless, passwords have always been criticized about their security flaws (Bonneau et al. 2012). Various studies have been reported that underpin the necessity for secure and usable authentication mechanisms (Shay et al. 2012; Komanduri et al. 2011; Shay et al. 2010; Inglesant and Sasse 2010; Florencio and Herley 2007; Adams and Sasse 1999). The literature reveals many proposals for improving password security, such as educating and influencing users to create more secure passwords (Forget et al. 2008; Forget and Biddle 2008; Yan et al. 2004), improving existing recall-based password approaches with recognition of text (Wright et al. 2012), enforcing the creation of secure passwords through password policies (Komanduri et al. 2011; Inglesant and Sasse 2010; Vu et al. 2007), automatically generating secure passwords and mnemonic passphrases (Kuo et al. 2006; Leonhard and Venkatakrishnan 2007). Furthermore, password managers (Halderman et al. 2005; Chiasson et al. 2006) have been proposed to minimize users' cognitive load.

A great amount of research of knowledge-based authentication mechanisms has focused on the design and implementation of graphical authentication schemes (see Biddle et al. (2012) for a recent review). This is further strengthened by the technological shift of current computing systems toward touch-based devices in which entering textual information (in this case, text-based passwords) on touch-based keyboards is a demanding task (Findlater et al. 2011). In addition, graphical authentication mechanisms claim to preserve security and improve usability and memorability of user authentication as they leverage the vast capacity and capabilities of the human visual memory system (Angeli et al. 2005; Everitt et al. 2009; Biddle et al. 2012) and are memorable over extended periods of time (Tullis et al. 2011). Principally, graphical authentication mechanisms require from a user to enter an authentication key represented by images in a specific sequence. Graphical authentication schemes can be classified into three categories according to the memory task in remembering and entering the authentication key; *recall-based, cued-recall-based* and *recognition-based authentication.*

Recall-based authentication mechanisms require that users remember information and reproduce a secret drawing on a static image as their authentication key. The first recall-based authentication mechanism proposed was Draw-a-Secret (DAS – Jermyn et al. 1999) where users draw their authentication key on a two dimensional grid. Variations of the first DAS system that aimed to improve some of its usability issues include BDAS (Dunphy and Yan 2007) which added background images to the existing DAS to encourage the creation of stronger authentication keys, YAGP (Yet Another Graphical Password – Gao et al. 2008) that modified DAS to accept approximately correct drawings, Passdoodle (Varenhorst 2004) that added additional factors, such as, pen color, number of pen strokes, drawing speed for the matching process to add variability of drawings, Pass-Go (Tao and Adams 2008) where users draw their authentication key using grid intersection points, as well as commercial applications of Pass-Go, like Google Android mobile phones for unlocking screens by drawing an authentication key on a 3×3 grid.

Cued-recall authentication mechanisms require users to identify specific locations on a static image and are intended to reduce the memory load on users since specific cues are utilized in order to assist the recall of information. The dominant cued-recall authentication system is PassPoints (Wiedenbeck et al. 2005) and its variations (Biddle et al. 2012). In PassPoints, users click anywhere on a picture, with a tolerance metric defined around each click-point to avoid the need for pixel-perfect entries in the future. Variations include Persuasive Cued Click Points (Chiasson et al. 2008) that assists users to select random authentication keys by highlighting a random part of the picture where the click has to occur. Recently,

Bulling et al. (2012) have proposed a gaze-based authentication scheme that supports users in selecting secure gaze-based graphical passwords. In particular, the proposed authentication scheme uses saliency maps to mask out those areas of the image most likely to attract visual attention with the aim to increase the security of gaze-based cued-recall graphical authentication mechanisms.

Recognition-based authentication mechanisms require that the user creates an authentication key by selecting and memorizing specific images, and then recognize the images among decoys to authenticate. The most popular and extensively researched recognition-based graphical authentication system to date is Passfaces (2009) that uses human faces as part of the authentication key. Variations have been proposed that use different content in images, like the Story system (Davis et al. 2004) that uses everyday objects, places and people as the authentication key, and ImagePass (Mihajlov and Jerman-Blazic 2011) that utilizes single-object images as the authentication key. Another recent work proposed the Tiles system (Nicholson et al. 2012) in which users are assigned a target image and subsequently asked to select segments of that image with the aim to help mitigate the threat from verbal sharing and observation attacks.

To this end, knowledge-based user authentication mechanisms, and more specifically text-based passwords and graphical authentication mechanisms entail various design features. Based on the aforementioned analysis, we categorize important and widely used features as follows: (i) design type (e.g., text-based, picture-based); (ii) interaction design type (e.g., selecting images/text vs. typing text vs. touching visual images/text objects vs. drawing patterns); (iii) image type (faces, abstract or single-object); (iv) number of user-selected images/characters for the authentication key; (v) number of decoy images illustrated during graphical authentication; (vi) the policy of the authentication key (e.g., allow or not using the same image multiple times in a single key); (vii) the procedure for graphical authentication (e.g., showing more decoy images in one screen vs. showing less decoy images in multiple screens) (Ma et al. 2013).

8.2.2   Security Considerations in Knowledge-Based User Authentication

The literature reveals that various user authentication schemes entail different security strengths and weaknesses (Renaud et al. 2013; Biddle et al. 2012), since in each case different factors exist that affect the security of the authentication mechanisms. According to Biddle et al. (2012), attacks can be classified in two broad categories; *guessing attacks* or *capture attacks*. Guessing attacks are considered an important threat in user authentication. These are either performed online in which the attacker guesses and enters the authentication key through the live login interface or performed offline in which the attacker first gains full access to the system's database that contains verifiable authentication keys (e.g., hashes). In both text-based and graphical authentication, online guessing attacks can be prevented by using additional security measures that are enabled after consecutive unsuccessful logins (e.g., CAPTCHA). Offline guessing attacks are prevented by processing the authentication key through a hash function in case the attacker gains full access to the authentication keys. Thus, the attacker is required to check if an authentication key attempt is correct by first hashing the guessed key and then compare it to the value stored in the database. Accordingly, the theoretical space of an authentication key is vital for preventing offline guessing attacks. Thus, in both text-based and graphical authentication mechanisms, the number and type of images has a significant effect on guessing attacks (Komanduri et al. 2011; Biddle et al. 2012).

Capture attacks aim to acquire the authentication key by capturing data while the user enters the authentication key during login. Most common capture attacks include: (i) *shoulder surfing attacks* in which the attacker visually observes the user entering the authentication key; (ii) *phishing attacks* (password fishing); (iii) *social engineering* in which users might share their authentication key (either willingly or through phishing); and (iv) *malware attacks* (malicious software). A high number of research works have focused on minimizing threats of shoulder surfing attacks, such as De Luca et al. (2013) that proposed an approach using fake cursors in on-screen password mechanisms and Winkler et al. (2015) that proposed a hybrid approach for preventing shoulder surfing attacks on smartphones by leveraging a private near-eye display (i.e., Google Glass). Researchers have also focused to prevent social engineering by assisting users to create secure and memorable passwords (Nelson and Vu 2010; Wright et al. 2012) as well as investigating the type of image used in graphical authentication mechanisms (Mihajlov and Jerman-Blazic 2011).

8.2.3 Design Considerations in CAPTCHA

An acceptable CAPTCHA solution should embrace both security and usability aspects as its purpose is to provide safety of operation to Web application providers but as well usability and transparency to its end users, aiming to minimize the added cognitive effort of a casual user interacting with it. Various studies have been reported that underpin the necessity for increasing usability of current CAPTCHA implementations. A study of Yan and El Ahmad (2008) raised the usability issues of CAPTCHA and proposed a framework for evaluating various designs. A recent study which investigated users' perceptions towards CAPTCHA challenges underpinned the necessity for user friendly CAPTCHA challenges as current implementations do not provide an acceptable trade off solution with regards to usability (Fidas et al. 2011). Results have shown that even experienced users expressed their difficulties in solving a CAPTCHA challenge during their first attempt (Fidas et al. 2011).

In this context, research on CAPTCHA mechanisms has received significant attention lately aiming to increase security but at the same time usability. Researchers promote among others interaction with pictures, audio and video as a possible alternative to text-based CAPTCHA (Elson et al. 2007; Vikram et al. 2011; Ross et al. 2010; Gossweiler et al. 2009; Kluever and Zanibbi 2009). Accordingly, current CAPTCHA implementations can be classified into three broad categories: *text-recognition*, *image-recognition*, and *speech-recognition*.

Text-recognition CAPTCHA, which are also the most widely used today, require from a legitimate user to type letters or digits based on a distorted image that appears on the screen. Popular text-recognition CAPTCHA include among others reCAPTCHA (von Ahn et al. 2008), BaffleText (Chew and Baird 2003) and Gimpy (von Ahn et al. 2004). Furthermore, major Web service providers such as Google, Facebook, Microsoft and many others utilize text-recognition CAPTCHA to protect their services against automated software attacks (Bursztein et al. 2010).

Image-recognition CAPTCHA are usually based on image puzzle problems and annotation of static and animated images. For example, in ASIRRA (Elson et al. 2007), users are required to select pictures that illustrate cats among dogs. SEMAGE (Vikram et al. 2011) similarly requires users to recognize the content of a set of images, but as well understand and identify the semantic relationship between a subset of them. Other popular examples include IMAGINATION (IMAge Generation for INternet AuthenticaTION) (Datta et al. 2005), that uses a two-round click-and-annotate process in which a user needs to first click on the geometric centre of an image among a composite image tiled with multiple distorted images, and then annotate a distorted image of a simple object with one word of an available list of words, ARTiFACIAL (Rui and Liu 2004), where users are required to identify a single human face in a challenge, and click the six facial corners (four eye corners and two mouth corners) on the face to pass the challenge, Sketcha (Ross et al. 2010) and What's Up CAPTCHA (Gossweiler et al. 2009), that require users to adjust randomly rotated images to their upright orientation.

Finally, *speech-recognition CAPTCHA* are usually based on audio comprehension which principally require users to enter the words and numbers listened from a re-cording of a combination of simple words and numbers where disturbance and noise has also been added. Speech-recognition CAPTCHA are more difficult to solve and internationalize, and more demanding in terms of time and efforts in comparison with text-recognition and image-recognition CAPTCHA. However, audio-based CAPTCHA challenges have become an alternative for visually-impaired people. Examples include Text-to-Speech (Chan 2003) and human in contrast to synthetic voice recognition (Gao et al. 2010). In this chapter we primarily focus on text- and image-recognition CAPTCHA rather than speech-recognition CAPTCHA since these considered a significantly more demanding task in terms of solving time and is mostly used for users with physical impairments which is out of the scope of this chapter (Bigham and Cavender 2009).

8.2.4 Security Considerations in CAPTCHA

The success rate of an attack is the primary metric to evaluate CAPTCHA attack effectiveness (Zhu et al. 2010) and several research works have investigated the impact of specific design factors on CAPTCHA security (Bursztein et al. 2011, 2014; Golle 2008; Zhu et al. 2010). The work of Bursztein et al. (2014, 2011) has shown that specific text features in text-recognition CAPTCHA challenges affect the security of the mechanism. In particular, the following features affect the security (and the usability) of the challenge: (i) the length and font size used in the challenge; (ii) the rotation and collapse of the characters; and (iii) the number, width and color of lines illustrated in the challenge. The work of Bursztein et al. (2011) also showed that incorporating background images with noise is ineffective to attacks.

The works of Golle (2008) and Zhu et al. (2010) revealed that the security of image-recognition CAPTCHA challenges are affected by the following factors: (i) number, type and color of objects used in the challenge; (ii) the semantic meaning of the objects used in the challenge; and (iii) the source and generation of the objects (i.e., new challenges should be independent to past challenges). Furthermore, the work of Golle (2008) revealed that degrading the quality of the object or using distortion (as in text-recognition challenges) is ineffective to attacks, but rather decreases the usability of the challenge.

Finally, based on the work of Bigham and Cavender (2009), the security of speech-recognition CAPTCHA is affected by the number of characters used in the challenge, the alphabet and the added background noise in the narration.

8.3 Human-Centred Design Guidelines

Prior targeted and stand-alone research attempts have shown several interaction effects between several cognitive factors and design characteristics of user authentication and CAPTCHA mechanisms. According to the main findings and effects of these studies, we have chosen to map specific human factors with design characteristics of user authentication and CAPTCHA mechanisms as follows: (i) map human cognitive style differences (Verbal/Imager and Wholist/Analyst) with the type of the security mechanism (textual and graphical) since cognitive styles have shown to correlate with the type of information presented and processed in these mechanisms (Belk et al. 2012, 2013b, 2014a, b, 2015); and (ii) map human cognitive processing abilities (limited/enhanced) with the complexity of the mechanism (number of characters/images) since results have shown that specific elementary cognitive processes have an effect on task performance, problem solving and overall efficiency of processing and controlling information cognitively in such tasks (Belk et al. 2013a, 2014a, 2015).

Figure 8.3 illustrates the proposed mapping between the main factors of the user model. Accordingly, the mapping between the factors is performed on a two-level

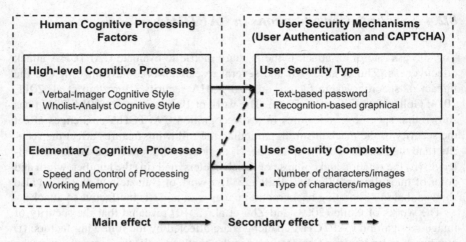

Main effect ⟶   Secondary effect ⇢

Fig. 8.4 Mapping between human factors and design factors of user security mechanisms

concept; in the first level, the high-level cognitive processes (cognitive styles) are used to decide the type of the security mechanism (textual or graphical), and in the second level, the elementary cognitive processes (i.e., speed and control of processing and working memory) decide the complexity level of the security mechanism (e.g., number and type of characters/images). Furthermore, given that our previous studies have shown that working memory capacity affects the task performance of different user authentication types (i.e., users with limited working memory capacity did not perform efficiently with graphical authentication mechanisms), a secondary mapping between elementary cognitive processes is additionally performed with the security type (Fig. 8.4).

In this section we will present a set of human-centred design guidelines for personalizing user authentication and CAPTCHA mechanisms. Table 8.1 summarizes the main criteria in order to analyze and document the usefulness of adopting a personalized approach in user authentication and CAPTCHA mechanisms. Accordingly, given existing usability, user experience and user acceptance issues in user authentication and CAPTCHA mechanisms, we propose to adapt and personalize the type and complexity level (How) of user authentication and CAPTCHA tasks (Where) based on a set of human cognitive factors (What), with the aim to assist the users during information processing and prevent cognitive load and eventually improve task completion efficiency, effectiveness and provide a positive user experience (Why).

In the following sections we describe in detail each guideline of Table 8.1 and their corresponding adaptation effects and human cognitive factors. For each guideline we also provide a visual illustration of the respective security mechanism and the triggered mapping of human cognitive factors and design characteristics for both user authentication and CAPTCHA mechanisms. In cases of a logical disjunc-

Table 8.1 Guidelines for personalizing security-related tasks according to human cognitive factors

Where	Why	What	How	Guideline
User authentication	Assist information processing Prevent cognitive load Improve task completion time Improve task effectiveness Improve user experience	Verbal Wholist Limited CPE Limited WMC	Textual Standard complexity	1A (Fig. 8.7)
		Imager Analyst Limited WMC	Textual Standard complexity	1B (Fig. 8.8)
		Verbal Wholist Enhanced CPE Enhanced WMC	Textual Higher complexity	2 (Fig. 8.9)
		Imager Analyst Enhanced WMC	Graphical Standard complexity	3 (Fig. 8.10)
		Imager Analyst Enhanced CPE Enhanced WMC	Graphical Higher complexity	4 (Fig. 8.11)
CAPTCHA		Verbal Wholist Limited CPE Limited WMC	Text-recognition Standard complexity	5 (Fig. 8.14)
		Verbal Wholist Enhanced CPE Enhanced WMC	Text-recognition Higher complexity	6 (Fig. 8.15)
		Imager Analyst Limited CPE Limited WMC	Image-recognition Standard complexity	7 (Fig. 8.16)
		Imager Analyst Enhanced CPE Enhanced WMC	Image-recognition Higher complexity	8 (Fig. 8.17)

tion (*OR*) of two or more human factors (i.e., in case that the decision for a design factor is dependent either on the one or the other factor, e.g., a user being Verbal *OR* Wholist), we do not explicitly provide multiple guidelines, but rather we present one mutual guideline indicating the logical disjunction between the factors and the design factor decision on the figure.

8.3.1 User Authentication Mechanisms

The user authentication mechanism communicates to the users the personalized authentication task. Two types of user authentication are used: a text-based password mechanism (Fig. 8.5) and a recognition-based graphical authentication mechanism (Fig. 8.6). The text-based password mechanism requires from users to recall and enter alphanumeric characters (including numbers, a mixture of lower- and upper-case letters) and special keyboard characters in a specific sequence. The graphical authentication mechanism requires from users to recall and enter single-object images in a specific sequence (e.g., tennis ball, teddy bear, etc.). The design and development of the graphical authentication mechanism is based on well reputed recognition-based graphical authentication mechanisms; such as DejaVu (Dhamija and Perrig 2000), PassFaces (2009) and ImagePass (Mihajlov and Jerman-Blazic 2011). In case users forget their authentication key, an option for resetting the key is available in which a hyperlink is sent to the users' email that redirects to a form for resetting their authentication key.

Following existing research works on design and security issues in user authentication (Renaud et al. 2013; Biddle et al. 2012; Komanduri et al. 2011), we suggest two different user authentication policies for each user authentication type; a stan-

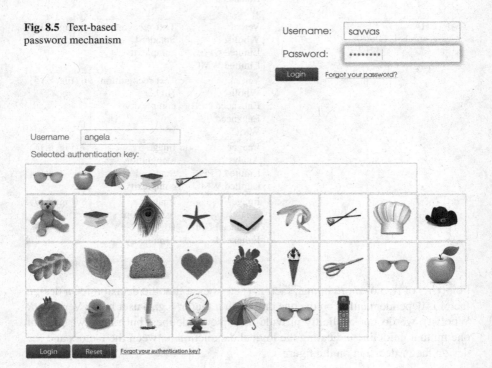

Fig. 8.5 Text-based password mechanism

Fig. 8.6 Recognition-based graphical authentication mechanism

dard and a higher complex user authentication policy. In the case of text-based passwords, a standard policy requires the creation of a password key that consists of eight alphanumeric characters with no further restrictions applied, whereas an enhanced policy requires similarly eight alphanumeric characters, entailing at least one upper-case letter and lower-case letter and special character. Both policies do not allow the creation of a dictionary word by performing a dictionary check based on a method widely used in practice[1] (Komanduri et al. 2011). In the case of graphical authentication mechanisms, a standard and a higher complex policy respectively requires users to enter five and eight unique, user-selected images that are shuffled within 25 stable, system-assigned decoy images. Although the theoretical key space is smaller compared to traditional text-based passwords, the particular design choice is typical for recognition-based graphical authentication (Biddle et al. 2012; Renaud et al. 2013; Ma et al. 2013).

8.3.1.1 Guideline #1: Text-Based Password with Standard Complexity

Guideline #1 entails communicating a text-based password with standard complexity. This guideline is split in two sub-guidelines; Guideline #1A (Fig. 8.7) and Guideline #1B (Fig. 8.8). Both guidelines follow a two-step adaptation process. In Guideline #1A, at a first level, in case users have a Verbal or Wholist cognitive style we suggest to provide a text-based password mechanism since this particular type of authentication is best matched to the habitual approach of users' cognitive processing styles. The reasoning behind this choice is based on existing theory on cognitive styles and prior studies that have shown that Verbals and Wholists are more efficient in completing text-based password tasks than graphical authentication tasks (Belk et al. 2014a, b). On the one hand, Verbals are more efficient in

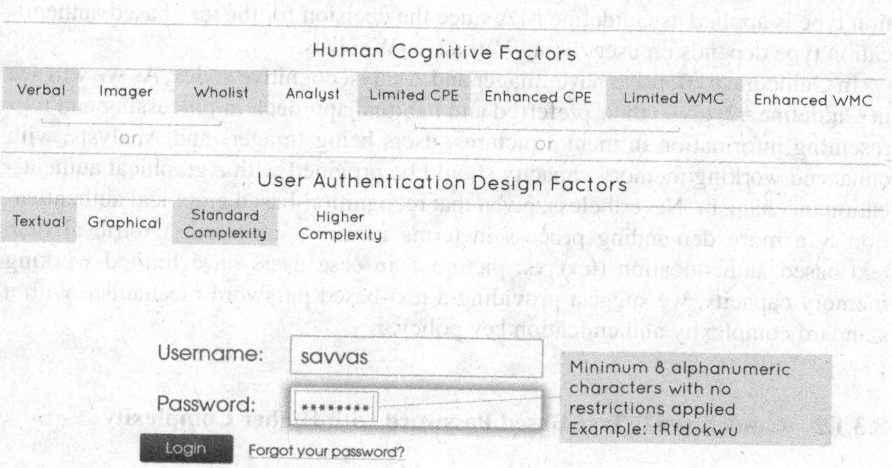

Fig. 8.7 Guideline #1A: Text-based password with standard complexity

---

[1] http://download.openwall.net/pub/wordlists

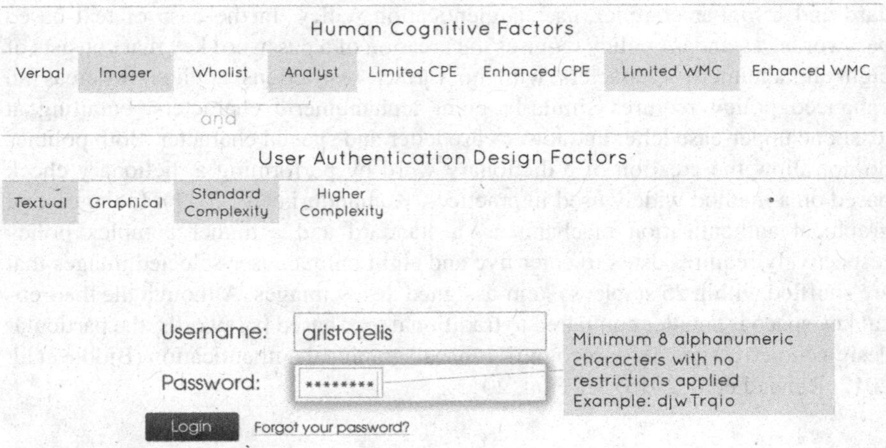

Fig. 8.8 Guideline #1B: Text-based password with standard complexity

processing textual information since they process and represent information in words, whereas prior studies have shown that Wholists are not efficient and effective in visual search tasks in picture-based grids, such as recognition-based graphical authentication (see Sect. 2.2.6). At a second level, in case users have limited cognitive processing efficiency (CPE) or limited working memory capacity a standard complexity policy will be provided to them, which requires the creation of a password key of a minimum of eight alphanumeric characters with no further restrictions applied. Given the logical disjunction between the cognitive styles and cognitive processing factors (Verbal *OR* Wholist, Limited CPE *OR* Limited WMC), for alternative cases such as a user being Verbal *AND* Analyst, the same authentication type is applied as Guideline #1A since the decision for the text-based authentication type depends on users being Verbals or Wholists.

In Guideline #1B, users have Imager and Analyst cognitive styles. As we will see in Guideline #2, given their preferred and habitual approach in processing and representing information in mental pictures, users being Imagers and Analysts, with enhanced working memory capacity should be provided with a graphical authentication mechanism. Nevertheless, given that recognition-based graphical authentication is a more demanding process in terms memory information retrieval than text-based authentication (text vs. pictures), in case users have limited working memory capacity, we suggest providing a text-based password mechanism with a standard complexity authentication key policy.

8.3.1.2 Guideline #2: Text-Based Password with Higher Complexity

Guideline #2 suggests providing a text-based password with higher complexity (Fig. 8.9). Similar to Guideline #1, Verbal or Wholist users are provided with a text-based password mechanism given their cognitive styles' characteristics. On the

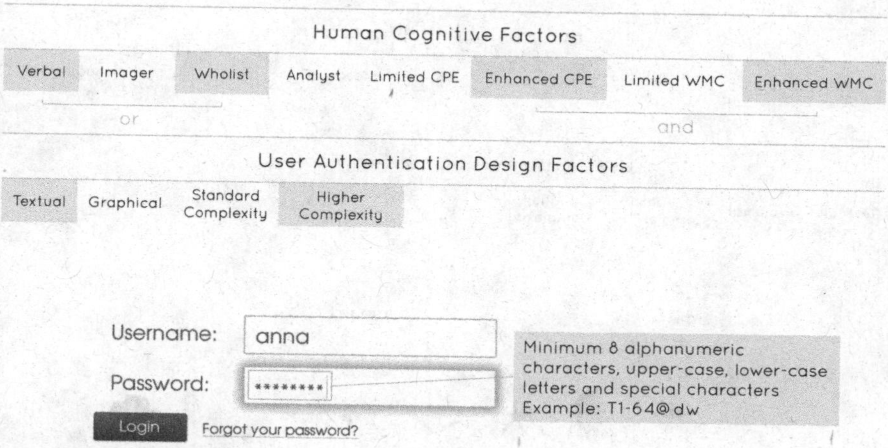

Fig. 8.9 Guideline #2: Text-based password with higher complexity

other hand, in case these users have enhanced cognitive processing efficiency and enhanced working memory capacity, it is suggested to provide a higher complexity policy. Although a higher complex policy might demand more cognitive processing and eventually more time to complete the task, studies have shown that users with enhanced cognitive processing abilities are as efficient and effective in completing high complex and less complex user authentication tasks (Belk et al. 2014a). This way, depending on custom requirements of service providers, a higher complex policy can be provided to these types of users, increasing the security of the authentication key, at a rather minimum cost to usability.

8.3.1.3   Guideline #3: Recognition-Based Graphical Authentication with Standard Complexity

Guideline #3 entails communicating a recognition-based graphical authentication with standard complexity (Fig. 8.10). In this case, users are Imagers and Analysts, and have enhanced working memory capacity. The reasoning behind this guideline is based on the following hypotheses which have been validated in prior studies (Belk et al. 2013b, 2014a, b). Imagers process and represent information in mental pictures and thus are efficient in recalling and processing graphical information (see Sect. 2.2.6), while Analysts perform efficiently on visual search tasks (Messick 1993; Goodenough and Karp 1961; Reardon and Moore 1988). In the context of recognition-based graphical user authentication, Analysts perform efficiently since recognition-based graphical authentication mechanisms entail primarily a visual search task (i.e., users are required to search for and recognize their graphical authentication key). Furthermore, Analysts have an improved visual working memory and are thus positively affected in graphical authentication tasks since the

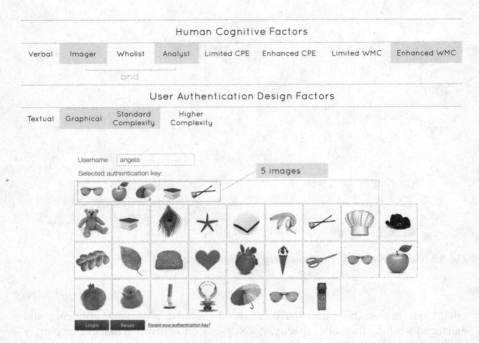

Fig. 8.10 Guideline #3: Recognition-based graphical authentication with standard complexity

recognition and recall of images are primarily processed by utilizing the visual working memory sub-system. Furthermore, given that recognition-based graphical authentication is a more demanding process in terms memory information retrieval than text-based authentication (text vs. pictures), a prerequisite for providing a graphical authentication mechanism is that users should have enhanced working memory capacity in order to better handle and process information during the recall process. Finally, a standard complexity policy is provided in which users are required to create an authentication key entailing a minimum of five images, which is typical for recognition-based graphical authentication mechanisms.

8.3.1.4   Guideline #4: Recognition-Based Graphical Authentication with Higher Complexity

Guideline #4 suggests providing a recognition-based graphical authentication mechanism with higher complexity (Fig. 8.11). The same principle and reasoning is followed as in Guideline #3, however in this case a higher complex policy is provided to users, requiring the creation of a graphical authentication with a minimum of eight images. The same rules apply as in Guideline #3, with an additional prerequisite of the user having both an enhanced cognitive processing efficiency and enhanced working memory capacity.

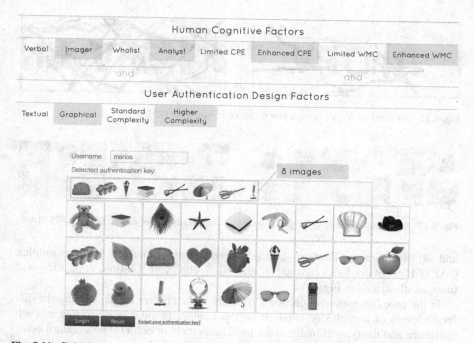

Fig. 8.11 Guideline #4: Recognition-based graphical authentication with higher complexity

8.3.2   *CAPTCHA Mechanisms*

The CAPTCHA mechanism communicates to the users the personalized CAPTCHA challenge. Two types of CAPTCHA mechanisms are used: A text-recognition CAPTCHA that requires from users to recognize and enter distorted alphanumeric characters, and an image-recognition CAPTCHA that requires from users to recognize and select specific images of a particular theme. The design and development of the text-recognition CAPTCHA mechanism is based on a similar technical approach followed by reCAPTCHA (von Ahn et al. 2008) as well as freely available open-source software (Securimage 2014). The image-recognition CAPTCHA mechanism is based on Microsoft ASIRRA which presents to the users images illustrating cats and dogs requiring from them to recognize and select the images that display cats (Elson et al. 2007). Both CAPTCHA mechanisms include a refresh button that initialize a challenge by reloading a new set of characters/images.

Following the design and security guidelines proposed in Bursztein et al. (2011), Zhu et al. (2010) and Golle (2008) we have designed two different complexity levels for each CAPTCHA type; a design with standard complexity and a higher complex design. In the case of text-recognition CAPTCHA, the criteria for developing the different levels of complexity are based on the number of characters presented, and the percentage of text distortion and noise illustrated in each CAPTCHA challenge. The standard complexity CAPTCHA entails a random number of 5–7 characters

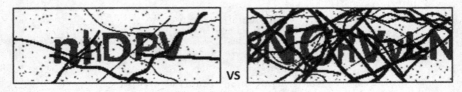

Fig. 8.12 Standard vs. higher complexity text-recognition CAPTCHA

Fig. 8.13 Standard (*colored*) vs. higher (*greyscale*) complexity image-recognition CAPTCHA

and 40 % character rotation, collapsing and lines, while the higher complex CAPTCHA entails 8–10 characters, and 60 % character rotation, collapsing and lines, as illustrated in Fig. 8.12.

In the case of image-recognition CAPTCHA, the criteria for developing the different levels of complexity is based on the number of images illustrated in each challenge and the type of image color used (greyscale or color). The standard complexity CAPTCHA illustrates a 12-image challenge with colored images while the higher complexity CAPTCHA illustrates a 14-image challenge with greyscale images, as illustrated in Fig. 8.13. The rationale behind the color change is based on the research work reported in Golle (2008), that suggests illustrating greyscale images for decreasing the attach success rate for the ASIRRA challenge. Given that a greyscale image removes important information for the efficient and effective recognition of the image, we suggest providing this type of image to users with enhanced cognitive processing abilities, since providing this to users with more limited cognitive abilities would probably hinder the efficiency and effectiveness of processing information and eventually decrease the usability of the task.

8.3.2.1 Guideline #5: Text-Recognition CAPTCHA with Standard Complexity

Guideline #5 suggests providing a text-recognition CAPTCHA mechanism with standard complexity (Fig. 8.14). In this case users can have a verbal cognitive processing style or holistic cognitive processing style. The primary reason behind this suggestion is based on the fact that users are Verbals and thus have improved abilities in processing textual information (see Sect. 2.2.6). In addition, given that Wholist users do not have improved visual search abilities, which is required in image-recognition CAPTCHA, these types of users are provided with a text-recognition CAPTCHA. Furthermore, a text-based challenge with standard complexity is provided due to the fact that users have both limited cognitive processing

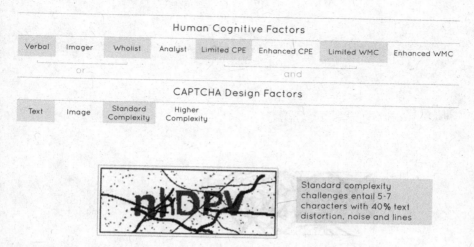

Fig. 8.14 Guideline #5: Text-recognition CAPTCHA with standard complexity

efficiency and working memory capacity. Thus, providing a higher complex challenge which requires improved cognitive processing abilities might decrease the usability of the task.

8.3.2.2 Guideline #6: Text-Recognition CAPTCHA with Higher Complexity

Guideline #6 involves a text-recognition CAPTCHA with higher complexity. Figure 8.15 illustrates an example text-based CAPTCHA challenge with high levels of text distortion, noise and lines. The same reasoning is followed for the CAPTCHA type recommendation (Verbal or Wholist), however in this case, given that users have either enhanced cognitive processing efficiency or enhanced working memory capacity, a higher complex challenge can be provided. The rationale behind this suggestion is based on prior studies that have shown that users with enhanced cognitive processing abilities perform equally well in higher and less complex CAPTCHA challenges (Belk et al. 2013d). This way, higher complex CAPTCHA challenges can be provided to users, increasing the security of the mechanisms at a minimum cost to usability. Nevertheless, given this unequal treatment between users with limited and enhanced cognitive processing abilities (since users with enhanced abilities are provided with a more demanding CAPTCHA challenge), we suggest enhancing the CAPTCHA challenge with a user feedback mechanism for eliciting the user's preference and perceived usability of the challenge. This way, users with enhanced cognitive processing abilities, that are required to solve more demanding and highly complex CAPTCHA challenges can explicitly adapt the complexity level. Apparently, such a feedback mechanism is also dependent on the custom security requirements of the service provider, since different requirements apply in different

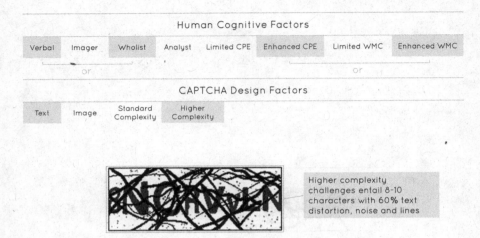

Fig. 8.15 Guideline #6: Text-recognition CAPTCHA with higher complexity

domains and contexts of use. Given the logical disjunction between the cognitive styles and cognitive processing factors (Verbal *OR* Wholist, Enhanced CPE *OR* Enhanced WMC), for alternative cases such as a user having enhanced CPE *AND* limited WMC, the same guideline is applied as Guideline #6 since the decision for the higher complex text-based challenge depends on the prerequisite that the user should have either enhanced CPE or enhanced WMC.

8.3.2.3   Guideline #7: Image-Recognition CAPTCHA with Standard Complexity

Guideline #7 suggests an image-recognition CAPTCHA mechanism with standard complexity levels (Fig. 8.16). In this case, users have imager and analytic cognitive processing styles, providing thus an advantage in processing visual and pictorial information as well as in visual search tasks. In particular, given that image-recognition CAPTCHA entail a visual search task for distinguishing cats among dogs, Analysts have an advantage since they have improved visual search task abilities and dis-embedding skills. In addition, given that the image-recognition challenge primarily entails information processing of pictures, the Imagers' habitual and preferred approach in processing graphical information provides a cognitive processing advantage during that task. Furthermore, a standard complexity CAPTCHA challenge entailing 12 colored images is based on the fact that users have limited cognitive processing abilities or limited working memory capacity, and might be thus overwhelmed when solving more images and with greyscale color illustrations.

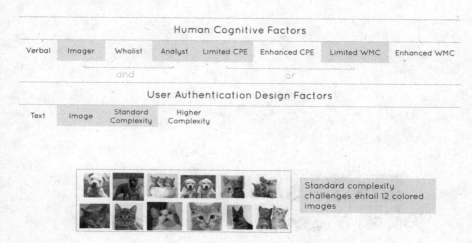

Fig. 8.16 Guideline #7: Image-recognition CAPTCHA with standard complexity

8.3.2.4 Guideline #8: Image-Recognition CAPTCHA with Higher Complexity

Guideline #8 suggests an image-recognition CAPTCHA challenge with higher complexity (Fig. 8.17). Similarly to Guideline #7, an image-recognition CAPTCHA is provided due to the fact that users have an imager and analytic cognitive style providing thus an advantage in cognitive processing over text-based information. Furthermore, in this case a higher complex challenge is provided since users have enhanced cognitive processing abilities and enhanced working memory capacity.

8.3.3 Adaptation Paradigm in mapU Based on Guidelines

Based on the aforementioned guidelines and using as an example Guideline #2, we further provide in Fig. 8.18 an adaptation paradigm at an implementation level. Main aim is to illustrate and make more clear to the reader how the guidelines and adaptation effects (from a user interface design level) can be realized and applied to a more technical perspective using the respective algorithms and formalizations in the mapU framework (see Chap. 5). The adaptation paradigm follows a three step process: (1) the user's model characteristics are initially retrieved from the database; (2) depending on the pool of available adaptation rules, specific rules are applied and adaptation decisions are taken (e.g., whether a textual or graphical authentication mechanism should be used); and (3) based on the generated set of adaptation decisions, a rule-based mechanism is run in which the personalized security type and complexity is communicated to the user interface.

According to Fig. 8.18, in Step 1 a client-side script calls the Web server for retrieving the user model characteristics of the user. In this particular example the

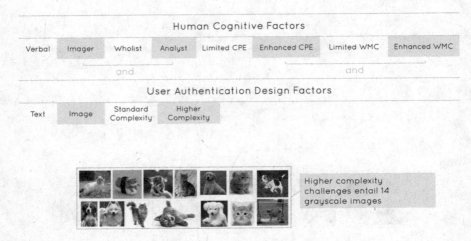

Fig. 8.17 Guideline #8: Image-recognition CAPTCHA with higher complexity

1. User Model

$um(u_i) = \{$
$\quad (d, age, 25),$
$\quad (cc, vi, verbal), (cc, wa, wholist),$
$\quad (cc, cpe, enhanced), (cc, wm, enhanced)$
$\}$

Client-side call to get user model

```
$.ajax({
  type: "GET",
  dataType: "json",
  url: "um.php",
  success: function (response) {
    um = response;
  },
  error: function (jqXHR, textStatus, errorThrown){
    console.log(jqXHR.status);
  } });
```

2. Recommendations

$r(um(u_i), AR) = R', R' \subseteq R$

$AR = \begin{cases} \{(vi, verbal) \text{ OR } (wa, wholist), \{(stype, textual)\}\} \\ \{(wm, enhanced) \text{ AND } (vi, imager) \text{ AND } (wa, analyst), \{(stype, graphical)\}\} \\ \{(cpe, limited) \text{ OR } (wm, limited), \{(cpx, standard)\}\} \\ \{(cpe, enhanced) \text{ AND } (wm, enhanced), \{(cpx, higher)\}\} \end{cases}$

$R' = \{(stype, textual), (cpx, higher)\}$ *Guideline #2*

Client-side call to get recommendations

```
$.ajax({
  type: "GET",
  dataType: "json",
  url: "recommendations.php",
  success: function (response) {
    recommendations = response;
  },
  error: function (jqXHR, textStatus, errorThrown){
    console.log(jqXHR.status);
  } });
```

3. Adaptation and Personalization

Minimum 8 alphanumeric characters, upper-case, lower-case letters
and special characters
Example: f1@ 43!er

Username: anna

Password: ....

Login   Forgot your password?

Client-side call to get recommendations

```
$.ajax({
  type: "GET",
  data: "recommendations=" + recommendations
  url: "ua.php",
  success: function (response) {
    $("#divAuthentication").html(response);
  },
  error: function (jqXHR, textStatus, errorThrown){
    console.log(jqXHR.status);
  } });
```

Fig. 8.18 An adaptation paradigm based on Guideline #2

user is 25 years old, has Verbal and Wholist cognitive styles and has enhanced cognitive processing abilities and working memory capacity. In Step 2, the system calls the adaptation engine *r* which is responsible to generate a set of recommendations

(R') for a user u_i using the user model $um(u_i)$ and a set of adaptation rules (AR) which are based on the abovementioned design guidelines. According to the set of all available recommendations R in the system, a subset R' is retrieved for that particular user. In this case, Guideline #2 is chosen and applied which entails communicating a text-based password mechanism with a higher complexity policy level. Finally, in Step 3, the generated recommendation R are sent to a server-side script in order to generate the personalized user authentication mechanism based on the suggested recommendations.

8.4 Evaluation

In further support of the abovementioned guidelines, but also in order to make the reader more familiar with experimental validation methods and analysis that could be used in the context of user authentication and CAPTCHA mechanisms in combination with human cognitive factors, we next present a related user study. Main aim is to practically recognize the added value of aligning these mechanisms to the unique intrinsic characteristics of users based on the suggested design conditions and adaptation effects. In this respect, a within-subjects study based on a match-mismatch approach was followed, evaluating the users' task completion efficiency and effectiveness when interacting with the personalized and non-personalized security task. We further present the method and developed hypotheses of the study.

8.4.1 Study Design Methodology

The user study was applied in a number of laboratory sessions for a specific computer science module for a period of three months. Both user authentication and CAPTCHA mechanisms were embedded in the laboratory's Web-site in which students were required to interact for viewing and downloading their material related to their daily course. Main aim of this process was to increase the ecological validity of the users' interactions with the two security mechanisms since the Web-site would be used by the students in a real-life scenario. Thus, their interactions with the security mechanisms would be performed as usual without the intervention of any experimental equipment or person. The participation of the students was voluntary and all participants agreed to a consent form that their interactions with the course's Web-site would be recorded as part of an experimental user study of the researchers' group. No further details about the aim of the study and the interaction data recorded (e.g., time to complete the tasks) were provided to the students in order to avoid bias effects. The user study lasted for three months and was split in four phases based on a within-subjects design as follows.

8.4.1.1 Phase A: User Modeling

The first month of the study was dedicated to classify the participants into different groups based on their performance scores on a series of specially designed cognitive factor elicitation tools which were part of the user modeling module of the mapU framework (see Chap. 5). Controlled laboratory sessions with a maximum of 10 participants were conducted with the aim to apply the psychometric tests in a scientific right manner. Participants were first guided through an online consent form and agreed to participate in the study. Then they enrolled in the study by initially choosing a unique username and then providing demographic information (i.e., age, gender, department of studies and major). Then the participants interacted with the developed online psychometric tests to elicit their cognitive processing characteristics. For the purpose of the study, in order to proceed with Phase B, all participants had to interacted first with the user modeling module in order to elicit their scores for all cognitive factors and further process the data and perform a cluster analysis for mapping each security type and complexity level to users based on the generated clusters.

8.4.1.2 Phase B: Initial User Interactions

In Phase B participants created their authentication key. In this stage, the adaptation module mapped a specific type (text-based or graphical) and complexity level (standard or higher) to each user account based on the cluster each user was assigned according to his/her responses to the psychometric test in Phase A. We followed a match-mismatch mapping condition aiming to evaluate the formulated adaptation rules. Within each formed user group, the conditions were randomly applied on the adaptation rules so that half of the participants would first interact with a personalized mechanism (matched condition), and half of the participants would first interact with a non-personalized mechanism (mismatched condition).

The mapped condition was constant throughout Phase B. Participants interacted with the assigned user authentication and CAPTCHA mechanisms as follows: (i) during user login in the course's laboratory course, participants were required to interact with the user authentication mechanism; and (ii) during a user action (e.g., uploading their daily lab exercise), participants were required to interact with the CAPTCHA mechanism by solving a challenge. Specific IP address monitoring techniques were applied in the course's Web-site so that it would be accessible only from the computers located at the laboratory room. The main aim of this process was to control the frequency of user interactions with the security mechanisms (the laboratory course was held twice a week). The users' interactions with the security mechanisms were recorded for one month (two sessions per week; a maximum of eight sessions for each user).

8.4.1.3   Phase C: Swapping the Security Mechanism

After Phase B, the system swapped the participants' security mechanism. In particular, participants that interacted with a matched (personalized) security mechanism in Phase B were prompted to create a new authentication key based on the mismatched condition, and vice versa. The new authentication key would be used for the same period as in Phase B (one month; two sessions per week; a maximum of eight sessions for each user). In the case of CAPTCHA mechanisms, similarly, the condition was swapped for all users and kept constant throughout Phase C. The main aim of Phase C was to engage the whole sample in both conditions for the same period of time.

8.4.1.4   Phase D: Post-study Survey

At the end of the study, a post-study questionnaire was provided to all participants aiming to elicit their perceived usability regarding their interactions with both conditions of the user authentication and CAPTCHA mechanisms. Main aim was to increase our understanding about the users' interactions with the security mechanisms and triangulate the quantitative results with qualitative measures.

8.4.2   Participants

A total of 135 students of social sciences participated in the study (62 males, 73 females, mean age 20.14). All participants had prior experience with text-based password and text-recognition CAPTCHA mechanisms. No participant had prior experience with recognition-based graphical authentication mechanisms and image-recognition CAPTCHA mechanisms.

8.4.3   User Interaction Metrics

Client-side and server-side scripts were developed to monitor the users' behavior during interaction with the user authentication and CAPTCHA mechanisms. In particular, the total time required for successful authentication (task efficiency) was recorded from the time users entered their username for identification, until they successfully completed the authentication process, as well as the total attempts required for successful authentication for each session (task effectiveness). Similarly, in the case of CAPTCHA mechanisms, task efficiency and effectiveness was respectively measured based on the total time and number of attempts required to solve the CAPTCHA challenge.

8.4.4   Hypotheses

The following hypotheses were formulated for the purpose of our research:

H1. The time needed (efficiency) to solve a personalized security mechanism is reduced compared to a non-personalized mechanism.

H2. The total number of attempts (effectiveness) to solve a personalized security mechanism is reduced compared to a non-personalized mechanism.

H3. Users' perceived task usability is improved when interacting with the personalized condition compared to the non-personalized condition.

8.4.5   Analysis of Results

The main aim of the study is to assess the added value of applying the suggested guidelines and adaptation rules in terms of users' task completion efficiency and effectiveness. Based on the within-subjects study design, several paired samples *t*-test analyses were run to determine differences in terms of time to complete and required attempts between user interactions with the matched (personalized) and mismatched (non-personalized) condition. Throughout the study, a total of 2016 authentication sessions (sessions per user: $M=7.56$; $SD=0.85$; $MIN=4$; $MAX=8$) have been recorded. In the case of CAPTCHA, a total of 1916 CAPTCHA sessions (sessions per user: $M=6.99$; $SD=0.86$; $MIN=5$; $MAX=8$) have been recorded.

8.4.5.1   User Modeling

A total of 135 user accounts have been created during Phase A in which controlled laboratory sessions were conducted aiming to elicit the participants' cognitive characteristics. The participants' scores on each psychometric test were processed as described in Chap. 5 and further fed to the classification engine of mapU in order to generate groups of users for each cognitive factor. The cluster analysis of the user modeling module separated users into clusters based on their processed scores of the psychometric tests. Figure 8.19 illustrates the participants' user model characteristics.

Several independent-samples *t*-tests were conducted to determine mean differences on the processed values (e.g., cognitive style ratios) between the generated cluster groups (e.g., Verbal and Imager group). Homogeneity of variances was not violated in all cases, as assessed by Levene's test for equality of variances. Results indicate that there were significant differences among the processed values between all the clusters, indicating that the user modeling module grouped effectively the users into different clusters, and could be thus safely used in the main data analysis.

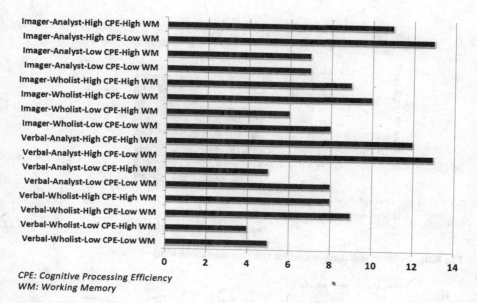

CPE: Cognitive Processing Efficiency
WM: Working Memory

Fig. 8.19 Distribution of participants' user models

8.4.5.2 Personalized Versus Non-personalized User Authentication

Task Completion Time Comparisons A paired-samples t-test was conducted to determine whether there are significant differences between the time needed to authenticate through the personalized and non-personalized user authentication mechanism. Accordingly, if cognitive styles and cognitive processing abilities are of any importance, these two groups should have statistically significant different scores.

The analysis revealed that interactions with personalized user authentication mechanisms were more efficient ($M = 11.88$, $SD = 2.59$) than non-personalized user authentication mechanisms ($M = 14.47$, $SD = 2.64$). These results were statistically significant different ($t(134) = -7.816$, $p < 0.001$). Figure 8.20 illustrates the means of performances of each condition. Accordingly, the results indicate that individual differences in cognitive processing could be a determinant factor on the adaptation of user authentication mechanisms as they improve task completion efficiency and thus support Hypothesis #1.

Furthermore, Fig. 8.21 illustrates the time to login per session for users that interacted first with the matched condition in Phase B and then with the mismatched condition in Phase C (Match-Mismatch group, Fig. 8.21 left) and vice versa (Mismatch-Match group, Fig. 8.21 right). Descriptive statistics reveal that users of the mismatched condition recorded consistently the highest times to authenticate over all sessions, compared to the matched condition. Such a result indicates the

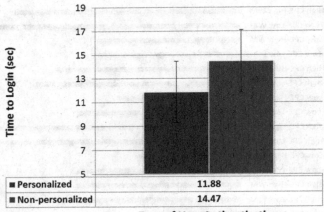

Fig. 8.20   Means of task completion time (sec) per user authentication condition

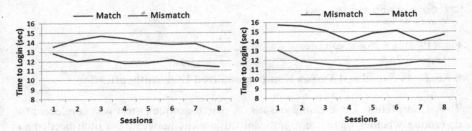

Fig. 8.21   Means of task completion time per session for the match-mismatch group and mismatch-match group

increased difficulty of users in interacting with the mismatched condition further supporting Hypothesis #1.

Failure Rate   Based on the number of attempts required to login, the number of sessions with failed attempts was counted. Sessions are considered as failed when more than one attempt is required by the participant to successfully authenticate. In contrast, successful sessions are the ones in which participants authenticate successfully at first attempt. The failure rate of each user was calculated as the number of failed sessions divided by all sessions of the user. Among 2016 user authentication sessions, 172 attempts failed (11.72 % overall failure rate). A paired-samples t-test was conducted to determine whether there are significant differences between the failure rate through the personalized and non-personalized user authentication mechanism. The analysis revealed that the mean failure rate for personalized conditions was 8.04 % ($SD=13.04$ %) and for non-personalized conditions 9.43 % ($SD=15.20$ %). Descriptive statistics indicate an increase of failure rate in the non-personalized condition, however inferential statistics revealed that these differences were not significantly different ($t(134)=-.825$, $p=0.416$). In this respect, no safe

Table 8.2 Number of
authentication key resets

	Textual	Graphical
Matched	2	5
Mismatched	4	8
Total	6	13

conclusions can be drawn for supporting Hypothesis #2 since no significant differences in failure rate have been observed.

Authentication Key Resets The total number of authentication key resets was counted along the study. Table 8.2 summarizes the total number of authentication key requests per condition and authentication type. In total, 19 authentication key requests were initiated throughout the study, among those requests, two users requested the authentication key reset three times, and the rest users requested the key reset one time. Results reveal a higher number of authentication key resets in graphical authentication across conditions compared to text-based password.

8.4.5.3 Personalized vs. Non-personalized CAPTCHA

Task Completion Time Comparisons A paired-samples t-test was conducted to determine whether there are significant differences between the time needed to solve a CAPTCHA challenge through the personalized and non-personalized mechanism. The analysis revealed that users needed significant less time to solve the personalized CAPTCHA challenge ($M = 14.6$, $SD = 3.07$) than the non-personalized CAPTCHA challenge ($M = 16.74$, $SD = 3.03$). These differences were statistically different ($t(134) = -5.526$, $p = 0.01$). Figure 8.22 illustrates the means of performances of each condition. Accordingly, the results indicate that individual differences in cognitive processing improve task completion efficiency of personalized CAPTCHA challenges and further support Hypothesis #1.

Furthermore, Fig. 8.23 illustrates the time to solve the CAPTCHA challenge per session for users that interacted first with the matched condition for one month and then with the mismatched condition (Match-Mismatch group, Fig. 8.23 left) and vice versa (Mismatch-Match group, Fig. 8.23 right). Accordingly, no significant differences were observed for users that started interacting for one month with the matched condition and then with the mismatched condition. On the other hand, higher differences were observed for users that started interacting with the mismatched condition and then with the matched condition. A possible interpretation might be based on the experience factor that could have positively affected users' interactions with the mismatched condition since users first interacted with the matched condition and then with the mismatched condition. Nonetheless, descriptive statistics indicate that across groups, users were solving the personalized CAPTCHA challenge faster than the non-personalized challenge.

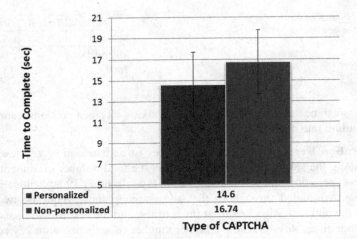

Fig. 8.22 Means of task completion time (sec) per CAPTCHA condition

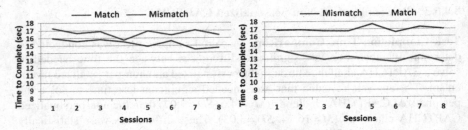

Fig. 8.23 Means of task completion time per session for the match-mismatch group and mismatch-match group

Failure Rate Similarly to the user authentication analysis, the number of sessions with failed attempts was counted. Among 1916 CAPTCHA sessions, 97 attempts failed (5 % overall failure rate). A paired-samples t-test was conducted to determine whether there are significant differences between the failure rate through the personalized and non-personalized CAPTCHA mechanism. The analysis revealed that the mean failure rate for personalized conditions was 3.98 % ($SD = 9.13$ %) and for non-personalized conditions 6.33 % ($SD = 10.94$ %). Inferential statistics revealed that these differences were significantly different ($t(134) = -1.975$, $p = 0.05$). Such a result supports Hypothesis #2 suggesting that the personalized CAPTCHA mechanism improves task effectiveness (less failure rate) compared to the non-personalized CAPTCHA mechanism.

Table 8.3 Participants that chose a specific authentication condition as their first choice for each evaluation factor

	Matched	Mismatched
User authentication preference	98	37
User authentication efficiency	92	43
User authentication effectiveness	81	54

Table 8.4 Participants that chose a specific CAPTCHA condition as their first choice for each evaluation factor

	Matched	Mismatched
CAPTCHA preference	106	29
CAPTCHA efficiency	88	47
CAPTCHA effectiveness	66	69

8.4.5.4 Post-study Survey

At the end of the study, we conducted a survey aiming to validate findings of the quantitative analysis as well as to enrich our understanding about the users' perceptions and perceived usability based on their interactions with the security mechanisms. All participants were asked to rank the two conditions of both security mechanisms (user authentication and CAPTCHA) based on the following aspects: (i) the condition that the users prefer; (ii) the condition that was more efficient; and (iii) the condition that was more effective. Example questions were *"Which CAPTCHA type do you prefer?"*, *"In which authentication type did you need less time to complete the task?"*, and *"In which authentication type did you need less attempts to complete the task?"*. For each question, participants ranked the two methods with 1 and 2 to represent their first and second choice. Tables 8.3 and 8.4 respectively list the number of participants who chose a specific user authentication and CAPTCHA condition as their first choice for each factor.

Factors Related to User Authentication A binomial statistical test was conducted to examine whether there is a preference relating personalized and non-personalized authentication mechanisms (H_0: p(personalized) = 0.5 and p(non-personalized) = 0.5). The result revealed that there is significant preference towards personalized mechanisms ($p < 0.001$). In particular, the majority of users (72.5 %) preferred the matched user authentication mechanism. In combination with the quantitative analysis that revealed significant better performance in the matched condition, such a result is promising for the applicability of the design guidelines and adaptation rules since the suggested recommendations have positively affected the users' preference. Regarding perceived usability, there was also a statistical significant choice towards the personalized condition ($p < 0.001$). A total of 92 participants thought that the personalized condition was the most efficient while 43 chose the mismatched condition. Such a result further supports the quantitative results which revealed that task efficiency was improved in the personalized condition. Finally, users found the personalized condition more effective to use ($p = 0.025$), although the quantitative analysis did not reveal significant differences in failure rates between the two conditions.

To this end, results partially support Hypothesis #3 since users perceived the usability (in terms of efficiency) and preferred the personalized user authentication mechanism.

Factors Related to CAPTCHA   The results revealed a high number of participants (106 participants) preferring the personalized CAPTCHA mechanism. The differences between the users' choices were significant ($p < 0.001$). Similarly to the user authentication mechanism, such a result is promising for the applicability of the suggested approach since the recommendation based on the design guidelines and the adaptation rules has positively affected the users' preference. Regarding perceived usability, there was also a statistical significant choice towards the personalized condition ($p = 0.001$). A total of 88 participants thought that the personalized condition was the most efficient while 47 chose the mismatched condition. Such a result further supports the quantitative results which revealed that task efficiency was improved in the personalized condition. Finally, there was no clear choice towards a condition in regards with perceived effectiveness ($p = 0.863$). This might be based on the fact that the majority of users solved the CAPTCHA challenge at first attempt, making it difficult to compare the effectiveness of one of the two conditions. In this context, results partially support Hypothesis #3 since users perceived the usability (in terms of task completion efficiency) and preferred the personalized CAPTCHA mechanism.

8.5   Benefits, Impact and Limitations

User security interactions over the World Wide Web are commonly related to user authentication and CAPTCHA mechanisms (Florencio and Herley 2007; Bursztein et al. 2014). Research works have shown that having a usability flaw during such user interactions could decrease the usability of the primary task (users might even abandon the task), overwhelm the users cognitively and eventually decrease the overall user experience with the system. Accordingly, the impact of the reported research primarily lies on the proposed interdisciplinary approach of mapping human cognitive characteristics with appropriate design factors of user security mechanisms, aiming to provide the most appropriate type and complexity level of the mechanism and thus assist the users' information processing during such tasks. The results reported in this chapter provide initial evidence that personalizing the user authentication and CAPTCHA task based on human cognitive differences could improve the usability and user experience since the users' performances when interacting with the personalized security mechanism were improved compared to the non-personalized mechanism. In particular, the personalized security mechanism substantially increased users' ability to complete the task faster as well as to complete the task with less attempts when using the personalized mechanism in contrast to the non-personalized. Furthermore, it is worth to mention that triangulation of results revealed that the users perceived the usability of the personalized condition.

We envision that the reported research will provide useful insights for practitioners and researchers to design and develop more human-centred and usable authentication and CAPTCHA mechanisms taking into consideration heterogeneity of users with unique preferences and characteristics. Considering current "one-size-fits-all" delivery approaches of user authentication and CAPTCHA, and the diversity of users, the added value of such an endeavor entails many benefits both from the users' perspective as well as from the service providers' perspective. From the users' perspective, the design and the deployment of personalized authentication and CAPTCHA tasks to the users' cognitive characteristics would assist the cognitive processing of information as well as the task execution performance, and eventually lead to a positive user experience. From the service providers' perspective, such an approach would increase user acceptance and thus provide a competitive advantage through the provision of personalized services.

Although the study yielded statistical significant results, the study itself and the proposed approach entails limitations that are inherent to the multi-dimensional character and complexity of this research work. An important limitation is related to the recruitment and sample of the study. The sample included a rather limited number of participants with similar profiles and educational backgrounds (i.e., undergraduate students). Furthermore, participants were more experienced with text-based passwords and text-recognition CAPTCHA than with recognition-based graphical authentication and image-recognition CAPTCHA challenges. On the other hand, we aimed to increase the internal validity of the study by recruiting participants that were experienced, rather than novice, with computer usage, user authentication and CAPTCHA tasks. Another limitation concerns the classification of users into two extreme user groups (e.g., Verbals and Imagers). Although a number of existing research works have used a cut-off score for grouping users into two distinct groups (Hong et al. 2012; Altun and Cakan 2006), this approach might not classify individuals that fall in between the two end points (e.g., intermediates). Nevertheless, based on the formalization of mapU in Chap. 5, we aimed to formalize an open and extendable user modeling module that models the users' cognitive characteristics along a continuum scale, and depending on the application domain, set the desired number of user groups (k) for mapping these with the appropriate design factors (in our case, a text-based or graphical security mechanism).

Furthermore, the suggested design guidelines and adaptation rules embrace new challenges from the user modeling and security perspective that need further investigation. From the user modeling perspective, a limitation of the current implementation of mapU is based on the explicit nature of the user data collection method that requires users to conduct a series of psychometric tests in order to elicit their cognitive characteristics which might decrease user acceptance and the practical feasibility of the proposed approach. In this context, there is a need to transparently elicit the users' cognitive characteristics based on their interactions and behavior in the system. Recently, we proposed a user data collection method (Belk et al. 2013c; Papatheocharous et al. 2014) that implicitly infers the user's cognitive characteristics by tracking their navigation sequence and behavior in particular sections of the system. Other related research works include the work of Chen and Liu (2008) that proposed tracking the users' behavior with navigation tools (hierarchical maps or alphabetical index) in order to elicit their cognitive styles, the work of Chang et al. (2013) that proposed an approach for detecting users' working memory capacity based on their behavior in interactive systems, and the work of Chan et al. (2014) that measured the usage of search tools in mobile interactive systems (basic vs. advanced search) in order to implicitly infer the users' cognitive styles.

From the security perspective, given that various user authentication and CAPTCHA schemes entail different security strengths and weaknesses (Renaud et al. 2013; Biddle et al. 2012; Bursztein et al. 2011, 2014), the recommendation of a particular type and complexity level would change the security metrics of the mechanism. For example, recognition-based graphical authentication schemes are more vulnerable to offline guessing attacks since these have a significant smaller theoretical key space than traditional text-based passwords (assuming that the level of usability remains at reasonable levels – Biddle et al. 2012). In this respect, depending on the application domain and custom requirements of the service provider, the recommendation rules of the mapU framework could be further extended with several security factors and policies (e.g., increase the number of images in the challenge) in order to meet the security requirements of the provider.

8.6   Summary

User security interactions over the World Wide Web are commonly related to user authentication and CAPTCHA mechanisms (Florencio and Herley 2007; Bursztein et al. 2014). Studies have already shown a number of usability and user experience issues in such human-computer interaction cycles and the research community has acknowledged the necessity for designing more usable security mechanisms (Fidas et al. 2011; Florencio and Herley 2007). Furthermore, a high number of research works have shown that human factors affect user interactions in both user authentication and CAPTCHA mechanisms in various contexts of use, suggesting that personalization strategies may assist the design and development of more usable security mechanisms.

In this respect we present an alternative approach to current state-of-the-art practices with the aim to achieve a balance between usability and security of two widely deployed and critical security mechanisms. In particular, the purpose of this chapter was to propose and evaluate a set of guidelines and adaptation effects that take into consideration a set of human cognitive processing factors and design characteristics for personalizing user authentication and CAPTCHA tasks. Our intention was to provide the most optimized condition, in terms of design type and complexity level, based on specific cognitive factors. The reader can further realize the adaptation effects and added value of this approach through the selected user study, that investigated user interactions on given security tasks, in which 135 users interacted with the personalized and the non-personalized version of user authentication and CAPTCHA mechanisms. Results revealed that matching the user security type (textual or graphical) and the complexity to users' cognitive styles and cognitive processing abilities improves task performance, primarily in terms of task completion efficiency. These findings are consistent with the theories of cognitive factors that are referred in our approach, and it seems that the challenging task of interpreting and applying these theories into adaptation rules for personalizing user authentication and CAPTCHA tasks has been at some extent successful and promising for the future.

References

Adams A, Sasse A (1999) Users are not the enemy: why users compromise security mechanisms and how to take remedial measures. Commun ACM 42(12):40–46

Albert D, Jeng B, Tseng C, Wang J (2010) A study of CAPTCHA and its application to user authentication. In: Proceedings of the international conference on computational collective intelligence (ICCCI 2010), Springer, Berlin/Heidelberg, pp 433–440

Altun A, Cakan M (2006) Undergraduate students' academic achievement, field dependent/independent cognitive styles and attitude toward computers. Educ Technol Soc 9(1):289–297

Angeli AD, Coventry L, Johnson G, Renaud K (2005) Is a picture really worth a thousand words? Exploring the feasibility of graphical authentication systems. Int J Hum Comput Stud 63(1–2):128–152

Baecher P, Buscher N, Fischlin M, Milde B (2011) Breaking reCAPTCHA: a holistic approach via shape recognition. In: Camenisch J, Fischer-Hbner S, Murayama Y, Portmann A, Rieder C (eds) Future challenges in security and privacy for academia and industry, vol 354, LNCS. Springer, Berlin/Heidelberg, pp 56–67

Belk M, Fidas C, Germanakos P, Samaras G (2012) Do cognitive styles of users affect preference and performance related to CAPTCHA challenges? In: Extended abstracts of the ACM SIGCHI conference on human factors in computing systems (CHI 2012), ACM Press, New York, pp 1487–1492

Belk M, Germanakos P, Fidas C, Samaras G (2013a) Studying the effect of human cognition on user authentication tasks. In: Proceedings of the conference on user modeling, adaptation, and personalization (UMAP 2013), Springer, Berlin/Heidelberg, pp 102–113

Belk M, Fidas C, Germanakos P, Samaras G (2013b) Security for diversity: studying the effects of verbal and imagery processes on user authentication mechanisms. In: Proceedings of the IFIP TC13 conference on human-computer interaction (INTERACT 2013), Springer-Verlag, Berlin/ Heidelberg, pp 442–459

Belk M, Papatheocharous E, Germanakos P, Samaras G (2013c) Modeling users on the world wide web based on cognitive factors, navigation behaviour and clustering techniques. J Syst Softw 86(12):2995–3012

Belk M, Germanakos P, Fidas C, Holzinger A, Samaras G (2013d) Towards the personalization of CAPTCHA mechanisms based on individual differences in cognitive processing. In: Proceedings of the international conference on human factors in computing & informatics (SouthCHI 2013), Springer, Berlin/Heidelberg, pp. 409–426

Belk M, Germanakos P, Fidas C, Samaras G (2014a) A personalisation method based on human factors for improving usability of user authentication tasks. In: Proceedings of the conference on user modeling, adaptation, and personalization (UMAP 2014), Springer, Berlin/Heidelberg, pp 13–24

Belk M, Fidas C, Germanakos P, Samaras G (2014b) A personalised user authentication approach based on individual differences in information processing. Interact Comput. doi:10.1093/iwc/iwu033

Belk M, Fidas C, Germanakos P, Samaras G (2015) Do human cognitive differences in information processing affect preference and performance of CAPTCHA? Int J Hum Comput Stud 84:1–18

Biddle R, Chiasson S, van Oorschot P (2012) Graphical passwords: learning from the first twelve years. ACM Comput Surv 44(4):41

Bigham J, Cavender A (2009) Evaluating existing audio CAPTCHAs and an interface optimized for non-visual use. In: Proceedings of the ACM SIGCHI conference on human factors in computing systems (CHI 2009), ACM Press, New York, pp 1829–1838

Bonneau J, Herley C, van Oorschot P, Stajano F (2012) The quest to replace passwords: a framework for comparative evaluation of web authentication schemes. Symposium on security and privacy, IEEE Computer Society, Washington, pp 553–567

Bulling A, Alt F, Schmidt A (2012) Increasing the security of gaze-based cued-recall graphical passwords using saliency masks. In: Proceedings of the ACM international conference on human factors in computing systems (CHI 2012), ACM Press, New York, pp 3011–3020

Bursztein E, Bethard S, Fabry C, Mitchell J, Jurafsky D (2010) How good are humans at solving CAPTCHAs? A large scale evaluation. In: Proceedings of the international symposium on security and privacy, IEEE Computer Society, Washington, pp 399–413

Bursztein E, Martin M, Mitchell J (2011) Text-based CAPTCHA strengths and weaknesses. In: Proceedings of the conference on computer and communications security (CCS 2011), ACM Press, New York, pp 125–138

Bursztein E, Moscicki A, Fabry C, Bethard S, Mitchell J, Jurafsky D (2014) Easy does it: more usable CAPTCHAs. In: Proceedings of the ACM SIGCHI conference on human factors in computing systems (CHI 2014), ACM Press, New York, pp 2637–2646

Chan T (2003) Using a text-to-speech synthesizer to generate a reverse Turing test. In: IEEE conference on tools with artificial intelligence, IEEE Computer Society, Washington, pp 226–232

Chan C, Hsieh C, Chen S (2014) Cognitive styles and the use of electronic journals in a mobile context. J Doc 70(6):997–1014

Chang T, El-Bishouty M, Graf S, Kinshuk (2013) An approach for detecting students' working memory capacity from their behavior in learning systems. In: Proceedings of the international conference on advanced learning technologies (ICALT 2013), IEEE Computer Society, Washington, pp 82–86

Chellapilla K, Larson K, Simard P, Czerwinski M (2005) Designing human friendly human interaction proofs (HIPs). In: Proceedings of the ACM SIGCHI conference on human factors in computing systems (CHI 2005), ACM Press, New York, pp 711–720

Chen S, Liu X (2008) An integrated approach for modeling learning patterns of students in web-based instruction: a cognitive style perspective. ACM Trans Comput-Hum Interact, 15(1), Article 1, 28

Chew M, Baird H (2003) Baffletext: a human interactive proof. In: Proceedings of the international conference on document recognition and retrieval (DRR 2003), SPIE/IS&T, Bellingham, WA, pp 305–316

Chiasson S, van Oorschot P, Biddle R (2006) Usability study and critique of two password managers. In: Proceedings of the USENIX security symposium, USENIX Association, Berkeley, pp 1–16

Chiasson S, Forget A, Biddle R, van Oorschot P (2008) Influencing users towards better passwords: persuasive cued click-points. In: Proceedings of the BCS conference on people and computers, British Computer Society, Swinton, pp 121–130

Cranor L, Garfinkel S (2005) Security and usability. O'Reilly Media, Inc, Beijing/Farnham/Sebastopol

Datta R, Li J, Wang J.Z (2005) IMAGINATION: a robust image-based CAPTCHA generation system. In: ACM conference on multimedia, ACM Press, New York, pp 331–334

Davis D, Monrose F, Reiter M (2004) On user choice in graphical password schemes. In: Proceedings of the USENIX security symposium, USENIX Association, Berkeley

De Luca A, von Zezschwitz E, Pichler L, Hussmann H (2013) Using fake cursors to secure on-screen password entry. In: Proceedings of the ACM conference on human factors in computing systems (CHI 2013), ACM Press, New York, pp 2399–2402

Demetriou A, Spanoudis G, Shayer S, Mouyi A, Kazi S, Platsidou M (2013) Cycles in speed-working memory-G relations: towards a developmental-differential theory of the mind. Intelligence 41:34–50

Dhamija R, Perrig A (2000) DejaVu: a user study using images for authentication. In: Proceedings of the USENIX security symposium, USENIX Association, Berkeley

Dunphy P, Yan J (2007) Do background images improve "draw a secret" graphical passwords?. In: Proceedings of the ACM international conference on computer and communications security (CCS 2007), ACM Press, New York, pp 36–47

Elson J, Douceur J, Howell J, Saul J (2007) Asirra: a CAPTCHA that exploits interest-aligned manual image categorization. In: Proceedings of the international conference on computer and communications security (CCS 2007), ACM Press, New York, pp 366–374

Everitt K, Bragin T, Fogarty J, Kohno T (2009) A comprehensive study of frequency, interference, and training of multiple graphical passwords. In: ACM international conference on human factors in computing systems (CHI 2009), ACM Press, New York, pp 889–898

Fidas CA, Voyiatzis AG, Avouris NM (2010) When security meets usability: a user-centric approach on a crossroads priority problem. In: Proceedings of Panhellenic conference on informatics. PCI'10. IEEE Computer Society, Washington, pp 112–117

Fidas C, Voyiatzis A, Avouris N (2011) On the necessity of user-friendly CAPTCHA. In: Proceedings of the ACM SIGCHI conference on human factors in computing systems (CHI 2012), ACM Press, New York, pp 2623–2626

Fidas C, Hussmann H, Belk M, Samaras G (2015) iHIP: towards a user centric individual human interaction proof framework. In: Proceedings of the ACM conference extended abstracts on human factors in computing systems (CHI EA 2015), ACM Press,New York, pp 2235–2240

Findlater L, Wobbrock J, Wigdor D (2011) Typing on flat glass: examining ten-finger expert typing patterns on touch surfaces. In: Proceedings of the ACM SIGCHI conference on human factors in computing systems (CHI 2011), ACM Press, New York, pp 2453–2462

Florencio D, Herley CA (2007) Large-scale study of web password habits. In: Proceedings of the ACM conference on World Wide Web (WWW 2007), ACM Press, pp 657–666

Forget A, Biddle R (2008) Memorability of persuasive passwords. In: Extended abstracts of the ACM SIGCHI conference on human factors in computing systems (CHI 2008), ACM Press, pp 3759–3764

Forget A, Chiasson S, van Oorschot P, Biddle R (2008) Improving text passwords through persuasion. In: Proceedings of the ACM international symposium on usable privacy and security (SOUPS 2012), ACM Press, pp 1–12.

Forget A, Chiasson S, Biddle R (2014) Towards supporting a diverse ecosystem of authentication schemes. In: Proceedings of the who are you?! Adventures in authentication workshop (WAY 2014) at the symposium on usable privacy and security (SOUPS 2014), USENIX Association

Gao H, Guo X, Chen X, Wang L, Liu X (2008) YAGP: yet another graphical password strategy. In: Proceedings of the IEEE conference on computer security applications, IEEE computer society, pp 121–129

Gao H, Liu H, Yao D, Liu X, Aickelin U (2010) An audio CAPTCHA to distinguish humans from computers. In: Proceedings of the international symposium on electronic commerce and security (SECS 2010), IEEE Computer Society, pp 265–269

Golle P (2008) Machine learning attacks against the asirra CAPTCHA. In: Proceedings of the conference on computer and communications security (CCS 2008), ACM Press, pp 535–542

Gossweiler R, Kamvar M, Baluja S (2009) What's up CAPTCHA?: a CAPTCHA based on image orientation. In: Proceedings of the international conference on World Wide Web (WWW 2009), ACM press, pp 841–850

Halderman JA, Waters B, Felten E (2005) Convenient method for securely managing passwords. In: Proceedings of the ACM international conference on World Wide Web, ACM Press, pp 471–479

Hayashi E, Pendleton B, Ozenc F, Hong J (2012) WebTicket: account management using printable tokens. In Proceedings of the SIGCHI conference on human factors in computing systems (CHI'12). ACM Press, pp 997–1006

Herley C, van Oorschot P (2012) A research agenda acknowledging the persistence of passwords. IEE Secur Priv 10(1):28–36

Herley C, van Oorschot P, Patrick A (2009) Passwords: if we're so smart, why are we still using them? In: Dingledine R, Golle P (eds) Financial cryptography and data security, vol 5628, LNCS. Springer, Heidelberg

Holman J, Lazar J, Feng JH, D'Arcy J (2007) Developing usable CAPTCHAs for blind users. In: Proceedings of the ACM SIGACCESS conference on computers and accessibility (ASSETS 2007), ACM Press, pp 245–246

Hong J, Hwang M, Tam K, Lai Y, Liu L (2012) Effects of cognitive style on digital jigsaw puzzle performance: a GridWare analysis. Comput Hum Behav 28(3):920–928

Inglesant P, Sasse A (2010) The true cost of unusable password policies: password use in the wild. In: Proceedings of the ACM SIGCHI conference on human factors in computing systems (CHI 2010), ACM Press, pp 383–392

Jermyn I, Mayer A, Monrose F, Reiter M, Rubin A (1999) The design and analysis of graphical passwords. In: Proceedings of the USENIX security symposium (Security 1999), USENIX Association, pp 1–1

Kluever KA, Zanibbi R (2009) Balancing usability and security in a video CAPTCHA. In: ACM symposium on usable privacy and security, Article 14, ACM Press, 11 p

Kobsa A, Nithyanand R, Tsudik G, Uzun E (2013) Can Jannie verify? Usability of display-equipped RFID tags for security purposes. J Comput Secur 21(3):347–370

Komanduri S, Shay R, Kelley P, Mazurek M, Bauer L, Christin N, Cranor L, Egelman S (2011) Of passwords and people: measuring the effect of password-composition policies. In: Proceedings of the ACM SIGCHI conference on human factors in computing systems (CHI 2011), ACM Press, pp 2595–2604

Kozhevnikov M (2007) Cognitive styles in the context of modern psychology: toward an integrated framework of cognitive style. Psychol Bull 133(3):464–481

Kuo C, Romanosky S, Cranor L (2006) Human selection of mnemonic phrase-based passwords. In: Proceedings of the ACM international symposium on usable privacy and security (SOUPS 2006), ACM Press, pp 67–78

Leonhard MD, Venkatakrishnan VN (2007) A comparative study of three random password generators. In: Proceedings of the IEEE international conference on electro/information technology (EIT 2007), IEEE Computer Society, pp 227–232

Ma Y, Feng J, Kumin L, Lazar J (2013) Investigating user behavior for authentication methods: a comparison between individuals with down syndrome and neurotypical users. ACM Trans Access Comput, 4(4), Article 15, p 27

Mihajlov M, Jerman-Blazic B (2011) On designing usable and secure recognition-based graphical authentication mechanisms. Interact Comput 23(6):582–593

Messick S (1993) The matter of style: manifestations of personality in cognition, learning, and teaching. Educational Testing Service, Princeton

Nelson D, Vu K (2010) Effectiveness of image-based mnemonic techniques for enhancing the memorability and security of user-generated passwords. Comput Hum Behav 26(4):705–715

Nicholson J, Dunphy P, Coventry L, Briggs P, Olivier PA (2012) Security assessment of tiles: a new portfolio-based graphical authentication system. In: Extended abstracts of the ACM SIGCHI conference on human factors in computing systems (CHI 2012), ACM Press, pp 1967–1972

Papatheocharous E, Belk M, Germanakos P, Samaras G (2014) Towards implicit user modeling based on artificial intelligence, cognitive styles and web interaction data. Int J Artif Intell Tools 23(2):21

Passfaces Corporation (2009) The science behind Passfaces. White paper, http://www.passfaces.com/enterprise/resources/white_papers.htm

Proctor R, Lien MC, Vu KP, Schultz E, Salvendy G (2002) Improving computer security for authentication of users: influence of proactive password restrictions. Behav Res Methods 34:163–169

Reardon LB, Moore DM (1988) The effect of organization strategy and cognitive styles on learning from complex instructional visuals. Int J Instr Media 15:353–363

Renaud K, Mayer P, Volkamer M, Maguire J (2013) Are graphical authentication mechanisms as strong as passwords?. In: Proceedings of the federated conference on computer science and information systems (FedCSIS 2013), IEEE Computer Society, pp 837–844

Reynaga G, Chiasson S (2013) The usability of CAPTCHAs on smartphones. In: Proceedings of the conference on security and cryptography (SECRYPT 2013), pp 427–434

Riding R, Cheema I (1991) Cognitive styles – an overview and integration. Educ Psychol 11(3–4):193–215

Ross SA, Halderman JA, Finkelstein A (2010) Sketcha: a CAPTCHA based on line drawings of 3D models. In: ACM conference on World Wide Web, ACM Press, New York, pp 821–830

Rui Y, Liu Z (2004) ARTiFACIAL: automated reverse Turing test using FACIAL features. J Multimedia Systems 9:493–502

Securimage v.3.5.2 (2014). http://www.phpcaptcha.org

Shay R, Komanduri S, Kelley P, Leon P, Mazurek M, Bauer L, Christin N, Cranor L (2010) Encountering stronger password requirements: user attitudes and behaviors. In: Proceedings of the ACM symposium on usable privacy and security (SOUPS 2012), ACM Press, Article 2, 20 p

Shay R, Kelley P, Komanduri S, Mazurek M, Ur B, Vidas T, Bauer L, Christin N, Cranor L (2012) Correct horse battery staple: exploring the usability of system-assigned passphrases. In: Proceedings of the ACM symposium on usable privacy and security (SOUPS 2012), ACM Press, Article 7, p 20

Shay R, Bauer L, Christin N, Cranor L, Forget A, Komanduri S, Mazurek M, Melicher W, Segreti S, Ur B (2015) A spoonful of sugar? The impact of guidance and feedback on password-creation behavior. In: Proceedings of ACM conference on human factors in computing systems (CHI 2015), ACM Press, pp 2903–2912

Shirali-Shahreza S, Penn G, Balakrishnan R, Ganjali Y (2013) Seesay and hearsay CAPTCHA for mobile interaction. In: Proceedings of the ACM SIGCHI conference on human factors in computing systems (CHI 2013), ACM Press, pp 2147–2156

Tao H, Adams C (2008) Pass-go: a proposal to improve the usability of graphical passwords. Netw Secur 7(2):273–292

Tullis TS, Tedesco DP, McCaffrey KE (2011) Can users remember their pictorial passwords six years later. In: Proceedings of the ACM SIGCHI international conference on human factors in computing systems (CHI 2011), ACM Press, pp 1789–1794

Varenhorst C (2004) Passdoodles: a lightweight authentication method. MIT Research Science Institute, Cambridge, MA

Vikram S, Fan Y, Gu G (2011) SEMAGE: a new image-based two-factor CAPTCHA. In: Proceedings of the international conference on computer security applications (CCS 2011), ACM Press, pp 237–246

von Ahn L, Blum M, Langford J (2004) Telling humans and computers apart automatically. Commun ACM 47:56–60

von Ahn L, Maurer B, McMillen C, Abraham D, Blum M (2008) reCAPTCHA: human-based character recognition via web security measures. Science 321(5895):1465–1468

von Zezschwitz E, De Luca A, Hussmann H (2014) Honey, I shrunk the keys: influences of mobile devices on password composition and authentication performance. In: Proceedings of the

Nordic conference on human-computer interaction: fun, fast, foundational (NordiCHI 2014), ACM Press, pp 461–470

von Zezschwitz E, De Luca A, Brunkow B, Hussmann H (2015) SwiPIN: fast and secure PIN-entry on smartphones. In: Proceedings of the 33rd annual ACM conference on human factors in computing systems (CHI'15). ACM, New York, pp 1403–1406

Vu K, Proctor R, Bhargav-Spantzel A, Tai B, Cook J, Schultz E (2007) Improving password security and memorability to protect personal and organizational information. Int J Hum Comput Stud 65(8):744–757

Wiedenbeck S, Waters J, Birget J, Brodskiy A, Memon N (2005) Authentication using graphical passwords: effects of tolerance and image choice. In: Proceedings of the ACM symposium on usable privacy and security (SOUPS 2005), ACM Press, pp 1–12

Winkler C, Gugenheimer J, De Luca A, Haas G, Speidel P, Dobbelstein D, Rukzio E (2015) Glass unlock: enhancing security of smartphone unlocking through leveraging a private near-eye display. In: Proceedings of the ACM conference on human factors in computing systems (CHI 2015). ACM Press, pp 1407–1410

Wright N, Patrick A, Biddle R (2012) Do you see your password?: applying recognition to textual passwords. In: Proceedings of the ACM symposium on usable privacy and security (SOUPS 2012), ACM Press, Article 8

Yan J, El Ahmad AS (2008) A low-cost attack on a microsoft CAPTCHA. In: Proceedings of the ACM conference on computer and communications security (CCS 2008), ACM Press, pp 543–554

Yan J, Blackwell A, Anderson R, Grant A (2004) Password memorability and security: empirical results. IEEE Secur Priv Mag 2(5):25–31

Zhu B, Yan J, Li Q, Yang C, Liu J, Xu N, Yi M, Cai K (2010) Attacks and design of image recognition CAPTCHAs. In: Proceedings of the ACM conference on computer and communications security (CCS 2010), ACM Press, pp 187–200

Epilogue

Human-centred Web Adaptation and Personalization – From Theory to Practice presented the outcome of our research efforts towards the identification and analysis of factors that would add more value to current Web-based systems and/or applications. In the ever growing new digital ecosystem of ubiquity, high connectivity and sharability, where billions of entities (humans and/or devices) communicate and exchange data, the need for interdisciplinary research is highlighted in the intersection of Adaptive Hypermedia, Web Personalization, User Modeling and Cognitive Psychology research disciplines. Such an approach will bring the human in the "centre", and the produced methods, models, algorithms and designs will be able to more inclusively tackle a number of serious visual and interaction problems observed today with respect to user experience (i.e. usability, accessibility, pleasure, etc.).

Indisputably, this is an ongoing research endeavor that is found only at the very beginning. We regard though as fundamental to set solid grounds and embrace viewpoints that holistically capture the necessity for seamless end-to-end human-computer communications. Thereupon, the solutions will have the expected valuable meaning for the end-users and will not obstruct their daily activities or alter their perception and behaviors when interacting with hypermedia environments. In this respect, this book unfolds our research experiences and results that focused primarily on understanding users and investigating the feasibility of alternative approaches to current state-of-the-art practices by personalizing interactive systems to the users' cognitive and emotional processing characteristics, and diversified perceptual preferences. Main aim was to deploy adaptive and personalized mechanisms and user interfaces that will support, assist and enable usable human-computer interactions for effective and efficient tasks execution in the prominent application areas of E-Learning, E-Commerce, and Usable Security. The book underpinned throughout the standpoint that human-centred adaptation and personalization should guide the design of applications and services for an enhanced user experience.

© Springer International Publishing Switzerland 2016
P. Germanakos, M. Belk, *Human-Centred Web Adaptation and Personalization*,
Human–Computer Interaction Series, DOI 10.1007/978-3-319-28050-9

Hence, we decided to expand on our knowledge and lessons learned from a top-to-bottom approach, reflecting a consistent research journey starting from theoretical concepts, dimensions and models towards more technical and practical implementation issues. Human factors played the most important role during the entire process, incorporating theories of individual differences within the scope of adaptive interactive systems, with the biggest challenge of how to interpret the fuzzy human nature to more tangible and rigid computational rules and procedures. We are convinced that the extent to which this can be more effectively achieved will constitute a significant contribution that its impact will be two-fold: On the one hand we will be able to shed more light on the relationship dynamics between the human and the computer, and on the other hand we will witness a tighter synergy between the academic and the business sector, since it will become clearer how to transform more basic research results into sustainable business applications tackling a problem that remains intractable for years.

In principle, main success factor for our research (as for any research of this kind) is considered at first to which depth we can grasp and comprehend intrinsic human values that affect implicitly the interaction processes (i.e., assessment of individual differences with respect to different kinds of ability, cognition and emotion), how accurately we can model these aspects acquiring a sufficient know-how for the arising potential and limitations depending on the context of application, and lastly how we can create flexible, but at the same robust and transparent, mapping rules that adapt/personalize the users' activities, content and navigation accordingly. Such an endeavor is by definition influenced by many research directions since it embraces the combination of theories suggested by the academic disciplines of humanities and social sciences with technologies provided by the field of information science. In our opinion, the reader can benefit from the contents of this book in numerous ways receiving knowledge and insights on different levels. We summarize below the main takeaways of this book:

- We holistically re-approached the area of Human-Computer Interaction underlying the new user requirements that reinforce the design and development of human-centred interactive systems. Consequently, we underpinned the importance of adaptation and personalization in the delivery of hypermedia content in the context of E-Learning, E-Commerce and Usable Security;
- Driven by theories of individual differences, we identified the value of understanding and incorporating human factors in the process of Web adaptation and personalization, focusing on their dynamicity and how they can affect the design of user interactions and interfaces;
- We elaborated on the main principles of adaptive interactive systems. We extensively investigated the fields of adaptation and personalization, focusing on the main categories and technologies for adapting their content and functionality, and on the importance of user modeling;

- We designed a high-level adaptation and personalization schema that realizes the mapping of specific high-level theoretical human factors and dimensions, with low-level technical concepts, technologies and algorithms;
- We proposed a formalization of a human factor-based user model for personalizing content and functionality of interactive systems;
- We proposed a formalization of an adaptation engine and a set of adaptation rules for personalizing user tasks based on the combination and the interrelation of the user modeling characteristics;
- We proposed an open and interoperable adaptation and personalization framework, namely mapU. The outcome of mapU could serve as a guide for researchers and practitioners for integrating heterogeneous elements, attributes and functionalities under a unified personalization framework aiming to improve usability and user experience;
- We presented a thorough analysis of challenges and issues in the areas of E-Learning, E-Commerce and Usable Security. Furthermore, we identified and summarized the most important design characteristics and usability concerns of each area that can be used as a reference by the reader when developing design interventions and adaptation and personalization mechanisms;
- We studied the impact of a number of human factors on users' preference, task performance and accuracy in different application areas. Based on the results which include objective quantitative data measures (data captured during experimentation) as well as subjective qualitative self-reporting data (focus group studies), we came to the conclusion that it is vital for the designers and developers of today's interactive systems or hypermedia environments to follow a human-centred approach, which predominantly entails the study, analysis and incorporation of individual differences in any solution considering always the peculiarities and constraints of the context of use; and
- We proposed and evaluated a set of adaptation effects and design guidelines for personalizing content and functionality of interactive systems based on human cognitive and emotional processing differences. We have discussed these practical guidelines by elaborating on a step-by-step method of incorporating them into systems and applications. We explained how they are yielded from the respective human factors by giving examples and presented coding paradigms of how they can be realized at a more technical/implementation level, conveying the essence of an end-to-end process.

The aftermath of this research effort indicates, to our knowledge, the value of human-centred adaptation and personalization as a viable alternative direction to current "one-size-fits-all" practices of interactive systems, for supporting the users during information processing, decision making, problem solving and learning. As seen through the methods used in this book, the analyses and the user studies conducted, the suggested human factors figure as elements of paramount importance for the concept of personalization and the development of adaptive mechanisms, since they have a main effect on particular design characteristics of several application areas. By personalizing the visual experience and functionality to the users' cognitive and emotional processing characteristics, it has been revealed that users are able to complete their tasks faster and more accurately, as well as those sharing (to a measurable practical extent) the same intrinsic characteristics on the subsequent psychometric scales have a clear preference towards particular designs of interactive systems.

Human-computer interactions are performed on every moment worldwide by billions of users and thus it becomes evident that having a service or application with a usability flaw in an interaction step or even if not considering usability issues while designing their activity interaction flows, most probably will result in unacceptable trade-offs for the users and the providers in terms of time and resources. In this respect, we envision that the reported research could constitute the basis for researchers and practitioners and encourage them to design and develop usable interactive systems taking into consideration the diverse user population and their' unique preferences and characteristics. The added value of such an endeavor entails many benefits both from the users' as well as from the service providers' perspective. For the former, the design and the deployment of human-centred personalized interfaces and applications would support the processing of content and the tasks execution, providing more clarity and meaning on the required information. At the same time would reduce any unnecessary steps and/or complexities, increasing the decision making and eventually leading to a positive user experience. For the latter, such an (strategic) approach would increase user acceptance and satisfaction and thus would provide an enhanced branding experience, assisting organizations to gain the competitive advantage through the provision of personalized services. Inevitably, in this case more consistent (user) research is required, investing on the identification and documentation of users' behaviors and operations (e.g., building qualitative personas, activity flows, use cases, etc.) in order to obtain a complete understanding of how they work and consequently create designs that will match their profiles with the appropriate interaction styles.

As a final word, based on the work presented in this book, and the inherent challenges and requirements in the area of adaptation and personalization, future research prospects entail further increasing the external validity of the research conducted so far with extended samples and varying user profiles. An interesting implication of this work relates to the gradual universality of today's information technology applications and unification of services and interactions. The literature acknowledges that the differences in cognitive processing styles and abilities exist not only within the national boundaries, but as well across diverse nations as they are affected by the culture in which they are developed. In this context, research works like the one reported in this book could be replicated on a global scale in order to gain empirical knowledge and understand individual differences between different nations or ethnic groups, and further apply that knowledge for the design and development of globalized personalization schemes. As an example, prior research has shown cross-cultural differences in field dependence-independence (Western vs. Eastern societies, African American vs. South African), and therefore future work could investigate the effects of inter-cultural differences on human-centered personalization interactions across different countries and continents whose impact could affect a large number of individuals from different cultures. Furthermore, the proposed approach could also have strong implications on elderly people whose cognitive processing characteristics are limited and decline over time. In this context, future research scenarios include conducting further user studies with other samples and specialized profiles (including characteristics of older adults) with the aim to strengthen the validity of the reported results and enrich our understanding about the effects of the related users' cognitive processing factors on preference and performance during interaction.

Another timely future research direction would be to expand and further investigate other intrinsic human factors (e.g., personality) with respect also to new technologies (e.g., device types) and interactive systems. For example, increase our understanding about the effects of human factors on different interaction methods driven by the utilization of external devices such as advanced eye-tracking systems and wearable technologies and devices (e.g., wireless and body sensors, activity trackers, smart watches, etc.). Currently, being part of the network of physical objects or "things", we are certainly coming closer to the users and we are able to capture and correlate more data with respect to their activities and physiological responses to given stimuli or situations. For instance, we could identify correlations between specific cognitive mechanisms and generic somatic symptoms of anxiety triggered during an activity step, and as a result to regulate this relationship to the benefit of the end-users by providing personalization solutions that will reflect their current state/feelings; allowing them to continue dealing with their tasks without experiencing any negative emotions (e.g., worry, tension, nervousness, etc.).

In a parallel direction, in this era of big data produced from various and diverse sources, an open question that still remains is how to generate human-centred adaptive visualizations that can increase users' understanding and enable decision making during the interaction process with multi-purpose data representations (e.g., in the healthcare sector where a physician needs to make instantly a critical decision for a patient by looking at different formats of visualizations presented in most cases at different levels of detail). The requirement here is to identify potential correlations of cognitive factors referring to high-level information processes as well as elementary cognitive processes with different kinds (in terms of type and complexity) of data visualizations (e.g. network diagrams, area and radar graphs, bar and line charts, etc.), and consequently to suggest interventions that could increase the usability and satisfaction of users based on their role and/or levels of expertise.

To sum up, it is true that there are many opportunities ahead but also numerous constraints still in place, either engraved to the multi-dimensional character and complexity of these research attempts or induced by the technological limitations of today's advancements that in many cases might hinder the practical feasibility of solutions. However, we are convinced that the key to a viable co-existence of the human and the computer in today's technological ecosystem that will offer usable lasting interactions is to bring the *human* into the "centre" and design *from* and *with* him. The driving factor in this pursuit is the end-user who should always have the "benefit of doubt" in any requirements collection, analysis, or compromization that will eventually embody the design of an interface, service, system and/or application. Thus, we strongly believe that an effective "recipe" should always acknowledge the triptych from *theory* to *principles* and *practice*, and not vice versa.